The Men Who Made

BLACKBURN ROVERS FC
SINCE 1945

The Men Who Made

BLACKBURN ROVERS FC
SINCE 1945

Harry Berry

To Janette

First published in 2006 by Tempus Publishing

Reprinted in 2012 by
The History Press
The Mill, Brimscombe Port,
Stroud, Gloucestershire, GL5 2QG
www.thehistorypress.co.uk

Illustrations provided by Howard Talbot and Empics.

British Library Cataloguing in Publication Data.
A catalogue record for this book is available from the British Library.

ISBN 978 0 7524 3194 9

Typesetting and origination by
Tempus Publishing Limited
Printed and bound in Great Britain by
Marston Book Services Limited, Didcot

INTRODUCTION

Having been born within two miles, as the crow flies, from Ewood Park it was perhaps inevitable that I would became a Rovers supporter. My maternal grandfather had been a fan but he died before I was born and since my father had no interest in the game it was my mother's cousin's husband, Ken McMillan, who I have to thank for first taking me to Ewood. That was over fifty years ago, as a young Ronnie Clayton was starting his career, but I can still recall the magic of that first trip down Livesey Branch Road. Today, my son Karl has been accompanying me to the Rovers for over thirty years, my nephew Andrew travels from Derbyshire and my younger brother Ian from Sheffield. Blue and white runs deep in our family.

Thirty years ago I had the honour of writing the club's official centenary history and since then I have always had the ambition to be involved in a complete record of the players who have worn the blue-and-white halves. Any true supporter knows that the players are like your family. Good, bad and sometimes ugly, they become part of your life. Footballers should be remembered, all of them, not just the great ones. To some, Blackburn are a small club, but they have had players who were truly exceptional. I was fortunate enough to spend years watching the pure genius that was Bryan Douglas. In the last few years Henning Berg was, for me, the most perfect defender I have ever seen, technically near-flawless and with an attitude. Few scale these heights of perfection but that does not stop them being recalled with affection. My favourites include John Bray, never overawed by reputations or venues; Jim Branagan, who any winger could beat once but only the courageous beat twice; Mike Hickman, the bravest of them all and Derek Fazackerley, so supremely competent that no-one noticed him. Hopefully the details provided in this book will evoke memories of the men who were Rovers.

By any standards Blackburn Rovers is a club that has overachieved, given the size and economic background of the town and the counter-attractions of the area. This is why 1995 and the Premiership title was so special. Only the fans who have been there through all the bad times (Karl and I were 2 of that 2,161 record-low attendance in 1985) know how special. We also knew that it is not likely to be repeated. It does not matter. Once was enough. It is still annoying to hear claims that Jack Walker bought the title. The team that won the Premiership cost less than £15 million, no more than our rivals at the time. Also, during Jack's years, the total spent on transfer fees did not exceed those received.

This book represents many happy hours spent researching the careers of these players. I have detailed histories of every player that has played for the club but every year the list gets larger and it was only possible to fit into this edition the players who have turned out since the Second World War. The players before 1939? Now they were characters! Some of them are featured in a snapshot of the FA Cup winning sides at the end of the book.

KEY TO STATISTICS

All player information is correct up to 31st December 2005.

* indicates commonly used Christian name. ' ' indicates nickname
Height and weight are imperial measurements. Career shows club, date and transfer fee

Career Statistics Abbreviations
p-c player coach, *p-m* player manager, *am* amateur, *pro* professional, *ass sch* associate schoolboy, *sch* schoolboy, *non con* non contact, *app* apprentice

Appearances
Full + substitute goals
PL Premier League FL Football League L Premier & Football Leagues FAC FA Cup LC Football League Cup
EC European Cup UEFA UEFA Cup FMC Full Members' Cup

AGNEW, Steven Mark
Midfield

5'9" 10st 6lb
Born: Shipley 9, November 1965
Debut: 17 August 1991

CAREER: Barnsley Oct 1986; Blackburn Rovers Jun 1991 (£700,000); Portsmouth Nov 1992 (Loan); Leicester City Feb 1993 (£250,000); Sunderland Jan 1995 (£250,000); York City Jul 1998 (free); Gateshead May 2001; West Auckland Town Nov 2002-May 2004.

Don Mackay bought Agnew for a club-record transfer fee, but both men were to regret the transaction. A strong, hard-tackling midfielder, he sustained an ankle injury that required surgery almost immediately and his entire first-team career at the club was truncated into a period of less than two weeks. Suffering from the departure of Mackay, Agnew was never in Kenny Dalglish's plans and after two seasons almost inactive he was transferred to Leicester. Later he helped Sunderland to promotion to the Premiership and finished his league career with a troubled spell at York City. He became assistant manager at Gateshead but left when Paul Proudlock was dismissed and signed for West Auckland. He was then appointed coach to the Leeds United youth team.

FL	2 apps	0 gls
FLC	2 apps	0 gls
Total	4 apps	0 gls

AINSCOW, Alan
Midfield

5'6.5" 9st 4lb
Born: Bolton, 15 July 1953
Debut: 1 February 1986

CAREER: Bolton County Grammar School; Blackpool Jul 1971 (app. Jul 1970); Birmingham City Jul 1978 (£40,000); Everton Aug 1981 (£250,000); Barnsley Nov 1982 (loan); Eastern (Hong Kong) 1984; Wolverhampton Wanderers Aug 1984 (free); Blackburn Rovers Jan 1986 (non con) Jun 1987; Rochdale Jun 1989; Horwich RMI Aug 1990; Flint Town United 1991.

Once regarded as a future golden boy of English football, Ainscow's career never blossomed after a promising start at Blackpool. A quick, effusive ball player with energy to spare, he was particularly disappointing on Merseyside and a move to Wolverhampton was fraught since he kept his home in Ormskirk and travelled. Given fourteen days' notice he was signed by the Rovers on non-contract terms, ostensibly to help with the young reserve side. He was to stay three years and although he was used mainly as a substitute he was in the side when they won the Full Members' Cup in 1987. After his playing days were over he coached Ellesmere Port Town and later assisted in the hospitality suites at Ewood. For a time he was a postman, owned a newsagents in Ormskirk and now delivers fruit and vegetables around Merseyside.

FL	42+23 apps	5 gls
FLC	2+1 apps	1 gl
FMC	4+2 apps	1 gl
PO	1+2 apps	0 gls
Total	49+28 apps	7 gls

AIREY, John
Winger

5'10" 11st
Born: Bedford, 28 November 1937
Debut: 7 March 1959

CAREER: Blackburn Olympic; East Lancashire Coachbuilders; Blackburn Rovers Jan 1959; Morecambe Jul 1963; Blackburn Central 1965-Oct 1968.

Although born in Bedford Airey grew up in Blackburn and starred for East Lancashire Coachbuilders when they won the Cotton Cup in 1957. Although the Rovers recognised his promise as a right winger of dash and determination, Airey was reluctant to give up work and positioned himself in an echelon behind the incomparable Douglas and Roy Isherwood. His debut came on the other flank when he scored a goal of beauty against Burnley, waltzing around the full-back before firing home. Thereafter he had little opportunity but he made 53 appearances for Morecambe before breaking his leg. Back in the Blackburn Combination he appeared in the final of the Eddleston Cup, but retired from the game when he broke his leg for the third time.

FL	3 apps	1 gl
Total	3 apps	1 gl

ALCOCK, Terence
Central defender

6'0" 11st 8lb
Born: Hanley, 9 December 1946
Debut: 27 December 1976

CAREER: Port Vale Sep 1964 (app. May 1962); Blackpool Aug 1967; Bury Feb 1972 (loan); Blackburn Rovers Dec 1976 (loan); Port Vale Feb 1977; Portland Timbers (USA) Apr 1977; Halifax Town Sep 1977-Jun 1978.

Able to play at centre-back or midfield, his versatility enabled him to carve a career at Blackpool, where he had to contend with Peter Suddaby, Glyn James and Paul Hart. He was at his best paired with Suddaby, the pair starring in the Anglo-Italian tournament final victory against Bologna. Bob Stokoe was of the opinion that he lacked the aggression to be a top-class player but there was no sign of this in his brief loan spell at Ewood Park where he contributed an unexpected goal. After playing in America he became landlord of The Bull in Burscough.

FL	3 apps	1 gl
FAC	2 apps	0 gls
Total	5 apps	1 gl

AMORUSO, Lorenzo
Centre-back

5'11" 13st
Born: Palese (Italy), 28 June 1971
Debut: 16 August 2003

CAREER: Cucine del Levante; Bari 1981; Mantova Nov 1991 (loan); Vis Pesaro Nov 1992 (loan); Fiorentina 1996; Glasgow Rangers Jun 1997 (£4,000,000); Blackburn Rovers Jul 2003 (£1,400,000).

Born close to Bari, he started with that club but it was to be five years and two loan spells before he established himself in the first team. An emotional player with great strength, he was a rugged if erratic defender but an inspirational character. A move to Fiorentina brought him honours but it was his move to Rangers that established his reputation. A stuttering start, in which he underwent three sessions of surgery on his Achilles tendon, was forgotten as he led the club to successive Scottish championships. In his final season the club achieved the treble in domestic competitions and Amoruso said goodbye with the goal that completed the hat-trick in the Scottish cup final. His start with the Rovers was as traumatic as his first months in Glasgow. Troubled by knee problems, he appeared to find the pace of the English game too great but his early season departure for knee surgery left the situation unproven. Coming back for his second season, it was almost a mirror image and a three-month spell for further surgery resulted in him being left completely out of the picture. Ever a man for the flamboyant, he proposed to his model girlfriend during an edition of the Italian version of the reality TV show *The Farm*. He is probably the only Blackburn player ever to have his own cookery book published.

PL	16+2 apps	3 gls
LC	1 app.	0 gls
UEFA	2 apps	0 gls
Total	19+2 apps	3 gls

ANDERSON, Benjamin Cummings
Centre half/centre forward

6'0" 12st 3lb
Born: Aberdeen, 18 February 1946
Debut: 6 February 1965

CAREER: Peterlee Jnrs; Blackburn Rovers Mar 1964; Bury Jul 1968 (£10,000); Cape Town City (South Africa) 1970; Crystal Palace Nov 1973-Jun 1974; Cape Town City (South Africa)1975-1976.

'Big Ben' was signed from junior football in the North-East and placed immediately in the reserve team at left half. His impressive physique was put to good use and he made a surprisingly early debut, nominally on the left wing but dropping deep to cover the flank. A talent for goal-scoring emerged immediately and the following season his introduction as substitute at Anfield added another goal. In 1967 he was moved to centre half but before he could settle he was converted to centre forward. Although his strike rate was good his lack of technique showed and he drifted out of the team. Never harnessing his talents he emigrated to South Africa, where he spent four years, before returning to team up again with Frank Large at Crystal Palace, but returned to Cape Town for two more seasons. The South African league at the time went largely unnoticed but Anderson was remembered by the Manchester United goalkeeper, Gary Bailey, as one of the great players in the league.

FL	21+7 apps	7 gls
Total	21+7 apps	7 gls

ANDERSON, Christopher Shelly
Right winger

5'6" 9st 12lb
Born: Rosie, Fife, 28 January 1928
Died: Derby, 20 July 1996
Debut: 18 November 1950

CAREER: Lochore Welfare; Blackburn Rovers Aug 1950 (£150); Kidderminster Harriers; Nelson Feb 1953; Stockport County Jun 1953; Southport Jul 1954; Lion Brewery Nov 1955; Blackburn West Oct 1956; Highfield Athletic.

There was never a doubt that Anderson could dribble a football. An outstanding trial took him into the reserves where he quickly performed the feat that made him an Ewood legend. Losing his chewing gum, he retraced his steps with the ball under control and retrieved it, retaining possession the whole time. When he demoralised Manchester City on his debut spectators detected a second Stanley Matthews. The reality was that he was a maverick who liked the high life and had no discipline. Sent back into non-league football he resurrected his career at Stockport and Southport and once again squandered it. Back in Blackburn he worked at the Lion Brewery, playing locally as a permit player until an incident with a referee all but terminated his career. His private life was just as chaotic and after a life chasing pleasure he ended in an old people's home in Derby where he had a foot amputated because of gangrene.

FL	13 apps	1 gl
Total	13 apps	1 gl

ANDERSSON, Anders Per
Midfield

5'8.5" 11st 5lb
Born: Tomelilla (Sweden), 15 March 1974
Debut: 9 August 1997

CAREER: Svenstorps IF; Malmo FF Sum 1990; Blackburn Rovers Jul 1997 (£500,000); AAB Aalborg (Denmark) Oct 1998 (loan) Jun 1999 (£250,000); Benfica (Portugal) 2001 (free); Belenenses (Portugal) Jan 2004 (free). Malmo FF Jun 2005 (free).
INTERNATIONALS: Sweden 27 apps 2 gls.

Roy Hodgson first saw Andersson playing for his home village (population less than 250), where he had been spotted by Malmo's chief scout. The son of a local farmer, he was only fifteen and so had to wait a year before signing for the Swedish First Division club. By then Hodgson had moved on but within a year Andersson was playing in Malmo's midfield, partnering his namesake Patrick and later, when Patrick left for a bigger club, Patrick's brother Daniel. A neat, tidy, hard-working blond, Andersson was conspicuous enough to gain international honours but many respected Swedish football men believed that he lacked a ruthless edge and would struggle in the English Premiership. Nevertheless, when Hodgson took over at Ewood he remembered the youthful player and persuaded him to try his luck in English football. The Swedish experts were proved correct; the tidy, careful player was swept away in the maelstrom of English midfield war and never prospered. He slipped back into Scandinavian football in Denmark where he won championship honours but a Bosman move to Benfica did not greatly improved his reputation, although it has helped him back into the national squad.

PL	1+3 apps	0 gls
FAC	0+1 apps	0 gls
FLC	3 apps	1 gl
Total	4+4 apps	1 gl

ANDERSSON, Patrik Jonas
Central defender

6'1" 13st 11lb
Born: Borgeby (Sweden), 18 August 1971
Debut: 9 January 1993

CAREER: Bjarred 1985; Malmo FF 1988; Blackburn Rovers Jan 1993 (£800,000); Borussia Moenchengladbach (Germany) Nov 1993 (£425,000); Bayern Munich (Germany) Jun 1999 (£2,000,000); Barcelona (Spain) Jun 2001 (£5,000,000); Malmo FF Feb 2004 (free) Aug 2005.
INTERNATIONALS: Sweden 96 apps 3 gls.

Andersson's father, Roy, was one of the all-time greats of the Malmo club, having made the second-highest number of appearances. It was therefore not surprising that Patrik became a footballer (making his debut in the regionalised Swedish Fourth Division at the age of fourteen) nor that he quickly joined his father's old club. When Jonas Thern left for Benfica he established himself in the first team, playing a key role in their European victory over Inter Milan. There was competition for his signature when Kenny Dalglish brought him to Blackburn but he found no happy haven at Ewood Park. Unable to gel with Colin Hendry at the centre of the defence and lacking stamina when played in midfield he was discarded within a year but found the Bundesliga more to his liking. With the confidence of a third-place medal from the 1994 World Cup his international career blossomed and he was a stalwart in the defence for a decade. Calm, resolute and unflinching, he played with concentration and efficiency. A move to Bayern Munich brought league and cup medals and a financially lucrative move to Barcelona. For the last years he was dogged by injuries that forced him out of the 2002 World Cup and placed question marks over his future. A move back to Sweden brought him a championship medal, although recurring injuries prevented him playing the final weeks of the season. Returning to action in the European tie against FC Thun, he tore his cruciate ligaments and decided to retire after undergoing surgery.

PL	7+5 apps	0 gls
FAC	1 app.	0 gls
FLC	2 apps	1 gl
Total	10+5 apps	1 gl

ANDRESEN, Martin
Midfield

5'11" 11st 11lb
Born: Oslo, 2 February 1977
Debut: 28 February 2004

CAREER: Krakstad; Ski; Moss; Viking Stavangar; Stabaek; Wimbledon Oct 1999 (£1,800,000); Molde Jun 2000-Dec 2000 (loan); Stabaek Dec 2000 (free); Blackburn Rovers Jan 2004-Jun 2004 (loan); SK Brann Mar 2005 (£1,250,000).
INTERNATIONALS: Norway 19 apps 2 gls.

After working his way through several clubs Andresen established himself at Stabaek, who he helped to a cup-final victory. A solid box-to-box midfielder, he was brought over to Wimbledon when the club was acquired by Norwegian owners but started only 4 times for them before he was allowed to return on loan to his own country. His international career blossomed late after stagnating when he came to the end of the age group teams and when the Rovers became interested in him near to the January 2004 transfer window he had started to establish himself a reputation. This extended off the field because he was voted the sexiest man in Norway. Brought over for a week's trial at Brockhall he returned home with no concrete offer, but the Rovers' failure to sign Muzzy Izzet saw them readdress the situation and agree a loan deal until the end of the season. Although his play went unrecognised the run that saved the club from relegation coincided with the club opting for a diamond formation in midfield with Andresen playing in the holding role. Although there had been talk of a permanent deal neither party appeared to be keen and he returned to Norway to sign for Brann nine months later. Protected by the fact that his father is a multi-millionaire he has never been forced to accept moves that he was uncomfortable with and has expressed the view that he will never play outside Norway again.

PL	11 apps	0 gls
Total	11 apps	0 gls

APPLEBY, James Patrick
Centre half

6'1.5" 12st
Born: Shotton, Durham, 15 June 1934
Debut: 27 September 1958

CAREER: Shotton Jnrs; Wingate Welfare; Burnley Feb 1953; Blackburn Rovers Feb 1958; Southport Oct 1961; Chester Jun 1962; Horden CW 1963; Ryhope CW 1967.

Signed to provide cover for Matt Woods, the well-built but stiff-limbed player never really achieved this target. Both his first-team appearances were disappointing and he was not permitted any other chance. If the theory was that First Division football was too fast for him he struggled for pace in the lower leagues too and eventually moved back to his native North-East. A fitter at Blackhall Colliery, he remained in the game managing Horden Colliery Welfare for some ten years.

FL	2 apps	0 gls
Total	2 apps	0 gls

ARCHIBALD, Steven
Striker

5'10" 11st 2lb
Born: Glasgow, 27 September 1956
Debut: 19 December 1987

CAREER: Crofoot United; Fernhill Athletic; East Stirling; Clyde 1974; Aberdeen Jan 1978 (£25,000); Tottenham Hotspur May 1980 (£800,000); Barcelona (Spain) Jul 1984 (£1,150,000); Blackburn Rovers Dec 1987-Jun 1988 (loan); Hibernian Aug 1988 (free); Espanyol (Spain) Jan 1990 (free); St Mirren Nov 1990 (free); Reading Jan 1992 (free); Ayr United Feb 1992; Fulham

Sep 1992; East Fife Aug 1994 (player-manager); Home Farm Everton (Eire) Jan 1997.
INTERNATIONALS: Scotland 27 apps 4 gls.

Archibald was Don Mackay's prestigious investment, taken on loan from an unhappy spell at Barcelona, and the most renowned player to be acquired for some time. At his best he was a quick, instinctive player, difficult to mark and a regular, though not prolific, goalscorer. At White Hart Lane he had contributed to FA and UEFA Cup glory but after a Spanish league champions' medal in 1985 his career had stalled. His charisma brought the fans back for a spell but play-off failure ended the engagement and the expected impetus from Archibald was not as great as had been anticipated. He visited a few more clubs before hanging up his boots and embarked on a varied career. A Sky TV expert for a time, he also made a forty-five-minute comeback in the League of Ireland and was appointed an executive director of Benfica when Graeme Souness was their coach. In the summer of 2000 he stepped in to try and save the debt-ridden Scottish club Airdrie, but his status of preferred bidder hindered events and the club ultimately folded when he did not inject the necessary funds.

FL	20 apps	6 gls
FAC	1 app.	0 gls
PO	1 app.	0 gls
Total	22 apps	6 gls

ARDILES, Osvaldo Cesar 'Ossie'
Midfield

5'6" 9st 10lb
Born: Province of Cordoba (Argentina), 3 August 1952
Debut: 26 March 1988

CAREER: Red Star (Cordoba); Instituto (Cordoba) 1973; Belgrano (Cordoba) 1974; Huracan 1975; Tottenham Hotspur Jul 1978 (£350,000); Paris St Germain (France) Jul 1982 (loan); Blackburn Rovers Mar 1988 (loan); Queens Park Rangers Aug 1988 (free); Fort Lauderdale (USA) Jun 1989.
INTERNATIONALS: Argentina 50 apps 9 gls.

One of the most famous creative players in football, Ardiles joined Tottenham after gaining a winners' medal in the 1978 World Cup. With his neat, perceptive play he became a dominant influence in the First Division and helped Tottenham to FA and UEFA Cup success. Deceptively resilient, he had moral character too and against all expectations continued playing during the Falklands conflict. The influence of Steve Archibald brought him to Ewood for a brief loan spell that included an unsuccessful attempt to negotiate the play-offs. A target for the Second Division hardmen, he found the experience painful and had little opportunity to stamp his authority on proceedings. He took a step towards a future in the game when he became player-coach at Queens Park Rangers but broke a leg which ultimately persuaded him to stop playing. His subsequent career as manager or coach around the world has been chequered. He took both Swindon and West Brom to promotion but failed at Newcastle, Tottenham, Deportivo Guadalajara, Croatia Zagreb and Yokohama Marinos. Within this bad run he was a huge success with Shimizu Z-Pulse. After coaching Al Ittihad in Saudi Arabia (where he was dismissed with his club top of the league and unbeaten) he returned to his native country to take charge at Racing. His first act was to appoint his old Tottenham teammate Ricky Villa as his assistant. Successful at the club, he nevertheless resigned because he did not believe that the club could progress ,and moved back to Japan, the country where he was most at ease, to coach Tokyo Verdy. His undulating managerial career has clouded his illustrious pedigree as a player because there have been few greater creative talents than the man who summed up the game with one sentence, 'some play with a round ball, others use a square one.'

FL	5 apps	0 gls
PO	1+1 apps	0 gls
Total	6+1 apps	0 gls

ARENTOFT, Preben 'Ben'

Midfield/left-back

5'6.5" 10st 5lb
Born: Copenhagen (Denmark), 1 November 1942
Debut: 2 October 1971

CAREER: Bronshoj Boldklub; Greenock Morton Sep 1965; Newcastle United Mar 1969 (£18,000); Blackburn Rovers Sep 1971 (£15,000); Helsingborgs IF 1977-1980 (p-c).
INTERNATIONALS: Denmark 9 apps.

The only route for foreign footballers into the Football League in the 1970s was to pass through a Scottish club. Arentoft, a Danish international, signed for Hal Stewart's Morton and helped them to promotion while obtaining the residential qualifications for a move south of the border. He joined Newcastle, where he displayed thought and creativity in their midfield and gained great repute on Tyneside when his goal secured the club the Fairs Cup. Ken Furphy brought him to Ewood as he rebuilt the side that had been relegated to the Third Division but Arentoft was never comfortable among the chaos of a Third Division midfield scrap. Conversely he became a stylish left-back, unusually cultured for this level and when asked to play centre-back proved that intelligence and experience can overcome lack of physical dimensions. Never happy when Gordon Lee took over the club, he decided to return to Denmark to resume his old profession as an accountant. He subsequently became a senior manager with the Copenhagen City Council, was player-coach at Helsingor, and from his home in Stenlose had a sideline business dealing in works of art. Currently he is head of the juvenile probation service in Copenhagen.

FL	94 apps	3 gls
FAC	10 apps	0 gls
FLC	4 apps	0 gls
Total	108 apps	3 gls

ARNOLD, James Alexander

Goalkeeper

6'1" 11st 5lb
Born: Stafford, 6 August 1950
Debut: 18 August 1979

CAREER: Rising Brook; Stafford Rangers; Blackburn Rovers Jun 1979 (£20,000); Everton Aug 1981 (£175,000); Preston North End Oct 1982 (loan); Port Vale Jul 1985 (free); Kidderminster Harriers; Rochester; Workington; Blackburn Rovers Mar 1990-May 1990; Stoke City (reserves).

Statistically, Arnold's spell at Blackburn is never likely to be exceeded. His concession rate was a goal every 150 minutes, his clean sheet percentage was fifty-seven and he once went 556 minutes without conceding a goal. Defensively the club was impressive and some of the credit for that was due to Arnold. It appeared to be a huge gamble when the new manager, Howard Kendall, paid £20,000 for a man who was nearly twenty-nine and had never played in the Football League. However, as coach at Stoke he had observed him playing at nearby Stafford and was confident of his ability. He proved a good judge. Arnold was an immaculate goalkeeper, sure-handed, agile and confident of his angles and technique. Perhaps of all Blackburn goalkeepers he was the most error free. Promotion back to the Second Division came in his first season, the following year promotion to the First Division was lost on goal difference. There was to be no third season because Kendall moved to Everton and took Arnold with him. Strangely the player was never the same again and his career faded until he retired to become the recreation officer for Stafford Police. He had a last fleeting contact with the Rovers when he was signed to provide emergency cover in 1990, but he was never called upon.

FL	58 apps	0 gls
FAC	7 apps	0 gls
FLC	3 apps	0 gls
Total	68 apps	0 gls

ARNOTT, Kevin William
Midfield

5'10" 11st 12lb
Born: Bengham, 28 September 1958
Debut: 25 November 1981

CAREER: St Aidan's School, Sunderland; Sunderland Dec 1976; Blackburn Rovers Nov 1981 (loan); Sheffield United Jul 1982 (free); Blackburn Rovers Nov 1982 (loan); Rotherham United Mar 1983 (loan); Vasalunds (Sweden); Chesterfield Nov 1987 (free); Gateshead Nov 1990; Nly Karlby (Finland); Hebburn Sep 1982.

Once regarded as a prodigy at Roker Park, the elegant midfield man with classic distribution had lost his way by the time he came on loan to the Rovers. He added a new dimension to the side but funds were tight and the Rovers hesitated about taking him permanently. He was recalled by his club and the Rovers did not attempt to sign him when he became available in the close season. A year later he was back on loan at Ewood and once again his silky skills stood out, but finances were no better and he was again allowed to leave. After summer football in Sweden he found an acceptable home at Chesterfield where, despite the bustle of the division, his cool composure made him an outstanding player. Troubled by a persistent ankle injury he gave up league football but played on for sometime for the enjoyment.

FL	28+1 apps	3 gls
FAC	2 apps	0 gls
Total	30+1 apps	3 gls

ASTON, John
Left winger

5'9.5" 11st 6lb
Born: Manchester, 28 June 1947
Debut: 19 August 1978

CAREER: Seymour Rd Jnrs; Wheeler St Sec Mod; Manchester United Jul 1964 (app. Jun 1963); Luton Town Jul 1972 (£30,000); Mansfield Town Sep 1977; Blackburn Rovers Jul 1978-Jun 1980 (£20,000).

Sons who take the route of their father run a hard road and as the son of the Manchester United international, John Aston was not guaranteed an easy ride. Fortunately he was a vastly different player from his father, who had been a full-back. Aston was a touchline-hugging left winger, fleet of foot who deemed it his major role to stay wide and cross often. It brought him an Under-23 cap but more memorably a place in United folklore as the man who destroyed the Benfica right-back Adolfo in the 1968 European Cup final. Soon after he broke a leg and, with his place gone at Old Trafford, he moved for a spell of gainful employment with Luton. His move to Ewood was to accommodate a desire to play nearer to his home in Ashton. It brought limited benefit to the Rovers. Although he had occasional flashes of speed he lacked stamina and contributed little before retiring to his pet shop business in Stalybridge.

FL	12+3 apps	2 gls
LC	1 apps	0 gls
Total	13+3 apps	2 gls

ATHERTON, Dewi Lewis
Midfield

6'0" 11st 2lb
Born: Penmaenmawr, 6 July 1951
Died: Colwyn Bay, September 1987
Debut: 28 April 1969

CAREER: Blackburn Rovers Jul 1968 (ass sch Jul 1967); Bangor City Sep 1971.

There was much competition for the signature of Atherton, a tall Welsh boy who clearly had qualities as a industrious midfield forager. He contributed to a good youth team during the 1968/69 season and it was no surprise that he was given an extended run in the first team the year after. The arrival of a new manager, Ken Furphy, changed all that. He had little time for Atherton's more precise play and promoted the younger Bradford and McDonald ahead of him. Within a matter of months his contract was cancelled. Returning to north Wales he played for Bangor City but was diagnosed with motor neurone disease, which brought a premature death at the age of thirty-six.

FL	9+1 apps	0 gls
LC	1 app.	0 gls
Total	10+1 apps	0 gls

Mark Atkins in action against Oxford United, December 1991.

ATKINS, Mark Nigel
Full-back/Midfield

6'0" 12st 5lb
Born: Doncaster, 14 August 1968
Debut: 27 August 1988

CAREER: Hatfield Main; Scunthorpe United Jul 1988; Blackburn Rovers Jun 1988 (£45,000); Wolverhampton Wanderers Sep 1995 (£1,000,000); York City Aug 1999 (free); Doncaster Rovers Nov 1999 (free); Hull City Mar 2001 (free); Shrewsbury Town Jul 2001 (free); Harrogate Town Jul 2003; Stalybridge Celtic Jan 2005.

Recruited from Scunthorpe, Atkins was signed to replace Chris Price at right-back, and initially was often moved to the centre of the defence when the team was reshuffled. For a young man he displayed an admirable temperament, never allowing the fact that a winger could beat him to rattle him and distributing the ball with calm. He also had an unexpected eye for goal, spotting the opportunity to run from deep and finish with poise. It was Tony Parkes, in one of his spells as caretaker manager, who had the inspired idea that Atkins could play in midfield. The handicap of not being a great ball winner was compensated by an ability to follow instructions to the letter. Atkins stayed on his feet, was mobile and always positioned himself between his opponent and the goal, bringing solidity and balance to the team. Able to get into the penalty area more often he provided many important goals. When, in 1994/95, David Batty missed almost the entire season, Atkins slotted in alongside Tim Sherwood to fuel the engine room that brought the Premiership title to Ewood. No-one should underestimate his contribution to this achievement. Immediately surplus to requirements when Batty was fit, Atkins had a productive spell with the Wolves before dropping out of the Football League with Doncaster. However, he still had admirers and in early 2003 contributed to the Shrewsbury team that shocked Everton in the FA Cup. He became assistant manager to John Reed at Harrogate and moved on with him to Stalybridge at the start of 2005.

L	224+33 apps	34 gls
FAC	11+3 apps	0 gls
FLC	20+4 apps	4 gls
PO	8 apps	1 gl
FMC	6 apps	0 gls
EC	1 app.	0 gls
UEFA	1+1 apps	0 gls
CS	1+1 apps	0 gls
Total	272+42 apps	39 gls

B

BAAH, Peter Hayford
Left-back/left midfield

5'9" 10st 4lb
Born: Littleborough, 1 May 1973
Debut: 5 October 1991

CAREER: Shadsworth School; Accrington/Rossendale College; Blackburn Rovers Jun 1991 (YTS Jul 1989); Rotherham United Apr 1992 (loan); Fulham Jul 1992; Wycombe Wanderers Sum 1994 (trial); Northwich Victoria Sum 1994; Columbus Xoggz (USA) 1995; Ohio Xoggz (USA) 1996; Burnley Nov 1996 (trial); Bury (trial); Indiana Blast (USA) 1998; Indiana Reggae Boys (USA); Cincinnati Kings (USA) Jul 2005.

A left winger whose father came from Ghana, he was spotted at Shadsworth school and was taken on the YTS scheme. Temporarily converted to left-back he made an unexpected debut against Fulham in an unorthodox line-up. Injured when Kenny Dalglish took over, he was immediately made surplus to requirements when Alan Wright was signed and later joined his old manager, Don Mackay, at Fulham. Released after two seasons at Craven Cottage he struggled to find a club and decided to coach in the USA in Hawaii and New York. He also played professionally in the USISL and at both clubs he served he was in the company of an Ewood youth team colleague, Jon Pickup. At present he is still playing in the USA and has a coaching role with Hamilton Southeastern school.

FL	1 app.	0 gls
Total	1 app.	0 gls

BABBEL, Markus
Defender

6'3" 12st 13lb
Born: Munich (Germany), 8 September 1972
Debut: 30 August 2003

CAREER: TSV Gilching Argelsried; Bayern Munich 1991; Hamburg SV 1992; Bayern Munich 1994; Liverpool Jun 2000 (free); Blackburn Rovers Aug 2003 (loan); VfB Stuttgart Jun 2004 (free).
INTERNATIONALS: Germany 51 apps 1 gl.

A towering player who is at home at right-back or in the centre of defence, he made such little progress with his home town club that he was allowed to join Hamburg. He returned to Munich two years later, still as elegant in style, but with a professional, ruthless efficiency that guaranteed that he would play at the highest level. International caps and championship medals followed but despite this success he took advantage of being out of contract to join Liverpool, just in time to contribute to the historic three cups season. At the peak of his profession he developed the sometimes fatal Guillain-Barre syndrome but although it took over a year, during which time he spent time in a wheelchair unable to walk, he recovered and started playing again. He found that Liverpool had moved on without him and, unable to establish a regular place, he was allowed to join the Rovers on a season-long loan. After a promising start his form slumped alarmingly, which he subsequently blamed on the drinking culture at the club. To support his claims, when he moved back to Germany he recovered his panache and was brought back into the international squad.

PL	23+2 apps	3 gls
FAC	1 app.	0 gls
FLC	1 app.	0 gls
UEFA	1 app.	0 gls
Total	26+2 apps	3 gls

BAGGIO, Dino

Midfielder

6'2" 12st 8lb
Born: Camposaniero, Padova (Italy), 24 July 1971
Debut: 13 September 2003

CAREER: AS Torino 1989; Inter Milan 1991; Juventus 1992; Parma 1994; Lazio 2000; Blackburn Rovers Aug 2003 (loan); Ancona Calcio Jan 2004-Jun 2004 (loan); Trieste Jul 2005.
INTERNATIONALS: Italy 60 apps 7 gls.

An elegant but competitive central midfielder, Baggio came to Ewood on loan in the twilight of a career that has brought him huge honours. Apart from appearing in a World Cup final (1994) he gained three UEFA Cup winners' medals (with Juventus and Parma), was capped 60 times for his country and played with most of the top Italian clubs. No relation to the more famous Roberto Baggio, he was viewed by many critics as more valuable to the national team because of his ability to adapt to the team's needs and play a defensive or offensive role as dictated by the circumstances. His move to Lazio resulted in him playing little football for two seasons and when he came to Ewood the rustiness was evident. He was only given one start, in the UEFA Cup, and his appearances from the substitute's bench were unremarkable. It was a relief to all when his loan contract was taken over by Ancona in the January transfer window, but that club's subsequent relegation and bankruptcy ensured that he would have to return to Lazio the following season. Here the financial situation was just as bleak and because he refused to negotiate a reduction in his wages he was excluded from the squad and his wages were left unpaid.

PL	0+9 apps	1 gl
FAC	0+1 app.	0 gls
UEFA	1+1 apps	0 gls
Total	1+11 apps	1 gl

BAILEY, John Anthony

Left-back

5'8" 10st 9lb
Born: Liverpool, 1 April 1957
Debut: 19 August 1975

CAREER: Everton; Blackburn Rovers Apr 1975; Everton Jul 1979 (£300,000); Newcastle United Oct 1985 (£100,000); Bristol City Dec 1988-Jan 1992.

After being rejected by Everton Bailey was given an apprenticeship by the Rovers. Initially the club could not make up their mind whether his future lay in defence or on the left wing, because he was speedy and ran with enthusiasm. Given an early debut, he settled into the team at left-back, forming with Kevin Hird the most adventurous full-back pairing the club had ever fielded. Confident in everything he did and a cocky, ebullient improviser, it was obvious that the arrival of freedom of contract would signal his departure, ironically to the club that had first rejected him. He gathered medals during his spell at Goodison but a move to Newcastle was fraught with personal problems. After a spell coaching at Everton he returned briefly to the Football League as assistant to Howard Kendall at Sheffield United.

FL	115+5 apps	1 gl
FAC	7 apps	0 gls
FLC	7 apps	0 gls
Total	129+5 apps	1 gl

BALDWIN, James
Wing half

5'6.5" 10st 6lb
Born: Blackburn, 12 January 1922
Died: Blackburn, 13 February 1985
Debut: 1 January 1946

CAREER: Mill Hill St Peter's; Blackburn Rovers Aug 1943 (am) Dec 1945 (pro); Leicester City Feb 1950 (£10,000); Great Yarmouth (p-m) Apr 1956.

Baldwin arrived on the scene with his local club just as the Second World War had ended. He established himself as a left-sided player with industrious habits and strength. His Ewood career was forever blemished by an incredible miss in the dying minutes of a cup tie at Charlton, which, if scored, would have advanced the club to the next round. Instead, Charlton recovered and won the trophy. A long spell at Leicester increased his reputation and he had a spell in management at Great Yarmouth and then Yeovil when his playing career ended.

FL	88 apps	0 gls
FAC	8 apps	1 gl
Total	96 apps	1 gl

BARKER, Simon
Midfield

5'9" 10st 11lb
Born: Farnworth, 4 November 1964
Debut: 29 October 1983

CAREER: Blackburn Rovers Nov 1982 (app. Jul 1981); Queens Park Rangers Jul 1988 (£400,000); Port Vale Sep 1998-Dec 1999.

Barker made his name as a right-sided midfield player who was an adept passer, particularly with his speciality, the angled ball played past the inside of the left-back to free his right winger. A competitive individual, marking was not his strongest point but he could shoot with power and missed only two of fifteen competitive penalties. Recognition came in the form of England Under-21 caps and in the final of the Full Members' Cup in 1987 he was deservedly named Man of the Match for a performance of both fire and culture. With the club failing to make progress it was inevitable that he would move and he joined Queens Park Rangers for a large fee. In all he was to remain with them for ten years and received a testimonial game against Jamaica's World Cup team in recognition of his outstanding contribution as a leader of the team. After a brief spell with Port Vale he retired but joined the PFA agency that assisted with player contracts.

FL	180+2 apps	35 gls
FAC	11 apps	0 gls
FLC	9 apps	4 gls
FMC	6 apps	2 gls
PO	2 apps	0 gls
Total	208+2 apps	41 gls

BARTON, David 'Dick'
Centre-back

6'0" 11st 7lb
Born: Bishop Auckland, 9 May 1959
Debut: 28 August 1982

CAREER: Newcastle United May 1977; Blackburn Rovers Aug 1982 (loan); Darlington Jul 1983 (free); Blyth Spartans 1984; Counden (Co. Durham) 1985.

Having made the grade with his local side, Barton became surplus to requirements when they signed Jeff Clarke. Although several clubs were interested he came on loan to the Rovers because he was aware that Keeley had refused to sign a new contract and the possibility existed of a permanent move. There was never much doubt about his wholehearted commitment (his celebrations on finding the net against his old club were memorable until he found the referee had disallowed it, and he also managed to get himself sent off for dissent). However, the Rovers had no funds and when his loan period expired he was allowed to return to his club. Although he subsequently moved to Darlington a knee injury forced him into non-league football and ultimately led to his retirement. After a brief spell away from the game he returned as manager of Newton Aycliffe and then moved up the non-league ladder as assistant manager of Spennymoor United.

FL	8 apps	1 gl
Total	8 apps	1 gl

BARTON, John Birchall
Goalkeeper

5'10" 13st 4lb
Born: Orrell, 27 April 1942
Debut: 20 August 1966

CAREER: Billinge & Upholland Sec Mod; Wigan Boys' Club; Preston North End May 1959 (app. May 1957); Blackburn Rovers Jun 1966-Jun 1972 (£5,000); Mar 1973-Jun 1973.

Barton never lived up to the youthful promise that brought him a First Division debut at sixteen and youth international honours. Not ideally built for the position of goalkeeper, he had rubber-ball agility but never commanded the penalty area with real authority. Deemed the designated successor to Fred Else, he lost out to Alan Kelly and in seven years at Deepdale did not make fifty appearances. Ironically the Rovers signed him to replace the aging Else but, although an ever present in his first season, his inability to deal with the crossed ball cost the club and led to the acquisition of first Adam Blacklaw and then Roger Jones. Unexpectedly he triumphed over Blacklaw in the choice as Jones' deputy but played little until given a free transfer in 1972. He decided to retire and went into lorry driving, but was briefly back at Ewood a year later as emergency cover.

FL	68 apps	0 gls
FAC	1 app.	0 gls
FLC	3 apps	0 gls
Total	72 apps	0 gls

BATTY, David
Midfield

5'5" 10st
Born: Leeds, 12 December 1968
Debut: October 30 1993

CAREER: Horse & Groom; Tingley Athletic; Shakespeare Middle School; Pudsey Jnrs; Leeds United Aug 1987 (app. Aug 1985); Blackburn Rovers Oct 1993 (£2,750,000); Newcastle United Feb 1996 (£3,750,000); Leeds United Dec 1998-Jun 2004 (£4,400,000).
INTERNATIONALS: England 42 apps.

Small in stature but physically strong, the abrasive player became a folk hero with his home town club, gaining a championship medal and England caps. Disenchantment at having to restrict his style so that Gary Speed and Gary McAllister could play with more freedom led to him leaving Leeds unexpectedly and Kenny Dalglish seized the opportunity to pair him with Tim Sherwood in the Ewood engine room. A dictator of play, forever wanting the ball and playing it around, he demonstrated that he was not simply a tough-tackling destructive force and helped elevate the Rovers to become one of the top teams in England. Ironically a broken bone in his foot removed him for most of the Premiership-winning season of 1994/95 and by the time he returned Ray Hartford was in charge. He introduced the silkier skills of Lars Bohinen and Batty was often a reluctant outcast on the left side. This had repercussions during the European Cup campaign because it placed him in front of Graeme Le Saux, and the pair were suspended after exchanging punches on the field in Moscow. Unhappy and not shy of showing it, he was sold to Newcastle where he continued to excel. Moving back to Leeds, he catalogued an horrendous succession of misfortunes that included pericarditis following a rib injury and crippling Achilles tendon injuries. When his contract ended it was not renewed and he decided to stop playing, although he had an occasional advisory role with Harrogate Town.

P	53+1 apps	1 gl
FAC	5 apps	0 gls
FLC	6 apps	0 gls
EC	5 apps	0 gls
CS	1 app.	0 gls
Total	70+1 apps	1 gl

BEAMISH, Kenneth George
Striker

6'0" 12st 6lb
Born: Birkenhead, 25 August 1947
Debut: 17 August 1974

CAREER: Stork; Tranmere Rovers Jul 1966; Brighton & Hove Albion Mar 1972 (£25,000+Duffy); Blackburn Rovers May 1974 (£25,000); Port Vale Sep 1976 (£12,000); Bury Sep 1978 (£3,000); Tranmere Rovers Nov 1979 (£10,000); Swindon Town May 1981 (free).

Ken Beamish came to Ewood because Brian Clough had taken over at Brighton and was not impressed with the player's lack of balance or poise. Conversely, Gordon Lee had taken over at Blackburn and was more used to life in the Third Division and saw Beamish's hustle, effort and physical qualities as ideal for the task ahead. Despite being erratic in front of goal he contributed to the club's immediate championship, even finding quasi-cult status among the fans, who for years after chanted 'Beamo' whenever anyone missed badly. In the Second Division he struggled but still found plenty of clubs looking for his particular qualities over the next six years. A brief try at management with Swindon was sufficient to tell him he had no gift for this and he returned to live locally. When he had played for the Rovers he had lived in Euxton where he became a huge favourite due to his involvement in local charity work. This experience proved ideal for his future role down at Ewood where for many years he has been involved as manager of the promotional side.

FL	86 apps	18 gls
FAC	3 apps	2 gls
FLC	9 apps	5 gls
Total	98 apps	25 gls

BEAN, Alan
Centre half

5'10.5" 11st 4lb
Born: Doncaster, 17 January 1935
Died: Sheffield, 25 February 1961
Debut: 15 November 1952

CAREER: Blackburn Rovers Apr 1952-Jun 1955; Worksop Town; Wisbech Town; Retford Town.

Spotted playing for Doncaster Boys he became a member of the ground staff at Ewood. Along with Bryan Douglas, he was regarded as the most promising of all the club's juniors but an early debut was traumatic. A knee injury forced him out of the Football League and he was playing in the Yorkshire League at Abbeydale Park when he collapsed and died. It was his first game back following a Christmas knee injury and he had only had the chance for a few hours' sleep after working the night shift.

FL	2 apps	0 gls
Total	2 apps	0 gls

BEARDALL, James Thomas
Centre forward

5'11" 12st 3lb
Born: Salford, 18 October 1946
Debut: 20 April 1968

CAREER: Albert Rd Sec Mod (Whitefield); Bury Jan 1962-Dec 1963; Prestwich United; Bury Aug 1964 (am); Blackburn Rovers May 1967 (am) Mar 1968 (pro); Oldham Athletic May 1969 (free); Great Harwood Mar 1970; Radcliffe Aug 1973; Great Harwood to May 1976.

An apprenticeship at Bury ended without the offer of a professional contract, but Beardall continued to represent the youth team as an amateur while playing park football. Eddie Quigley knew of Beardall due to his connections in the Bury area and invited him to sign amateur terms and play with the reserves. Although he was promising, Quigley would not elevate him until he signed professional, which he did when he had finished his apprenticeship in the printing trade. In the first team Beardall still had his trademark eye for goal but he struggled with the increased pace of play and never looked like achieving the necessary sharpness in his movements. A short-term scoring sensation at Oldham, he drifted back into the non-league world, playing for some time at Great Harwood.

FL	4+2 apps	1 gl
Total	4+2 apps	1 gl

BEARDSMORE, Russell Peter
Winger

5'6" 9st
Born: Wigan, 28 September 1968
Debut: 26 December 1991

CAREER: Atherton Collieries; Manchester United Oct 1986 (app. Jun 1985); Blackburn Rovers Dec 1991 (loan); Bournemouth Jun 1993-Dec 1999 (free).

It was ironic that after Manchester United found the frail but talented winger not robust enough for the top flight and Kenny Dalglish echoed the sentiments when he took him on loan, Beardsmore eventually made a career for himself in the lower divisions at full-back. As a creative defender he was a fixture for Bournemouth before chronic back trouble caused his retirement. He was immediately offered the position of Assistant Community Development officer at the Fitness First Stadium.

FL	1+1 apps	0 gls
Total	1+1 apps	0 gls

BEATTIE, James Scott
Striker

6'1" 12st
Born: Lancaster, 27 February 1978
Debut: 12 October 1996

CAREER: Queen Elizabeth GS; Blackburn Rovers Aug 1994; Southampton Jul 1998 (£1,000,000); Everton Jan 2005 (£6,000,000).
INTERNATIONALS: England 5 apps.

Beattie's father Mick, a lorry driver in Blackburn, made many sacrifices so that his son could attend the town's top school, Queen Elizabeth Grammar School. Academically bright, he gained 9 GCSEs and might have studied medicine. He instead chose to accept the traineeship with the club on whose terraces he had stood. Even at that tender age it represented a change in career because Beattie had been an outstanding swimmer with Wigan Wasps and was ranked second in the country at butterfly when he was fourteen. A serious shoulder injury forced him to concentrate on football and he proved that he could score goals as he worked his way through the youth teams into the reserves. His career appeared to plateau as he left his teens and before he had a chance to recover he was sold to Southampton, who needed him to replace

Kevin Davies who was moving the opposite way, for a phenomenal and as it transpired excessive sum. Given a chance to develop, he grew into a fearsome old-fashioned centre forward, a great leaper and header and with the lung power to run perpetually. Although he was recognised as the most promising young striker of his time there was some doubt about a lifestyle that included close friendships with recording stars such as Craig David and the members of Artful Dodger. Anxious to improve his status with the national side and return north, he signed for Everton in January 2005 for £6,000,000, but suspension and injury prevented him making much contribution that season.

P	1+3 apps	0 gls
FAC	0+1 app.	0 gls
FLC	2 apps	0 gls
Total	3+4 apps	0 gls

BECKFORD, Jason Neil
Winger

5'9" 12st 4lb
Born: Manchester, 14 February 1970
Debut: 16 March 1991

CAREER: Burnage HS; Manchester City Aug 1987:Blackburn Rovers Mar 1991 (loan); Port Vale Sep 1991 (loan); Birmingham City Jan 1992 (£50,000); Bury Mar 1994 (loan); Stoke City Aug 1994; Millwall Dec 1994; Northampton Town May 1995; Burnley Jul 1996 (trial); Halifax Town Oct 1996; Altrincham 1996.

Jason Beckford and his brother Darren were regarded as potentially good players at Manchester City but neither harnessed natural talent to achievement. A thickset, powerful man who played wide on the right, he often found the game eluded him; certainly it was always the case in his loan spell at Ewood, and his lack of a settled home thereafter appears to confirm that this was often the case. After a downward spiral among many clubs he retired and was appointed to a coaching position at Manchester City's School of Excellence. In 2002 he became assistant to Ally Pickering at Mossley, combining this with his employment as a senior counsellor in the Manchester Drugs Unit.

FL	3+1 apps	0 gls
Total	3+1 apps	0 gls

BEE, Francis Eric
Inside forward

5'11.5" 10st 9lb
Born: Nottingham, 23 June 1927
Debut: 5 March 1949

CAREER: Nottingham Forest (am); Sunderland Jun 1947; Blackburn Rovers Mar 1949 (£6,000); Peterborough United Jul 1950 (free); Boston United 1954.

In 1949 the Rovers were desperate for an inside forward and wanted to sign either Aitken of Glasgow Rangers or Ivor Broadis. Outbid by Sunderland for the talented Welsh international, they asked if the Roker club would be in a position to release their young prospect Frank Bee. Unfortunately desperation inflated the fee and it was found that Bee was a rough diamond who the club simply did not have time to hone. It was not long before he was released and he never played in the Football League again, finishing his career at wing half with Peterborough before playing 5 games for Boston.

FL	4 apps	0 gls
Total	4 apps	0 gls

BEGLIN, James Martin
Left-back

5'11" 11st
Born: Waterford, 29 July 1963
Debut: 13 October 1990

CAREER: Bolton; Bohemians; Shamrock Rovers; Liverpool May 1983; Leeds United Jul 1989 (free)-Jul 1991; Plymouth Argyle Nov 1989 (loan); Blackburn Rovers Oct 1990 (loan).
INTERNATIONALS: Eire 15 apps.

Having started his career with Shamrock Rovers when the club was having financial troubles, Beglin provided them with the lifeline of his transfer fee to Liverpool. Frustrated by the presence of Alan Kennedy, he spent much time in the reserves but his sweet left foot and the coolness with which he performed marked him as an asset for the future. When Kennedy was injured he stepped in and was immediately at home in a side that had been league champions the previous year. Present in the tragic European Cup final at the Heysel Stadium, the subsequent ban on English clubs prevented him playing in European competition, but he gained international experience with the Republic of Ireland. In 1987 he broke his leg in the Merseyside derby and subsequently never played to the same standard. His spell on loan at Ewood added stability to a suspect position but was brief. Articulate and informed, he took readily to broadcasting and obtained positions commenting on the game with RTE and Granada.

FL	6 apps	0 gls
Total	6 apps	0 gls

BELL, John Eric*
Left half

5'8.5" 9st 9lb
Born: Bedlington, 13 February 1922
Died: Heysham, 22 February 2005
Debut: 1 September 1945

CAREER: Blyth Shipyard; Blackburn Rovers Aug 1945-May 1957.

Perhaps the most underrated Rover of all time, Eric Bell came from the shipyards of the North-East as the Second World War ended to bring deceptive hardness to his role of efficient covering and tough tackling. Competing for a half-back position with the youthful prodigy Ronnie Clayton and the raucous Jack Campbell, he served a succession of managers who all saw him as their first choice on the left side. In emergencies he played left-back and left wing but for a decade he formed with the man behind him, Bill Eckersley, one of the most solid left-sided partnerships in football. When he retired he was found a coaching role at Ewood where he proved his worth when his side lifted the FA Youth Cup and later when he twice coached the reserves to the Central League title. He had become a sub-postmaster in Darwen and later he moved to take a similar position in the Morecambe area.

FL	323 apps	9 gls
FAC	10 apps	0 gls
Total	333 apps	9 gls

BELL, Norman
Striker

6'1" 13st 1lb
Born: Hylton Castle, Sunderland, 16 November 1955
Debut: 25 November 1981

CAREER: Monkwearmouth GS; Wolverhampton Wanderers Nov 1973 (app. Jul 1971); New England Teamen (USA) Apr 1980, Apr 1981 (loan); Blackburn Rovers Nov 1981 (£70,000)-Jun 1985; Darwen.

Bell had gained an impressive reputation as a goalscorer at Wolverhampton, where his ability to come off the bench and change the game had made him the original super-sub. A gangling, energetic player, good in the air and ideal as a partner for a predatory sharp shooter, he might have proved an ideal accompaniment for Simon Garner if he had not been frequently troubled by a knee injury that eventually terminated his career. He remained in the area where he went into business and had a spell as player-manager at Darwen. His son Andrew gained schoolboy international honours and became a trainee with the Rovers before playing for Wycombe Wanderers and York City.

FL	57+4 apps	10 gls
FAC	2 apps	0 gls
FLC	2 apps	0 gls
Total	61+4 apps	10 gls

BELL, Robert Charles
Centre half

6'0" 11st 11lb
Born: Cambridge, 26 October 1950
Debut: 11 September 1971

CAREER: Tottenham Hotspur (app. May 1966); Ipswich Town Nov 1968 (app. Sep 1967); Blackburn Rovers Sep 1971 (with £50,000 for Hunter); Crystal Palace Sep 1971 (£50,000); Norwich City Feb 1972 (loan); Hellenic (South Africa) 1973; York City Feb 1977; Fort Lauderdale Strikers (USA) Apr 1977-Aug 1978.

When Allan Hunter decided that the Third Division was no place for an international of his promise Ipswich won the bidding war for his services. In addition to a fee they offered Bell, a raw-boned, rugged individual who could slot straight into his spot. Less than two weeks later Crystal Palace offered £50,000 for Bell and Ken Furphy, who wanted to rebuild his side, accepted the offer. Perhaps the decision was shrewd, for no club ever extracted the latent promise from the player and he ended his career in the USA.

FL	2 apps	0 gls
Total	2 apps	0 gls

BELLAMY, Craig Douglas
Striker

5'9" 10st 12lb
Born: Cardiff, 13 July 1979
Debut: 13 August 2005

CAREER: Rumney High School; Norwich City Jan 1997; Coventry City Aug 2000 (£6,500,000); Newcastle United Jul 2001 (£6,000,000); Glasgow Celtic Jan 2005 (loan); Blackburn Rovers Jul 2005 (£5,000,000).
INTERNATIONALS: Wales 34 apps 9 gls.

A small, waspish striker with great pace and poise, able to get behind defences and create goalscoring opportunities, he started his career at Norwich and quickly attracted the attention that brought big-money moves to Coventry and Newcastle. His progress has only been limited by recurring knee injuries and a temperament that has sometimes created conflict, most famously at Newcastle, where his public feud with Graeme Souness resulted in his exit. Never a man to take the conventional option, he had a successful half season on loan at Celtic before deciding to join his old international manager, Mark Hughes, at Blackburn. Although his injury worries have continued he has brought a cutting edge and decisive movement that the team was badly in need of.

PL	8+3 apps	5 gls
FLC	2+1 apps	2 gls
Total	10+4 apps	7 gls

BENT, Marcus Nathan
Striker

6'2" 12st 4lb
Born: Hammersmith, 19 May 1978
Debut: 25 November 2000

CAREER: St Augustine's; St Paul's Sch (Sunbury); Sunbury Celtic; Brentford Jul 1995 (app. Jul 1994); Crystal Palace Jan 1998 (£150,000); Port Vale Jan 1999 (£375,000); Sheffield United Oct 1999 (£300,000); Blackburn Rovers Nov 2000 (£2,500,000); Ipswich Town Nov 2001 (£2,800,000); Leicester City (loan) Aug 2003; Everton Jun 2004 (£450,000).

During his schooldays Bent represented England in the 100 metres and was also selected for the

England Catholic Schools' football team. Taken on as an apprentice at Brentford, who spotted him playing junior football at Sunbury, his career meandered through Crystal Palace and Port Vale, at every point never fully achieving his potential. It took a move to Sheffield United to change his future because at Bramall Lane he was at last able to ally his physical tools to an effective game. Fast, mobile and strong in the air he became a much more potent scoring threat and caught the eye of Graeme Souness, who required a more aggressive leader of the line. In the promotion season of 2000/01 Bent played his part with vital goals but it was obvious that Souness had doubts about whether he could make the Premiership grade and the following season he was largely sidelined until Ipswich agreed to pay the asking price and involve him in their battle against relegation. Ironically, although this fight was unsuccessful, Bent proved that he could cope with the Premiership and score goals. He remained in the Premiership, signing for Everton, where he earned respect playing in an improved side where he was the lone striker.

L	22+15 apps	8 gls
FAC	5+1 apps	3 gls
FLC	0+1 app.	0 gls
Total	27+17 apps	11 gls

BENTLEY, David Michael
Midfield

5'10" 11st
Born: Peterborough, 27 August 1984
Debut: 11 September 2005

CAREER: Charlton Youth; East Anglia Youth; Wormley Youth; Arsenal School of Excellence 1996; Arsenal Sep 2001; Norwich City Jun 2004-Jun 2005 (loan); Blackburn Rovers Aug 2005 (loan).

Born in Peterborough and raised in Cheshunt, he joined the Arsenal school of excellence at twelve and moved through the England international age groups. A natural athlete with quick feet, fine skills and vision, he found that making the breakthrough to the Arsenal first-team squad was difficult and accepted season-long loans, first at Norwich and then with the Rovers. Despite a fine debut at Bolton, he has not consolidated his position in the Blackburn team and remains a fringe player, mostly found on the substitutes bench.

PL	10+2 apps	
FLC	3 apps	1 gl
Total	13+2 apps	1 gl

BERG, Henning
Right-back/central defender

6'0" 11st 9lb
Born: Eidsvell (Norway), 1 September 1969
Debut: 2 February 1993

CAREER: KFUM (Oslo); Valerengen Aut 1988 (£2,000); Lillestrom 1992 (£20,000); Blackburn Rovers Jan 1993 (£400,000); Manchester Utd Aug 1997 (£5,000,000); Blackburn Rovers Sep 2000 (loan) Dec 2000-Jun 2003 (£1,750,000); Glasgow Rangers (free) Aug 2003-Jun 2004.
INTERNATIONALS: Norway 100 apps 9 gls.

Only one man participated in both of the club's greatest triumphs in recent years, the Premiership championship of 1995 and the Worthington Cup victory of 2002, Henning Berg. This was not coincidental because Berg is, despite a three-year break in the middle of his service, one of the club's all-time greats. He arrived at Ewood in late 1992 when the club trained beside the river at Pleasington and Berg was a lonely figure as he waited for the work permit that would allow him to play. When it arrived he proved a sound, consistent right-back, perhaps the greatest stand-up tackler the club has ever fielded, with balance and power and great calm. After the championship season he was moved to his preferred position at the centre of the defence and proved to be superb, a born leader, a competitor and driving force able to read play and organise. Much of this was down to his fitness and timing and his departure to Manchester United contributed to the club's decline and relegation. Three years later he was able to remedy this as he returned to transform a drifting side into one that was promoted back to the Premiership. At Cardiff, in the absence of the suspended Short, Tugay and Flitcroft, he warranted the captaincy with his leadership. In the last season of his contract he decided to return to Norway but later changed his mind. Graeme Souness was unwilling to accommodate this reversal and, out of contract, he joined Glasgow Rangers. The Rovers' subsequent defensive weaknesses demonstrated just what a loss he was to the club. At the end of his first season in Scotland he retired and returned to Norway where he wrote his autobiography and worked with the media. Just before he hung up his boots he had been awarded his 100th cap for his country. By the start of the next Norwegian season he was back in football as coach to SFK Lyn.

L	244+7 apps	7 gls
FAC	16 apps	0 gls
FLC	19 apps	0 gls
UEFA	3+1 apps	0 gls
EC	6 apps	0 gls
CS	1 app.	0 gls
Total	289+8 apps	7 gls

BERKOVIC, Eyal

Midfield

5'7" 10st 2lb
Born: Regba (Israel), 2 April 1972
Debut: 10 February 2001

CAREER: Maccabi Haifa; Southampton Oct 1996-May 1997 (loan); West Ham United Jul 1997 (£1,700,000); Glasgow Celtic Jul 2000 (£5,500,000); Blackburn Rovers Feb 2001 (loan); Manchester City Jul 2001 (£1,600,000); Portsmouth Jan 2004-Jan 2005 (free); Maccabi Tel Aviv Jun 2005.
INTERNATIONALS: Israel 78 apps 9 gls.

Born in the hot, dusty wastelands of Nahrya, Berkovic was fortunate that his first club, Maccabi Haifa, recognised that, despite the slight physique, they had a player of supreme artistry with a burning desire to succeed. Introduced into the first team at twenty, the club won the Israeli championship the following season with a record number of points. With Atar and Hazan he formed a midfield that was truly dominant and inevitably this took him into the national side. Success in his homeland continued but, driven by ambition, he spent a season on loan at Graeme Souness's Southampton. By the end of it he had made a reputation that meant that Southampton could not afford to sign him and instead he joined West Ham, where he settled down well in the Golders Green area. Dynamic, kinetic and a true playmaker there was also a theatrical edge to the player that promoted drama and controversy. It was this that forced him to leave for Scotland where he found a change of management excluded him from the side. Brought on loan to Blackburn to give impetus to a final push for promotion, Berkovic brought not just class but passion to the task. Undecided as to whether the player would be a luxury in a Premiership side which might require strong backs and consistency, Souness decided not to take the option of signing him but Kevin Keegan happily accepted the chance and his judgement proved correct as Berkovic's leadership helped establish Manchester City in the Premiership. A move to Portsmouth saw him less influential and his contract was cancelled so that he could find a club back in Israel.

FL	4+7 apps	2 gls
FAC	3 apps	0 gls
Total	7+7 apps	2 gls

BIMPSON, James Louis*

Right winger/centre forward

6'1.5" 12st 2lb
Born: Rainford, 14 May 1929
Debut: 21 November 1959

CAREER: Bushey Lane CoE School; Rainford Sec Mod; Rainford North End 1946; Burscough Sum 1952; Royal Engineers (Villack, Austria); British Troops (Austria); Liverpool Jan 1953; Blackburn Rovers Nov 1959 (£60,000); Bournemouth & Boscombe Athletic Feb 1961; Rochdale Aug 1961; Wigan Athletic Jul 1963; Burscough.

Born and raised in Rainford, Bimpson's career was not helped by the fact that the local pitch was commandeered for the 'dig for victory' campaign, so at least national service in Austria allowed him to play the game regularly. Returning home he moved just down the road to Burscough and, when given his debut in the Liverpool Combination, he was such a sensation that it was inevitable that he would find his way to Anfield. He scored seven goals on his debut and did not play a full season before he was transferred. A deputy to Billy Liddell, he tallied an impressive goal total and earned respect as a powerful, committed, honest player who could provide muscle and application. He came to Ewood to add cover to a talented team who had no depth, but found himself immediately introduced on the right wing because of the transfer of Roy Vernon. Sadly his best days were behind him and, although he ran honestly, he brought no great pace or game-breaking talent. Ironically, in the downside of his career he started to collect medals, playing on the losing side in the FA Cup final (with the Rovers) and the FL Cup final (with Rochdale).

FL	22 apps	5 gls
FAC	7 apps	3 gls
Total	29 apps	8 gls

BINNS, Eric
Centre half

6'0" 12st 6lb
Born: Halifax, 13 August 1924
Died: Burnley, 22 September 2007
Debut: 27 August 1955

CAREER: Huddersfield Town; Halifax Town May 1946; Goole Town; Halifax YC; Burnley Mar 1949; Blackburn Rovers May 1955, Kettering Town Aug 1957; Runcorn.

Having failed to make the grade as a centre forward at Halifax, Binns was converted to the centre of the defence where he demonstrated that he was calm, composed and solid. Rediscovered at Burnley, he could not displace Tommy Cummings but the Rovers admired his play in the reserves so much that they paid a small fee for him with the intention of him taking over immediately from Willie Kelly. Being carried off in the public trial game did not help his cause but since the team, without him, lost the first 2 games and conceded 5 goals it was not a great setback. In the next 11 games only 12 goals were conceded and Binns appeared to be the difference. During this time he had looked vulnerable to the fast-breaking forwards but he had used his positional sense so well that only Billy Liddell had discomforted him. However, his vulnerability was exposed rapidly and in the next 9 games 22 goals were conceded and Kelly returned. In the close season Matt Woods arrived to effectively end Binns's Rovers career. A keen cricketer with Burnley CC, he later became steward at the club.

FL	23 apps	0 gls
Total	23 apps	0 gls

BIRCHENALL, Alan John
Midfield

6'0" 11st 3lb
Born: East Ham, 22 August 1945
Debut: 30 September 1978

CAREER: Haydn Rd Jnr Sc; Claremont Sec Mod; Bestwood YC; Parliament St Methodists; Bartons Transport; Stamford; Thorneywood Athletic; Notts County (jnrs); Sheffield United Jun 1963; Chelsea Nov 1967 (£100,000); Crystal Palace Jun 1970 (£100,000); Leicester City Sep 1971 (£100,000);

Notts County Mar 1976 (loan); San Jose Earthquakes (USA) Apr 1977 (loan); Notts County Sep 1977; Memphis Rogues (USA) Apr 1978; Blackburn Rovers Sep 1978; Luton Town Mar 1979; Hereford United Oct 1979; Trowbridge (p-c) 1980.

Born in London but raised in Nottingham, Birchenall joined Sheffield United from school and was given an early first-team debut. He quickly established himself as an elegant player equally at home in midfield or up front. After completing a century of appearances and winning Under-23 international caps he became Dave Sexton's first signing at Chelsea. With his platinum blond hair and penchant for publicity, Birchenall was happy at Stamford Bridge and continued to be in demand and popular at Crystal Palace and Leicester. By then he had dropped deeper, bringing stability and balance to the team, and off the field he had become respected as a dressing room guru. He intended his spell in America to be his swansong but the Rovers were desperate for a man of influence and brought him home. Unhappily, he was not accustomed to relegation dogfights and looked ill at ease. Never a man to be unoccupied he bought the Griffin Inn in Swithihead (a 300-year-old public house) and started a business importing ladies' footwear. He also coached Trowbridge into the Alliance Premier League and became public relations officer at Leicester.

FL	17+1 apps	0 gls
FAC	2 apps	0 gls
Total	19+1 apps	0 gls

BJORNEBYE, Stig-Inge

Left-back

5'10" 11st 9lb

Born: Elverum (Norway), 11 December 1969

Debut: 12 August 2000

CAREER: Elverum IL 1986; Strommen IF 1988; Kongsvinger IL 1989 (£12,000); Rosenborg BK 1992 (£33,000); Liverpool Dec 1992 (£600,000); Rosenborg BK Mar 1994 (loan); Brondby IF (Denmark) Mar 2000 (loan); Blackburn Rovers Jun 2000-Mar 2003 (£300,000).

INTERNATIONALS: Norway 75 apps 1 gl.

The son of Jo-Inge Bjornebye, who competed in the ski jump at the Olympics of 1968 and 1972, Bjornebye commenced playing with his local side when still a teenager. His steady, positionally sound play, and the attacking options he gave by his delivery of the ball from the wide left, convinced newly promoted Strommen that he would bolster their side. Continuing to climb the ladder, he arrived at one of the country's top sides, Rosenberg, and honours started to accumulate. He was called into the national side, won a championship medal and scored the winning goal in the cup final. A move abroad was inevitable but his choice of Liverpool looked less than ideal for a time. Pushed into a side that was losing defenders rapidly, he formed with Torben Piechnik a central defensive partnership that was much derided. Patience, though, is one of Bjornebye's qualities and he worked diligently until he won a place at left-back and won a League Cup winners' medal. After breaking a leg he was never in Gerard Houllier's plans and the chance to link up again with Graeme Souness brought him to Ewood. Part of the side that won promotion to the Premiership, he won another League Cup winners' medal at Cardiff in 2002, returning after a spell out with illness to be one of the top performers on the day. His appearances were restricted by continual injuries (he had a back problem) and illness but they were nothing to the disastrous spell he struck after the final victory. A training injury fractured his eye socket and almost cost him this sight in one eye, and then he had to undergo surgery because a condition in his leg might have resulted in amputation. After taking medical advice he retired from the game, becoming trainer to SFK Lyn and taking up a role scouting for the

Rovers in Norway before he was appointed assistant coach of the national side.

L	53+3 apps	1 gl
FAC	4+1 apps	0 gls
FLC	7 apps	0 gls
Total	64+4 apps	1 gl

BLACKLAW, Adam Smith

Goalkeeper

5'11.5" 14st 6lb
Born: Aberdeen, 2 September 1937
Died: Barnoldswick, 28 February 2010
Debut: 19 August 1967

CAREER: Frederick St School; Burnley Oct 1954; Blackburn Rovers Jul 1967 (£15,000); Blackpool Jun 1970 (free); Great Harwood 1971; Clitheroe (p-m) Dec 1976.
INTERNATIONALS: Scotland 3 apps.

Present throughout Burnley's glory years but displaced by Harry Thomson, a move to Ewood appeared ideal for all parties because Blacklaw at his best had been a formidable presence. A huge man, dominant in the goalmouth and deceptively agile, the truth was that he was in the downswing of his career. Although sometimes he looked the part (he once went 582 minutes between conceding goals) he had become vulnerable to the long shot and was suffering health-wise. When Roger Jones was signed he had reached the end, even losing his place as deputy to John Barton. He managed Clitheroe for a time, playing occasionally, but became the licensee of a public house. Later he became the caretaker/handyman at Nelson and Colne College at Barrowford.

FL	96 apps	0 gls
FAC	5 apps	0 gls
FLC	9 apps	0 gls
Total	110 apps	0 gls

BLAKE, Nathan Alexander

Striker

5'11" 13st 12lb
Born: Cardiff, 27 January 1972
Debut: 31 October 1998

CAREER: Chelsea (trainee); Cardiff City Aug 1990 (free); Sheffield United Feb 1994 (£300,000); Bolton Wanderers Dec 1995 (£1,500,000); Blackburn Rovers Oct 1998 (£4,000,000); Wolverhampton Wanderers Sep 2001 (£1,500,000); Leicester City Aug 2004-Jun 2005 (free); Leeds United Dec 2004 (loan).
INTERNATIONALS: Wales 29 apps 4 gls.

After failing to make the grade at Tottenham Blake returned to his home-town team. He was then a right-back, and played for the Welsh 'B' team in that position, but Cardiff noticed that he had the build of a sprinter and at times was equally explosive. Trying him up front, they discovered he had an eye for goal and the ability to lurk with intent in the danger areas. These qualities took him to Sheffield United, Bolton and the Rovers, although in every case he could not prevent his team being relegated from the Premier League. Never settled at Ewood, his lack of work rate did not endear him and his move to Wolverhampton was no surprise. Although he helped the Wanderers to promotion he continued to struggle with injury and was released and joined Leicester. His chances of finding a new club in 2005 were ended when he received a suspension for testing positive for a recreational drug.

L	37+17 apps	13 gls
FAC	5+3 apps	2 gls
FLC	3 apps	1 gl
Total	45+20 apps	16 gls

BLORE, Reginald
Forward

5' 9" 12st
Born: Sesswick, Wrexham, 18 March 1942
Debut: 30 November 1963

CAREER: Liverpool May 1958 (am) May 1959 (pro); Southport Jul 1960 (free); Blackburn Rovers Nov 1963 (£6,000); Oldham Athletic Dec 1965 (£8,000); Bangor City 1970; Ellesmere Port Town 1971.

Although born in Wales Blore grew up near Goodison Park. Taken into Liverpool's youth scheme, he scored seven goals in one FA Youth Cup tie against Chester but the odds on making the grade appeared stacked against a player who was not tall enough for a striker and not constructive enough for an inside forward. At Southport he found his niche and became a stalwart until the Rovers decided that he was worth a gamble to add depth. He never established himself but moved on to become a regular at Oldham. When his playing days were over he moved into the insurance trade where no doubt he was able to utilise the skill that brought him the PFA golf championship.

FL	11 apps	0 gls
Total	11 apps	0 gls

BOGAN, Thomas
Right winger

5' 9" 11st 6lb
Born: Glasgow, 18 May 1920
Died: Wilmslow, 23 September 1993
Debut: 26 September 1953

CAREER: Strathclyde 1937; Blantyre Celtic 1938; Renfrew Jnrs 1943; Hibernian; Glasgow Celtic Jan 1946; Preston North End Sep 1948; Manchester United Aug 1949; Aberdeen Mar 1951; Southampton Dec 1951; Blackburn Rovers Aug 1953; Macclesfield Town Jun 1954.

By the time that he was signed Bogan had lost the characteristic speed and nimbleness that marked his best football. At his most effective during the war years, even they were blighted by a broken leg received after ninety seconds of a wartime international against England. A persistent knee injury marred his first spell south of the border, with Preston, but he recovered at Old Trafford. By the time he came to Ewood he was working as a linotype operator on the compositors' room at *The Guardian* and *Manchester Evening News* and he was to spend most of the remainder of his working life there. He died of a heart attack while enjoying a game of golf at Wilmslow.

FL	1 app.	0 gls
Total	1 app.	0 gls

BOHINEN, Lars
Midfield

5'11" 12st 2lb
Born: Vadso (Norway), 8 September 1969
Debut: 14 October 1995

CAREER: Langnes; Baerum Sportsklubb 1986; SFK Lyn; Valerengens Idrettsforening; Young Boys of Berne (Switzerland) Nov 1989 (£40,000); Viking Stavanger Apr 1990 (loan); Lillestroem Sportsklubb Jan 1993 (loan); Nottingham Forest Oct 1993 (£450,000); Blackburn Rovers Oct 1995 (£700,000); Derby County Mar 1998 (£1,450,000); Lyngby FC (Denmark) Jan 2001 (free); Forum BK (Denmark) Dec 2001-Aug 2002; Valerengens Aug 2003-Dec 2003.
INTERNATIONALS: Norway 49 apps 10 gls.

Born in the Finnmark county of northern Norway, Bohinen grew up in Mo i Rana (Lagnes), which is not far from the Arctic circle. Fortunately he moved near Oslo at the age of fourteen and commenced playing for his local side, making his debut in the Second Division in 1986. Although he progressed and moved accordingly he was ill at ease when he ventured abroad and was loaned out by his Swiss club. It was not until he signed for Nottingham Forest that the football world was shown what a true talent he was. With complete mastery of the ball he was able to perform perfect cameos of casual trickery, could ease elegantly through a defence and could also shoot with power. Conversely he was inconsistent, sometimes refrained from tracking back and suffered frequent niggling thigh injuries. A revelation when he arrived at Ewood, he was never accommodated in the 'hole' that Ray Harford believed was his true position. When relegation loomed Tony Parkes preferred the 'dogs of war' across his midfield and Bohinen was left an isolated and somewhat dispirited individual. Never one to suffer silently, he was in trouble with Harford and then with Jim Smith at Derby because of his inability to accept situations he did not appreciate. His last playing days were spent in Denmark. Here he had the misfortune to first play for a club that went bankrupt and then received a career-ending injury with his next club in only his second game. Returning to Norway he was appointed assistant coach with Valerengens, making a brief playing comeback before injury again intervened.

FL	40+18 apps	7 gls
FAC	2+1 apps	1 gl
FLC	3+2 apps	1 gl
Total	45+21 apps	9 gls

BOTHROYD, Jay
Striker

6'3" 13st 6lb
Born: Islington 7 May 1982
Debut: 11 September 2004

CAREER: Westward School; Arsenal Jul 1999; Coventry City Jul 2000 (£1,000,000); Perugia (Italy) Jun 2003 (free); Blackburn Rovers Aug 2004 -Jun 2005 (loan); Hertha Berlin (Germany) Jul 2005 (trial); FSV Mainz 05 (Germany) Aug 2005 (trial); Charlton Athletic Aug 2005.

Acknowledged as an exciting talent with fine skills for a tall player he has displayed a remarkable ability to self destruct. After helping Arsenal to win the FA Youth Cup he was put up for sale for disciplinary reasons after throwing his shirt at the coach when he was substituted. Even so Coventry paid a million pounds for him, an astonishing fee for a player who had not played a first-team game. Nursed carefully, he flashed talent but his casual style irritated the fans and a new manager (Gary McAllister) refused to use him. Bothroyd took the unusual step of joining a run-of-the-mill Italian side (Perugia) but in his first season achieved little beyond a dramatic goal that in the end merely delayed the club's relegation. Surplus to requirements, he joined Blackburn on a season-long loan but did nothing to suggest that his career had turned around. Although he appeared to be on the point of being given the chance to play regularly alongside Paul Dickov, a serious thigh injury virtually ended his season. Curiously, his friends include Colonel Gaddafi's son, who played with him at Perugia, and Jade Goody from Big Brother.

PL	6+5 apps	1 gl
FAC	0+1 app.	0 gls
FLC	1 app.	0 gls
Total	7+6 apps	1 gl

BOYD, Leslie Munro 'Lee'
Centre-back

5'11" 12st 1lb
Born: Newcastle 7 September 1952

CAREER: New Hartley Juniors; Leeds United (app.); Blackburn Rovers May 1972-Jun 1973 (free).

The son of a miner from East Holywell, Shiremoor he became an apprentice at Leeds but was not offered professional terms. He was given a season's contract at Ewood and although athletic and tough he proved erratic and inconsistent. He was named substitute for an end-of-season game but did not get on the field. His most memorable impact was the day when, travelling to training from the North-East with teammate Geoff Dale, he was stranded in thick snow and was stuck in his car for several hours.

FLC	4 apps	0 gls
Total	67+6 apps	3 gls

BRADFORD, David William

Midfield

5'5" 9st 8lb
Born: Manchester, 22 February 1953
Debut: 14 August 1971

CAREER: Manchester City (ass sc); Blackburn Rovers Aug 1971 (app. Nov 1969); Sheffield United Jul 1974 (£20,000); Peterborough United Oct 1976 (loan); West Bromwich Albion Dec 1976 (loan) Feb 1977; Detroit Express (USA) Apr 1978; Washington Diplomats (USA) Apr 1981; Coventry City Aug 1981 (£60,000); Tulsa Roughnecks (USA) Apr 1982; Seattle Sounders (USA) Apr 1983; Tulsa Roughnecks Apr 1984; Rossendale United Sep 1985.

Dubbed 'the first million-pound footballer' by his manager Ken Furphy, the dynamic, bouncy, red-headed midfield player never translated his youthful promise into maturity. It did not stop Furphy believing in him (he took him to Sheffield United and then the USA) but Bradford lacked the stamina to be a really great player. He found a niche in indoor soccer in the USA, where his sublime skills were fully demonstrated in the penalty shoot-outs that decided drawn games. Married to Jack Campbell's daughter he returned locally, living in Withnell, and then taking a sub post office in the Brownhill region.

FL	58+6 apps	3 gls
FAC	5 apps	0 gls

BRADSHAW, Alan

Inside forward

5'8" 10st 8lb
Born: Blackburn, 14 September 1941
Debut: 1 September 1962

CAREER: Audley Jnrs; Queen Elizabeth GS; Blackburn Rovers Jan 1960 (non con) May 1962 (am); Loughborough College; Blackburn Rovers Mar 1964; Crewe Alexandra May 1965; Macclesfield Town; Great Harwood (p-m) Apr 1976; Chorley (p-c) 1978.

When Trevor Rimmer received an injury in the first leg of the FA Youth Cup semi-final the team was reshuffled to bring in the schoolboy Alan Bradshaw. His goal in the first leg of the final contributed to the club winning the trophy for the only time in their history. Soon after, Bradshaw enjoyed a good run in the FA Amateur Cup with Loughborough University. A tidy, intelligent inside forward, he made a scoring debut at Everton but struggled to break into a good side, perhaps not helped by the fact that he was a part-timer, having qualified as a PE teacher. He carved out a career for himself at Crewe and then had managerial and coaching experience at a variety of locations locally with Great Harwood, Chorley, Padiham, Clitheroe and the Rovers' youth team and abroad in Malaysia. Outside football he had an interest in a nursing home in Clitheroe.

FL	11 apps	2 gls
Total	11 apps	2 gls

BRADSHAW, Paul William

Goalkeeper

6'2.5" 12st 1lb
Born: Altrincham, 28 April 1956
Debut: 17 February 1974

CAREER: Blackburn Rovers Jul 1973; Wolverhampton Wanderers Sep 1977 (£140,000); Vancouver White Caps (Canada) May 1984; West Bromwich Albion Aug 1985; Walsall Jun 1986; Bristol Rovers Apr 1987; Newport County Aug 1987; West Bromwich Albion Aug 1988; Peterborough United Aug 1990; Kettering Town Jul 1991.

Bradshaw should have been one of England's greatest goalkeepers. From the moment he signed for the Rovers after playing at Ewood for the Altrincham Schools' team he had everything. A dominating physical specimen with great reach, agility, sure hands and a positive, calm approach, he played the game naturally but still looked like he had absorbed lessons on technique. It is unusual for a goalkeeper to make his debut while still eligible for the youth team but Bradshaw did and coped well. When the legendary Roger Jones had to be sold he took over without the slightest hitch. When big money took him to Wolverhampton he played well but never matured into an international with his dedication sometime questioned. The victim of an assault in a Midlands nightclub in which he almost lost an eye, he recovered to eke out his career in unlikely venues before becoming a security advisor in Wolverhampton.

FL	78 apps	0 gls
FAC	4 apps	0 gls
FLC	5 apps	0 gls
Total	87 apps	0 gls

BRANAGAN, James Patrick Stephen

Full-back

5'10" 11st 5lb
Born: Barton, 3 July 1955
Debut: 27 October 1979

CAREER: De La Salle School; Cadishead FC; Oldham Athletic Jul 1973 (ass sch Nov 1971); Cape Town City (South Africa) May 1977; Huddersfield Town Nov 1977; Blackburn Rovers Oct 1979 (£20,000); Preston North End Jul 1987 (free); York City Sep 1987-Dec 1988; Chorley-May 1989.

The son of the Manchester City full-back Ken Branagan, he struggled during the early part of his career and even took the route of playing in South Africa to try and make a career. Signed by Howard Kendall to play left-back, he proved emphatically that he could not play on his wrong side but when switched with Mike Rathbone he was a revelation. A true hard man who never took a backward step, rock solid in the tackle and a born competitor, he allied great intelligence to his conviction. Occasionally opponents ghosted past him but they seldom did it twice in the same game and if they did the fear factor multiplied because Branagan was never a man to surrender. An on-field leader, it was no surprise that he was appointed club captain. When he finished playing professionally he worked in insurance and financial services in Salford and was still playing parks football when he had turned forty.

FL	290+4 apps	5 gls
FAC	20 apps	0 gls
FLC	18 apps	0 gls
FMC	5 apps	0 gls
Total	333+4 apps	5 gls

BRAY, John 'Tank'

Right-back

5'10" 12st
Born: Rishton, 16 March 1937
Died: Rainford, 29 September 1992
Debut: 21 September 1959

CAREER: Norden School, Rishton; Clayton Schools; Bangor St YC; Blackburn Rovers Mar 1954 (ground staff May 1953); Bury Apr 1965; Drumcondra (Eire) Sep 1956; Great Harwood.

Bray had two uncles who had played top-class football, for Burnley and Manchester City

John Bray in August 1963. (Howard Talbot Photography)

respectively, so his pedigree was established well before he started appearing with the Rovers' youth teams. A wing half of enormous energy and a sheer power that outstripped most contemporaries, he played the game the way most fans would have done so, with total commitment. No cause was ever lost, he was never in awe of any player, he would crunch into the tackle, chase any ball and was a true players' player. Fortunate enough to make his debut in the season when Blackburn reached the FA Cup final, he had established himself at right-back by the time the club played at Wembley. Like many big men he suffered persistent leg injuries and this limited his career and eventually led to him joining Bury. He had a spell as player manager at Great Harwood and guided them into the first round of the FA Cup. He then worked as a foreman at Jackson Steel in Blackburn. During a time when he was driving a lorry it was discovered that he had heart trouble and he retired early and went to live at the Isle of Whithorn in Scotland. It was on a visit to his old teammate Louis Bimpson in 1992 that he collapsed and died.

FL	153 apps	2 gls
FAC	19 apps	0 gls
FLC	12 apps	0 gls
Total	184 apps	2 gls

BRIGGS, Thomas Henry
Centre forward

6'0" 12st 7lb
Born: Chesterfield, 27 November 1923
Died: Grimsby, 10 February 1984
Debut: 29 November 1952

CAREER: Plymouth Argyle Nov 1945 (am) Mar 1946 (pro); Grimsby Town May 1947; Coventry City Jan 1951 (£18,550); Birmingham City Sep 1951; Blackburn Rovers Dec 1952 (£15,000); Grimsby Town Mar 1958 (£2,000); Glentoran (p-m) May 1959-Jun 1961.

When Tommy Briggs was signed he had already scored 110 league goals in 177 appearances but still had his critics. Many said that he was not a footballer, that he had no ball skills and couldn't truly lead the line. A big lump of a man, he ran powerfully if without grace, but he was a hard man to dispossess and single minded

Tommy Briggs in November 1955. (Howard Talbot Photography)

about his purpose. He had a hammer in both feet and if the ball was lofted his heading was just as lethal. Slotting into a team that loved to pour forward, he simply harvested a goal tally that will never be equalled. In just short of five full seasons he scored 140 goals in 194 league games, without fuss, almost unnoticed. On the unforgettable day when he had already scored six goals against Bristol Rovers the club was awarded a last-minute penalty. Since he was not the penalty taker he made no effort to take the responsibility but eventually he was led to the spot. Carefully he struck his seventh of the afternoon, turned on his heel and jogged back to the halfway line with an odd handshake from the nearest players. He returned to live in Grimsby where he resumed his old profession of master butcher, later working in the electrical supply industry and scouting for the Rovers.

FL	194 apps	140 gls
FAC	10 apps	3 gls
Total	204 apps	143 gls

BRITT, Martin Charles
Centre forward

5'10.5" 12st 4lb
Born: Leigh-on-Sea, 17 January 1946
Debut: 19 March 1966

CAREER: Eastwood School; West Ham United Jan 1963 (app. Jul 1961); Blackburn Rovers Mar 1966-Jun 1967 (£17,000).

Britt appeared to have the football world at his feet at the time that he scored four goals in the second leg of the FA Youth Cup final to help West Ham overturn Wolves' pre-game lead. A regular youth international at a club where talent was always given a chance, his failure to mature was surprising. Signed by the Rovers as a last-gasp move to avoid relegation, he was already suffering from an arthritic knee condition that ended his career before he could play ten games for the club. Returning to college, he worked for the electricity board before setting up his own very successful textile company.

FL	8 apps	0 gls
FLC	1 app.	0 gls
Total	9 apps	0 gls

BROOMES, Marlon Charles
Central defence

6'0" 12st 12lb
Born: Meriden, 28 November 1977
Debut: 17 September 1997

CAREER: New Oscott Lions; Blackburn Rovers Nov 1994; Swindon Town Jan 1997 (loan); Queens Park Rangers Oct 2000 (loan); Grimsby Town Sep 2001 (loan); Sheffield Wednesday Dec 2001 (free); Burnley Jul 2002 (trial); Preston North End Aug 2002 (free); Stoke City Aug 2005 (ex Neal).

A regular international at schoolboy level, Broomes was hunted by all the major clubs so it was considered a coup when he signed for the Rovers. A left-sided central defender, he had athleticism, composure on the ball and could use possession well. His career with the Rovers was dogged by misfortune. He missed huge amounts of playing time with hamstring injuries that were later diagnosed as being caused by an ankle irregularity. When he did finally break into a struggling side he was playing well when he was unlucky to be sent off at Chelsea. With the experience of Peacock being preferred for the rest of the dogfight he found the door closed to him, particularly when the new manager, Graeme Souness, decided to opt for experience. When he left the club he continued to struggle with injury and did not settle until Craig Brown eased him patiently into the Preston line-up, but still he has not fulfilled his youthful promise.

L	24+7 apps	1 gl
FAC	4 apps	0 gls
FLC	3 apps	0 gls
Total	31+7 apps	1 gl

BROTHERSTON, Noel
Winger

5'10" 10st 6lb
Born: Dundonald, 18 November 1956
Died: Blackburn, 6 May 1995
Debut: 20 August 1977

CAREER: North Down Schools; Tottenham Hotspur Apr 1974 (app. 1972); Blackburn Rovers Jul 1977 (free); Bury Jul 1987 (free); Scarborough Oct 1988 (loan); Motala (Sweden) 1989; Chorley 1990.
INTERNATIONALS: Northern Ireland 27 apps 3 gls.

Although he was a product of a successful youth crop at White Hart Lane the sheer volume of talent made Brotherston surplus. Blackburn found they had a right winger who was a tricky, mercurial ball player who could change a game and initially also had an eye for goal. When, in 1980, he scored the goal that clinched the Home International championship for his country it appeared likely that a lucrative move was in the offing but, despite foreign interest, nothing materialised. As the seasons wore on Brotherston appeared to show the frustrations. Sometimes playing on the left wing he became inconsistent and often infuriating as he squandered his talent. He remained in the town, working as a painter and decorator but, in 1995, at the age of thirty-eight, he was found dead in his bed from heart failure.

FL	307+10 apps	40 gls
FAC	24+1 apps	4 gls
FLC	22 apps	2 gls
FMC	2+1 apps	1 gl
Total	355+12 apps	47 gls

BROWN, John Keith
Centre-back

6'0" 11st
Born: Edinburgh, 24 December 1979

CAREER: Blackburn Rovers; Barnsley Sep 1999-Oct 1999 (loan) Dec 1999 (£100,000); Oxford United Nov 2000-Dec 2000 (loan); Falkirk Feb 2002 (free); Portadown Sep 2002; Berwick Rangers Oct 2002-Jun 2003; ECU Joondalup (Australia) 2004.

The much sought-after captain of the Scottish schoolboy international side he came to Ewood because Kenny Dalglish was a boyhood idol. A centre-back with great perception, he formed a great partnership with Martin Taylor in the team that reached the semi-final of the FA Youth Cup. With a plethora of centre-backs he went on loan to Barnsley but on his return he was substitute for a League Cup and then a league game, but before he could make his first-team debut he was sold to Barnsley. Unexpectedly he failed to settle at any club and emigrated to Australia, where he played in the SWC Premier League.

BROWN, Richard Anthony
Right-back

5'10.5" 12st 12lb
Born: Nottingham, 13 January 1967
Debut: 11 September 1991

CAREER: Nottingham Forest (sch); Derby County; Ilkeston Town; Sheffield Wednesday Dec 1984 (£10,000); Ilkeston Town Jul 1986; Grantham Town Jan 1987; Boston United Jul 1987; Kettering Town Jul 1988 (£500); Blackburn Rovers Sep 1990 (£10,000); Maidstone United Feb 1991 (loan); Stockport County Mar 1995 (free); Blackpool Aug 1995; Kettering Town Dec 1995; Stalybridge Celtic; Gainsborough Trinity; Altrincham Mar 1997; Salford City.

When Tony Parkes said that his right-back Richard Brown reminded him of Djalma Santos, the great Brazilian, he was being less fanciful than it appeared. Brown had great skill for a defender, able to bring a high ball under control with one deft flick of the boot and capable of dropping a pinpoint pass down the channel. He also lacked concentration and at times let his opponent lose him much too easily. After his career had failed to get underway he had become a printer and it was work commitments that caused complications in his transfer from Kettering. Carefully eased into the team, he played well during the club's promotion to the Premier League only to lose his place to David May at the death. Serious health problems then restricted his opportunity and his career once again faded away. In between his spells in non-league football he has coached in Boyle County, Kentucky.

L	26+2 apps	0 gls
FAC	2 apps	0 gls
FLC	1+1 app.	0 gls
FMC	1 app.	0 gls
Total	30+3 apps	0 gls

BURGESS, Benjamin Keiron
Striker

6'4" 14st 4lb
Born: Buxton, 9 November 1981
Debut: 15 April 2000

CAREER: New Mills; Oldham Athletic; Stoke City; Everton; Blackburn Rovers Nov 1998 (trainee); Northern Spirit (Australia) Oct 2000 (loan); Brentford Aug 2001 (loan); Stockport County Jul 2002 (£4000,000); Oldham Athletic Jan 2003 (loan); Hull City Mar 2003 (£100,000).

After playing as a schoolboy for several clubs Burgess was granted a traineeship at the Rovers (with compensation paid to Everton). A huge but athletic player, he had jumped 1.95 metres in the high jump and opened the bowing for Buxton. His size and goal-scoring ability made him a prospect and he was fast tracked with a loan spell in Australia (where he was voted the national Under-21 player of the year) and at Brentford (where he scored 17 goals). Despite this Souness had given up on him making a Premiership player and he was moved on to Stockport, where he struggled to make an impact. His situation appeared bleak when he struggled at Oldham but he found form at Hull and established himself in the Republic of Ireland Under-21 side.

FL	1+1 app.	0 gls
FLC	1 app.	0 gls
Total	2+1 apps	0 gls

BURGIN, Andrew
Left-back

5'8.5" 9st 8lb
Born: Sheffield, 6 March 1947
Debut: 7 September 1974

CAREER: Sheffield Wednesday Mar 1964 (app. Aug 1962); Rotherham United Aug 1967; Detroit Cougars (USA) Mar 1968; Halifax Town Dec 1968 (loan) Mar 1969; Blackburn Rovers Sep 1974-Jan 1977 (£15,000).

After failing to establish himself with his first two clubs Burgin became a fixture at Halifax, a steady, sure-tackling, speedy full-back who positioned himself well and brought balance to a team. Initially he was brought to Ewood by Gordon Lee to play at right-back but when Mick Heaton could not switch to the left-hand side Burgin moved and settled in comfortably. The Rovers were promoted to the Second Division in his first season but it was not anticipated that he would have any trauma adjusting to the higher division. Unhappily, no-one found out because Burgin collided with his teammate Mick Hickman in an early game and received a career-ending knee injury. He became a licensee, then a driver for the sweets manufacturer Barker & Dobson but later became janitor at Queen Elizabeth Grammar School.

FL	45 apps	1 gl
FAC	3 apps	0 gls
FLC	2 apps	0 gls
Total	50 apps	1 gl

BURKE, Marshall
Midfield

5'7" 9st 1lb
Born: Glasgow, 26 March 1959
Debut: 13 December 1980

CAREER: Burnley Mar 1977; Leeds United May 1980 (free); Blackburn Rovers Dec 1980 (free); Lincoln City Oct 1982 (£2,500); Cardiff City Dec 1983 (loan); Scarborough 1984; Tranmere Rovers Sep 1984; (Portugal); Scarborough; Northwich Victoria; Colne Dynamoes Aug 1986; Blackburn Rovers Aug 1986 (non con); Morecambe; Colne Dynamoes; Darwen; Bacup; Clitheroe.

Burke always attracted attention because of his busy style, his ball skill and his energy and he was considered an outstanding prospect at Burnley. Given a first-team opportunity, he failed to replace Peter Noble and a brief spell at Leeds failed to recover his prospects. In less-exacting surroundings at Ewood he proved to be a grafter and displayed an ability to obtain some well-struck goals. Dissatisfied with the terms offered to him he sought a move, which started a period of wanderlust in his career. Returning local, he actually started appearing for the Rovers' reserves when he did not have a first-team game with Colne. He also played at Wembley in 1987 when Colne won the FA Vase.

FL	34+5 apps	7 gls
FAC	1 app.	1 gl
FLC	3 apps	0 gls
Total	38+5 apps	8 gls

BUSBY, Vivian Dennis
Striker

6'0" 11st 12lb
Born: High Wycombe, 19 June 1949
Debut: 14 February 1981

CAREER: Hatters Lane School; Terriers (High Wycombe); Wycombe Wanderers 1966; Queens Park Rangers (trial); Chelsea (trial); Fulham Nov 1969 (trial); Luton Town Jan 1970 (£1,300); Newcastle United Dec 1971 (loan); Fulham Aug 1973 (£35,000); Norwich City Sep 1976 (£50,000); Stoke City Nov 1977 (£50,000); Sheffield United Jan 1980 (loan); Tulsa Roughnecks (USA) Mar 1980; Blackburn Rovers Feb 1981 (exchange McKenzie); York City Aug 1982 (free).

A conventional striker who had depths of creativity, he built up a reputation as a journeyman who brought a touch of class wherever he played. He came to Ewood at the tail end of his career, for no other reason than it was the only compensation the club could obtain when Duncan McKenzie decided to play in the USA. Busby cut an unhappy figure with the Rovers, often injured and generally out of touch. Making his way as a coach, he was Dennis Smith's right-hand man at York, Stoke and Sunderland and performed a similar role for Howard Kendall at Sheffield United and Everton. His one attempt to manage on his own ended in failure at Hartlepool but he has always found someone who believed in his coaching ability, acting as reserve team coach at Fulham and youth team coach at Swindon. Sandwiched in this spell was a period where he worked with Metro Radio. He later acted as assistant and temporary manager with York City.

FL	8 apps	1 gl
Total	8 apps	1 gl

BUTCHER, John Melvin

Goalkeeper

6'2.5" 12st 3lb
Born: Newcastle, 27 May 1956
Debut: 8 March 1977
CAREER: Blackburn Rovers 1974 (am) Mar 1976 (pro); Darwen Feb 1976 (loan); Oxford United Aug 1982 (free); Halifax Town Sep 1982 (loan); Bury Dec 1983 (loan); Chester City Aug 1984; Bury Oct 1985 (loan); Altrincham 1987; Macclesfield Town 1989; Rhyl.

The 'enfant terrible' of Rovers' goalkeeping, Butcher had an ideal build, athleticism and had all the basics of a good goalkeeper. Occasionally he looked impressive but his consistency was poor, he was vulnerable from long range and he dropped crosses. It is one of the game's mysteries how he appeared in 100 games but there was always the belief that he was about to turn the corner. He was also an ideal club man, representing them with credit at local functions and training diligently.

FL	104 apps	0 gls
FAC	5 apps	0 gls
FLC	7 apps	0 gls
Total	116 apps	0 gls

BUTT, Leonard

Inside forward

5'5.5" 10st 1lb
Born: Wilmslow, 26 August 1910
Died: Macclesfield, June 1994
Debut: January 23 1937

CAREER: Wilmslow Albion; Alderley; Ashton National Gas; Stockport County Jun 1929 (am); Aug 1929 (pro); Macclesfield Town May 1932; Huddersfield Town Aug 1935; Blackburn Rovers Jan 1937; York City Jan 1947; Mansfield Town Oct 1947; Mossley (p-m) Jun 1948.

The double signing of Butt and Jock Wightman in January 1937 was one of the key building blocks that led to the club's promotion in 1939. After a stuttering career, where he had dropped out of the Football League and worked as a stonemason playing part-time with Macclesfield, Butt had rehabilitated himself in Huddersfield. Even so it was a surprise that Blackburn had acquired a complete inside forward who could forage effectively and keep his winger supplied but also displayed a previously hidden talent for clinical finishing. There was serious conjecture that he would play for England but the Second World War prevented this although the player kept active enough playing for both Manchester clubs, Huddersfield, Wrexham, York, Chelsea, Stockport and Aldershot. Football's resumption came too late to enable him to further his career but he moved into management at Mossley and then his hometown, Wilmslow.

FL	10 apps	0 gls

Pre-war

FL	100 apps	44 gls
FAC	7 apps	4 gls
Total	117 apps	48 gls

BYRNE, David Stuart

Right winger

5'8" 11st
Born: Hammersmith, 5 March 1961
Debut: 25 February 1989

CAREER: Brentford; Southall; Hounslow 1980; Chiswick Albion; Harrow Borough Aug 1981; Hounslow Sep 1981; Kingstonian Oct 1983; Gillingham Jul 1985; Millwall Aug 1986 (£5,000); Cambridge United Sep 1988 (loan); Blackburn Rovers Feb 1989 (loan); Plymouth Argyle Mar 1989 (free); Bristol Rovers Feb 1990 (loan); Watford Nov 1990 (£50,000); Reading Aug 1991 (loan); Fulham Jan 1992 (loan); Shamrock Rovers (Eire) Jan 1993 (loan); St Johnstone Mar 1993; Partick Thistle Jul 1993; Walsall Feb 1994 (loan); St Mirren Feb 1995; Tottenham

Hotspur Jun 1995 (non con); Ayr United Aug 1995; Albion Rovers (p-c) Jan 1996.

The brother-in-law of Gerry Francis, Byrne was a right-wing flyer who broke into the Football League late in his career. He was at his peak with Millwall and it was from there that he came to Ewood on loan. It was thought that he added some pace and attacking options in his games for Blackburn but funds were scarce and Don Mackay waited until the expiration of the loan period before making a decision. He was then beaten to the punch by Plymouth, who had opposed him when they played the Rovers. Ironically, three years later, Mackay took the player on loan again, this time for Fulham. Byrne's long career was studded with oddities; he scored with his last kick for Watford and he was taken on as a non-contract player by Tottenham to play in the Inter Toto Cup. He ended his playing days as player-coach of Albion Rovers.

FL	4 apps	0 gls
Total	4 apps	0 gls

BYROM, John

Inside forward

5'9" 11st 12lb

Born: Blackburn, 28 July 1944

Debut: 11 November 1961

CAREER: St Peter's Sec Mod; Blackburn Rovers Aug 1961; Bolton Wanderers Jun 1966 (£25,000); Blackburn Rovers Sep 1976 (free); Hare & Hounds (Sunday Lge).

A lean, goal-hungry inside forward he was given his first-team debut at the age of seventeen and immediately looked at home, scoring regularly but above all playing with a maturity that belied his years. Competition for places in a good team was fierce and it was not until Fred Pickering was sold to Everton that Byrom finally blossomed. Moved to centre forward he scored 25 league goals in 1964/65 and if not ideally built for the position was effective. Relegation the following season was a surprise and Byrom suffered more than most from the absence of Bryan Douglas. He became a victim of the clear out that followed but the decision to allow him to move down the road to Bolton proved a huge error. Despite moving back to a more withdrawn position, he scored 113 league goals for his new club. Ten years later he was brought back to Ewood to try and add his experience to a faltering side. By now age was catching up with him and despite cameo flashes he was not effective.

FL	121+3 apps	50 gls
FAC	16 apps	12 gls
FLC	9 apps	2 gls
Total	146+3 apps	64 gls

CAIRNS, Ronald

Inside forward

5'7" 10st 4 lb

Born: Chopwell, 4 April 1934

Debut: 26 December 1955

CAREER: Chopwell Jnrs; Consett; Blackburn Rovers Sep 1953; Rochdale Jun 1959 (£2,500); Southport Jul 1964; Wigan Athletic 1965; Hyde United; Darwen.

An energetic, dark-haired player who took time to settle in at Ewood following his arrival from junior football in the North-East. Never more than a deputy, he found a permanent home at Southport where he proved that the embryonic goal talent that he had hinted at was tangible. He later crossed the Rovers' path again when he was a member of the Rochdale team that beat them in the semi-final of the League Cup. He continued to live in Darwen where he played as an all rounder for the Carus cricket team.

FL	26 apps	7 gls
Total	26 apps	7 gls

CALLOWAY, Laurence John
Left-back

5'11" 12st 9lb
Born: Birmingham, 17 June 1945
Debut: 24 April 1968

CAREER: West Bromwich Albion (ass sc); Queen's Colts YC; Wolverhampton Wanderers Oct 1962 (app. Jul 1961); Rochdale Jul 1964 (free); Blackburn Rovers Mar 1968 (£5,500); Southport Aug 1970 (ex Russell); York City Jun 1971 (£6,000); Shrewsbury Town Dec 1972; San Jose Earthquakes (USA) Apr 1974-Aug 1979.

In the late 1990s a body named the World Sports Humanitarian Hall of Fame appointed a selection committee. Its members were Gerald Ford, Nadia Comaneci, Jackie Joyner-Kersee, Jerry Kramer, Floyd Patterson, Stan Smith, Bill Steinkraus and Laurie Calloway. No-one would have believed that the rugged, enthusiastic left-back who came to Ewood in 1968 as an understudy for Keith Newton would end up in such exalted company. His English career was spent in the lower realms of the Football League but five years of NASL football in San Jose changed his life. By the end he was given the key to the city of San Jose, had become a close friend of Pelé and embarked on a coaching career that took in California Surf, Seattle Sounders, Salt Lake City Sting, San Francisco Blackhawks and San Diego Clash. For a time he was executive vice-president of the Brazilian Youth FA in the USA. When he remarried Marcella Spinazze, co-owner of the Café Marcella in San Jose, he embarked in another career in upmarket dining and opened an eponymous deli-restaurant in Capitola Village. Later he returned to coaching with Des Moines Menace, Syracuse Salty Dogs and Rochester Raging Rhinos.

FL	17+8 apps	1 gl
FAC	2 apps	0 gls
FLC	1+1 app.	0 gls
Total	20+9 apps	1 gl

CAMPBELL, John 'Nudger'
Wing half/right winger

5'6.5" 10st 10lb
Born: Liverpool, 17 March 1922
Died: Mijas, Spain, 10 February 2007
Debut: 13 October 1945

CAREER: Liverpool Apr 1943; Blackburn Rovers Nov 1945 (free); Oldham Athletic Jul 1956-Mar 1957 (free).

A product of school football in Bootle, Campbell joined Liverpool during the war years but came to Ewood as the war ended. A right winger with no great speed or trickery, he earned his place by graft and commitment. His conversion to wing half was natural given his physical abilities and this gave an ideal platform to harness his vigour and stamina. With Eric Bell and the young Ronnie Clayton at the club, competition for places was difficult but Campbell's adaptability kept him involved. After brief service with Oldham he returned to the Rovers, combining work with the club's reserves and youngsters with employment as a brewery representative.

FL	224 apps	19 gls
FAC	21 apps	1 gl
Total	245 apps	20 gls

CARSLEY, Lee Kevin
Midfield

5'10" 11st 11lb
Born: Birmingham, 28 February 1974
Debut: 3 April 1999

CAREER: Derby County Jul 1992; Blackburn Rovers Mar 1999 (£3,300,000); Coventry City Dec 2000 (£2,500,000); Everton Feb 2002 (£1,950,000).
INTERNATIONALS: Eire 29 apps.

Of Irish extraction and raised in the tough Sheldon area of Birmingham, he made a reputation at Derby as a hard-working, tough-tackling player who performed the predictable with strength and enthusiasm. His initial performances with the Rovers were not impressive (he was brought in to provide the bite that had been lacking since McKinlay was a regular) but the following season he became popular as one of the few bright spots in a dreadful season. He also became the club's first reliable penalty taker since Alan Shearer had left. After relegation he antagonised the fans by demanding a transfer on the grounds that he belonged in the Premiership and there was a certain amount of satisfaction when his new club, Coventry, was relegated and Blackburn promoted. Ultimately Carsley was proved right, because he did not remain outside the Premiership, Everton stepping in and taking him to Merseyside where he displayed an ability to play wide right as well as centre midfield. A model professional, who successive managers believed in, raising a son who has Down's Syndrome appears to have focused him on the important issues in life and apart from leaving Blackburn he has never been involved in controversy or histrionics.

L	40+6 apps	10 gls
FAC	4 apps	1 gl
FLC	4 apps	1 gl
Total	48+6 apps	12 gls

CARTER, Donald Frederick

Left winger

5'8" 11st
Born: Midsomer Norton, 11 September 1921
Died: Bath, January 2002
Debut: 21 August 1948

CAREER: Welton School; Norton St John's; Stourbridge Apr 1938; Bury Jan 1939 (£250); Blackburn Rovers Jun 1948 (£5,000); New Brighton Nov 1948; Northwich Victoria 1951.

Although Carter signed for Bury before the Second World War he did not make his debut until the resumption of the Football League. Originally a wireless operator, he transferred to the Tank Corps and experienced much action. Cartilage trouble threatened his career when he played again but he overcame it in style, scoring 18 goals in his first season. Lacking in speed, he compensated by crafty footwork and bustle but was used by Bury at inside forward. The Rovers signed him to play on the left wing but gave him only two opportunities before they rejected him. New Brighton got the best out of him (fortunately, because they had paid out a sum four times greater than their previous record transfer) . He played in four out of the five forward positions during his stay at the club, where he played more than a hundred league games.

FL	2 apps	0 gls
Total	2 apps	0 gls

CHADWICK, Francis Robert

Wing half

5'10" 10st 1lb
Born: Blackburn, 9 November 1927
Debut: 5 March 1949

CAREER: Harrison Gymnasium; Blackburn Rovers 1942 (am) 1947 (pro); York City Jul 1955-Jun 1956 (£250).

A plumber from Mill Hill, he converted from full-back, making his first-team debut as deputy for Jimmy Baldwin. Opportunities were few, although when he played his work rate impressed and his only goal was an explosively struck twenty-yard shot. By misfortune he was around at the same time that Ronnie Clayton arrived on the scene and inevitably he was denied opportunities. When he left for York he was the club's longest-serving player despite having only made a handful of first-team appearances. He played only one season in York, returning locally where he resumed his

cricketing career with Mill Hill Congregation in the Blackburn Sunday School League.

FL	11 apps	1 gl
Total	11 apps	1 gl

CHAPPELL, Leslie Alan
Striker

5'8" 10st 5lb
Born: Nottingham, 6 February 1947
Debut: 21 September 1968

CAREER: Rotherham United Feb 1965 (app. Apr 1963); Blackburn Rovers May 1968 (ex Gilliver); Reading Jul 1969; Doncaster Rovers Dec 1974; Swansea City Jul 1976-Jun 1981.

Although he was a young man Chappell had built a reputation at Rotherham as a mobile goalscorer. He was never comfortable in his role at Ewood but proved at Reading that he was a natural predator. Taking to coaching at Swansea, he had the rare distinction of playing in the Welsh Cup for them at the age of forty-two and was a substitute in the league the following season. After finishing in football he moved to live in Torquay, where he was involved in industrial cleaning.

FL	7 apps	0 gls
Total	7 apps	0 gls

CHARTER, Raymond
Full-back

5'8.5" 10st 6lb
Born: Ashton 10 January 1950
Debut: 14 March 1970

CAREER: Blackburn Rovers Jan 1968 (app. Jul 1966); Stockport County Jul 1971; Northwich Victoria 1974; Stalybridge Celtic 1975; Ashton United 1976; Hyde United 1978.

Starting at the club as a creative inside forward good enough to be selected for special training at Lilleshall he lost his way, overshadowed by his close friend Stuart Metcalfe. The club converted him to right-back where, surprisingly, his main defect was a vigorous approach that exceeded the permissible. He spent three good seasons with Stockport before entering the non-league scene with several clubs close to his home town.

FL	13+5 apps	0 gls
FAC	0+1 app.	0 gls
Total	13+6 apps	0 gls

CLAYTON, Kenneth
Wing half

5'9" 11st 2lb
Born: Preston, 6 April 1933
Debut: 22 November 1952

CAREER North Cliff; Preston North End; Blackburn Rovers Jul 1949 (am); May 1950 (pro); Ashton United 1961.

Forever remembered as the brother of the legendary Ronnie Clayton, Ken was considered the better prospect as a schoolboy. He would have joined Preston North End but the club rejected Ronnie, who was a year younger, so his father sent the pair to Ewood. A year later Ronnie had matured rapidly and made his first-team debut, and it was to be little more than a year later that Ken did the same. At home on the left-hand side, he was a tough-tackling, industrious player with great consistency. The brothers had established themselves at wing half when, in 1957, Ken Clayton broke his leg in a jarring tackle. Physically he never recovered and although he remained at the club until 1961 he never saw much first-team action.

FL	72 apps	0 gls
FAC	5 apps	0 gls
Total	77 apps	0 gls

CLAYTON, Ronald
Wing half

5'10" 11st 4lb
Born: Preston, 5 August 1934
Died: Blackburn, 29 October 2010
Debut: 25 April 1951

CAREER: Ribbleton Ave Meth Sc; Fishwick Sec Mod; North Cliff; Blackburn Rovers May 1950; Morecambe (p-m) Jul 1969; Great Harwood 1970.
INTERNATIONALS: England 35 apps.

An immortal at the club, Clayton made his first-team debut at sixteen and, but for national service, would have exceeded 700 appearances. At his peak he was the complete old-fashioned wing half; strong, tireless and with the virtue of timing that allowed him to tackle hard but cleanly and out-jump taller men to the high ball. Carefully nurtured by England from the Under-23 ranks to the national team, he succeeded Billy Wright as captain. He also led the Rovers to promotion to the First Division and to the FA Cup final. Unfortunate to lose his national spot, he continued as consistently as ever for the club. At the end of his career his future was challenged by the movements in the game that brought 4-2-4 formations. Slotting easily into the back four, he demonstrated that sheer class will prevail and added a timely reminder of just what a strong and superbly conditioned athlete he was. When still in the middle of his career he opened a newsagent's shop in Darwen and, after an unproductive spell managing Morecambe, worked as a sales representative. When Jack Walker assumed control of the club he brought Clayton back to assist in club promotions and with his association with the club he became a popular tour guide at Ewood.

Ronnie Clayton in August 1963. (Howard Talbot Photography)

FL	579+2 apps	15 gls
FAC	56 apps	1 gl
FLC	28 apps	0 gls
Total	663+2 apps	16 gls

CLINTON, Thomas Joseph
Left-back

5'7" 10st 12lb
Born: Dublin, 13 April 1926
Debut: 26 December 1955

CAREER: Dundalk; Everton Mar 1948; Blackburn Rovers Apr 1955; Tranmere Rovers Jun 1956 (free); Runcorn 1957.
INTERNATIONALS: Eire 3 apps.

Clinton left Dublin to work on the Dundalk railway station when he was in his teens. Playing with the local side, he attracted the attention of Everton whose chief scout, Noel Kelly, actually signed him on the station, the form being pushed through the train window as it pulled away. At Goodison he formed a sound partnership with Jones and earned respect as a reliable penalty taker, although he is best remembered for one he missed in the 1953 FA Cup semi-final. The move to Ewood was a strange one since, although he was known to be a classy player, his chances of supplanting Bill Eckersley were negligible. After football he was a newsagent for a time before working in insurance.

FL	6 apps	0 gls
FAC	2 apps	0 gls
Total	8 apps	0 gls

CODDINGTON, John William
Centre half

6'1" 12st 4lb
Born: Worksop, 16 December 1937
Debut: 19 August 1967

CAREER: Worksop BC; Huddersfield Town Jan 1955 (ground Sep 1953); Blackburn Rovers Jun 1967 (£19,000); Stockport County Jan 1970 (loan) Mar 1970; Great Harwood Jul 1971; Drogheda (Eir) Feb 1973.

The powerful, raw-boned sandy haired centre half was brought to Ewood because although the defensive pairing of Clayton and Sharples was effective they lacked height. Abrasive and wholehearted, he was at his best when strong limbs and courage were the requisites, but up against skilful or speedy opponents he struggled. Made club captain, he became a focus for those disappointed at the club's lack of progress and will be forever remembered for a ludicrously bad penalty, taken from the longest run seen at Ewood and hit with probably the least venom. Even worse, he was allowed to take it again because of an infringement and replicated the movement perfectly. Well respected as a coach, he worked with Bradford City and Middlesbrough and later managed Horden Colliery Welfare.

FL	72+1 apps	3 gls
FAC	5 apps	0 gls
FLC	6 apps	0 gls
Total	83+1 apps	3 gls

COLE, Andrew Alexander
Striker

5'11" 11st 12lb
Born: Nottingham, 15 October 1971
Debut: 1 January 2002

CAREER: Douglas Rd Primary Sc; Sandfield Sec Mod; Parkhead Academicals; Emkals; Arsenal Oct 1989 (app. Jul 1988); Fulham Sep 1991 (loan); Bristol City Mar 1992 (£500,000); Newcastle United Mar 1993 (£1,750,000); Manchester United Jan 1995 (£6,250,000+Gillespie); Blackburn Rovers Dec 2001 (£8,000,000); Fulham Jul 2004 (free); Manchester City Jul 2005 (free).
INTERNATIONALS: England 14 apps 1 gl.

The son of Jamaican immigrants who came to Nottingham, where his father worked in the mines, Cole's precocious footballing talent enabled him to escape a hard future in a deprived area. Chosen for training at the

Andy Cole in action against Manchester United in 2003.

FA School of Excellence he opted to join Arsenal but found his chances limited and was eventually offloaded to Bristol City. Here he developed into a goalscorer but it was at Newcastle that he took this art to new heights, having a strike rate that can seldom have been bettered. In less than two years his transfer value quadrupled and even Newcastle were powerless to resist the spending power of Manchester United. At Old Trafford Cole won championship, FA Cup and European Cup medals, scored prolifically and when teamed with Dwight Yorke formed a mobile, instinctive partnership that defences found difficult to handle. Unperturbed by lack of success with England he lost his United place when Van Nistelrooy was acquired and, anxious to play regularly, joined the Rovers even though they were fighting relegation. Within two months he had completed a full set of medals, scoring the winning goal in the League Cup final, and then helped the club avoid relegation by scoring regularly. Reacquainted with Yorke at Ewood, their partnership was disappointing and relations with Graeme Souness grew so acrimonious that Cole reported him to the PFA. Inevitably his departure followed, the club allowing him to leave on a free transfer so that they could save on his wages, which had been the highest ever paid to a Blackburn player. At Fulham he settled in comfortably although his best days are now clearly behind him.

PL	74+9 apps	27 gls
FAC	5 apps	3 gls
FLC	8 apps	7 gls
UEFA	2+2 apps	0 gls
Total	89+11 apps	37 gls

COLEMAN, Christopher

Central defence

6'2" 12st 10lb

Born: Swansea, 10 June 1970

Debut: 16 December 1995

CAREER: Manchester City Nov 1984 (ass sc); Swansea City Aug 1987 (trainee Jun 1987); Crystal Palace Jul 1991 (£275,000); Blackburn Rovers Dec 1995 (£2,800,000); Fulham Dec 1998-Oct 2002 (£2,100,000).

INTERNATIONALS: Wales 31 apps 4 gls.

Coleman first came north to take up a traineeship at Maine Road but, homesick, he walked out and moved to his home town club. A reputation for using his exceptional physique well and keeping calm brought him a transfer to Crystal Palace, where he was often used as an emergency striker. When his club was relegated he decided to leave and was about to sign for Coventry when the Rovers decided they could use him as a replacement for Ian Pearce. Within a week Graeme Le Saux received a crippling injury and so Coleman slotted in alongside Hendry at the centre of the defence. Despite his promise he never cemented his place and a year's lay off because of Achilles tendon trouble relegated him well down the list of potential central defenders. Realising that he had to move he took the unusual step of dropping two divisions to join Kevin Keegan's Fulham. At least his ability to spot potential was acute because, two seasons later, they were in the Premiership, although the last games were played without his services. A horror crash while driving his high-powered car at night almost cost him a leg and although he bravely fought his way through a series of operations he was forced to give up the game, remaining with his club on the coaching staff. Thrust into the final games of the season as acting manager, following the departure of Jean Tigana, he displayed sufficient acumen for the club to hand him the role permanently and he is now recognised as one of the most promising young managers in the Premiership.

L	27+1 apps	0 gls
FAC	2 apps	0 gls
FLC	2 apps	0 gls
Total	31+1 apps	0 gls

COLLIER, Darren James
Goalkeeper

6'0" 12st 6lb
Born: Stockton, 1 December 1967
Debut: 13 May 1989

CAREER: Middlesbrough (non con); Blackburn Rovers Dec 1987 (non con) Jun 1988; Darlington Jul 1993 (free); Sing Tao (Hong Kong); Berwick Rangers Nov 1996-1997; Billingham Town May 2005.

A young goalkeeper who failed to make the grade at Middlesbrough, he was a regular in the Rovers' Central League side that gained promotion in 1989. When Vince O'Keefe left he became the understudy to Terry Gennoe, but his first-team appearances were punctuated by error and the team lacked confidence in him. He became a regular at Darlington but lost his place to Mike Pollitt and then had dreadful luck with injury. Playing in Hong Kong he tore a ligament so badly that a pin had to be inserted. Returning to England he was recruited by Berwick and had become the first-choice goalkeeper when another serious leg injury ended his career. Having taken his PFA pension in 2002 he rehabilitated himself sufficiently to resume playing with Billingham. Somewhere through the years his calm temperament appears to have been eroded and he was twice sent off in 2004/05 for arguing after receiving a yellow card, which prompted him to retire.

FL	27 apps	0 gls
FLC	3 apps	0 gls
FMC	1 app.	0 gls
Total	31 apps	0 gls

COMSTIVE, Paul Thomas
Midfield

6'0" 12st 12lb
Born: Southport, 25 November 1961
Debut: 7 October 1980

CAREER: Plymouth Argyle (ass sc); Blackpool (trial); Chorley FC Youth; Blackburn Rovers Dec 1978 (non con) Oct 1979; Rochdale Sep 1982 (loan); Feb 1983 (loan); Wigan Athletic Aug 1983 (free); Wrexham Nov 1984 (free); Burnley Aug 1987 (£8,000); Bolton Wanderers Sep 1989 (£37,500); Chester City Nov 1991 (£10,000); Southport (p-c) Aug 1993; Morecambe Mar 1995; Chorley Mar 1996; Congleton Town Feb 2004.

Comstive was living testament to perseverance. Spotted at an early age by Plymouth's northern scout, Tony Waiters, he was not offered terms and had an unsuccessful trial at Blackpool. At the time he was playing on the left wing but his qualities of superb physique, industry and determination did not wholly ally themselves to the position. Trying to break into the game through the Chorley youth team, he had a fortunate break when the Rovers' chief scout, Fred O'Donoghue, made an unscheduled call at Eccleston. The resulting trial with the Rovers went well until it was found he was too old for a traineeship, so he was given non-contract terms and later, when converted to left-back, signed a professional contract. Used occasionally by the Rovers he was loaned out and in doing so caught the eye of Wrexham, where he went on to gain a Welsh Cup winners' medal and played in European competition. From then on he found a succession of clubs who liked his tough tackling and fearsome dead-ball shooting. Returning to the non-league, he helped coach Southport to the Vauxhall Conference and, settling back in his home town, found work as a delivery officer for the Royal Mail.

FL	3+3 apps	0 gls
Total	3+3 apps	0 gls

CONLON, Bryan
Striker

6'1" 12st 7lb
Born: Shildon, 14 January 1943
Died: Shildon, 11 October 2000
Debut: 15 August 1970

CAREER: Shildon Morden Council Sc; Sheffield Wednesday (trial); Newcastle United May 1961; South Shields May 1962; Darlington Aug 1964; Millwall Nov 1967 (£16,000); Norwich City Dec 1968; Blackburn Rovers May 1970 (ex Darling); Crewe Alexandra Jan 1972 (loan); Cambridge United Mar 1972 (£5,000); Hartlepool United Sep 1972 (free); Shildon Athletic Jul 1974-Dec 1975.

Lean and hard, Conlon had served several clubs before he came to the Rovers, his virtues being his honesty and effort. Like so many transfers at the club around this period the deal revolved not so much around who was coming in but who was leaving in exchange, in this case the talented but inconsistent Malcolm Darling. Conlon removed the uncertainty but he was never a prolific scorer and was even moved to play centre-back when the club had problems. After over a decade of wandering he finished his playing career back in his home town.

FL	43+2 apps	7 gls
FAC	2 apps	0 gls
FLC	3+1 apps	0 gls
Total	48+3 apps	7 gls

CONNELLY, John Michael

Winger

5'8.5" 11st 2lb
Born: St Helens, 18 July 1938
Debut: 24 September 1966

CAREER: St Teresa' Sc; St Teresa's OB; Southport Jnrs; St Helens Town; Burnley Nov 1956; Manchester United Apr 1964 (£60,000); Blackburn Rovers Sep 1966 (£40,000); Bury Jun 1970-Jun 1973.
INTERNATIONALS: England 20 apps 6 gls.

Connelly was a slick-haired winger who could fly, cross from any angle – often at the last moment as the ball reached the dead-ball line and cutting in could spit venom with either foot. With an illustrious career at Burnley and Manchester United Connelly was a long way from the end when he came to Ewood, and he shared in a side that threatened a return to the First Division, but this never materialised. A spell at Bury completed his footballing career although he was still playing five-a-side football in the Thompson Centre when in his forties. By then he was the proprietor of a fish and chip shop in Brierfield.

FL	148+1 apps	36 gls
FAC	6 apps	2 gls
FLC	9 apps	1 gl
Total	163+1 apps	39 gls

COOK, Leslie

Left-back

5'8" 11st
Born: Blackburn, 11 November 1924
Died: Leicester, September 1996
Debut: 6 April 1940

CAREER: St Barnabas's School; Blakey Moor School; Blackburn Rovers Jun 1939 (am) Feb 1943 (pro); Coventry City Jul 1949; Rugby Town 1955; Bedworth Town Jul 1956.

Only the second Blackburn-born player to be selected for the England Schoolboy side his development was delayed by the Second World War. With a good left foot the blond player might have expected a long run in the side but the sudden appearance of Bill Eckersley forced him to search for a future elsewhere. Eventually he signed for Coventry, which meant that he had to sell his shop in Oswaldtwistle, but he had four good years in the Midlands.

FL	76 apps	0 gls
FAC	8 apps	0 gls
Total	84 apps	0 gls

CORBETT, James John

Winger

5'9" 10st 12lb
Born: Hackney, 6 July 1980

CAREER: Gillingham Jan 1998; Blackburn Rovers May 1998 (£525,000); FC Royal Antwerp (Belgium) Nov 2001 (trial); Darlington Mar 2003-May 2003 (loan); Southend United Jul 2003 (free); Margate Sum 2005; Dagenham and Redbridge Nov 2005 (trial).

Although he had been only a professional for a few months, and had been a programme seller quite recently, the Rovers paid a considerable fee to win the race for his signature. Capable of beating an opponent on either side and with a reputation for being able to score goals on his debut, he was hampered by initial muscle strains and then a broken leg. Named as substitute in an understrength side for the League Cup he received no other call up for the first team and has played much fewer games in the Football League than was prophesied when he was a teenager.

COUGHLAN, Graham

Centre-back

6'2" 14st
Born: Dublin, 18 November 1974

CAREER: Cherry Orchard; Bray Wanderers Jul 1995; Blackburn Rovers Oct 1995 (£100,000); Swindon Town Mar 1997-Apr 1997 (loan); Livingston Mar 1999 (free); Plymouth Argyle May 2001 (free); Sheffield Wednesday Jul 2005 (free).

Although he had only been at Bray for a matter of months Coughlan came to Ewood on the recommendation of the Bray manager, Pat Devlin. In his three seasons at Ewood he emerged as a towering centre-back but was some way off first-team standard. He was twice named to the substitute's bench in an injury crisis, the latter time preventing him joining Rotherham on loan. His contract was cancelled so that he could join Livingston, and playing first-team football changed his career. After appearing in the Bell's Scottish Cup final he joined Plymouth where he was a revelation. The team won Divisions Two and Three and Coughlan was an inspired defender who contributed many goals when he came up for set pieces.

COUGHLIN, Russell James

Midfield

5'8" 11st 6lb
Born: Swansea, 15 February 1960
Debut: 28 March 1979

CAREER: Manchester City Jul 1976 (am) Mar 1978 (pro); Blackburn Rovers Mar 1979 (£35,000); Carlisle United Oct 1980 (£20,000); Plymouth Argyle Jul 1984 (£20,000); Blackpool Dec 1987 (£75,000); Shrewsbury Town Sep 1990 (loan); Swansea City Oct 1990 (£10,000); Exeter City Jul 1993 (£18,000+Hodge); Torquay Utd Oct 1995; Dorchester Town 1995; Gretna 1997.

A playmaker who specialised in controlling the centre of midfield and hitting long, telling balls, he came to the Rovers when extremely young and was probably not mature enough to assume the responsibility. A suspect temperament did not aid his struggle to establish himself and the club simply could not wait for his development, which came later in his career with a variety of clubs. The owner of a powerful shot, he played too deep to fully utilise it. Despite a roly-poly physique he lasted well, playing the game for more than twenty years.

FL	22+2 apps	0 gls
FLC	1+1 app.	0 gls
Total	23+3 apps	0 gls

COWANS, Gordon Sidney
Midfield

5'9" 10st 7lb
Born: Durham, 27 October 1958
Debut: 16 November 1991

CAREER: Aston Villa Sep 1976; Bari (Italy) Jun 1985 (with Rideout for £850,000); Aston Villa Jul 1988 (£250,000); Blackburn Rovers Nov 1991 (£200,000); Aston Villa Jun 1993 (free); Derby County Jan 1994 (£80,000); Wolverhampton Wanderers Dec 1994 (£20,000); Sheffield United Dec 1995 (free); Bradford City Jul 1996 (free); Stockport County Mar 1997 (free); Burnley Jul 1997-Jun 1998.
INTERNATIONALS: England 10 apps.

One of the most complete midfield players England has produced, he was groomed through all the grades of the international game. If he had not twice broken a leg he would probably have established himself as a fixture in the national side. Perceptive, patient and a leader, he perpetually demanded the ball, playing it long or short and was always moving in order to make himself available for the pass. For one who employed the sliding tackle to such good effect he had a remarkable ability to recover to the vertical, an asset limited to good athletes. He was recruited by Kenny Dalglish to mastermind the attempt to gain promotion and was probably the key player when the club achieved this in 1992. Expected to be omitted in the upper flight, he wrestled a place for himself but when his contract expired he returned home for his third spell with Aston Villa. After wandering from club to club he took over as reserve coach at Burnley but inevitably found himself playing again. Unsurprisingly, when he left he returned again to Villa on the coaching staff.

L	49+1 apps	2 gls
FAC	5 apps	1 gl
FLC	4 apps	0 gls
PO	3 apps	0 gls
Total	61+1 apps	3 gls

COXON, Eric Gary*
Right-back

5'7.5" 10st 8lb
Born: Liverpool, 31 May 1946
Debut: 6 May 1967
CAREER: Everton Jul 1961 (app); Blackburn Rovers Dec 1963; Northwich Victoria Aug 1969-1972.

When clubs have no great resources it is often advisable to look for players discarded by the larger clubs. Coxon was such a player and by dint of steady application in the reserves earned himself a first-team chance. This was slightly more than might have been expected but the Rovers had a need for drive in midfield and liked to move their international right-back, Keith Newton, upfield. For all his endeavour Coxon looked limited and it was no surprise when he was released and joined Northwich. For reasons never hinted at during his stay at Ewood he attracted a bad disciplinary record in Cheshire and left when the manager, Jim Green, was replaced by Terry Bradbury.

FL	10 apps	0 gls
Total	10 apps	0 gls

CRAIG, Joseph
Striker

5'9" 11st 2lb
Born: Bridge of Allan, 14 May 1954
Debut: 30 September 1978

CAREER: Hawkshill Sc; Lornshill Academy; Sauchie Jnrs; Partick Thistle Feb 1972; Glasgow Celtic Sep 1976 (£80,000); Blackburn Rovers Sep 1978 (£40,000); Hamilton Academicals Mar 1981 (£10,000); Armadale Thistle Nov 1987.
INTERNATIONALS: Scotland 1 app. 1 gl.

Craig will be remembered as the one-cap wonder who scored in his only international appearance, when he came on as a substitute.

His early career was hampered by his pragmatism in not leaving his job as a motor mechanic in Bathgate. When he eventually concentrated on football he became an enthusiastic and courageous leader of the line, technically adept despite an awkward style and limited athleticism. Failure to obtain goals limited his chances and he eventually returned to Scotland. He remained in the game as manager of Cowdenbeath and Armadale Thistle and coach of Aidrieonians before working for the Royal Mail in their sorting office on Glasgow Airport.

FL	44+4 apps	8 gls
FAC	3 apps	1 gl
FLC	3+1 apps	1 gl
Total	50+5 apps	10 gls

CRAIG, Robert McAllister

Inside forward

5'5" 10st 12lb
Born: Airdrie, 8 April 1935
Died: Toronto, 1 October 2010
Debut: 26 April 1962

CAREER: Bicester; Blantyre Celtic; Third Lanark; Sheffield Wednesday Nov 1959; Blackburn Rovers Apr 1962 (£18,000); Glasgow Celtic Nov 1962 (£15,000); St Johnstone 1963 (ex Young); Oldham Athletic Mar 1964 (£5,000); Toronto City (Canada) May 1965; Johannesburg Wanderers (South Africa) 1966; Third Lanark Feb 1967.

A chunky, competitive inside forward who had often appeared a resilient opponent, Craig's transfer to the Rovers was one that retrospectively appeared a puzzle. He was a chief playmaker and with Bryan Douglas in the side the Rovers had no need for another one. From the start he never appeared attuned to the club and despite opening his first full season with a hat-trick he displayed a lethargy that prompted the *Blackburn Times* to state 'Craig once more showed his distaste for hard graft or spirited exchange.' The player admitted he was not enjoying his Ewood career, blaming the style of play and his wife's dislike of the area. Blackburn accepted the first bid for his services and the local paper cited his signing as one of the worst deals in the club's history.

FL	8 apps	3 gls
FLC	2 apps	0 gls
Total	10 apps	3 gls

CRAWFORD, Andrew

Striker

5'7" 10st 4lb
Born: Filey, 30 January 1959
Debut: 6 October 1979

CAREER: Filey Town 1976; Derby County Jan 1978 (app Sep 1975); Manawatu (New Zealand) 1979 (loan); Blackburn Rovers Oct 1979 (£50,000); AFC Bournemouth Oct 1982 (£35,000); Cardiff City Aug 1983 (trial); Scarborough Town Oct 1983 (non con); Middlesbrough Oct 1983-Jun 1984); Stockport County Dec 1984; Torquay United Feb 1985 (non con); Tennyson 1985; Edgehill 1988; Poole Town 1988; Bournemouth Sports 1989; Swanage Town & Herston 1989; AFC Lymington; Bridlington Town; Pickering Town 1994; Hunmanby United.

A small, self-obsessed left-sided striker, Crawford was signed by Howard Kendall to score sufficient goals to lift the side from the Third Division. He performed the task to the letter, with 18 league goals scored from all ranges, distinguished only by his manic desire to inscribe his name on the scoresheet. Unpopular in the dressing room, he succeeded in alienating the fans when immediately after promotion he submitted a transfer request on the grounds that he was worthy of a better club. Pushing the self-destruct button, he committed a breach of discipline on Bournemouth's tour of New Zealand and from then on his career spiralled downwards. Still playing in 2001 alongside his son Ryan, they played for Hunmanby United in the

Scarborough & District FA Harbour Cup final. Later in the year a confrontation with Filey Town's Paul Bowes provoked a mass brawl that forced the abandonment of a tie in the Scarborough District Cup.

FL	56 apps	21 gls
FAC	8 apps	5 gls
FLC	4 apps	0 gls
Total	68 apps	26 gls

CROFT, Gary
Left-back

5'9" 10st 8lb
Born: Burton on Trent, 17 February 1974
Debut: 28 September 1996

CAREER: Port Vale; Grimsby Town Jul 1992; Blackburn Rovers Apr 1996 (£1,000,000); Ipswich Town Sep 1999 (£800,000); Wigan Athletic Mar 2002 (loan); Cardiff City Mar 2002 (loan) Jul 2002 (free); Grimsby Town Aug 2005 (free)

Croft will forever be remembered as the first professional footballer to play the game wearing an electronic tag. Imprisoned for motoring offences, he was released under electronic surveillance and returned to the game sporting the requisite appendage for a period. By then he was an Ipswich player but he joined the Rovers in 1996 as part of Ray Harford's plans to strengthen the championship-winning team. Enthusiastic, quick into the tackle and with the ability to cover vast areas when exposed, he had talent but was often indecisive. Although naturally left-footed he looked more composed on the other flank in brief appearances there. Over several seasons he never cemented a starting place, nor did he at Ipswich or Cardiff.

L	33+7 apps	1 gl
FAC	4+2 apps	0 gls
FLC	6 apps	0 gls
Total	43+9 apps	1 gl

CROMPTON, Alan
Inside forward

5'9" 10st 8lb
Born: Manchester, 6 March 1958
Debut: 12 March 1977

CAREER: Sunderland Mar 1975 (app Feb 1975); Blackburn Rovers Jul 1976 (free); Wigan Athletic Jul 1978 (free); Runcorn 1981; Telford 1986; Northwich Victoria 1987; Accrington Stanley.

A stocky inside forward who had struggled at Sunderland, he made progress with the reserves and scored frequently. Despite his opportunism he did not adjust to the greater pace of the first team and joined Wigan, helping them gain admission to the Football League. In 1986 he played at Wembley when he came off the bench in the final of the FA Trophy.

FL	2+2 apps	0 gls
Total	2+2 apps	0 gls

CROOK, Walter
Left-back

5'8.5" 10st 9lb
Born: Whittle le Woods, 28 April 1912
Died: Mellor, 27 December 1988
Debut: 19 March 1932

CAREER: St Aidan's; Blakey Moor; Blackburn Shopkeepers; Blackburn Nomads; Blackburn Rovers Jan 1931; Bolton Wanderers May 1947-May 1948.

Although he was born south of the Blackburn boundary Crook was raised in Mill Hill and went to work as a butcher's boy. The Rovers noticed his strong, no-nonsense approach to junior football and quickly signed him, grooming him to take over from Taffy Jones. Not only did the club find they had a hard, consistent player, they also found a man who was virtually indestructible. He created a club record of 193 successive appearances, including the promotion season of 1938/39. During wartime football with Aldershot, Chelsea and Blackpool he suffered his first injury problems and when the league resumed, he missed several games with leg injuries. Falling into dispute over contract terms he left for Bolton, a move that opened a new career. After one season he embarked for the continent where he became trainer for Ajax, helping them to eleven Dutch championships. He also coached at Sparta Rotterdam but returned to England for a spell with Accrington, starting as trainer and ending up also as manager and club secretary. Following a return to Ajax he managed Wigan and for eighteen years was trainer at Preston North End.

FL	21 apps	0 gls
FAC	2 apps	0 gls
Total	23 apps	0 gls

Pre-war

FL	197 apps	2 gls
FAC	17 apps	0 gls
Total	214 apps	2 gls
Grand Total	237 apps	2 gls

CROSSAN, Edward
Inside forward

5'6" 10st
Born: Derry, 17 November 1925
Died: Derry, 16 June 2006
Debut: 31 January 1948

CAREER: Glentoran; Derry City; Blackburn Rovers Nov 1947 (£3,000); Tranmere Rovers Aug 1957; Cork Hibernians (Eire) Sep 1958.
INTERNATIONALS: Northern Ireland 3 apps 1 gl.

The capture of Crossan was one of the most astute pieces of business the club ever performed. Although he was permitted a gradual introduction to first-team football the club obtained a player of scintillating ability. His quick

Eddie Crossan in November 1955. (Howard Talbot Photography)

feet could dance through the tightest defences, he had stamina and although his shooting was regarded as a weakness he was still proficient enough to score 18 league goals in a season. He also scored some of the most magical solo goals the club has ever witnessed, elaborate efforts where he took on opponents for the sheer thrill of dribbling past them. Sometimes whimsical, he never gained recognition in his own country, gaining just 3 international caps, less than his young brother John, who seldom looked as good a player.

FL	287 apps	73 gls
FAC	15 apps	1 gl
Total	302 apps	74 gls

CROWE, Christopher
Inside forward

5'7" 10st 10lb
Born: Newcastle, 11 Jun 1939
Died: Bristol, May 2003
Debut: 19 March 1960

CAREER: St John's Sc; Edinburgh; Heart of Midlothian (trial); Leeds United Oct 1954 (am) Jun 1956 (pro); Blackburn Rovers Mar 1960 (£25,000);

Wolverhampton Wanderers Feb 1962 (£28,000); Nottingham Forest Aug 1964 (£30,000); Bristol City Jan 1967 (£15,000); Auburn (Aus) May 1969 (£4,000); Walsall Sep 1969 (£1,000); Bath City Feb 1971; Greenaway Sports.
INTERNATIONALS: England 1 app.

With the money from the sale of Roy Vernon Blackburn brought the Leeds player Chris Crowe to Ewood. He had blond hair, pace and an explosive shot, exactly the same qualities as the club's other inside forward Peter Dobing. The result was that they never gelled and Crowe increasingly looked a misfit. For a time an experiment was made with him playing on the right wing. Perhaps this should have been persevered with because, when he left the club, he started playing in this position and gained a cap for England. However, no club ever fully harnessed his massive potential and his career faded dramatically. He had been born in Newcastle when his father was briefly employed there but when he was three months old the family moved to Edinburgh and he played for the Scottish Schools' side. He would have joined Hearts but the Scottish system at the time did not offer traineeships and, knowing that he would be farmed out to a junior club, he opted to go to England and join the Leeds ground staff. He retained an affection for the city and moved back after he had finished playing, working in a variety of jobs (shoe shop manager, taxi driver, licensee of a public house and estate agent).

FL	51 apps	6 gls
FAC	5 apps	1 gl
FLC	6 apps	4 gls
Total	62 apps	11 gls

CURRY, Sean Patrick
Striker

5'7" 11st 7lb
Born: Liverpool, 13 November 1966
Debut: 24 January 1987

CAREER: Liverpool Jun 1983; Blackburn Rovers Jan 1987 (£5,000); Hartlepool United Aug 1989 (free); Preston North End Oct 1989-Mar 1990.

Spotted playing in the Liverpool reserves, Curry was brought to Ewood by the caretaker manager, Tony Parkes. Small for a striker, he had quick reactions and found occasional use as a replacement player. Having just struck a prolific spell with the reserves he began to absent himself from the club because of travelling problems. His contract was cancelled and although he was subsequently reinstated he soon moved on.

FL	25+13 apps	6 gls
FAC	0+1 app.	0 gls
FLC	3+2 apps	0 gls
FMC	2+1 apps	1 gl
PO	0+2 apps	0 gls
Total	30+19 apps	7 gls

CURTIS, John
Right-back

5'9" 11st 4lb
Born: Poulton le Fylde, 2 September 1954
Debut: 20 August 1977

CAREER: Blackpool Sep 1972 (app Jul 1970); Blackburn Rovers Jul 1977 (free); Wigan Athletic Mar 1979 (loan) Jun 1979; Morecambe Dec 1981-Jan 1984.

A free transfer signing designed to fill a gap left by the sale of Kevin Hird, he was a plucky, hard tackler but found the pace of the game hard to cope with. This was surprising since he had much experience at Blackpool but he also struggled when he moved on to Wigan. Part of the reason for this was that he sustained a badly broken leg and never fully recovered. A transfer to Southport fell through when he could not pass the medical and at Morecambe recurring knee trouble ended his career after approximately 100 games. As

a schoolboy he was a champion hurdler who won the All England championship.

FL	9+1 apps	0 gls
FLC	2 apps	0 gls
Total	11+1 apps	0 gls

CURTIS, John Charles
Right-back

5'10" 11st 9lb
Born: Nuneaton, 3 September 1978
Debut: 12 August 2000

CAREER: Manchester United Oct 1995; Barnsley Nov 1999 (loan); Blackburn Rovers Jun 2000 (£1,500,000); Sheffield United Mar 2003 (loan); Leicester City Aug 2003 (£500,000); Preston North End Sep 2004-Nov 2004 (loan); Nottingham Forest Feb 2005 (free).

Groomed by Manchester United and by England through its age group teams, Curtis appeared assured of an illustrious career. A dogged, steady right-back who could move into the centre as part of a back three, he was consistent and enthusiastic. The first signs of doubt about his ability arose when he was given first-team exposure at Old Trafford. After a bad performance he was written out of their future and shipped out on loan to Barnsley, where he was a huge success and helped them reach the play-off final. Immediately he was brought to Ewood by Souness and in his first season the club was promoted. Curtis played his part and his career looked promising. Once again exposure to the Premiership produced limitations and the arrival of Lucas Neill reduced him to a bit part. Despite continuing interest he was unable to obtain a move until Sheffield United took him on loan in March 2003. In the summer he opted to join Leicester, a move that brought him little opportunity and injury curtailed his chance of obtaining a permanent contract at Preston. Snapped up by Nottingham Forest to bring experience to their fight against relegation, he ironically scored the own goal that condemned the club to relegation to the third tier of the English league system.

L	61 apps	0 gls
FAC	6 apps	0 gls
FLC	10 apps	0 gls
UEFA	1 app.	0 gls
Total	78 apps	0 gls

D

DAHLIN, Martin Nathaniel
Striker

6'1" 13st 1lb
Born: Uddevalla (Sweden), 16 April 1968
Debut: 9 August 1997

CAREER: Lunds BK; Malmo FF 1987; Borussia Mönchengladbach (Germany) Sep 1991 (£750,000); AS Roma (Italy) Jun 1996 (£2,875,000); Borussia Mönchengladbach (Germany) Oct 1996-May 1997 (loan); Blackburn Rovers Jul 1997-Jul 1999 £2,000,000); Hamburg SV (Germany) Oct 1998-May 1999 (loan).
INTERNATIONALS: Sweden 60 apps 29 gls.

Dahlin's father, Nat Akins, was a drummer from Venezuela who played with the Edmundo Ross Orchestra. On a trip to Sweden he met a Swedish girl and their son, Martin, was born in Uddevalla, 50km north of Gothenburg. Akins could not obtain work in Sweden and lost contact with his family. Martin's mother, Lisa, became a psychologist and married the man who gave Dahlin his name by adoption. Starting his career in Lund, Dahlin moved steadily up the football ladder, so that by 1988 he was included in the national team that played Brazil as part of their Olympic preparations. A marvellously free-running striker with immense upper-body strength that allowed him to ride challenges and shield the ball, he also had a rare eye for a goal chance. Consistency was not one of his qualities and his elevation to the national side was delayed until 1991 by a sudden loss of form. Finally elevated, he had to handle the pressure of being his country's first black player, but he coped well and was part of the side that reached the semi-finals of the European Championship in 1992 and the World Cup of 1994, where he was arguably the best player on view. Reasoning that the Swedish game was modelled on the long ball found in England, he moved to the Bundesliga to develop a greater technical game and became a better all-round player. Strangely he never prospered in Italy and was on the downswing of his career when Roy Hodgson brought him to Ewood. Although there were occasional reminders of his illustrious past he never came to terms with English football, hampered by back trouble and hamstring strains that frequently sidelined him. Loaned out to Germany, he found his back problems had become chronic and he had to retire from the game. He subsequently became a football agent, a commentator for Swedish television and launched his own brand of clothes.

P	13+13 apps	4 gls
FAC	0+1 app.	0 gls
FLC	2 apps	2 gls
UEFA	0+1 app.	0 gls
Total	15+15 apps	6 gls

DAILLY, Christian Eduard

Centre-back

6'0" 12st 10lb

Born: Dunde,e 23 October 1973

Debut: 29 August 1998

CAREER: Downfield Primary; Harris Academy; Sporting Club (Dundee); Dundee United Aug 1990; Derby County Aug 1996 (£1,000,000); Blackburn Rovers Aug 1998 (£5,300,000); West Ham United Jan 2001 (£1,750,000).

INTERNATIONALS: Scotland 58 apps 3 gls.

A utility defender capable of playing at left-back or in the centre of defence, Dailly has prompted varied opinions wherever he has played the game. An intelligent man who plays with care and comprehension, he can dominate in the air and is mobile and strong enough. Consistency is probably his failing but Roy Hodgson believed in him sufficiently to pay a huge fee when he brought him to replace Henchoz. Two-and-a-half years later his value had dropped by two thirds and there are those at West Ham who would argue that this still over-priced him, but he remains a defender of huge, classical potential who has never matured into the commanding figure he might have become.

L	60+10 apps	4 gls
FAC	4 apps	0 gls
FLC	5+1 apps	0 gls
UEFA	2 apps	0 gls
Total	71+11 apps	4 gls

DALY, Patrick John

Inside forward

5'5" 10st 2lb

Born: Manchester, 3 January 1941

Debut: 16 January 1960

CAREER: St Cuthbert's (Manchester); Blackburn Rovers May 1957 (non con) Jan 1958; Southport Feb 1962; Hyde United Aug 1962; Runcorn Oct 1962; Witton Albion 1964-Oct 1966; Rhyl Dec 1966; Witton Albion 1967; Altrincham; Chorley; Northwich Victoria; Dunlops (Liverpool Lge).

A prominent schoolboy footballer in Manchester, he gained notice in 1955 when he was a member of the city side that reached the final of the national schools' competition, gained county honours, represented the Manchester Catholic boys and was reserve for the England Under-14 side. His local progress was obscured by the presence of Nobby Lawton and Roy Cheetham, who had better physiques. Johnny Carey saw the talent in his quick feet and shrewd brain and, despite his obvious frailty, was not afraid to bring him to Ewood. Among the junior sides he excelled, being best remembered for scoring the goal that brought the Rovers their only success in the final of the FA Youth Cup. Sadly the doubts about his lack of strength and durability were not refuted when he received first-team opportunity at the Rovers and then Southport, and he drifted into non-league football.

FL	3 apps	0 gls
FLC	1 app.	0 gls
Total	4 apps	0 gls

DANNS, Neil Alexandre
Midfield

5'9" 12st 1lb
Born: Liverpool, 23 November 1982
Debut: 19 September 2002

CAREER: Liverpool (sc); Blackburn Rovers 2000 (trainee) Sep 2002; Blackpool (loan) Aug 2003-Nov 2003; Colchester United Sep 2004-Dec 2004 (loan) Dec 2004 (£50,000).

The son of a man who is a skateboard legend (European champion, four times British champion and manager of Team Extreme) Danns was nearly lost to sport in his teenage years when a bicycle accident almost severed his Achilles tendon. Although brought up in the wildest part of Liverpool his parents managed to keep him away from detrimental influences and he signed schoolboy forms for Liverpool. However, he agreed a traineeship with the Rovers, convinced that he would have a better chance of success away from Anfield. One of the best Rovers' youth team players ever, he captained the side in the 2001 FA Youth Cup final. A midfield player who plays with aggression and power he served an apprenticeship playing wide right or as a striker but found a home in the centre of midfield. Although he made his debut in the UEFA Cup tie against CSKA Sofia, few opportunities followed and he was forced to obtain much-needed first-team football at Blackpool, although he exhibited a tendency to incur the wrath of the official with two red cards in a three-month loan spell. The following season he was loaned out to Colchester but, as previously, he found that the experience he had gained did not produce first-team opportunities when he returned, and he took the offer of the permanent contract Colchester.

PL	1+2 apps	0 gls
FAC	1 app.	0 gls
FLC	2 apps	0 gls
UEFA	1 app.	0 gls
Total	5+2 apps	0 gls

DARLING, Malcolm
Forward

5'7.5" 10st
Born: Arbroath, 4 July 1947
Debut: 13 November 1965

CAREER: Errol; Luncarty Jnrs; Blackburn Rovers Oct 1964; Norwich City May 1970 (ex Conlon); Rochdale Oct 1971; Bolton Wanderers Sep 1973 (£14,000); Chesterfield Aug 1974; Stockport County Mar 1977 (loan); Sheffield Wednesday Aug 1977; Hartlepool Sep 1977; Morecambe Nov 1977; Bury Mar 1978; Morecambe Oct 1978; California Sunshine (USA); Darwen 1980-1981.

Starting as a right winger, Darling was one of the most exciting youth prospects the club had signed. Slight of build, he was as waspish as his red hair hinted, a fair athlete and owner of a venomous shot. Able to play with equal facility in most forward positions, he never developed into the class player he appeared capable of being and his exchange for the orthodox Conlon was simply the club's response to a player who flattered to deceive. He remained in the game for a long time, although his chief legacy is that he is best remembered for his outrageous ability to fall dramatically in the penalty area, which enraged opponents but often managed to find sympathetic referees. In 1981 he had his first spell in management as assistant to Jimmy Birkett at Darwen and later managed Great Harwood Town.

FL	114+14 apps	30 gls
FAC	8 apps	4 gls
FLC	4+1 apps	0 gls
Total	126+15 apps	34 gls

DAVIDSON, Callum Iain
Left-back

5'10" 12st 2lb
Born: Stirling, 25 June 1976
Debut: 13 April 1998

CAREER: St Johnstone; Heriot-Watt University; Blackburn Rovers Feb 1998 (£1,750,000); Leicester City Jul 2000 (£1,700,000); Preston North End Jul 2004 (free).
INTERNATIONALS: Scotland 15 apps.

The son of a merchant seaman, Davidson was born in Stirling but grew up in a village outside Perth. His footballing progress was limited by his involvement with other sports (he had a golf handicap of two and played for Scotland's boys' team and represented his area at squash) and his part-time civil engineering studies at Edinburgh University. St Johnstone nursed him carefully into first-team football and, after receiving Under-21 caps, several clubs began to watch him. A speedy player who tackled fiercely and had a confidence on the ball, his early Ewood career was punctuated by injuries and changes of management affected his confidence. A new career with struggling Leicester was not ideal to rediscover his abilities but in Division One he prospered and became an integral part of the team. Unhappily his stay at the club attracted adverse publicity from the blow to his face, in an off-field incident, that led to the dismissal of Dennis Wise by the club's management. Craig Brown, his old international manager, recruited him for Preston, where he has played well despite suffering from recurring hamstring problems.

L	63+2 apps	1 gl
FAC	6 apps	0 gls
FLC	3+1 apps	0 gls
UEFA	1+1 app.	0 gls
Total	73+4 apps	1 gl

DAVIES, Kevin Cyril
Striker

6'2" 13st
Born: Sheffield, 26 March 1977
Debut: 15 August 1998

CAREER: Chesterfield Apr 1994; Southampton May 1997 (£700,000); Blackburn Rovers Jun 1998 (£7,250,000); Southampton Aug 1999 (Ostenstad+£1,200,000); Millwall Sep 2002 (loan); Bolton Wanderers (free) Aug 2003.

Destined to be remembered as the club's most expensive mistake, Davies came north regarded by Roy Hodgson as the man who could replace Alan Shearer. A teenage sensation who helped Chesterfield reach the FA cup semi-final he had power, fire and physique. Unhappily at Ewood, even the physique looked doubtful. He was slow, both in thought and action, could not hit the target and never appeared likely to become a first-team regular. Ironically a future England striker, James Beattie, had been allowed to go south for just a fraction of the price. A move back to Southampton was a relief for Davies and the Rovers' fans but in four seasons away from the Rovers, Davies did little to rehabilitate his career. Down to what was probably his last chance he has found a sympathetic home at Bolton and has rewarded them with two seasons of old-fashioned centre forward play that has made him a firm favourite at the Reebok.

L	11+12 apps	1 gl
FAC	2 apps	1 gl
FLC	3 apps	0 gls
UEFA	1 app.	0 gls
Total	17+12 apps	2 gls

DAWSON, Alistair John

Defender

5'10" 11st 10lb
Born: Johnstone, 25 February 1958
Debut: 15 August 1987

CAREER: Johnstone HS; Glasgow Rangers 1975; Blackburn Rovers Aug 1987 (£50,000); Airdrieonians 1989.
INTERNATIONALS: Scotland 5 apps.

Dawson was winding down an illustrious career that had seen him appear in nine cup finals in Scotland when he was signed in a hurry by the Rovers when Glen Keeley suddenly left for Oldham. Although he had a reputation as a calm, reliable defender who could play at both full-back or in the centre his Ewood days started with a carry-over suspension about which the club was caught unawares, and then punctuated by frequent absence for attention to knee injuries. By this time his mobility was suspect, although there was never a doubt about his positional sense or authority. Released because he was seldom able to play for regular spells, he played briefly for Airdrie before managing St Andrew's in Malta. Later he was assistant manager at Ayr United and then manager of Hamilton Academicals. He subsequently coached in the Street League in Scotland and his team reached the semi-final of the world cup for homeless people in 2003.

FL	32+8 apps	0 gls
FAC	1 app.	0 gls
FLC	3 apps	0 gls
FMC	1+1 app.	0 gls
PO	1+1 app.	0 gls
Total	38+10 apps	0 gls

DE PEDRO (Francisco Javier De Pedro Falque)

Left winger

5'11" 12st
Born: Logrono (Spain), 4 August 1973
Debut: 14 August 2004

CAREER: Real Sociedad 1989; Blackburn Rovers Jun 2004 (free); Perugia (Italy) Jan 2005 (free); IFK Gothenburg Oct 2005.
INTERNATIONALS: Spain 12 apps 2 gls.

A Basque brought up in the Riojo, De Pedro had spent his entire career at Real Sociedad, working his way through the junior and 'B' side. Capable of playing on the extreme left but more accustomed to working infield, he possessed a left foot that could open a defence up with a quick flick. A dead-ball expert, he was given his international debut in 1998 but fell out of favour until he was recalled for the 2002 World Cup. Having turned down several transfer opportunities because he wanted to remain in his home area he became embroiled in a dispute with his club and was left out of the side. This gave Blackburn the opportunity to sign him on a free transfer but his lack of match fitness was immediately apparent. He started on the opening day of the season but was taken off at half-time and, apart from a brief substitute appearance and a League Cup start, he never played for the first team again. By the time he left for Perugia in the winter transfer window he had played just 116 minutes' first-team football.

PL	1+1 app.	0 gls
FLC	1 app.	0 gls
Total	2+1 apps	0 gls

DERBYSHIRE, Matthew

Striker

5'10" 11st 11lb
Born: Blackburn, 14 April 1986
Debut: 7 May 2005

CAREER: Our Lady & St John's; Darwen FC; Great Harwood Town; Blackburn Rovers Nov 2003 (£20,000); Plymouth Argyle Aug 2005 (loan).

A slim, mobile goalscorer, he slipped through the local scouting net until he graduated from the Great Harwood youth team and started scoring an impressive amount of goals for the first team. Although he was watched by several Premiership clubs it was the Rovers who moved in for him, discovering that he was already employed at Ewood with the community development scheme. He was a member of the side that reached the semi-final of the FA Youth Cup and the following season as a reward for scoring 6 goals in 13 starts, he was given a first-team squad number towards the end of the season and a week later made his debut when he came on as substitute against Fulham.

PL	0+1 app.	0 gls

DEVINE, Peter
Striker

5'7.5" 12st
Born: Blackburn, 25 May 1960
Debut: 2 May 1983

CAREER: Witton Park Sc; Brooklands; Mill Hill Old Boys; Mill Hill WMC; Bury (trial); Blackburn Rovers (trial); Mill Hill St Peter's; Chorley; Vancouver Whitecaps (Canada) Apr 1981(£20,000); Bristol City Aug 1981; Unknown (Finland); Blackburn Rovers Sep 1982 (non con); Chorley; Burnley Jul 1984-Jul 1986; Chorley; Horwich RMI; Clitheroe; Lancaster City; Workington Town; Lancaster City; Rossendale United; Haslingden.

Devine was the (mercifully) anonymous star of a video of unusual football clips. Taking a penalty for Lancaster against Whitby, he developed cramp in both legs as he was about to shoot and the ball was propelled with such lack of force that the goalkeeper had to wander off his line to retrieve it. This was the most bizarre feature of an unusual career that saw him fail to make the grade locally before finally starring with the neighbouring non-league side, Chorley. Spotted by Tony Waiters and taken to play in the NASL, he failed to make the starting line-up in Canada but made the acquaintance of Dick Dinnis, who recruited him for Bristol City when he returned to England. A further misadventure followed in Finland where he signed but never played for a club in Helsinki, the name of which even the player cannot recall. Incredibly, his hasty return from Scandinavia brought him an invitation to play as a non-contract player with the Rovers. A left-sided player with mobility, he had a few first-team games but managed far more with Burnley two years later. Later he served a variety of non-league sides and worked as a Sports Development officer in a 'football in the community' scheme at Ewood.

FL	8 apps	2 gls
Total	8 apps	2 gls

DE VRIES, Roger Stuart
Left-back

5'8.5" 11st 5lb
Born: Willerby, Hull, 25 October 1950
Debut: 9 August 1980

CAREER: Hull City Aug 1967; Blackburn Rovers Jul 1980 (free); Scunthorpe United Oct 1981-1982.

After making over 300 league appearances for Hull City, De Vries was a short-term solution to the left-back problem with the Rovers. Positionally sound and strong in the tackle, he had lost pace by the time he came to Ewood and was never going to be anything other than a stopgap. Ironically, with his next club Scunthorpe, he finally scored the maiden goal that had eluded him in fourteen seasons in the Football League. He subsequently taught in a primary school in Hull and was still playing five-a-side football at the Woodford complex in Hull in 2004.

FL	13 apps	0 gls
FAC	1 app.	0 gls
FLC	3 app.	0 gls
Total	17 apps	0 gls

DEWHURST, Robert Matthew
Centre-back

6'3" 13st 1lb
Born: Keighley 10 September 1971
Debut: 28 August 1990

CAREER: Blackburn Rovers Feb 1989 (trainee) Oct 1990; Darlington Dec 1991 (loan); Huddersfield Town Nov 1992 (loan); Wycombe Wanderers Jan 1993 (loan); Hull City Nov 1993 (free); Exeter City Jul 1999 (free); Scunthorpe United Aug 2000-Sep 2000; Gainsborough Trinity Sep 2000; North Ferriby United Sep 2000.

A Yorkshire lad from the Ilkley area, Dewhurst was conspicuous because of his height and his determination in the tackle. Hampered because the club had aspirations that prevented them playing untried youngsters, he was loaned around before finally joining Hull City. Under manager Terry Dolan he became a cornerstone of the defence and a frequent goalscorer with his powerful left foot at set pieces. Injury finally ended his career at Hull but he has spent five seasons at North Ferriby. A fine fast bowler, he played for Blackburn Northern during his stay in Blackburn.

FL	13 apps	0 gls
FLC	1 app.	0 gls
FMC	1 app.	0 gls
Total	15 apps	0 gls

DIAMOND, Anthony John
Striker

5'10" 10st 4lb
Born: Rochdale, 23 August 1968
Debut: 6 September 1986

CAREER: Blackburn Rovers Jul 1984 (non con) Jun 1986; Wigan Athletic Oct 1988 (loan); Blackpool Aug 1989-Jun 1991 (free); Chorley Sep 1990 (loan); Atherton LR; Castleton Gabriels 1994; Top House (Rochdale Sunday Lge).

The son of a club scout, Diamond qualified to play for the Northern Ireland Under-21 team because of his parentage. He was a strong, bustling striker who found difficulty adjusting to the pace of the first-team game. Exposure to league football tempted him to turn down a contract offer and leave for Blackpool, but the move proved disastrous and he ended playing non-league football. At Castleton he enjoyed some managerial experience, although only on a temporary basis. He is one of only two players who represented the club in the FA Youth Cup in four different seasons.

FLM	9+17 apps	3 gls
FMC	1+1 app.	0 gls
Total	10+18 apps	3 gls

DIAWARA, Kaba
Striker

5'11" 11st 8lb
Born: Toulon (France), 16 December 1975
Debut: 26 August 2000

CAREER: Toulon 1993; Girondins de Bordeaux Jun 1994; Stade Rennes FC Jan 1998 (loan); Arsenal Jan 1999 (£2,500,000); Olympique de Marseille Jun 1999 (£3,000,000); Paris St Germain Dec 1999 (1m FFR+Leroy); Blackburn Rovers Aug 2000 (loan); West Ham United Sep 2000-May 2001 (loan); Racing Ferrol (Spain) Jan 2002-Jun 2002 (loan);

OGC Nice Aug 2002-May 2003 (loan); Al-Ittihad (Quatar) Sep 2003; AC Ajaccio Jun 2005.
INTERNATIONALS: Guinea 6 apps 5 gls.

When Arsenal paid £2.5 million for Diawara it was in belief that they were signing a player whose strong running and physical ability might adapt well to the English game. Never a regular goalscorer in French football, there was always the possibility that he might mature. In fact, he had incredible bad luck at Highbury, striking the woodwork so regularly that it became a talking point. It was to set the template for a career in England, France and Spain where he was never to achieve what the club foresaw. However, after undergoing knee surgery he was loaned out to Nice, a newly promoted club with horrific financial difficulties that made their survival doubtful. The team commenced playing inspired football, sparked by Diawara's goal-snatching instincts and remained among the leaders of the French league. Returning to Paris St Germain, Diawara found himself a hot property but settled for the financial reward of a move to Qatar. He also availed himself of the amnesty given to players who had represented a country at age-group level to change their allegiance and commenced a successful international career with Guinea, the country his parents left when his father came to France and found work on the docks at Toulon.

FL	1+4 apps	0 gls
FLC	1 app.	1 gl
Total	2+4 apps	1 gl

DICKINS, Matthew James
Goalkeeper

6'4" 14st
Born: Sheffield, 3 September 1970
Debut: 14 April 1992

CAREER: Sheffield United Jul 1989; Orient Jan 1990 (loan); Lincoln City Feb 1991 (free); Blackburn Rovers Mar 1992 (£250,000); Blackpool Jan 1993 (loan); Lincoln City Nov 1993 (loan); Grimsby Town Sep 1994 (loan); Rochdale Oct 1994 (loan); Stockport County Feb 1995 (loan) Mar 1995; Lincoln City 1996; Altrincham 1996; Boston United Sep 1998 (loan); Sheffield FC Jan 1999.

Dickins was discovered playing for Lincoln, having failed to make the grade in Sheffield. A hugely built young man with all the apparent attributes for a goalkeeper, he came to Ewood on the eve of the transfer deadline. His debut was traumatic from the opening moment, when he failed to catch a huge punt upfield, to the final minutes, when he misjudged a harmless shot that became the winning goal. Loaned out to recover his composure, his erratic form reappeared at most of his subsequent clubs, with the exception of Blackpool. Eventually he continued his career at the country's oldest club, Sheffield FC.

FL	1 app.	0 gls
Total	1 app.	0 gls

DICKOV, Paul
Striker

5'6" 11st 9lb
Born: Livingston, 1 November 1972
Debut: 14 August 2004

CAREER: Arsenal Jun 1989 (Trainee) Dec 1990; Luton Town Oct 1993-Jan 1994 (loan); Brighton Mar 1994-Apr 1994 (loan); Manchester City Aug 1996 (£1,000,000); Leicester City Feb 2002 (£100,000); Blackburn Rovers Jun 2004 (£150,000).
INTERNATIONALS: Scotland 10 apps 1 gl.

The son of Polish immigrants who settled in Livingston, he made a name for himself early and was the only one of the Scottish side that reached the final of the Under-16 World Cup in 1989 to make the grade at senior level. This was despite the fact that he played striker and never grew beyond 5'6". To compensate for his lack of stature he developed a waspish attitude, never stopped chasing and hounded opponents constantly. This brought him little opportunity at Arsenal but after loan spells had emphasised his worth he was signed by Manchester City. At Maine Road and then with Leicester he proved that no matter how hard pressed his club was he could obtain goals and proved a cult hero with both sets of fans. His last-second goal in the play-off final against Gillingham was voted the greatest goal ever scored by a City player and he subsequently scored again when his club clinched promotion to the Premiership. When Leicester were relegated he joined the Rovers and in an uneasy season his efforts were astonishing. Even playing with a groin strain he ran non-stop, always offering himself for the pass and closing defenders down with phenomenal effort.

PL	35+5 apps	13 gls
FAC	6 apps	1 gl
FLC	3 apps	2 gls
Total	44+5 apps	16 gls

DJORKAEFF, Youri
Midfield

5'11" 11st 6lb
Born: Bayonne (France), 9 March 1968
Debut: 2 October 2004

CAREER: USG Decines; Saint Priest; Villeurbanne; FC Grenoble 1984; RC Strasbourg Aug 1989; AS Monaco Nov 1990; Paris St Germain Jul 1995; Inter Milan (Italy) Jul 1996; FC Kaiserslautern (Germany) Jul 1999; Bolton Wanderers Feb 2002-Jun 2004 (free); Blackburn Rovers Sep 2004-Dec 2004 (free); Metro Stars (USA) Feb 2005.
INTERNATIONALS: France 82 apps 28 gls.

A legendary French international who won a World Cup winners' medal in 1998, his father Jean had gained 48 international caps during a career that saw him play for Lyon, Marseilles and Paris St Germain. Although he played for France, Djorkaeff's paternal side were ethnic Kalmouk, a Mongol tribe from Russia. Intermarried with French and Polish blood, Djorkaeff's pedigree was further complicated by the fact that his maternal line was pure Armenian. Whatever the resultant mix it produced in Youri a player of rare subtlety and all-round capabilities whose deft touches could undermine a defence. It was a surprise in 2002 that a player of such pedigree joined a struggling club like Bolton, but he was perhaps more instrumental than anybody else in establishing the Wanderers as a Premiership side. Unable to agree a new contract, he stopped playing but was brought to Ewood by Mark Hughes to try and turn Blackburn's fortunes around at a time outside the transfer window when only free agents could be signed. After a promising debut he faltered and a long-term injury kept him out of the game so long that the Rovers declined to renew his contract, which expired at the end of December. Two months later he signed to play in Major League Soccer in the USA.

PL	3 apps	0 gls
Total	3 apps	0 gls

DOBING, Peter Alan
Inside forward

5'9.5" 11st 9lb
Born: Manchester, 1 December 1938
Debut: 29 September 1956

CAREER: Blackburn Rovers Dec 1955; Manchester City Jul 1961 (£37,000); Stoke City Aug 1963-Jun 1973.

Unusually, Dobing was the son of a Salford rugby league player and his brother was a goalkeeper with Chester. Spotted playing for Crewe schools, he was brought to Ewood and emerged as one of the club's most promising prospects, who made his league debut at the

Peter Dobing in April 1960. (Howard Talbot Photography)

age of seventeen. A punchy, pacy inside forward who could shoot with venom, particularly cutting in from the right-hand side, he was also a complete player who could play as an out-and-out centre forward if required. A regular Under-23 international, apparently being groomed for England, it remains a mystery why he never fully blossomed. Sold to Manchester City because the club found him a difficult character to handle, he prospered and at Stoke had a ten-year career in which as he grew slower he moved deeper to provide know-how and panache. Once on the Lancashire ground staff, he could possibly have made the grade as a leg spinner. When he retired he lived in Swynnerton and developed a business selling crockery to hotel chains.

FL	179 apps	88 gls
FAC	22 apps	16 gls
FLC	4 apps	0 gls
Total	205 apps	104 gls

DOBSON, Anthony John
Defender

6'1" 12st 10lb
Born: Coventry, 5 February 1969
Debut: 19 January 1991

CAREER: Coventry City Jun 1985 (app) Jun 1986; Blackburn Rovers Jan 1991 (£300,000); Portsmouth Sep 1993 (loan) Dec 1993 (£150,000); Oxford United Dec 1994 (loan); Peterborough United Feb 1996 (loan); West Bromwich Albion Aug 1997 (free); Gillingham Sep 1998 (£25,000); Northampton Oct 1998 (£22,500); Forest Green Rovers Aug 2000; Rugby United (p-m).

After joining Coventry as a schoolboy he made rapid progress through their youth ranks and into the England Under-21 team. Signed with Steve Livingstone, he was the first big-money signing made by the Rovers for years. Initially signed to play at centre-back he impressed with his reading of the game, his coolness and the strength of his tackling. Moved to left-back, he tidied up a problem position but fell foul of referees and was sent off three times. These were caused by slowness of acceleration rather than undue roughness but the club was sufficiently concerned to replace him with Alan Wright. Apart from a spell at Portsmouth his career disintegrated rapidly and he ended up as player-manager at Rugby United. Later he became the manager of Solihull Borough.

L	36+5 apps	0 gls
FAC	2 apps	0 gls
FLC	5 apps	0 gls
FMC	1 app.	0 gls
Total	44+5 apps	0 gls

DONIS, Yorgis 'George'
Right winger

6'0" 12st
Born: Frankfurt (Germany), 22 October 1969
Debut: 17 August 1996

CAREER: Doxa Nikopolis; Pavio Melas (Thessalonika); Panathinaikos 1987; Athinaikos 1988 (loan); Panargiakos Argos 1989-Dec 1990 (loan); Ioannina Dec 1990-91 (loan); Blackburn Rovers Jun 1996 (free); AEK Athens Jan 1998 (free); Sheffield United

Mar 1999-May 1999 (trial); Huddersfield Town Jun 1999-Jul 2000 (£1,000,000).
INTERNATIONALS: Greece 24 apps 5 gls.

Although born in Germany, where his parents ran a bar in Frankfurt, Donis was brought up in Salonika among fellow Greeks who were descended from those born around Constantinople. Starting his football with a Salonika, team he moved to another small club in Thessalonika but was spotted by a journalist and recommended to Panathinaikos. Although given an immediate debut in the Greek cup he served a typical apprenticeship, being loaned out to several clubs. Even after gaining national honours he had not progressed beyond being third choice (behind the Pole Warzycha and Alexoudis) but injuries gave him opportunity and he participated fully in a championship victory and a European Cup campaign that ended at the semi-final stage. In this he demonstrated his qualities. Being fleet of foot, strong and able to cross with precision he also displayed a refreshing ability to beat his opponent on any side. Available on a Bosman free transfer he was persuaded to join the Rovers because he could see the value in acting as a supply line for Alan Shearer. Before he could pull on a blue and white shirt, Shearer was gone and little time after so was the manager , Ray Harford. The caretaker manager, Tony Parkes, did not want a winger who was reluctant to track back in a relegation fight and the next manager, Roy Hodgson, did not value the player. Released back to play in Greece he suffered again when the coach was changed. Persuaded by Steve Bruce to return to England, he followed the manager from Sheffield United to Huddersfield but trauma pursued him. He could not settle, was gazumped attempting to buy a home, was detained in Athens because of a national service commitment and eventually agreed with the club that his contract should be cancelled so that he could return to Greece. He subsequently became coach of Larissa who he guided to promotion to the top division.

PL	11+11 apps	2 gls
FAC	0+1 app.	0 gls
FLC	3 apps	0 gls
Total	14+12 apps	2 gls

DONNELLY, Darren Charles
Striker

5'10" 11st 6lb
Born: Liverpool, 28 December 1971
Debut: 13 April 1991

CAREER: Blackburn Rovers Jul 1988 (trainee) Jun 1990; Chester City Jul 1993-Jun 1994 (free); Holywell Town.

After progressing through the youth team Donnelly was given one first-team game. During it he demonstrated surprising poise and technique but lacked pace. When Kenny Dalglish arrived and started introducing new players he was lost in the maelstrom and was released. Recruited by Chester City, he found it hard to break into the first team and was again released. He moved into the Welsh League with Holywell Town but made only a handful of appearances.

FL	1+1 app.	0 gls
Total	1+1 app.	0 gls

DOUGAN, Alexander Derek* 'Cheyenne'
Centre forward

6'3" 12st 6lb
Born: Belfast, 20 January 1938
Died: 24 June 2007
Debut: 14 March 1959

CAREER: Mersey St Sch (Belfast); Belfast Tech HS: Mersey St BC; Cregagh BC; Linfield 1952 (sc); Distillery 1953; Preston North End (trial); Bury (trial); Portsmouth Aug 1957 (£4,000); Blackburn Rovers Mar 1959 (£11,000); Aston Villa Aug 1961 (£12,000); Peterborough United Jun 1963 (£21,000);

Leicester City May 1965 (£21,000); Wolverhampton Wanderers Mar 1967 (£50,000); Kettering Town (p-m) Dec 1975-77.
INTERNATIONALS: Northern Ireland 43 apps 8 gls.

Blackburn had been interested in Dougan when he was a raw, gangling centre half with Distillery but the asking price was too great. By the time he had been successfully honed by Portsmouth, Blackburn's status had improved and they required a goal-scorer to cement their position in the First Division. They acquired a man of many facets, a rangy, mobile, awkward opponent with a facility to undermine defences and harvest goals but a player of whimsical moods and uncertain application. By modern standards his off-field activities may look normal but for a conservative small town in Lancashire his eccentric driving of a top-of-the-range sports car, his well-publicised romance with a beauty queen and his liking for the high life were not usual. A shaven head was novel and while some supporters found him endearing and christened him 'Cheyenne', traditionalists questioned his application and commitment. When he declared himself fit for the biggest game in the club's contemporary history, the 1960 FA Cup final, and in doing so placed his personal wishes in front of the club's, the end of his time in east Lancashire was at hand. Obviously unable to perform to anything like his capabilities, he contributed hugely to the debacle that resulted. Later he was to resurrect his career, notably with the Wolves, where he acquired cult status and later returned as chairman and chief executive. As his career declined he had moved into management but changed directions to become a sports presenter with Yorkshire Television. Developing many business interests he was also for a time executive officer of a charitable foundation connected with sport.

FL	59 apps	26 gls
FAC	14 apps	4 gls
FLC	3 apps	4 gls
Total	76 apps	34 gls

DOUGLAS, Bryan

Right winger/inside left

5'5" 9st 10lb
Born: Blackburn, 27 May 1934
Debut: 4 September 1954

CAREER: St Bartholomew's Sc; Blakey Moor Sc; Lower Darwen YC; Blackburn Rovers Apr 1952; Great Harwood Jun 1969.
INTERNATIONALS: England 36 apps 11 gls.

The son of a Blackburn train driver and one of eight children, the only doubts about whether Bryan Douglas was destined for greatness lay in his small stature. From the minute he arrived at his home-town club as a schoolboy the sheer genius in his quick, bewitching feet was obvious. He could trick and tantalise but beyond that had vision and clarity of thought that created opportunity for those around him. To watch him lay a ball to a winger in flight was to watch perfection. The passes were perfect to an inch, requiring the player to reach peak momentum but never stepping over the narrow line that produced a 'hospital' pass. Worried about his frail physique, the club nurtured him carefully but Douglas was always more than just a dribbling right winger. He never shirked a challenge, competed fiercely and could tackle with the best. He also kept cool in front of goal and could be relied upon to score regularly. In addition he had a tactical brain, not only acting as fulcrum of the attack but quick to spot when a defensive colleague was caught out of position. When danger suddenly threatened the first to track back and fill the breach was usually Douglas. After carving himself a reputation as a Matthews-style right winger, he was moved to inside left where he was even more at home, supplying the quick though balls for the strikers, carrying the ball huge distances, manipulating it with mesmeric feet. At a time when genius went unprotected he survived despite severe punishment and it was a measure of his resilience that he

Bryan Douglas in August 1963. (Howard Talbot Photography)

endured so long at the top level. Still resident in his home town, he worked as sales manager for the Star Paper Mill and continues to watch his only club week after week.

FL	438 apps	101 gls
FAC	39+1 apps	9 gls
FLC	25 apps	5 gls
Total	502+1 apps	115 gls

DOUGLAS, Jonathan
Midfield

6'0" 12st 12lb
Born: Clones, 22 November 1981
Debut: 31 October 2000

CAREER: Clones Town; Monaghan United 1993; Glasgow Celtic (trials); Largy Coll, Clones; Glasgow Celtic (trial); Blackburn Rovers Feb 2000; Chesterfield Mar 2003-May 2003 (loan); Blackpool Aug 2003-Nov 2003 (loan); Gillingham Mar 2005-May 2005 (loan); Leeds United Aug 2005 (loan).
INTERNATIONALS: Eire 2 apps.

A strongly built midfield player from the Irish borderland, Douglas has come back well from horrific ligament damage that threatened his future. A defensive player who will carry out his instructions to the letter and tackle all day, he played a prominent part in the fight against relegation in 2004, operating on the left-hand side of midfield. This led to his inclusion in the Republic of Ireland squad but his breakthrough was short lived and he was once again forced to go on loan in order to experience first-team football. As a youngster he played Gaelic football but moved to football and at the age of sixteen made his debut for Monaghan in the League of Ireland.

PL	13+2 apps	1 gl
FAC	1+4 apps	0 gls
FLC	1+2 apps	0 gls
Total	15+8 apps	1 gl

DOWNES, Steven Fleming
Striker

5'10" 11st 7lb
Born: Leeds, 2 December 1949
Debut: 13 March 1976

CAREER: Leeds MDBC; Rotherham United Apr 1967; Sheffield Wednesday Dec 1969; Chesterfield Aug 1972; Halifax Town Jul 1974 (free); Blackburn Rovers Mar 1976 (loan); Scarborough; Gainsborough Trinity.

It was a sign of the times that the Rovers had to borrow Downes to assist in a fight against relegation. He had been playing with Halifax but was about to be released and had never fully translated the goal-scoring promise he had displayed with the reserves at Rotherham, into first-team achievement. A big, energetic striker his physical qualities committed defenders but his technique and finishing were not of the same order. He performed for the Rovers exactly to his capabilities but was never a candidate for a permanent transfer.

FL	6 apps	0 gls
Total	6 apps	0 gls

DUFF, Damien
Left winger

5'10" 9st 7lb
Born: Ballyboden, 2 March 1979
Debut: 11 May 1997

CAREER: Leicester Celtic; St Kevin's Boys; Lourdes Celtic; Blackburn Rovers Mar 1996; Chelsea Jul 2003 (£17,000,000).
INTERNATIONALS: Eire 57 apps 6 gls.

When Kenny Dalglish was the Rovers' manager the club's Irish scout was the Bray Wanderers' manager, Pat Devlin. A legend in the country, he had access to the brightest talent, which was how Damien Duff ended up at Ewood. He had attended De La Salle College in Churchtown where he played rugby but started playing football with junior clubs around Dublin. Frail in appearance and looking perpetually drained he was always destined to become a major star because he possesses ball skills that are hard to defend against. So quick is his control, so fast his acceleration that he alters defensive situations in a split second. Despite being double marked he can ease effortlessly past defenders, twisting quickly and always having the time to pick out a target for a cross. A star of the 2002 World Cup, he has the ability to disrupt any defence in the world and is one of the few world players who can demoralise the opposition. A negative has been persistent hamstring problems that have severely curtailed his availability. With the spending power of their Russian owner, Chelsea were able to acquire his services in 2003, but despite the huge fee he proved to be a bargain as the club cemented a position among the world's elite clubs.

Damien Duff in 2003.

L	157+27 apps	27 gls
FAC	13+5 apps	2 gls
FLC	16+1 apps	5 gls
UEFA	4 apps	1 gl
Total	190+33 apps	35 gls

DUNN, David John Ian
Midfield

5'10" 12st 3lb
Born: Blackburn, 27 December 1979
Debut: 26 September 1998

CAREER: St Wulfstan's, Great Harwood; Burnley (sc); Huncoat United; Merrie England; St Augustine's; Blackburn Rovers Sep 1997; Birmingham City Jul 2003 (£5,500,000).
INTERNATIONALS: England 1 app.

Belying his imposing physique Dunn's game is in fact based on technical ability, which he employs best in the last third of the field. With quick feints, jinks and sudden acceleration he can take on defenders in the danger area and is capable of finishing himself because of his explosive shooting. Brought through the ranks of local schools and Sunday football, and carefully nurtured in the youth teams, his progress has been steady but he is capable of becoming a regular international if he develops. Not at his best tracking back, he had to pay attention to the defensive side of the game but remains a true game breaker. Adored by the public who saw him as the player who used to stand on the Ewood terraces, he frequently encountered the wrath of Graeme Souness, who was not impressed by his off-the-field lifestyle that incorporated celebrity girlfriends. This led to his departure in the summer of 2003, his acquisition being a club record for Birmingham City, but recurring hamstring problems have resulted in drastic surgery and limited his appearances.

L	120+16 apps	30 gls
FAC	11+2 apps	3 gls
FLC	14+3 apps	5 gls
UEFA	3+1 apps	0 gls
Total	148+22 apps	38 gls

DUNNING, Darren
Midfield

5'6" 11st 12lb
Born: Scarborough, 8 January 1981
Debut: Oct 31 2000

CAREER: Malton School; Blackburn Rovers Feb 1999; Bristol City Aug 2000 (loan); Rochdale Nov 2001 (loan); Blackpool Mar 2002 (loan); Torquay United Nov 2002 (loan); Macclesfield Town Jan 2003 (loan); York City Aug 2003 (free).

The stocky, aggressive midfield man was identified by Souness as having the attitude and desire to play league football. Tough in the tackle and a leader and organiser he found chances few and far between but was loaned out frequently to increase his chances. Many clubs have benefited from his ideal approach but his permanent move to York City saw him present when they dropped out of the Football League. One of the few players retained in their Conference debut, Dunning has laboured hard for the club in adverse circumstances.

FL	1 app.	0 gls
FAC	1 app.	0 gls
FLC	2 apps	1 gl
Total	4 apps	1 gl

DUNNING, William Samuel
Inside forward

5'9" 10st
Born: Bury, 15 November 1952
Debut: 14 November 1970

CAREER: Blackburn Rovers Jul 1968 (app) Nov 1970-Jun 1974; Johannesburg Rangers (SA) 1973-Jul 1974; Darwen Aug 1974-75.

An outstanding player in the club's youth side, playing when he was still at school, he was given an early first-team debut. A natural goal-poacher's instincts and quick reactions appeared likely to give him a good career but a bad car accident, where he was thrown through the car windscreen, changed his prospects. Unable to overcome back problems he did not develop and had to return from South Africa when his injuries flared again. He ended with Darwen, a sad loss of a footballer who had all the potential of a good player.

FL	10+3 apps	2 gls
Total	10+3 apps	2 gls

DUXBURY, Michael
Full-back

5'9" 11st 2lb
Born: Accrington, 1 September 1959
Debut: 15 September 1990

CAREER: St Mary's College; Manchester United Jul 1976 (app) Oct 1976; Blackburn Rovers Aug 1990 (free); Bradford City Jan 1992 (loan) Mar 1992-May 1994 (free); Golden Football Team (Hong Kong) 1994; Accrington Stanley Aug 1996.
INTERNATIONALS: England 10 apps.

Although he played with the Blackburn schools side there was never a chance that Duxbury would join the Rovers. Spotted at an early age by Manchester United he graduated through their sides, in the process picking up international honours. A steady, consistent utility defender, always able to perform the role asked, he made a career out of his dependability. Unfortunately, by the time he came home to Blackburn he was unable to provide any inspiration and, devoid of talented players around him, looked very ordinary. After a spell in Hong Kong, where he played in a league selection against England, he took over from Paul Mariner as director of football at Bolton School and later returned to Hong Kong as head of the Manchester United academy.

FL	25+2 apps	0 gls
FAC	2 apps	0 gls
FLC	1 app.	0 gls
FMC	0+1 app.	0 gls
Total	28+3 apps	0 gls

ECCLES, Terence Stewart 'Tex'
Centre half/centre forward

6'0.5" 13st
Born: Leeds, 2 March 1952
Debut: 31 January 1970

CAREER: Pudsey Jnrs; Blackburn Rovers Aug 1968 (app) Aug 1969; Mansfield Town Jul 1973; Huddersfield Town Jan 1977 (£8,000); Ethnikos (Greece) Jul 1978; York City Sep 1979-Apr 1981; Scarborough.

Eccles attended Temple Moyle Grammar School, where they only played rugby, and he played for the English schoolboys against Wales. However, his footballing performances with Pudsey juniors brought him trials at Leeds and Chelsea. Eventually he signed for the Rovers, where he was groomed to play centre half. His debut came at right-back but it was as a stop-gap striker that he made his reputation. A chance appearance as a substitute brought a career change and his worth as a hard, competitive player was to further his career longer than it might have done if he had remained a defender.

FL	33+13 apps	6 gls
FAC	1 app.	0 gls
FLC	2 apps	1 gl
Total	36+13 apps	7 gls

ECKERSLEY, William
Left-back

5'6" 10st 2lb
Born: Southport, 16 July 1925
Died: Blackburn, 25 October 1982
Debut: 1 May 1948

CAREER: High Park; Blackburn Rovers Nov 1947 (am) Mar 1948-Feb 1961.
INTERNATIONALS: England 17 apps.

It is ironic that Bill Eckersley played only one game in the country's top division, his debut coming when the Rovers were already relegated. Good enough to play regularly for his country, Eckersley played his entire career in the Second Division with the Rovers, a remarkable demonstration of loyalty. He was spotted by the club after only a few appearances in junior football in Southport, where he drove a lorry, but had gained experience in wartime football, playing with Wilf Mannion for the Palestine United Services team. An airborne member of the Royal Ulster

Bill Eckersley in August 1959. (Howard Talbot Photography)

Rifles, he served most of the war in the Middle East. This developed him into a left-back who oozed confidence. He had great quickness, tackled ferociously and brought the ball from the back far more than full-backs of the time. A dressing room humorist about whom there are scores of anecdotes, he enjoyed life and more than the occasional beer and cigarette. Despite his repute as a supreme classical footballer he found off-field employment challenging and was a shopkeeper and then an insurance agent before he became a chauffeur. He died of cancer at a tragically early age, his ashes being scattered on the Ewood pitch.

FL	406 apps	20 gls
FAC	26 apps	1 gl
Total	432 apps	21 gls

EDDS, Ernest Frederick

Left winger

5'7.5" 11st

Born: Portsmouth, 19 March 1926

Debut: 24 December 1949

CAREER: Portsmouth Apr 1944 (am); Plymouth Argyle Oct 1946; Blackburn Rovers Dec 1949 (£8,000); Torquay United Jun 1951; Plymouth Argyle Oct 1953; Swindon Town Jul 1955.

Ernest Edds was due to attend his engagement party shortly before the Rovers started negotiations to bring him to Ewood. He signed for the Rovers on Friday, raced north, missing Christmas Day at home, played three games in four days and had to wait until the Tuesday to explain events to his girlfriend. Ironically he was not destined to play twenty games for the Rovers. Although he had played most of his career at inside or centre forward the Rovers saw him as a left winger, but he never compensated for the departed Langton.

FL	18 apps	3 gls
FAC	1 app.	1 gl
Total	19 apps	4 gls

ELSE, Frederick

Goalkeeper

5'10" 11st 4lb

Born: Golborne, 31 March 1933

Debut: 19 August 1961

CAREER: St Wilfred's, Standish; Wigan Athletic; St Wilfred's Standish; 81 Heavy Ack Ack Regiment; Axwell Park; Preston North End Aug 1953; Blackburn Rovers Aug 1961 (£20,000); Barrow (p-m) Jul 1966-May 1970.

For many seasons Else had earned the reputation of being one of the game's least spectacular but most reliable goalkeepers. A man who relied on positioning and working out the correct angles he seldom went for the flamboyant when the orthodox would serve. The abolition of the maximum wage created a valuation for performance and Else thought his ambitions would be best served at Ewood. For the Rovers it marked the first real upgrade in the position since the Second World War. For a time Else was as recommended; calm, efficient and almost unnoticed but in the last months of his career he began to show frailties in his game that had not previously existed. After a spell as player-manager at Barrow, where he also for a time ran the social club, he trained as a maths teacher and taught in the area for fifteen years. In 1999 he retired and bought a house in Peyia on the island of Cyprus.

FL	187 apps	0 gls
FAC	18 apps	0 gls
FLC	16 apps	0 gls
Total	221 apps	0 gls

ELVY, Reginald

Goalkeeper

6'2.5" 11st 7lb
Born: Churwell, 25 November 1920
Died: Kingsthorpe, 13 July 1991
Debut: 10 November 1951

CAREER: Churwell Council Sc; Halifax Town Mar 1944; Bolton Wanderers Mar 1947; Blackburn Rovers Nov 1951 (£3,000); Northampton Town Jul 1956-1959 (£500).

If the Australian cricketer Ken Grieves had not been ill, Elvy would never have become a Rover. Desperate for a player to start immediately they dashed to Bolton to sign Grieves but, finding him unwell, signed Elvy instead. In doing so they acquired the prototype goalkeeper. Tall, skeletal with huge hands, he was one of the few goalkeepers of the day comfortable with the high shot that needs tipping over the bar. He also got down quickly for a tall man but his eyesight, that required him to wear contact lenses, was his Achilles heel. Strangely, Elvy had commenced his schoolboy career on the wing, but genetics and family tradition had placed him between the posts before he played for Morley & District schools. For the Rovers he was a marvellous servant, unmoved by playing behind a team who always believed they could score one more than the opposition. He finished his playing days in Northampton, worked as a representative for a brewery and scouted occasionally for the Rovers.

FL	192 apps	0 gls
FAC	16 apps	0 gls
Total	208 apps	0 gls

EMERTON, Brett Michael

Midfielder

6'0.5" 13st 5lb
Born: Bankstown (Australia), 22 February 1979
Debut: 16 August 2003

CAREER: Macquarie Fields HS; MacArthur Rams; NSW Academy of Sport 1989; Marconi Fairfield; Leeds United (trial); Australian Institute of Sport 1994; Sydney Olympic 1996; Feyenoord (Holland) 2000 (£4,000,000); Blackburn Rovers Jul 2003 (£2,500,000).
INTERNATIONALS: Australia 45 apps 9 gls.

Born in Bankstown, he was raised in Macquerie Fields where his sporting prowess was visible from an early age. At the age of ten he was taken to the New South Wales Academy of Sport where his natural athleticism was channelled into football. At the age of fifteen he accompanied Harry Kewell for trials with Leeds United but returned to Australia to join the Australian Institute of Sport. From there he graduated to Sydney Olympic and saw national exposure with the Australian Olympic Games' team. Full international caps followed and he joined the flood of young Australians who were coming into European football. He joined Feyenoord and contributed to their UEFA Cup final victory in 2002, although he missed the final because of suspension. A player at home wide on the right-hand side and able to operate as a right wing-back, he has speed and deceptive trickery. Anxious to move into the Premiership, he almost joined Newcastle but the deal fell through at the last moment and he ended joining Blackburn at a fee that recognised he had only a year of his contract remaining. In his two seasons at Ewood he has remained an enigma, capable of brilliance but often disappointing with his final execution. However he has been a vital outlet for the defence and a non-stop worker with a high tackle count.

PL	75+16 apps	7 gls
FAC	4+1 apps	0 gls
FLC	4+2 app.	2 gl
UEFA	2 apps	1 gl
Total	85+19 apps	10 gls

ENCKELMAN, Peter
Goalkeeper

6'2" 12st 5lb
Born: Turku (Finland), 10 March 1977
Debut: 8 May 2004

CAREER: TPS Turku; Aston Villa Feb 1999 (£200,000); Blackburn Rovers Nov 2003 (loan) Jan 2004 (£150,000).
INTERNATIONALS: Finland 5 apps.

The son of the Finnish international goalkeeper Goran Enckelman, genetics dictated that Peter would follow in his footsteps. Taken on by Aston Villa to understudy David James, he soon found himself deputy to his boyhood hero Peter Schmeichel. When he took over in the first team he became accepted as a sound, unspectacular player, but his position was undermined when, in a derby game with Birmingham, he missed Mellberg's throw in and the referee decided that he had made contact and awarded an own goal. Although he was not immediately left out, the subsequent arrival of Thomas Sorensen and the advance of Stefan Postma made him third choice. A loan spell at Blackburn was followed by a permanent transfer, but he has had little opportunity behind Brad Friedel.

PL	2 apps	0 gls
FLC	1 app.	0 gls
Total	3 apps	0 gls

ENDEAN, Barry
Striker/midfield

5'10" 11st
Born: Chester le Street, 22 March 1946
Debut: 30 October 1971

CAREER: Black Horse; Pelton Fell; Watford Sep 1968; Charlton Athletic Feb 1971 (£10,000); Blackburn Rovers Oct 1971 (with £8,000 for Rogers); Huddersfield Town Mar 1975 (with £5,000 for Hoy); Workington Town Oct 1975 (loan); Hartlepool Mar 1976 (£3,000); Workington.

A late arrival to the Football League, he was brought to Ewood because the Rovers' manager Ken Furphy knew him well from Watford and because the club was anxious to unload the perpetually brooding Eamon Rogers. Team morale was aided by the arrival of the bustling, ever-committed Endean but his failure to find the net brought complaints. Once he started to hit the target the fans warmed to his enthusiasm but it was when he was unexpectedly moved to midfield that he started to enjoy celebrity status. His fierce tackling was unexpected and his ability to ruffle opponents endeared him. A local court case involving the illegal borrowing of a builder's vehicle brought him the nickname 'Dumper'. When he had finally finished playing he became manager at Chester le Street, his home-town club.

FL	65+14 apps	18 gls
FAC	5 apps	0 gls
FLC	3+1 apps	1 gl
Total	73+15 apps	19 gls

ENGLAND, Harold Michael*

Centre half

6'2" 13st 2lb
Born: Holywell, 2 December 1941
Debut: 3 October 1959

CAREER: Ysgol Dinas Basing (Holywell); Blackburn Rovers Apr 1959; Tottenham Hotspur Aug 1966 (£95,000); Seattle Sounders (USA) May 1975; Cardiff City Aug 1975; Seattle Sounders (USA) May 1976-Aug 1979.
INTERNATIONALS: Wales 44 apps 3 gls.

When England arrived for trials after starring for the Flintshire schoolboy side he was sent home. The judgement was that he was too slender to become a professional and would never have the strength to compete at top level. Fortunately somebody thought again and one of the club's greatest players was signed. Despite his height (he later filled out his physique so that he became a dominant central defender) England had the touch that would have found him a position anywhere on the field, a tactical brain and the ability to slide a pass with precision. He could also shoot, was supreme in the air and competed well. He was launched into the first team at the age of eighteen and was part of the team around 1963 that might, with fortune, have been truly exceptional. Exposure to international football and the narrow confines of a small-town club led to his inevitable departure. He continued to grace the game at Tottenham, became the Welsh team manager and in 1984 was awarded the MBE for his services to Welsh football. When at Blackburn he opened an eponymous woodyard at Hoghton, but sold this and invested in residential homes in north Wales.

FL	165 apps	21 gls
FAC	12 apps	0 gls
FLC	7 apps	0 gls
Total	184 apps	21 gls

F

FARRELL, Gerard William

Left-back

5'7" 10st 6lb
Born: Liverpool, 19 March 1952
Debut: 9 October 1971

CAREER: Everton 1967 (sc); Wolverhampton Wanderers 1968 (app) May 1970; Watford Aug 1971 (loan); Blackburn Rovers Oct 1971 (free); Johannesburg Rangers (South Africa) Feb 1973; Morecambe Aug 1978-1980; Workington; Lancaster City 1982.

Having failed to make the grade at both Wolverhampton and Watford a trial at Ewood, where Ken Furphy was demolishing the staff, represented Farrell's last chance of making it into the Football League. Despite his tempestuous nature his spirit and willingness impressed and he was given a contract. Time proved that his wild tendencies and mis-timed tackling made him a marked man and after a spate of bookings he lost his place to the far calmer Mick Wood. Given the opportunity to move to midfield he failed to impress and was allowed to leave on a free transfer. After a spell in South Africa he returned to Morecambe but wanderlust took over and he left for Canada, hoping to play for Toronto in the NASL. A hand injury terminated this venture and he moved back to Morecambe, becoming the club's commercial manager as well as playing. He opened up an estate agency in the town and later expanded into the city of Lancaster.

FL	21+1 apps	1 gl
FAC	2 apps	0 gls
Total	23+1 apps	1 gl

F

FAZACKERLEY, Derek William
Centre-back

5'11" 11st 6lb
Born: Preston, 5 November 1951
Debut: 23 February 1971

CAREER: Blackburn Rovers May 1969 (app) Jan 1970; Chester City Jan 1987 (free); York City Jul 1988 (free); Bury Dec 1988-Jul 1989; Workington Sep 1989; Darwen; Kumu Kwsankoski (Finland) (p-m); Darwen.

The first sign that Fazackerley was going to be exceptional came before he had kicked a ball. During his apprenticeship he lost a full season because of a leg injury but the manager, Eddie Quigley, was sufficiently impressed to send him scouting on future opponents during his inactivity. Recovered, he never looked back and settled into a place as one of the two centre-backs. Playing alongside a taller man he was the supreme team player, able to anticipate danger, playing to the strengths of his partner and with great speed that enabled him to tidy up. Despite his lack of extra inches he was seldom beaten in the air, his timing being perfection and he had a body strength that made him a bruising opponent. A ferocious tackler with inch-perfect precision he was master of his own penalty area. If his distribution was sometimes suspect it posed the conundrum of how a man who could judge a back pass to inches could be so wayward going forward. His ability was such that if he had played for a larger club he had the talent to have played internationally but in the relative obscurity of Blackburn he went unnoticed, although in breaking the record for appearances at the club he achieved a record that may never be broken. In all he appeared in seventeen seasons for the first team, leaving when displaced by the younger David Mail. Searching for managerial experience he was assistant manager at Chester, coach at Bury and player-manager with a newly promoted team in Finland. Appointed youth coach at Newcastle, his career flourished when Kevin Keegan arrived and promoted him to the first team. Resigning to return to Blackburn under Roy Harford he survived the managerial change that brought in Roy Hodgson but not the one that replaced Hodgson with Kidd. Bouncing back spectacularly, he followed Keegan first to coach the England national side and then to Manchester City.

Derek Fazackerley in 1978.

FL	593+3 apps	24 gls
FAC	40 apps	1 gl
FLC	38 apps	1 gl
Total	671+3 apps	26 gls

FEAR, Keith William
Striker

5'7" 10st 8lb
Born: Bristol, 8 May 1952
Debut: 26 December 1977

CAREER: Merrywood GS; Bristol City May 1966 (sc) Jun 1969; St Louis Stars (USA) Apr 1976 (loan); Hereford United Sep 1977 (loan); Blackburn Rovers Dec 1977 (loan); Plymouth Argyle Feb 1978; Brentford Nov 1979 (loan); Chester City Jan 1980-Jun 1981; Scarborough 1982; Bangor City 1983; Stafford Rangers.

The recipient of a reward from the *Hotspur* comic for his schoolboy achievements in football, athletics and basketball, his prowess was duly noted by his local club. Achieving international honours at youth level and playing in the FA Youth Cup semi-final he appeared to have great potential. Small but stockily powerful, his quick, darting style was difficult to counter but his potential remained unfulfilled. He arrived with the Rovers over a Christmas programme when the club had few resources and no money. An immediate hit because he scored on his debut at Burnley, he then undermined the good work by missing a penalty in the same game. The Rovers were interested in prolonging his stay but not at the asking price of £20,000 and Fear spent the rest of his career moving down the football pyramid while moving on the field to a midfield position.

FL	5 apps	2 gls
FAC	1 app.	0 gls
Total	6 apps	2 gls

FENTON, Graham Anthony
Striker/midfield

5'10" 11st 3lb
Born: Wallsend, 22 May 1974
Debut: 18 December 1995

CAREER: Cramlington Jnrs; Aston Villa May 1989 (ass sch) Feb 1992; Blackburn Rovers Nov 1995 (£1,250,000); Leicester City Aug 1997 (£1,100,000); Walsall Mar 2000 (loan); Barnsley Jul 2000 (trial); Stoke City Aug 2000; St Mirren Sep 2000; Blackpool Aug 2001-Jun 2003; Darlington Sep 2002-Jan 2003 (loan); Blyth Spartans (Jul 2003).

Capable of playing in every forward position, the stocky, aggressive player gained Under-21 honours but his career with Aston Villa drifted without him maturing into the prospect they had anticipated. Contributory to this was a troublesome groin strain problem that delayed the completion of his move to Blackburn. A natural predator, he suffered again from lack of regular opportunity and is best remembered for his two late goals that helped destroy Newcastle's quest for the Premiership title in 1996. A succession of clubs followed without his career blossoming but it was not until he arrived at St Mirren that an explanation was found. Tests proved that he was asthmatic and this is the reason why throughout his career he has seldom played for the full ninety minutes.

PL	9+18 apps	7 gls
FAC	0+1 app.	0 gls
FLC	0+2 apps	0 gls
Total	9+21 apps	7 gls

FENTON, William Hartas
Left wing

5'8" 10st 11lb
Born: Hartlepool, 23 June 1926
Died: York, 14 April 1973
Debut: 15 January 1949

CAREER: Barnsley Nov 1944; Horden CW; Blackburn Rovers Dec 1948; York City May 1951; Scarborough 1957.

Having dropped back into non-league football with Horden Colliery, Fenton was shrewd enough to qualify as a draughtsman and found employment in Blackburn when he was signed, so that he was only a part-time player. This probably hindered his development because when he left for York he matured into a sharp, penetrative player with a sound shot and, unusually for a left winger of the day, a definite goal-scoring flair. He scored 31 goals in his first season and retired with over 100 goals to his credit. The player of the year at the club still receives a trophy named in Fenton's honour. His son, Stephen, was a professional footballer with Bradford City.

FL	33 apps	7 gls
FAC	1 app.	0 gls
Total	34 apps	7 gls

FERGUSON, Barry
Midfielder

5'11" 11st 1lb
Born: Glasgow, 2 February 1978
Debut: 13 September 2003

CAREER: Glasgow Rangers SABC 1986; Glasgow Rangers Jul 1994; Blackburn Rovers Aug 2003 (£6,500,000); Glasgow Rangers Jan 2005 (£5,500,000).
INTERNATIONALS: Scotland 31 apps 1 gl.

Born and raised in Glasgow and a member of the Rangers from the age of eight, Ferguson followed his brother into the Rangers first team. A complete 'box-to-box' midfield player with great athleticism as well as being a natural leader he was well on his way into becoming a legendary figure at Ibrox when he decided that he wished to play in the Premiership. Despite the fact that he was captain of his country and had won every honour the Scottish game had to offer, he relished a stiffer challenge and in August 2003 decided to follow his old teammate Amoruso to Ewood. His transition to English football was difficult and he was only just getting used to the extra pace of the game when a broken kneecap kept him out for half a season. Returning to the side he was given the captaincy, but the decision of Souness to join Newcastle prompted Ferguson to think of returning to Rangers. By the winter transfer window he was sufficiently unsettled to ask for a transfer and having achieved little in his time at Ewood the Rovers consented.

PL	35+1 apps	3 gls
FAC	1 app.	0 gls
FLC	1 app.	1 gl
Total	37+1 apps	4 gls

FERGUSON, Michael Kevin
Right winger

5'10.5" 11st 7lb
Born: Burnley, 9 March 1943
Debut: 18 August 1962

CAREER: Plymouth Argyle Mar 1959 (am); Accrington Stanley Jul 1960; Blackburn Rovers Mar 1962 (£2,500); Aston Villa May 1968 (£50,000); Queens Park Rangers Nov 1969 (£15,000); Cambridge United Jul 1973; Rochdale Jul 1974; Los Angeles Aztecs (USA) Apr 1975 (loan); I A Akrannes (Iceland) (p-c) 1976; Halifax Town Dec 1976.

A mass of contradictions, Ferguson was a bewitching, leggy, dribbling machine who the Rovers rightly saw as a devastating force down the right flank, switching him from the inside forward position he had played at Accrington Stanley. Cast on the soccer scrapheap when Stanley folded, he made the short trip to Ewood and his conversion to the number seven shirt was such an overwhelming success that the Rovers were able to move Bryan Douglas inside without losing effectiveness on the flank. Never a man to accept mistreatment he dispensed his own justice, and in doing so he brought into play a ferocious tackling instinct that was surprising in such an artist. Extremely popular with the crowd, he became unsettled when many of the better players were allowed to leave, his situation not being aided by the club's desire to play him at right-back. He had every potential for the position except desire but he found a new home at Aston Villa, where he had once contributed the most amazing individual goal scored by the Rovers. Serving a managerial apprenticeship as player-coach with Akrannes he guided them to two national championships. He moved to Cyprus where he coached Apoel to a first and then second-place finish and also worked with Evagoras. In Turkey he coached Karsyaka and in Sweden, Vasterhaninge. For such a well-respected continental coach it is puzzling why he never succeeded in England.

Mike Ferguson in August 1963. (Howard Talbot Photography)

After a spell with Nelson he managed Rochdale and Enfield but was dismissed by both clubs for failure to meet expectations. Arthritis hit him at a relatively young age and hampered him so much that he was forced to forego any further involvement with the game.

FL	220 apps	29 gls
FAC	15 apps	1 gl
FLC	14 apps	6 gls
Total	249 apps	36 gls

FETTIS, Alan William
Goalkeeper

6'1" 11st 4lb
Born: Belfast, 1 February 1971
Debut: 26 December 1997

CAREER: Glentoran; Ards; Hull City Aug 1991 (£50,000); West Bromwich Albion Nov 1995 (loan); Nottingham Forest Jan 1996 (£250,000); Blackburn Rovers Sep 1997 (£300,000); Leicester City Sep 1999 (loan); York City Mar 2000 (£50,000); Hull City Jan 2003 (free); Sheffield United Dec 2003-Feb 2004 (loan); Grimsby Town Mar 2004 (loan); Macclesfield Town Jun 2004 (free).
INTERNATIONALS: Northern Ireland 25 apps.

Brought from his native Northern Ireland by Hull City he settled well on Humberside but it is perhaps indicative of his career that he is chiefly remembered for twice coming on as an outfield substitute and scoring. Down to third choice at Nottingham Forest he sought more opportunities at Ewood but, after a fine debut, he had a spell when it appeared that every shot at him landed in the net. At York he proved a fine, confident player who kept the struggling side competitive before he returned to his first English club where, unexpectedly, he was named to the PFA divisional team.

PL	9+2 apps	0 gls
FAC	1 app.	0 gls
Total	10+2 apps	0 gls

FIELD, Anthony
Striker

5'7" 11st
Born: Halifax, 6 July 1946
Debut: 23 October 1971

CAREER: Illingworth United; Halifax Town Jul 1963; Barrow Aug 1966; Southport Mar 1968; Blackburn Rovers Oct 1971 (£15,000+Goodwin); Sheffield United Mar 1974 (£75,000); New York Cosmos (USA) Apr 1976; Memphis Rogues (USA) Apr 1978-Aug 1980).

Many scouts dismissed Field in the early part of his career because he lacked physique and strength but the Rovers, who had fallen on hard times in the Third Division, were less judgemental. Dark and swarthy, favouring the left side, he had electric acceleration and a goal-scorer's obsession. He scored with sweetly struck long shots but harvested just as many creeping in unseen under the shadow of the posts. An efficient penalty expert, he ended his career with an impressive strike rate, rejoining his manager Ken Furphy at Sheffield United. He never prospered in the First Division but followed Furphy to America and established himself as a star of the NASL.

FL	104+2 apps	45 gls
FAC	10 apps	7 gls
FLC	4 apps	2 gls
Total	118+2 apps	54 gls

FILAN, John Richard
Goalkeeper

5'11" 12st 10lb
Born: Sydney (Australia), 8 February 1970
Debut: 9 August 1997

CAREER: St Michael's, Meadowcroft; Marist Brothers Eastwood 1987; Budapest St George 1989; Wollongong Wolves 1991; Budapest St George 1992; Wollongong Wolves 1992; Stoke City (trial); Southampton (trial); Peterborough United (trial) Cambridge United Mar 1993 (£40,000); Nottingham Forest Dec 1994 (loan); Coventry City Mar 1995 (£300,000); Blackburn Rovers Jul 1997 (£700,000); Wigan Athletic Dec 2001 (£400,000).
INTERNATIONALS: Australia 2 apps.

After a successful Olympic Games in which he played in the third-place play-off, Filan tried his luck in England. It took several trials at various clubs before he was signed by Cambridge and even when he made the starting line-up there, a move up the ladder to Coventry brought only more frustration. Spotted by Tony Parkes and Derek Fazackerley playing in the Coventry reserves, he was brought to Ewood because Shay Given was not prepared to understudy Tim Flowers and had moved to Newcastle. Although he was unknown, the first sight of Filan was sufficient to convince the fans they had an ample replacement and indeed he subsequently kept Flowers out of the first team. Not a tall man, he was superbly agile, left his line with conviction and when presented with a physical challenge he punched his weight. A dreadful broken arm sidelined him but he had regained his place when Souness decided that Brad Friedel was the man he wished to have between the Blackburn posts. Not a man to tolerate inactivity, Filan dropped down two divisions in search of regular football and was rewarded with a Division Two championship medal with Wigan and then helped them gain promotion to the Premiership.

L	61+1 apps	0 gls
FAC	5 apps	0 gls
FLC	6 apps	0 gls
Total	72+1 apps	0 gls

FINNIGAN, Anthony
Midfield

6'0" 12st
Born: Wimbledon, 17 October 1962
Debut: 27 August 1988

CAREER: Crystal Palace (jnrs); Fulham Oct 1980-Jul 1982; Leicester City 1982 (trial); Middlesbrough 1983 (trial); Corinthian Casuals 1983; Ravaniemi Lappi (Fin) 1984; Crystal Palace Mar 1985; Blackburn Rovers Jul 1988 (£45,000); Hull City Aug 1990 (£30,000); Swindon Town Mar 1991-Apr 1991 (free); Crystal Palace 1991 (non con); Brentford Jan 1992 (non con); Crystal Palace Apr 1992-Oct 1992; Fulham Nov 1992 (trial); Earnest Borel (HK) Feb 1993-Jun 1993; Brighton & Hove Albion Sep 1993 (trial); Barnet Sep 1993; Hendon; Dulwich Hamlet; Fulham Sep 1994-Jan 1996 (non con); Falkirk Jan 1996; Worthing 1996.

Despite an illustrious career with the England youth team Finnigan failed to harness his ability until Crystal Palace recruited him from non-league football. Well built and comfortable on the ball, he was versatile enough to play several positions and could change within the game without a problem. His move to Blackburn was a classic example of the wrong player at the wrong club. Hampered by injury, inconsistent and in a different culture from his native London he was ill at ease. He accused the fans of racism and certainly there was a lack of appreciation of his skills. A move to Hull increased the downward spiral of his career and in 1994 he was facing the Bow Street JPs charged with possessing heroin with intent to supply. Acquitted of intent to supply, he was convicted of the lesser charge of possession. Although Fulham stood by him during the trial it was deemed best if he left London and he finished his career in Scotland with Falkirk. Retiring, he opened a sports' agency with his old Palace teammate Andy Gray, using the name of 'Wright, Wright, Wright'.

FL	21+15 apps	0 gls
FAC	5 apps	1 gl
FLC	3 apps	0 gls
FMC	3+1 apps	1 gl
Total	32+16 apps	2 gls

FLITCROFT, Garry William
Midfield

6'0" 11st 7lb
Born: 6 November, 1972
Debut: 30 March 1996

CAREER: Turton HS; Turton Jnrs; Bolton Lads Club; Manchester City Jul 1989 (trainee) Jul 1991; Bury Mar 1992 (loan); Blackburn Rovers Mar 1996 (£3,200,000).

An energetic midfield man whose assets were his physical presence, desire to succeed and leadership. He made a highly unusual debut, being sent off within minutes, but the club was never unappreciative of the influence he brought to games. A ferocious tackler, he was less comfortable with the ball and preferred the safe pass to the perceptive. Possessing abundant energy, he was utilised to provide forward runs but lacked composure in critical positions. Despite having his critics it is now commonly accepted that the team was worse for his absence, although those absences were increased by his disciplinary record.

L	229+16 apps	14 gls
FAC	15+2 apps	4 gls
FLC	10+4 apps	1 gl
UEFA	4 apps	1 gl
Total	258+22 apps	20 gls

FLOWERS, Timothy David
Goalkeeper

6'2" 14st
Born: Kenilworth, 3 February 1967
Debut: 6 November 1993

CAREER: Wolverhampton Wanderers Mar 1981 (sc) Aug 1983 (app) Aug 1984; Southampton Apr 1986 (loan) Jun 1986 (£70,000); Swindon Town Mar 1987 (loan) Nov 1987 (loan); Blackburn Rovers Nov 1993 (£2,400,000); Leicester City Jul 1999-Jun 2003 (£1,100,000); Stockport County Oct 2001 (loan); Coventry City Feb 2002 (loan); Manchester City Aug 2002-Nov 2002 (loan).
INTERNATIONALS: England 11 apps.

It took a world-record fee for a goalkeeper to bring Flowers to Ewood but Kenny Dalglish wanted the best man he could buy to cement

Tim Flowers in 1994.

the Rovers' position in the Premiership. Payback was quick as the supremely professional Flowers established himself as a vital component of the team that took the Premiership title in 1995. Possessing great reflexes and a careful student of angles and technique, he might have enjoyed a longer career with the club if he had not suffered from injury and found John Filan a redoubtable opponent. A special place in the club's history will forever be reserved for Flowers and his performance on VE night when he was superb against Newcastle in preserving a lead will never be forgotten. He became the first person at the club to respond to Alex Ferguson's mind games with his famous 'bottle' interview that underlined the team's determination to hold on to their lead at the top of the table. Although he has had to undergo hip replacement surgery he has remained in the game as goalkeeping coach at Leicester and then Manchester City.

PL	175+2 apps	0 gls
FAC	13+1 apps	0 gls
FLC	14 apps	0 gls
UEFA	4 apps	0 gls
EC	6 apps	0 gls
CS	2 apps	0 gls
Total	214+3 apps	0 gls

FORBES, George Parrott
Left half

5'11.5" 11st 13lb
Born: Dukinfield, 21 July 1914
Debut: 30 January 1937

CAREER: Crescent Road Congregationalists; Mossley 1934; Hyde United; Blackburn Rovers Jan 1937; Barrow Jun 1946-1951.

Originally a strapping centre forward who brought energy and muscle to the game, he was signed from parks football by Mossley for whom he scored 2 goals in 3 games. Allowed to slip away to Hyde, he attracted the Rovers' interest but when signed received little opportunity until the war years, when he converted to left half. Although he was at Blackburn nearly ten years he made only 2 league appearances. In five years at Barrow he exceeded 100 appearances. His curious second forename came from taking his mother's maiden name.

FAC	1 app.	0 gls
Pre-war		
FL	2 apps	1 gl
Total	3 apps	1 gl

FOWLER, Martin
Midfield/Full-back

5'10" 11st 8lb
Born: York, 17 January 1957
Debut: 19 August 1978

CAREER: Huddersfield Town Apr 1972 (app) Jan 1974; Blackburn Rovers Jul 1978 (free); Hartlepool United Mar 1980-May 1980 (loan); Stockport County Aug 1980 (free); Scunthorpe United Jul 1982-Feb 1983.

By the time he arrived on a free transfer Fowler was attempting to rescue a career that began brightly at youth level and once made him the subject of a £100,000 enquiry from Manchester City. Extravagantly coiffeured, he brought effort and enthusiasm to midfield but the Rovers were quick to recognise that his mobility and vision were suspect. Converted to full-back, he never shirked a challenge or gave in but in the general shake up at Ewood he found himself surplus to requirements. He enjoyed the best days of his career at Stockport but became disillusioned and gave up the game to become a police officer.

FL	36+2 apps	0 gls
FAC	1 app.	0 gls

FLC	3 apps	0 gls
Total	40+2 apps	0 gls

FOYLE, Martin John
Striker

5'10" 11st 2lb
Born: Salisbury, 2 May 1963

CAREER: Southampton Aug 1980; Blackburn Rovers Mar 1984 (loan); Aldershot Aug 1984 (£10,000); Oxford United Mar 1987 (£120,000); Port Vale Jun 1991-Feb 2000 (£375,000).

Brought in on loan from Southampton when still only a prospect, he was substitute for one game but did not play. Although lacking in pace he proved to be a natural goalscorer who ended with 154 league goals in over 500 appearances before becoming the manager at Port Vale.

FRANDSEN, Per
Midfield

6'1" 12st 6lb
Born: Copenhagen (Denmark), 6 February 1970
Debut: 25 September 1999

CAREER: B 1903; Lille OSC (France) 1991; FC Copenhagen 1994; Bolton Wanderers Aug 1996 (£300,000); Blackburn Rovers Sep 1999 (£1,750,000); Bolton Wanderers Jul 2000 (£1,650,000); Wigan Athletic Jun 2004-Jun 2005 (free).
INTERNATIONALS: Denmark 22 apps.

In his first season Per Frandsen helped his small club to the runners-up spot, scored 15 goals and gained his first international cap before moving to further his career in France. In three seasons there he was transformed into a midfield playmaker who could hit all the passes in the range, was deceptively mobile and worked hard. Realisation that Lille would never be a power prompted him to return to Denmark but it was with Bolton that his career really blossomed. His move to the Rovers was one of those ill-fated decisions and he seldom appeared at ease in a blue and white shirt but recovered his form immediately when he made the return trip to Bolton. He was granted a free transfer by the Wanderers four years later but no sooner had he started at Wigan than his career was terminated by a knee injury. He has announced his intentions of returning to Denmark in the close season and starting up as a football agent.

FL	26+5 apps	5 gls
FAC	4 apps	1 gl
Total	30+5 apps	6 gls

FRIEDEL, Bradley Howard
Goalkeeper

6'3" 14st 3lb
Born: Lakewood, Ohio (USA), 18 May 1971
Debut: 18 November 2000

CAREER: Bay High School (Cleveland); UCLA1990; Dallas Sidekicks 1993; Newcastle United May 1994 (trial); Brondby IF (Denmark) 1995; Galatasaray (Turkey) Sep 1995; Columbus Crew (USA) Aug 1996; Liverpool Dec 1997 (£1,000,000); Energie Cottbus (Germany) Oct 2000 (trial); Blackburn Rovers Nov 2000 (free).
INTERNATIONALS: USA 81 apps.

Football is a game of opinions but there can be no argument on one subjective matter: Brad Friedel is the greatest goalkeeper ever to play for Blackburn Rovers. A superbly built player, with great agility and improvisation, his form since coming to Blackburn has been a revelation. No player has had a greater influence on his team in the Premiership than Friedel and his list of outstanding saves is endless. Equally importantly, the number of mistakes he has made have been few. Man of the Match in the club's Worthington

Brad Friedel celebrates in 2002.

Cup Final victory he has been amazingly consistent, disproving all the doubts that arose about him when he was at Liverpool. It was a surprise when Souness brought him to Ewood, since John Filan was a good and popular goalkeeper, but Souness knew his man well after a season spent with him in Turkey and his judgement has proved to be impeccable. In 2002/03 he touched pinnacles of perfection few goalkeepers reach and to no-one's surprise was voted to the PFA Premiership team. If he struggled for a time when the defence lost Henning Berg his form returned once Andy Todd and Ryan Nelsen struck up a partnership at centre-back. He also contributed the first goal from a club goalkeeper for 120 years when he came up for a corner against Charlton and turned in a cross from the left.

L	193 apps	1 gl
FAC	20 apps	0 gls
FLC	14 apps	0 gls
UEFA	6 apps	0 gls
Total	233 apps	1 gl

FRYATT, James Edward
Centre forward

6'0" 12st
Born: Southampton, 2 September 1940
Debut: 19 October 1968

CAREER: King Edward GS; Southampton; Moor End YC; Charlton Oct 1957; Southend United Jun 1960 (£600); Bradford PA Jun 1963 (£2,500); Southport Mar 1966 (£4,000); Torquay United Mar 1967 (£5,000); Stockport County Oct 1967 (£6,000); Blackburn Rovers Oct 1968 (£30,000); Oldham Athletic Feb 1970 (£8,000); Southport Nov 1971; Philadelphia Atoms (USA) May 1973; Southport Aug 1973; Philadelphia Atoms (USA) May 1974; Stockport County Sep 1974; Torquay United Dec 1974; Chorley Jan 1975; Hartford Bi-Centennials (USA) Apr 1975; Philadelphia Atoms (USA) Jul 1975-Aug 1975.

With a balding head and bushy sideburns Fryatt was easily recognisable. At home in the lower divisions, where size, heart and persistency can bring goals, his chief area of expertise was when the ball was in the air. Seldom involved otherwise, he contributed little to the Rovers and was soon experiencing football in the USA. It is stated he once scored a goal for Bradford within four seconds of the kick-off, although the claim may be apocryphal. He remained in the USA after retirement first as the assistant manager of Las Vegas Quicksilver and then as a croupier. His son Edward was raised in the country and became a golf professional on the PGA circuit. When Jim Fryatt finally returned to England he found employment with a firm who lay playing fields.

FL	29+8 apps	5 gls
FAC	4 apps	3 gls
Total	33+8 apps	8 gls

G

GALE, Anthony Peter
Centre-back

6'1" 12st 4lb
Born: Westminster, 19 November 1959
Debut: 20 August 1994

CAREER: Fulham Nov 1974 (sc) Jun 1976 (app) Aug 1977; West Ham United Aug 1984 (£150,000); Blackburn Rovers Aug 1994 (free); Crystal Palace Sep 1995; Maidenhead United 1996.

Bobby Moore's replacement at Fulham, he earned a reputation as a footballing defender with poise, mobility and good distribution. After seven years with the club he moved on to West Ham where he became Alvin Martin's partner. In all he stayed ten years with the Hammers but personal honours eluded him. Released in 1994, he was training with Barnet when the Rovers asked him to come north to replace the retired Kevin Moran and the absconded David May. A successful trial in a friendly against Celtic earned him a debut in the Charity Shield final and a regular place until the turn of the year in the side that ultimately won the Premiership. Although he lost his place to Ian Pearce he had sufficient appearances to qualify for a medal, his first major honour. Released at the end of the season he kept fit with Barnet until Crystal Palace offered him terms. Unhappily, he was injured for most of the time and saw out his playing days with Maidenhead. On retiring he was employed by Capital Radio as co-commentator with Jonathan Pearce and worked in the family business.

PL	15 apps	0 gls
FLC	2 apps	0 gls
UEFA	2 apps	0 gls
Total	19 apps	0 gls

GALLACHER, Bernard
Left-back

5'8" 11st 4lb
Born: Johnstone, 22 March 1967
Died: Sutton Coldfield, 28 August 2011
Debut: 17 November 1990

CAREER: Aston Villa Aug 1983 (app) Apr 1985; Blackburn Rovers Nov 1990 (loan); Doncaster Rovers Sep 1991; Brighton & Hove Albion Oct 1992-Jul 1993; Northampton Town Jan 1994-May 1994; Bromsgrove Rovers; (Hong Kong).

A stocky, red-headed left-back who came on loan from Aston Villa, he was tenacious and a good tackler but lacked invention going forward. The price quoted for a permanent move was sufficient to deter the Rovers but by the end of the season he was available on a free transfer. He briefly found a regular spot at Brighton but had moved into non-league football before moving to Hong Kong.

FL	4 apps	0 gls
Total	4 apps	0 gls

GALLACHER, Kevin William
Striker

5'8" 10st 10lb
Born: Clydebank, 23 November 1966
Debut: 3 April 1993

CAREER: St Andrew's HS, Clydebank; Duntocher BC; Dundee United Nov 1983; Coventry City Jan 1990 (£700,000); Blackburn Rovers Mar 1993 (ex Wegerle+cash, value £1,500,000); Newcastle United Sep 1999 (£700,000); Bolton Wanderers Jul 2001 (trial); Preston North End Aug 2001; Sheffield Wednesday Mar 2002-May 2002; Huddersfield Town Sep 2002-Oct 2002.
INTERNATIONALS: Scotland 53 apps 9 gls.

There was never a doubt that the waspish little striker would make a professional footballer

Kevin Gallacher celebrates in 1998.

despite his lack of stature. His father Willie and uncle Patsy both had played for Celtic and Gallacher had learned well the techniques and tricks that strikers without physical resources require. Able to play wide on either side he was best paired with a big man and found in his early days at the club that Mike Newell was the ideal complement. Successive broken legs and the arrival of Alan Shearer restricted his opportunities but when Shearer left he returned and in his sixth season (under Roy Hodgson) found the best goal-scoring form of his career. A regular for Scotland, he fell out of favour when Brian Kidd took over but was taken to Newcastle as stop-gap cover alongside Alan Shearer. In retirement he has remained in the Blackburn area and is often found giving expert analysis on BBC radio.

FL	132+12 apps	46 gls
FAC	13 apps	4 gls
FLC	8+2 apps	3 gls
EC	0+1 app.	0 gls
CS	1 app.	0 gls
Total	154+15 apps	53 gls

GALLAGHER, Paul
Forward

6'1" 12st
Born: Glasgow, 9 August 1984
Debut: 15 March 2003

CAREER: Our Lady & St John's; Blackburn Eagles; Blackburn Rovers Mar 2003; Stoke City Aug 2005 (loan).
INTERNATIONALS: Scotland 1 app.

Although born in Scotland Gallagher was brought to Blackburn as a young child and grew up in the Shadsworth district. A rangy left-sided player, able to play wide or up front he made his first impact with a FA Youth Cup hat-trick against Exeter. Before the end of the season he had obtained a hat-trick for the reserves at Bradford and another in the final of the national Under-19 competition. Sandwiched between was a first-team debut when he came on as substitute in the home victory over the champions Arsenal and an appearance for the Scottish Under-21 side.

He was fast tracked into the full Scottish side and started to appear more regularly with the Rovers, but even though he has proved to be a goal threat his career is currently side-lined by his inability to hold down a regular place.

PL	17+26 apps	5 gls
FAC	4+1 apps	0 gls
FLC	0+2 apps	1 gl
Total	21+29 apps	6 gls

GARBETT, Terence Graham
Midfield

5'9" 11st 2lb
Born: Malton, 9 September 1945
Debut: 11 September 1971

CAREER: Pelton Fell; Stockton; Middlesbrough Aug 1963; Watford Aug 1966; Blackburn Rovers Sep 1971 (£16,000); Sheffield United Feb 1974 (£35,000); New York Cosmos (USA) Apr 1976-Aug 1977 (£9,000).

The new Rovers manager Ken Furphy decided that he needed an onfield henchman, and so returned to his former club Watford to acquire Terry Garbett. A right-sided player with great drive, a fierce tackler and strong runner, Furphy looked to him for inspiration and for a time he provided it. Surgery on a cartilage and the departure of Furphy soured the end of his time at the club and he soon followed Furphy, first to Bramall Lane and then to the USA. After he retired he decided to stay in America and became a coach at the University of Southern California.

FL	90 apps	6 gls
FAC	9 apps	1 gl
FLC	4 apps	0 gls
Total	103 apps	7 gls

GARNER, Simon
Striker

Simon Garner in 1991.

5'8" 11st 3lb
Born: Fishtoft, Boston, 23 November 1959
Debut: 29 August 1978

CAREER: Boston GS; Boston Colts; Boston United (non con); Blackburn Rovers Jul 1978; West Bromwich Albion Aug 1992 (£50,000); Wycombe Wanderers Jan 1994 (free); Torquay United Feb 1996 (loan); Woking Jun 1996-Nov 1996 (free); Kirkham Open Prison Nov-Dec 1996; Wealdstone Feb 1997; Dagenham & Redbridge (loan); Windsor & Eton; Flackwell Heath-Jul 2000.

Never the definitive footballer, Garner arrived at Ewood from school in Boston and made moderate progress through the youth side. Stocky and not the most athletic of players, he was deceptively quick over the first five yards and had an innate ability to lose his marker and free himself near goal. His dislike of serious training and his enjoyment of more than the occasional cigarette and glass of beer raised a few eyebrows, even in the club, but Jim Smith was a shrewd judge of ability and realised that he had a man who could regularly do what few players can – score goals. By the time he finished his Rovers career he had shattered the club scoring record, endeared himself to the crowd and had achieved sufficient to guarantee that he will always be remembered when the club is discussed. Although he spent a few seasons playing with other clubs and played non-league football beyond his fortieth birthday he has remained uniquely blue and white to the fans and enjoys a rapport seldom accorded to any player. Sent to prison in 1996 for contempt of court when he disposed of matrimonial assets in breach of a court injunction, he found in his brief spell of incarceration that the public was still solidly behind him. After playing with Wycombe he remained in the South living in Cookham, working first as a postman then as a painter and decorator before taking on the role of house husband.

FL	455+29 apps	168 gls
FAC	24+5 apps	7 gls
FLC	32+2 apps	11 gls
FMC	10 apps	4 gls
PO	7+1 apps	2 gls
Total	528+37 apps	192 gls

GAYLE, Howard Anthony

Right winger/striker

5'10.5" 10st 9lb
Born: Liverpool, 18 May 1958
Debut: 15 August 1987

CAREER: Stanley House; Bedford (Liverpool Sunday League); Liverpool Jun 1974 (app) Nov 1977; Fulham Jan 1980 (loan); Newcastle United Nov 1982 (loan); Birmingham City Jan 1983 (loan) Jun 1983 (£75,000); Sunderland Aug 1984-Apr 1987(£75,000); Dallas Sidekicks (USA) 1986; Stoke City Apr 1987 (£125,000); Blackburn Rovers Aug 1987 (£5,000); Halifax Town Aug 1992 (non con); Carlisle United (trial); Wrexham (trial); Accrington Stanley Sep 1993.

Gayle arrived at Ewood and found he had problems – he never justified his initial promise that saw him star in a European Cup semi-final against Bayern Munich in his second first-team game, and he was Blackburn's first black player. Despite playing for five clubs after Liverpool he had failed to make any permanent impact, a failure ascribed to temperament rather than talent. On the field he was quick, athletic, ran strongly and had fair finishing abilities but was considered indisciplined, temperamental and was not inclined to back down when racially abused. At Ewood the cloud lifted from his career. He became a cult favourite and either playing wide right or up front scored goals. In 1988/89 he had his best season with 23 goals but unfortunately missed a penalty in the play-off final against Crystal Palace. Strangely, when he was released, he found difficulty finding a club and even at Accrington only played the 1 game. Having grown up in Liverpool 8 he was ultimately drawn back to the bleak streets of Toxteth where he achieved much as an unpaid counsellor, running the Stanley House youth scheme with ex-world karate champion Geoff Thompson. Thompson provided the contacts that brought premises and cash but it was Gale who confronted the drug gangs and vandals on the streets and that ensured that the work continued.

FL	97+19 apps	29 gls
FAC	5+2 apps	0 gls
FLC	6+3 apps	1 gl
FMC	3+1 apps	1 gl
PO	8 apps	3 gls
Total	119+25 apps	34 gls

1987. Howard Gayle celebrates.

GENNOE, Terence William

Goalkeeper

6'2.5" 13st 3lb
Born: Shrewsbury, 16 March 1953
Debut: 29 August 1981

CAREER: Meole Bruce JS; The Wakeman School; Bricklayers Sports; Bury Jun 1973; Blackburn Rovers Mar 1974 (loan); Leeds United Mar 1975 (loan); Halifax Town May 1975 (£3,000); Southampton Feb 1978 (£40,000); Everton Sep 1980 (loan); Crystal Palace Jan 1981 (loan); Blackburn Rovers Aug 1981-Jun 1992 (£60,000).

A chequered first two years in league football included a loan spell at Ewood when Roger Jones had to undergo knee surgery. He failed to make the first-team line-up (young Paul Bradshaw being preferred) and it was not until he joined Halifax on a free transfer that he gained a regular playing position. Signed for a large fee by Southampton, he had proved ideally built for his position with good reflexes and agility but a series of errors demoted him to third choice behind Wells and Katalinic. It was on potential that Blackburn signed him when they had lost Jim Arnold to Everton, but from the onset he was assured, a capable defensive organiser, commanding in reaching crosses and with soft hands. He slotted in so well that he broke the club record for appearances by a goalkeeper and also became the oldest man to keep goal for the club. Ironically, on this day, he sustained the injury that prompted the club to go out and sign his replacement, Bobby Mimms. Having already trained as a teacher he obtained a degree with the Open University. On retirement he was used by the club as a goalkeeping coach but left for Newcastle when the club delayed making the position permanent. He later followed Kenny Dalglish to Celtic in a similar role.

FL	289 apps	0 gls
FAC	18 apps	0 gls
FLC	15 apps	0 gls
FMC	4 apps	0 gls
PO	8 apps	0 gls
Total	334 apps	0 gls

GILL, Wayne John

Midfield

5'10" 11st 3lb
Born: Chorley, 28 November 1975
Debut: 14 September 1999

CAREER: Leyland St Mary's; Eccleston Jnrs; Blackburn Rovers; Dundee United Mar 1998 (loan); Blackpool Mar 2000 (loan); Tranmere Rovers May 2000 (free); Oldham Athletic Oct 2001-Jun 2003 (£70,000); Rochdale (trial) Jul 2003; Scarborough Aug 2003-Apr 2004; Droylsden Aug 2004.

A product of local football, his career was hampered by a serious leg injury during his early time at the club. Essentially a right-sided midfield player who likes to get forward and shoot, he was retained by the Rovers and was made reserve team captain even though his only experience of first-team football was when weakened sides were played in the League Cup. A loan spell with Blackpool produced an incredible strike rate, scoring with his first touch, but moving to Tranmere and onto Oldham his career was blighted by injury.

FLC	3 apps	0 gls
Total	3 apps	0 gls

GILLESPIE, Keith Robert

Right winger

5'10" 11st 3lb
Born: Bangor, 18 February 1975
Debut: 19 December 1998

CAREER: Bangor GS; West Bangor; St Andrews BC; Manchester United Feb 1993; Wigan Athletic Sep 1993 (loan); Newcastle United Jan 1995 (in the exchange for Cole); Blackburn Rovers Dec 1998-Jun 2003 (£2,350,000); Wigan Athletic Dec 2000-Jan 2001 (loan); Leicester City (free) Jul 2003-Jun 2005; Leeds United Jun 2005 (trial); Sheffield United Aug 2005.
INTERNATIONALS: Northern Ireland 65 apps 2 gl.

The son of a prison officer in The Maze he went to Old Trafford in his teens and graduated in the company of Beckham, Butt, Gary Neville and Giggs. He attracted attention as a winger of great speed, confident in taking players on and able to cross on the run. Thrown in as a makeweight in the deal that took Andy Cole to Old Trafford, Gillespie was to frustrate on Tyneside, seldom playing to his potential. Recruited by Kidd for the Rovers the story changed little and Souness was repeatedly frustrated with his unpredictability. Capable of backtracking, there was a time when his defensive qualities were better than his offensive ones, although the inconsistency of his defending tended to even matters on that score.

L	67+46 apps	5 gls
FAC	6+ 4 apps	1 gl
FLC	8+3 apps	0 gls
UEFA	0+3 apps	0 gls
Total	81+56 apps	6 gls

GILLIVER, Alan Henry

Centre forward

6'1" 13st 7lb
Born: Huddersfield 3 August 1944
Debut: 20 August 1966

CAREER: Swallow Dinnington School; Ruther Valley Schoolboys; Anston Jnrs (Worksop); Huddersfield Town Aug 1961; Blackburn Rovers Jun 1966 (£35,000 but reduced by tribunal); Rotherham United May 1968 (ex Chappell); Brighton & Hove Albion Jul 1969; Lincoln City Feb 1971; Bradford City Jun 1972; Stockport County Jun 1974; Baltimore Comets (USA) May 1975; Boston United; Buxton Mar 1976 (loan); Gainsborough Trinity Aug 1976; Bradford City Aug 1978 (non con).

Discovered by Huddersfield in the Sheffield Amateur league playing for his works team (where he was an apprentice dye sinker), he had commenced as a centre half but moved upfield where his barnstorming style and abundant energy could be better employed. A debutant at seventeen, he was eased slowly into the first team but caught Blackburn's attention immediately following their relegation to the Second Division. He quickly found himself in the headlines but not for positive reasons. A long-standing back injury had not been disclosed by his club at the time of the transfer negotiations and a tribunal decided that part of the fee should be returned to the Rovers, recommending that all future transfers should be the subject of a medical examination. He never truly recovered his mobility but was appreciated for his courage and endeavour. However, he was quickly exchanged for Les Chappell of Rotherham. An all-round sportsman, he played cricket for Hechmondwyke and was a noted golfer. He subsequently became the stadium manager at Valley Parade, Bradford.

FL	32+2 apps	9 gls
FAC	1 app.	0 gls
FLC	4 apps	0 gls
Total	37+2 apps	9 gls

GIVEN, Seamus John

Goalkeeper

6'1" 13st 4lb
Born: Lifford ,Co. Donegal, 20 April 1976
Debut: 24 September 1996

CAREER: St Columba's Coll (Stranorler); Lifford Celtic; Glasgow Celtic; Blackburn Rovers Aug 1994 (free); Swindon Town Jan 1995-Feb 1995 (loan) Aug 1995-Sep 1995 (loan); Sunderland Jan 1996-Apr 1996 (loan); Newcastle United Jun 1997 (£1,500,000). INTERNATIONALS: Eire 74 apps.

Given's father recognised from the start that his son was going to become a great goalkeeper and instructed his school in Lifford that he had only to be selected in goal. His college team was less amenable and he played midfield in an All Ireland Cup final but the steady stream of scouts were in no doubt that he was a great prospect between the posts. He ultimately chose Celtic, following in the footsteps of his hero Packy Bonner. Offered a derisory contract, he returned to work on his father's pitch and putt course but the offers came in. Pat Devlin brought him to Ewood and although he had a traumatic trial with the reserves he was offered a contract. Unable to make much impact at Ewood because of the queue of goalkeepers ahead of him, he enjoyed a loan spell at Sunderland where he helped them to promotion by keeping a record number of clean sheets. Only given 2 league games, when Flowers was unfit, he tired of waiting for an opportunity and turned down a contract offer to join Newcastle. He has since proved one of the best goalkeepers in the Premiership, unbelievably athletic, brave and secure in his positioning. Alongside this he has become the Republic of Ireland's regular goalkeeper, starring in the World Cup Finals.

FL	2 apps	0 gls
FLC	0+1 app.	0 gls
Total	2+1 apps	0 gls

GLAISTER, George
Inside forward

5'7" 9st 13lb
Born: Bywell, Northumberland, 18 May 1918
Died: Preston, 8 November 1966
Debut: 2 March 1940

CAREER: North Shields 1936; Blackburn Rovers May 1937; Stockport County Apr 1947; Halifax Town Aug 1950; Accrington Stanley Sep 1951; Witton Albion Aug 1952; Macclesfield Town Sep 1952; Bangor City Oct 1952.

Slim and stylish, he lost the best part of his career to the war years and in a struggling side found goals hard to come by. After sterling service with Stockport, Halifax and Accrington he drifted into the non-league, ending his career at Bangor where he played for the Welsh League representative team. A part-time groundsman at Ewood, he worked as a maintenance man on the Bangor ground but returned to live in Blackburn, working as a representative for Samlesbury Engineering Co. He died unexpectedly at work at the age of forty-eight.

FL	8 apps	1 gl
FAC	2 apps	0 gls
Total	10 apps	1 gl

GLENN, David Anthony
Right-back

5'10" 10st 10lb
Born: Wigan, 30 November 1962
Debut: Nov 19 1983

CAREER: Wigan Athletic Jul 1979 (app) Nov 1980; Chelsea Nov 1982 (loan); Blackburn Rovers Jul 1983 (free); Chester City Jul 1985 (free); Blacktown City (Australia) 1989; Blacktown City (Australia) 1989; Fleetwood Town; Chorley Jun 1992.

A fluid, intelligent player, Glenn suffered at Wigan from the fact that he was a local boy who lived yards from the ground and like many locals was unappreciated by the fans. At one stage his career appeared to be blossoming and Chelsea took him on loan for a look but a few months later he was available on a free transfer. Although he slotted in easily at Ewood he found difficulty coping with tricky wingers and after his initial season drifted out of the first-team picture. At home at Chester, he failed to consolidate his position and inexplicably ended playing non-league football.

FL	23+1 apps	0 gls
FAC	3 apps	0 gls
Total	26+1 apps	0 gls

GLOVER, Alexander
Winger

5'6.5" 10st 8lb
Born: Glasgow, 28 February 1922
Died: Ulverston, July 2000
Debut: 3 September 1951

CAREER: 256 Boys' Brigade, Glasgow; Linthouse Victoria; Partick Thistle May 1943; Bradford PA Mar 1948 (£8,000); Luton Town Sep 1949 (£8,000); Blackburn Rovers Sep 1951; Barrow Aug 1954-1958.

When the Rovers were deep in trouble in 1951 one of their new recruits was Glover, a diminutive, effervescent player who preferred to play on the right but moved to the left so that another new signing, Jackie Wharton, could play there. The pair were waspish and an irritant to full-backs with Glover playing conventionally wide to allow Wharton more freedom to improvise. As a consequence Glover seldom scored but he is best remembered for the clinching goal in the unforgettable cup tie with Burnley when he moved to the centre to convert Holmes' cross, after the centre forward had retrieved a seemingly lost ball. Displaced by the return of Langton, he moved on to play four seasons with Barrow. A skilled saxophonist he played on a programme transmitted by the BBC.

FL	64 apps	4 gls
FAC	7 apps	1 gl
Total	71 apps	5 gls

GODWIN, Verdi
Centre forward

5'8" 11st 8lb
Born: Blackburn, 11 February 1926
Debut: 2 February 1946

CAREER: Moss St Sc; Bangor St; Blackburn Rovers May 1945 (am) Mar 1946; Manchester City Jun 1948; Stoke City Jun 1949; Mansfield Town Jan 1950; Middlesbrough Nov 1951 (trial); Grimsby Town Jan 1952 (trial); Brentford Mar 1952; Southport Jul 1954; Barrow Aug 1955; Tranmere Rovers Aug 1956; Kings Lynn Jul 1957; Netherfield 1957; New Brighton 1958; Macclesfield Town 1959; Fleetwood Town; Colwyn Bay Aug 1960; Fleetwood Town 1961-1964.

Named after the composer, born locally but raised in Blackpool, he returned to Blackburn during the war as a conscript Bevin Boy, cycling the fourteen miles to Townley Pit every day and then returning in the evening. He also managed to train twice a week with the Rovers. Unsurprisingly his game was all about fitness and enthusiasm although sometimes he played in the skill position on the right wing. However it was for courage and robustness that he became noted and appeared to be establishing himself nicely when he made (in his words) the huge mistake of asking for a rise. The subsequent dispute ended in his transfer and commenced a career in which he became a soccer nomad, playing for whoever wanted strong legs and a great heart. He settled in Southport where he became a lifeguard, being awarded the British Empire Medal in 1987 in recognition of his service. It is, however, as a football scout that he will be best remembered. A prolific watcher of junior football, he was one of the most knowledgeable men in the game at assessing young talent. Working for Blackpool, Liverpool, Plymouth and Vancouver Whitecaps he unearthed many great young players, the best known perhaps being Peter Beardsley.

FL	27 apps	6 gls
Total	27 apps	6 gls

GOODWIN, Frederick James
Midfield/Full-back

5'10" 11st 1lb
Born: Stockport, 4 January 1944
Debut: 4 March 1970

CAREER: Wolverhampton Wanderers Apr 1959 (ground) Jan 1961; Stockport County Jan 1966; Blackburn Rovers Mar 1970 (exchange Coddington+£5,000); Southport Oct 1971 (with £17,500 in exchange for Field); Port Vale Aug 1972; Macclesfield Town Aug 1973; Stockport County Aug 1974; New Mills 1975; Stalybridge Celtic; British Rail (Stockport).

Having been groomed through the youth scheme at Wolverhampton it was a surprise that Goodwin never became a first-team regular. He was a sound, mobile, intelligent wing half with exemplary effort and consistency but lacked the spark to be comfortable at the highest level. At Stockport he was at home and helped the club to the Fourth Division title in 1967. The Rovers' manager, Eddie Quigley, had first-hand experience of his qualities at Edgeley Park and was happy to introduce him to Ewood. In his eighteen months with the Rovers he was a model professional, converting to right-back seamlessly before he was a makeweight in the transfer that brought Tony Field to Ewood. When his playing days were over he was a grocer in his home town, coached briefly at Ashton United and then uncharacteristically found himself in the spotlight. Playing in a local league he received a *sine die* suspension for violence involving a referee. His previous good character was recognised when this ban was appealed against and in 1980 he moved to New Zealand, coaching Stopout to two titles in five years. He also coached Papatoetoe, Hut Valley United and Columbus Waterside before he returned to England in 1993.

FL	63+1 apps	4 gls
FAC	1 app.	0 gls
FLC	4 apps	0 gls
Total	68+1 apps	4 gls

GRABBI, Corrado 'Ciccio'

Striker

6'0" 12st 13lb
Born: Turin (Italy), 29 July 1975
Debut: 18 August 2001

CAREER: Juventus 1992; Sparta Novara 1993; Juventus 1994; AS Lucchese 1995; AS Chievo Verona Nov 1995; FC Modena 1996; Juventus 1998; Ternana Calcio Sep 1998; US Ravenna 1999; Ternana Calcio 2000; Blackburn Rovers Jun 2001 (£6,750,000); FC Messina Jan 2002-Jun 2002 (loan); Ancona Calcio Jan 2004-Jun 2004 (free); Genoa Cricket & FC Sep 2005.

Grabbi was the third generation of his family to wear the black and white of Juventus but he spent most of his career in Italy farmed out to smaller clubs. Two seasons with Modena in Serie C increased his reputation as an instinctive goalscorer but a return to Juventus found him overawed and he was sent to Ternana. It was here that he cemented his reputation, scoring 20 goals in the season and starting a rush for his services. The Rovers won this but in two seasons with the club he seldom looked anything but an expensive misfit, too easily dismayed by misfortune and, although capable of working hard, inconsistent in his application. He was allowed to return on loan to Italy to see if it might reinvigorate his approach but nothing changed and he was eventually allowed to join Ancona on a free transfer. On brief occasions he showed flashes of ability inside the penalty area and for a striker was amazingly good at setting up chances for a teammate, but his confidence was never high. Ancona were bottom of the league when he joined and after their relegation went into bankruptcy, which meant that Grabbi's contract was cancelled. Overweight and injured, he has been unable to find a club, although he has been training with Ternana with a view to playing again.

PL	11+19 apps	2 gls
FAC	1+2 apps	1 gl
FLC	2+3 apps	1 gl
UEFA	2+2 apps	1 gl
Total	16+26 apps	5 gls

GRAHAM, Leslie

Inside forward

5'7.5" 10st 6lb
Born: Urmston, 14 May 1924
Died: Torfaen, January 1998
Debut: 20 September 1947

CAREER: Urmston; Blackburn Rovers May 1945 (am) Apr 1947; Newport County Feb 1953 (£2,500); Watford Jul 1955 (free); Newport County Sep 1957

(£1,250); Cambridge City Jul 1959; Merthyr Town (p-m) 1959-1960.

During the war Graham served in India, where he played for Mysore State and also for an all-Muslim team. He received his opportunity in the game directly as a result of this football because an Indian army major recommended him to the Rovers and they signed him after a trial. A small, inventive player, he knew where the goal was and despite his lack of physique played in all forward positions except for the left wing. The arrival of Eddie Quigley restricted his opportunities and he moved on, proving an ideal club man with Newport and Watford. As the years rolled on he lost speed and moved back to wing half, compensating for his lack of pace with his shrewdness.

FL	150 apps	42 gls
FAC	7 apps	2 gls
Total	157 apps	44 gls

GRAY, David
Full-back

5'7" 10st 6lb
Born: Coupar Angus, 8 February 1922
Died: Dundee, 17 May 2008
Debut: 21 August 1948

CAREER: Lochee Harp; Dundee Violets; Glasgow Rangers 1943; Preston North End May 1947; Blackburn Rovers Aug 1948 (with £16,000 for Langton); Dundee Jun 1954 (free); Dundee United 1956-58.

The makeweight in the transfer that took Bobby Langton to Preston, he was a right-back with speed and zest but was never more than a steady foil to the brilliant Bill Eckersley. A splendid striker of a dead ball, he became the penalty taker but was relieved of the role after blasting successive kicks against the crossbar. Replaced by the consistent and more defensive Ronnie Suart, Gray underwent spinal surgery in 1951 and with his playing time limited indicated a desire to return to Scotland. His three brothers, Stuart, Tom and Bruce, were all fine footballers who achieved good standards in the game.

FL	107 apps	5 gls
FAC	4 apps	0 gls
Total	111 apps	5 gls

GRAY, Michael
Full-back

5'7" 10st 10lb
Born: Castletown, Sunderland, 3 August 1974
Debut: 1 February 2004

CAREER: Castle View School; Manchester United 1990 (schoolboy); Sunderland 1990 (trainee) Jul 1992; Glasgow Celtic Sep 2003-Dec 2003 (loan); Blackburn Rovers Jan 2004 (free); Leeds United Jan 2005-Jun 2005 (loan).
INTERNATIONALS: England 3 apps.

An enthusiastic left-back who made it with his home-town side after being rejected by Manchester United, he led his side to promotion to the top division after crucially missing the vital penalty in the shoot-out the previous year. Much happier overlapping with enthusiasm than defending, he won international caps when Kevin Keegan was the England manager. He came to Blackburn when the club was fighting a battle against relegation and became the regular left-back, but the following season his defensive deficiencies were highlighted and he was allowed to have a long loan spell with Leeds United. .

PL	36 apps	0 gls
FLC	4 apps	0 gls
Total	40 apps	0 gls

GRAYSON, Simon Nicholas

Full-back

6'0" 12st 10lb
Born: Ripon, 16 December 1969
Debut: 7 August 1999

CAREER: Bedale Comprehensive; Leeds United Jun 1988; Leicester City Mar 1992 (£50,000); Aston Villa Jul 1997 (£1,350,000); Blackburn Rovers Jul 1999 (£750,000); Sheffield Wednesday Aug 2000 (loan); Stockport County Jan 2001-Apr 2001 (loan); Notts County Sep 2001-Nov 2001 (loan); Bradford City Feb 2002-Mar 2002 (loan); Blackpool Jul 2002 (free).

An effective utility player capable of playing all across the back or in midfield, he was most at ease in the right-back position where he tackled well, had sure positional sense and the ability to slide along the line and cover. Limited in his playing time at Aston Villa, he was Brian Kidd's choice to play right-back but found that Graeme Souness was not of the same opinion when he took over. Extremely well paid at the Rovers, he saw his contract out rather than take a salary drop before joining Blackpool when his contract at Blackburn had ended. He has been appointed the manager at Blackpool, succeeding Colin Hendry

FL	31+3 apps	0 gls
FAC	2+1 apps	0 gls
FLC	1+1 app.	0 gls
Total	34+5 apps	0 gls

GREEN, Alan

Left-back

5'8" 10st 12lb
Born: Chorley, 18 July 1924
Debut: Jan 13 1945

CAREER: Blackburn Rovers Oct 1944 (am) Sep 1945; Wigan Athletic Jul 1947-1947.

Green was working as a draughtsman when he came to the club on amateur terms as the Second World War was drawing to an end. Quickly promoted to the first team and signed on professional terms, his future appeared bright but the club's new manager, Eddie Hapgood, was not prepared to gamble on youth with First Division survival at stake. A move to Wigan produced only half a dozen appearances, curiously partnering his namesake Jack Green, the old Accrington and Manchester United right-back.

FAC	2 apps	0 gls
Total	2 apps	0 gls

GREER, Gordon

Centre-back

6'2" 12st 5lb
Born: Glasgow, 14 December 1980
Debut: 12 September 2001

CAREER: Port Glasgow; Clyde Jun 2000 (£1,500 with Cannie); Blackburn Rovers May 2001 (£200,000); Stockport County Mar 2003 (loan); Kilmarnock Sep 2003 (free).

When Greer was working as an electrician and playing for Port Glasgow, Clyde spotted him and took him and his teammate Phil Cannie. Greer immediately forced his way into the first team where, with his flowing locks and propensity for strolling upfield, he earned the nickname 'Amo', due to his likeness to Rangers' Italian Lorenzo Amoruso. The manager Alan Maitland not only advised him to change his hairstyle but restricted his forward charges so that he became a more reliable defender. Signed by the Rovers on his future potential, he failed to achieve an impact. His only first-team appearance was in an understrength team in the League Cup and his erratic play did not even cement him a reserve-team place. A loan spell at Stockport alerted clubs to his potential and soon after the start of the 2003/04 season he returned north of the border to join Kilmarnock.

FLC	1 app.	0 gls
Total	1 app.	0 gls

GREGORY, David Harry

Striker

5'9" 11st 6lb
Born: Peterborough, 6 October 1951
Debut: 19 August 1978

CAREER: Walton Sec Sc; Peterborough United; Chatteris Town; Peterborough United Aug 1973; Stoke City Jun 1977 (£55,000); Blackburn Rovers Jul 1978 (loan); Bury Sep 1978 (£30,000); Portsmouth Dec 1979 (£30,000); Wrexham Jul 1983 (free); Peterborough United Aug 1986; King Lynn Aug 1987; Holbeach United 1990; Watton United 1990; Spalding 1991; Holbeach United 1993-1996; The Crown (Sunday Lge).

Recruited by his local side from school, he was released because it was believed he did not have the physique for league football. He became a motor mechanic but played so well for Chatteris that the Peterborough manager, Noel Cantwell, changed his mind and re-signed a player who quickly demonstrated that he had goal-scoring ability. He was never happy after completing a move to Stoke that brought Peterborough much-needed revenue, and so became available on loan at a time when Blackburn were looking for a striker. In a short period of time he proved a real find, displaying a goal flair, quick control and an ability to pass tidily. A permanent deal appeared a formality. There are conflicting accounts about the next proceedings, suggesting that he demanded exorbitant terms or that he disliked playing for the new manager Jim Iley. Whatever the reason he signed for Bury (where the rewards can hardly have been huge). He remained in the Football League until well into his mid-thirties, despite a portliness that brought much crowd comment. Later he settled in Holbeach, continuing playing and working as a ceramic tiler.

FL	5 apps	3 gls
FLC	1 app.	1 gl
Total	6 apps	4 gls

GRESKO, Vratislav

Left-back

5'11" 11st 5lb
Born: Pressburg (Bratislava) Slovakia, 24 July 1977
Debut: 2 February 2003

CAREER: FK Dukla Banska Bystrica 1995; ASK Inter Slovnaft Bratislava 1997; Bayer 04 Leverkusen (Germany) 1999; Inter Milan (Italy) Oct 2000 (£5,000,000); Parma AC (Italy) Oct 2002 (ex Almeyda); Blackburn Rovers Jan 2003 (loan) Aug 2003 (£1,750,000).
INTERNATIONALS: Slovakia 27 apps 2 gls.

Gresko's break into first-team football in Slovakia came when he was undergoing national service and played for the army team. Returning to his home town, he was groomed for the national team via the Under-21s but was repeatedly well placed in the voting for Player of the Year. Spotted by Bayer Leverkusen, he was seldom used by the first team but his form in the European Under-21 Finals was sufficient to prompt Inter Milan to pay a large fee for him. Converted from his early position in midfield he became a complete left-back, strong in the tackle, shrewd in positioning and with an easiness on the ball that permitted him to link with the attack. An error in the final game that cost Inter the *Scudetto* prompted an astonishing display of fan power that saw him hounded from the club and sent to Parma. Struggling with a club who had run out of money and ideas, he was amenable to a move for first-team football and so came to Ewood, despite the fact that he spoke no English. This did not deter him settling into the side and he looked a fine player until he suffered fractures to three metatarsal bones followed a year later by a cruciate ligament injury that required surgery.

PL	35+4 apps	1 gl
FAC	1 app.	0 gls
FLC	2 app.	0 gls
UEFA	2 apps	0 gls
Total	40+4 apps	1 gl

GREW, Mark Stuart

Goalkeeper

5'11" 12st 8lb
Born: Bilston, 15 February 1958
Debut: 13 October 1990

CAREER: West Bromwich Albion Jun 1976; Wigan Athletic Dec 1978 (loan); Notts County Mar 1979 (loan); Leicester City Jul 1983 (£25,000); Oldham Athletic Oct 1983 (loan); Ipswich Town Mar 1984 (£60,000); Fulham Sep 1985 (loan); West Bromwich Albion Jan 1986 (loan); Derby County Mar 1986 (loan); Port Vale Jun 1986 (free); Blackburn Rovers Oct 1990-Jan 1991 (loan); Cardiff City Jul 1992 (free); Stafford Rangers 1994.

Despite gaining a FA Youth Cup winners' medal with West Brom, Grew found it hard to compete with Tony Godden but like many promising young goalkeepers found relief in spells out on loan. Permanent transfers increased his frustration since at Leicester and Ipswich he found himself understudying fine goalkeepers (Mark Wallington and Paul Cooper). A free transfer move to Port Vale brought regular football but when he lost his place to Thomas Wood he came on loan to the Rovers who had Gennoe injured and his deputy, Collier, struggling. In a poor side, Grew briefly became a cult favourite, brave to the point of foolhardiness, agile and confident. A permanent move would have been popular but Port Vale asked for so much that Blackburn switched their attentions to Bobby Mimms. Later in his career Grew was dismissed by Cardiff for allegedly selling his allocation of cup-final tickets but was later reinstated. Returning to Port Vale, he took over as youth-team coach from Ian Miller and later moved up to be first-team coach.

FL	13 apps	0 gls
FLC	1 app.	0 gls
Total	14 apps	0 gls

GRIFFITHS, Barry

Goalkeeper

5'11" 11st 6lb
Born: Manchester, 21 November 1940
Died: Rochdale, September 1997
Debut: 9 April 1960

CAREER: Newton Heath Tech Coll; Sheffield Wed; Blackburn Rovers 1959 (am) Jul 1962; Altrincham; Witton Albion; Stalybridge Celtic.

After playing for the Manchester Schools side he signed for Sheffield Wednesday and played in the semi-final of the FA Youth Cup. The following season he went one better, being a member of the Rovers' side that won the trophy for the only time in their history. His fabulous penalty save in the second leg of the final will long be remembered as a vital contribution to victory. An early debut found him tidy but his goalkeeping was always somewhat erratic. In his second game he was not as fortunate. He had developed a weakness with the lob shot and Blackpool exposed him mercilessly. Consequently he received no other first-team chances and soon was playing non-league football.

FL	2 apps	0 gls
Total	2 apps	0 gls

GUDMUNDSSON, Lars Roger Niklas* 'Gudis'

Striker/Left winger

5'11" 12st 9lb
Born: Trönninge (Sweden), 29 February 1972
Debut: 20 January 1996

H

CAREER: Tronninge IF; Halmstads BK; Norwich City 1995 (trial); Blackburn Rovers Dec 1995-Mar 1996 (loan) Mar 1996 (£700,000); Ipswich Town Mar 1997-May 1997 (loan); Malmo FF Jul 1997 (£300,000); Elfsborg IF Mar 2001; Malmo FF Nov 2002; Angelhoms FF.
INTERNATIONALS: Sweden 7 apps.

A smooth technician, admired by Ray Harford for his play on the left side of the field, he had made a successful entry into football when he helped a young Halmstads side to a Swedish Cup final victory. After a successful run in the European Cup Winners' Cup he sought opportunity abroad but struggled at Blackburn with the formation. In Sweden he had played as a left-sided midfield player who went forward but, when played as a left-sided striker, he lacked the desired skills. Surprisingly, he was signed after a mediocre loan spell but quickly became superfluous. After a loan spell with Ipswich he returned to his homeland but faded out of the picture apart from a Swedish Cup victory with Elfsborg that went to penalties and was decided with the twenty-fourth one taken.

PL	1+5 apps	0 gls
Total	1+5 apps	0 gls

GUEST, William Francis
Left wing

5'8.5" 10st 11lb
Born: Brierley Hill, 8 February 1914
Died: Blackburn, 21 November 1994
Debut: 23 January 1937

CAREER: Brierley Hill Jnrs; Bromley Rovers (Kingswinford); Birmingham City Aug 1928 (am) Feb 1932; Blackburn Rovers Mar 1937 (ex Beattie); Walsall Aug 1947; Peterborough United 1949-1951; Kidderminster Harriers; Lovells Athletic; Hinckley United; Bilston United.

Connected with Birmingham from the age of fourteen he was converted from a bustling centre forward to the left wing, although he still liked to move inside and have attempts on goal. The loss of his place to Morris prompted him to seek a move and he was exchanged for Jack Beattie. To a club passing through a bad spell his urgency and goal-scoring were invaluable, but he found himself on the sidelines as young Bobby Langton commenced an illustrious career. With the Second World War following it was not anticipated that Guest would return but he had always been a fitness fanatic who kept fit during the summer playing cricket as a professional for Moseley, and for a time was on the ground staff of Warwickshire County Cricket Club. Guest had a brief swansong with the Rovers when football resumed and later his physical condition stood him in good stead as he prolonged his playing career until he was approaching forty. While working as a storeman at GEC Witton he coached Brandwood Rovers but spent the last twenty years of his life back in Blackburn.

FL	22 apps	3 gls
FAC	2 apps	0 gls
Total	24 apps	3 gls

Pre War		
FL	66 apps	27 gls
FAC	4 apps	2 gls
Grand Total	94 apps	32 gls

HAMILTON, David
Midfield/Full-back

5'9" 10st 2lb
Born: South Shields, 7 November 1960
Debut: 10 January 1981

CAREER: Sunderland Sep 1978; Blackburn Rovers Jan 1981 (free); Cardiff City Mar 1985-May 1985 (loan); Wigan Athletic Aug 1986 (£11,000); Chester City Aug 1989 (free); Binche (Bel) (trial); Burnley Aug 1990 (free); Chorley Aug 1992 (free); Barrow Dec 1993; Accrington Stanley Aug 1994-Feb 1995; Great Harwood 1995; Mossley 1995; Accrington Stanley Jan 1998-Mar 1998; Atherton LR; Ramsbottom United Mar 1998.

Although he had been an England youth international his career in senior football appeared to be destined to be hampered by his frail appearance. Spotted by Howard Kendall and introduced to the first team via the substitute bench, he proved that looks were deceptive. He was indefatigable in midfield and was capable of converting to full-back without any loss of effectiveness. Established as one of the team's most versatile players, his departure was unexpected when he could not agree personal terms. After he tried his luck abroad, playing with his brother in Belgium, he returned locally and was establishing himself with Burnley when he was badly injured challenging Stuart Pearce. At the end of his career he was coach and then player-manager at Accrington before joining Preston's coaching staff. He left to work for Parcel Force, resuming playing with Great Harwood and then was joint manager of Accrington with Jim McCluskie. Since then he has been youth coach at Rochdale and is currently chief scout at Wigan Athletic.

FL	104+10 apps	7 gls
FAC	1+1 app.	0 gls
FLC	7 apps	0 gls
Total	112+11 apps	7 gls

HAMILTON, Gary Ian
Striker

5'9" 11st 10lb
Born: Banbridge (Northern Ireland), 6 October 1980
Debut: 26 September 2000

CAREER: Lisburn Youths; Blackburn Rovers Oct 1997; Rochdale Aug 2000 (loan); Wigan Athletic Apr 2001 (trial); Raufoss (Norway) May 2001-Jul 2001 (loan); Brentford Aug 2001 (trial); Portadown Aug 2001; MetroStars (USA) Mar 2004 (trial).
INTERNATIONALS: Northern Ireland 4 apps.

The son of an Irish farmer, he was brought to Ewood by the club's Irish scouts Norman Boyd and Derek Langley. A mobile front man, he scored in every round of the FA Youth Cup but generally, scoring goals was a problem. Great positioning brought him many chances but his finishing was often wayward. A brief appearance as substitute in a below-strength League Cup team was all he achieved and despite several trials elsewhere he never found an English club sufficiently interested in him. After spending some months at a Norwegian club (a move orchestrated by Henning Berg) he returned to his homeland, immediately having astonishing success with Portadown, who he helped to the championship and to a cup-final appearance. Having made many Under-21 appearances for his country he moved up in May 2003 to the Irish 'B' side and then made appearances for the full team. In 2005 he gained a cup winners' medal but his attitude has been called into question and he no longer commands a regular first-team place at the club.

FLC	0+1 app.	0 gls
Total	0+1 apps	0 gls

HARFORD, Paul Raymond Thomas
Midfield

6'3.5" 14st
Born: Chelmsford, 21 October 1974

CAREER: Arsenal Jul 1991 (trainee) Sep 1993; Blackburn Rovers Jun 1994-Jun 1996; Wigan Athletic Aug 1994-Sep 1994 (loan); Shrewsbury Town Dec 1994-Feb 1995 (loan); Farnborough Town Jun 1996-Nov 1998; Sacramento (USA) Sum

1997 (loan); Welling United Nov 1998; Sutton United Nov 1998; Aldershot Town May 2001; Bracknell Town May 2002-Dec 2002; Leatherhead Town (p-m) Dec 2002.

The Arsenal management were not pleased when the well-built utility Paul Harford decided to leave and join Blackburn, where his father was first-team coach. He never flourished at Ewood and when his father became manager his position worsened. His choice as substitute for the 1995 Charity Shield game raised a few eyebrows because attempts to place him on loan had been short lived. His father took the decision to release him and he continued to play in non-league football in the South.

HARGREAVES, David George 'Haggis'
Centre forward

5'8.5" 11st 4lb
Born: Rough Lee, Colne, 27 August 1954
Debut: 4 February 1978

CAREER: Accrington Stanley; Blackburn Rovers Dec 1977-Jun 1978; Accrington Stanley; Padiham; Whinney Hill; Oswaldtwistle St Mary's.

A corporation gardener, he became a legend in Accrington with his scoring exploits. Not particularly robust, he had an eye for goal and the ability to get his shot off quick and accurately. The change of regimen when he came into professional football at the age of twenty-three contributed to a series of injuries that restricted his chances and he was soon back with Accrington. He continued to play in junior football and at the age of forty-four was still playing for Oswaldtwistle St Mary's reserves. A legend in the Accrington area, it was sad to see him fall on hard times when he was working as a rent collector locally.

FL	2 apps	0 gls
Total	2 apps	0 gls

HARKNESS, Steven
Left-back

5'10" 11st 2lb
Born: Carlisle, 27 August 1971
Debut: 14 September 1999

CAREER: Newlaithes School; Carlisle United Mar 1989; Liverpool Jul 1989 (£75,000); Huddersfield Town Sep 1993 (loan); Southend United Feb 1995 (loan); Benfica (Portugal) Mar 1999 (£750,000); Blackburn Rovers Aug 1999 (£500,000); Sheffield Wednesday Sep 2000 (£200,000); Chester City Jul 2002-Oct 2002 (free).

A teenage prodigy snapped up by Liverpool, he never established himself at Anfield despite his competitive qualities and strong running. Sometimes utilised as a central defender, he was rescued from obscurity when Graeme Souness took him to Benfica, but the British experience at the Estadio do Luz ended badly and Harkness was one of the chief sufferers, suspended for showing disrespect to the chairman. A forced loan move to Aves was contemplated when Brian Kidd brought him to Ewood, but he never showed anything like acceptable form. The arrival of Souness looked to signal a fresh start for Harkness but Souness brought in Bjornebye and Harkness moved on. A move to the Conference with Chester ended when the player decided to concentrate on business interests.

FL	17 apps	0 gls
FAC	1 app.	0 gls
FLC	2+1 apps	0 gls
Total	20+1 apps	0 gls

HARRIS, Joseph
Centre forward

5'10" 11st 10lb
Born: Belfast, 8 April 1929
Debut: 13 January 1951

CAREER: Distillery; Larne; Blackburn Rovers Jan 1951 (£2,300); Oldham Athletic Mar 1953; Belfast Crusaders Jul 1954.

After starting with Distillery his opportunities were so limited that he had drifted out of the Irish League and was playing with Larne when the Rovers spotted him. At the time he was working at a Ministry of Food store and had never in his life left Ulster. After only two days in Blackburn he was chosen for the first team and proved to be quick and mobile. More chances would have come his way but the club signed Bill Holmes around the same time and he became the side's talisman. In 1952 Harris broke his leg in the pre-season trial and, because Tommy Briggs was subsequently signed, never received any other opportunity.

FL	35 apps	14 gls
FAC	1 app.	0 gls
Total	36 apps	14 gls

HARRISON, Michael John

Left winger

5'10" 11st 8lb
Born: Ilford, 18 April 1940
Debut: 22 September 1962

CAREER: Chelsea Apr 1957; Blackburn Rovers Sep 1962 (£20,000); Plymouth Argyle Sep 1967 (£20,000); Luton Town Jun 1968; Dover Town Jul 1970.

Harrison had been carefully groomed through the Chelsea youth team and had progressed to the point where he gained Under-23 international honours, but competition for places was intense and Harrison could not obtain regular first-team football. On the left wing at Ewood he was an immediate success, benefitting from playing inside Bryan Douglas, and proved a strong and deceptively fast winger with a curious high knee lift. He also had a left foot that spat venom and was the surest of penalty takers (one miss in fourteen), with the same technique every time (low to the goalkeeper's right) but struck with such power and accuracy that the goalkeeper seldom had a chance. Able to put a cross over with precision, he lost his place when John Connelly was signed, which gave the Rovers a winger who could play on either side of the field.

FL	160 apps	40 gls
FAC	14 apps	2 gls
FLC	7 apps	1 gl
Total	181 apps	43 gls

HAVERTY, Joseph

Left winger

5'3.5" 9st 9lb
Born: Dublin, 17 February 1936
Died: London, 7 February 2009
Debut: 19 August 1961

CAREER: Home Farm; St Patrick's Athletic; Arsenal Jul 1954; Blackburn Rovers Aug 1961 (£12,000); Millwall Sep 1962; Glasgow Celtic Sep 1964 (trial); Bristol Rovers Dec 1964; Shelbourne Dec 1964; Chicago Spurs (USA) Feb 1967; Kansas City Spurs (USA) Mar 1968; Dallas Tornado (USA) 1968.
INTERNATIONALS: Eire 32 apps 3 gls.

With his size and approach it became a cliché that the word 'leprechaun' would be employed whenever Haverty played. He was a conventional outside left who hugged the touchline, his play full of tricks and feints from staccato feet and sheer impudence. Strangely, his main purpose was to beat men wide and furnish crosses for the men inside, but he was brought to Ewood at a time when the forward line might have auditioned for *Snow White*. In his years at Highbury he had become a much-loved favourite but at Ewood, where he was not even the cleverest dribbler (Bryan Douglas was in the line up), he was misplaced and ineffective. After little more than a year he embarked on a peripatetic career that ultimately finished in an apt setting, amid the razzle-dazzle of the NASL

FL	27 apps	1 gl
FLC	4 apps	0 gls
Total	31 apps	1 gl

HAWKINS, Graham Norman
Centre half

6'0" 11st 10lb
Born: Darlaston, 5 March 1946
Debut: 17 August 1974

CAREER: Wednesbury HS; Wolverhampton Wanderers Aug 1962 (app) Jun 1963; Preston North End Jan 1968; Blackburn Rovers Jun 1974 (£15,000); Port Vale Jan 1978-Apr 1980.

Groomed by Wolves after being spotted with East Staffordshire schoolboys, he made his reputation in six years with Preston North End. A commanding, dominant figure with natural authority, good in the air and well versed in reading the game, he was signed by Gordon Lee because he felt the team needed a leader. It was a surprise when North End allowed him to depart but the move was ideal for the player who lived in Lytham and had a partnership in a Preston garage with the ex-boxer, Bob Rhodes. Captain of the team that gained promotion from the Third Division, he was troubled by recurring muscle injuries and to help prolong his career he elected to move down a grade to Port Vale. On retirement he became coach at Shrewsbury and when appointed manager at his first club, Wolves, he led them to promotion. Two years later he was dismissed and moved to coach in Bahrain where he led his team to the national title. For a spell he returned to act as development scout at Ewood but was coach of the Kuweit national team at the time of the Gulf War.

FL	108+1 apps	4 gls
FAC	4 apps	0 gls
FLC	8 apps	0 gls
Total	120+1 apps	4 gls

HAYHURST, Stanley Henry
Goalkeeper

5'10" 10st 9lb
Born: Leyland, 13 May 1925
Died: Leyland November 1998
Debut: 14 December 1946

CAREER: Leyland Motors; Blackburn Rovers Nov 1942 (am) Jan 1943; Tottenham Hotspur Oct 1948 (ex Hughes); Barrow Jun 1950 (£1,500); Grimsby Town Jan 1951 (£3,500); Weymouth Town.

Signed as a youngster during the Second World War he was introduced to the team as deputy and then successor to George Marks. The elevation came at a bad time for the player since he was troubled by his wife's poor health. Despite his agility he was uncertain on the line and glaring errors in the game against Tottenham resulted in the club signing the Tottenham reserve, Bill Hughes. Despite his performance the Londoners saw enough to persuade them to take Hayhurst in exchange but his spell at White Hart Lane never brought a senior appearance. Ted Ditchburn was a splendid first choice but when Tottenham played him with a broken hand Hayhurst decided that the time had come to leave and he played regularly with Barrow and Grimsby. He returned to live in Bent Lane, Leyland, and worked at the rubber works. He became manager at Chorley and in 1968 took the club into the Northern Premier League.

FL	27 apps	0 gls
Total	27 apps	0 gls

HEATON, James Michael*
Full-back

5'6" 10st 10lb
Born: Sheffield, 15 January 1947
Died: Blackburn, 11 April 1995
Debut: 9 October 1971

CAREER: Sheffield United Apr 1962 (app) Nov 1964; Blackburn Rovers Oct 1971-Jan 1977 (£8,000); Great Harwood Jan 1978; Morecambe.

An effusive, gymnastic right-back, he was signed by Ken Furphy and was one of the few such signings that was retained by the next manager Gordon Lee. With an improbable head of hair and ability to clear from positions that looked physically impossible, Heaton was an enthusiast who aided team spirit by his effort and drive. Appointed captain, he led his side to promotion but never reaped the reward because, shortly after, he sustained a serious leg injury that terminated his career. After a long battle against the odds he retired and ran a sports shop in town but was recalled to the club to act as assistant to temporary manager John Pickering. He stayed in this capacity under Howard Kendall and forged such an understanding that he followed him to Goodison Park. He was later to serve under Kendall at Maine Road. In between he was involved in the Football in the Community project and managed Workington. Tragically, he died from head injuries sustained in a motor accident on Grane Road in Haslingden at a time when he was working as a debt collector.

FL	169+2 apps	1 gl
FAC	9 apps	0 gls
FLC	10 apps	0 gls
Total	188+2 apps	1 gl

HELLIWELL, David 'Spider'

Inside forward

5'8" 9st 12lb
Born: Blackburn, 28 March 1948
Died: Blackburn, 22 March 2003
Debut: 3 September 1966

CAREER: Mill Hill; Blackburn Rovers Jun 1964 (app) May 1966; Lincoln City May 1969; Workington Jul 1970; Rochdale Jul 1976; Morecambe 1977.

Although his brother Frank had not progressed beyond the Rovers' youth team David Helliwell ensured that a similar fate did not befall him when he produced a magical display for the reserves, which made it impossible to stop him making his first-team debut as soon as possible. This performance, based on baffling ball skills that made him appear to have more than the usual number of legs and led to his nickname, was seldom reproduced with the senior side. His frame was slender and his durability questionable and he drifted into the lower divisions, proving, however, with nearly 200 games at Workington that even in the lower divisions class will tell. He returned to his home town, dying unexpectedly at an early age at his home in Isherwood Street, Ewood.

FL	15 apps	1 gl
FLC	1 app.	0 gls
Total	16 apps	1 gl

HENCHOZ, Stéphane

Centre-back

6'1" 12st 4lb
Born: Billens (Switzerland), 7 September 1974
Debut: 9 August 1997

CAREER: Fetigny; Stade Payerne 1984; Bulle 1988; Neuchatel Xamax 1991; Hamburger SV (Germany) Jun 1995 (£625,000); Blackburn Rovers Jun 1997 (£3,500,000); Liverpool Jul 1999 (£3,500,000); Glasgow Celtic Jan 2005-Jun 2005 (free); Wigan Athletic Jul 2005 (free).
INTERNATIONAL: Switzerland 69 apps.

The son of a Swiss train driver, Henchoz was heading for a career in banking if his football skill had not intervened. Introduced by Roy Hodgson to the national team at the age of eighteen he had Hodgson to thank again when he entered the Premiership. He had struggled in his first season in the Bundesliga and his second was terminated by injuries to his ankles which required surgery. It was therefore an act of faith by Hodgson to step in and pay a huge fee to bring him to Blackburn. Once again he took a season to settle in but once he accustomed himself he proved a commanding defender, extremely intelligent in his positioning, solid in all aspects of his defensive duties and very calm. Unfortunately the rest of the side were poor and the subsequent relegation ensured that Henchoz would move on. At Liverpool he confirmed his position as one of the best defenders in the Premier League and with a successful club accumulated some of the honours that players value so much.

PL	70 apps	0 gls
FAC	6 apps	0 gls
FLC	3+1 apps	0 gls
UEFA	2 apps	0 gls
Total	81+1 apps	0 gls

Colin Hendry in 1992.

HENDRY, Edward Colin * James

Centre half

6'1.5" 12st 2lb
Born: Keith, 7 December 1965
Debut: 14 March 1987

CAREER: Keith GS; Isla Vale; Motherwell (trial); Dundee; Blackburn Rovers Mar 1987 (£30,000); Manchester City Nov 1989 (£700,000); Blackburn Rovers Nov 1991 (£700,000); Glasgow Rangers Aug 1998 (£3,750,000); Coventry City Feb 2000 (£750,000); Bolton Wanderers Dec 2000 (loan) Feb 2001-Jun 2003 (free); Preston North End Feb 2002 (loan); Blackpool Dec 2002 (loan).
INTERNATIONALS: Scotland 51 apps 3 gls.

No-one realised when Don Mackay signed Hendry that they were being introduced to a man destined to become one of the club's most iconic figures. He had never won a regular place in the Dundee side, split his time between defence and attack and was unheard of south of the border. Within two months his right foot had brought a late winner in the Wembley final of the Full Members' Cup and the platform for cult status had been created. Moving back to defence, he proved a magnificent acquisition. With his flowing blond hair, aerial supremacy and ability to throw his body anywhere (no matter how painful the consequences) he cut a swashbuckling, inspiring figure. Dissatisfied with the club's failure to progress, he was transferred to Manchester City but was never comfortable away from Ewood and two years later was back, helping drive Kenny Dalglish's reconstructed side to promotion and memorably to the Premiership title. The fans had always had a special relationship with Hendry, who had lived locally and participated to the full in local affairs. It was therefore seen as a betrayal when he opted for the money available in a switch to Glasgow Rangers and, although he also gained honours, he soured his unique local relationship. His spell in Scotland was brief and he returned to play locally with Bolton, Preston and Blackpool but his hoped for return to Ewood never materialised. After a spell out of the game, when his wife was extremely ill following surgery, he became manager of Blackpool and guided them through a satisfactory first season.

L	328+8 apps	34 gls
FAC	20+1 apps	0 gls
FLC	27 apps	0 gls
FMC	7 apps	1 gl
PO	9 apps	0 gls
UEFA	2 apps	0 gls
EC	5 apps	0 gls
CS	1 app.	0 gls
Total	399+9 apps	35 gls

HERRON, Alan
Centre half

6'0" 12st 2lb
Born: Ashington, 6 October 1932
Debut: 28 April 1956

CAREER: Newcastle United; Ashington; Blackburn Rovers Aug 1950; Wigan Athletic May 1959-1960.

Brought to Ewood after failing to impress at Newcastle, he was groomed to be the successor to the ageing Willie Kelly. Fair haired, strongly built and dour, he received his first chance when Kelly was moved to left-back, and coped well. However, the unexpected arrival of the magnificent Matt Woods effectively strangled his career. Although sought after by league clubs he was induced to sign for Wigan by the presence of manager Pat Murphy and played either at right-back or in the centre for a season. Perhaps the first Rover to be prosecuted for a motoring offence, he was fined for driving a car before he had passed his test without being accompanied by a qualified driver.

FL	4 apps	0 gls
Total	4 apps	0 gls

HICKMAN, Michael Frederick Thomas
Striker/midfield

5'8" 10st 8lb
Born: Elstead, 2 October 1946
Debut: 4 February 1975

CAREER: Brighton & Hove Albion Sep 1963 (am) Jun 1965; Grimsby Town Jun 1968; Blackburn Rovers Feb 1975 (£10,000); Torquay United Oct 1975-1977 (£2,500).

Nicknamed 'Harpo' by his teammates because of his resemblance to the Marx brother he was a surprise signing by Gordon Lee to strengthen a team pushing for promotion. Although he was carrying a serious knee problem that ultimately ended his career, no-one would have guessed that from his on-field performance. Brave, a genuine hard man and with energy to burn, he made up for his lack of skill with constant action, throwing himself into the conflict and bringing swashbuckling bravado to the side. In helping the club to promotion he proved himself but an immediate change of manager, and with it a change of coach, effectively ended his Rovers career. A move to Torquay brought further injury and he joined their coaching staff. Moving to Australia, he managed Sydney Olympic to the national title and was made assistant manager of the national team before returning to Reading to work under Paul McGhee. He followed McGhee to Leicester and Wolves but when McGhee left the latter he returned to the other side of the world, coaching Sanfrecce Hiroshima in Japan and then assisting Graham Arnold with the Australian side Northern Spirit. When Arnold moved to assist Frank Farina with the national side, Hickman was promoted to head coach.

FL	23+3 apps	8 gls
FLC	2 apps	0 gls
Total	25+3 apps	8 gls

H

HIGGINS, George

Full-back

5'7" 10st 7lb
Born: Dundee, 16 February 1925
Died: Grimsby, 13 April 1993
Debut: 18 January 1947

CAREER: Lochee Harp; Blackburn Rovers Oct 1946; Bolton Wanderers Jul 1951 (£9,000); Grimsby Town May 1954 (free); Scarborough (p-m).

A tough, hard-tackling player who served as a marine commando on convoys to Russia during the Second World War, he was spotted by accident when the Rovers went to watch a teammate named Wallace. Brought in to replace the unsettled Walter Crook, he later did the same at Bolton after he had lost his Rovers place to the emerging Bill Eckersley. In 1953 he played in the Bolton side that was victorious in a FA Cup semi-final but lost his place to Ralph Banks before the big day. After experience in management at Scarborough he returned to the Football League as Grimsby's assistant trainer in 1960 and subsequently was Graham Taylor's assistant at Lincoln.

FL	53 apps	0 gls
FAC	3 apps	0 gls
Total	56 apps	0 gls

HIGNETT, Craig John

Midfield

5'9" 11st 10lb
Born: Prescot, 12 January 1970
Debut: 15 October 2000

CAREER: Liverpool; Crewe Alexandra May 1988 (free); Stafford Rangers (loan); Middlesbrough Nov 1992 (£500,000); Aberdeen Jul 1998 (free); Barnsley Nov 1998 (£800,000); Blackburn Rovers Jul 2000 (£3,250,000); Coventry City Nov 2002-Jan 2003 (loan); Leicester City Jul 2003 (free); Crewe Alexandra Feb 1904-May 1904 (loan); Leeds United Jun 2004 (trial) Aug 2004; Darlington Sep 2004.

Glandular fever at an important time during his development years at Liverpool left Hignett contemplating his future. He was rescued by Dario Gradi at Crewe who teased out of him the talents others had not seen, a coolness in possession, unflappability in front of goal and an ability to exploit space. Middlesbrough recognised these qualities and he shared in good years with the club before moving to Aberdeen. With Barnsley he struck the best scoring form of his life and it was this that prompted Souness to spend a great deal of money on his transfer. The return was disappointing. Never recovering from a false start caused by Achilles problems, he failed to establish himself as anything other than a situational substitute and as the squad grew stronger these opportunities disappeared. Attempting to attract the attentions of other clubs he went on loan to Coventry but broke his leg, though he recovered well and joined newly promoted Leicester in the close season. Released at the end of the season, he had a spell on temporary contract with Leeds before signing for Darlington.

L	20+33 apps	8 gls
FAC	4+4 apps	3 gls
FLC	5+1 apps	3 gls
UEFA	1 app.	0 gls
Total	30+38 apps	14 gls

HILDERSLEY, Ronald

Midfield

5'5" 10st
Born: Kirkcaldy, 6 April 1965
Debut: 27 August 1988

CAREER: Manchester City Jul 1981 (app) Apr 1983; Chester City Jan 1984 (loan); Chester City Jul 1984; Rochdale Aug 1985 (free); Preston North

End Jun 1986; Cambridge United Jan 1988 (loan); Blackburn Rovers Jul 1988 (free); Wigan Athletic Aug 1990; Halifax Town Nov 1991; East Fife Sep 1993-Sep 1995; Montrose Aug 1997-Sep 1997; Castleton Gabriels 1998; Wardle (p-m) 1999.

Despite a surprise first-team debut with Manchester City, his career was drifting until he unexpectedly found a home at Deepdale. There, his rubber-ball resilience, lifting effect on the team and enthusiasm made him popular and he converted from out-and-out left winger (where he lacked speed) to the midfield. Released by Preston, it appeared unlikely that he would move up a grade but he did so when he signed for the Rovers and for a time injected a similar uplift to the team's morale. When John Millar was converted to the left side of midfield he lost his spot and after lodging at Halifax moved north of the border, although he subsequently returned to non-league football in the Greater Manchester area.

FL	25+5 apps	4 gls
FAC	3 apps	1 gl
FLC	0+1 app.	0 gls
Total	26+6 apps	5 gls

HILL, Brian

Left wing

5'9.5" 10st
Born: Mansfield, 15 December 1942
Debut: 9 August 1969

CAREER: Ollerton Colliery; Grimsby Town Aug 1960; Huddersfield Town Nov 1966 (£20,000); Blackburn Rovers Jun 1969 (£30,000); Torquay United Jul 1971 (free); Boston United Jun 1973; Market Rasen (p-m).

A stand-out performer at Grimsby who had also served Huddersfield well, he was brought to supply balance to the line-up. Built along classical greyhound lines, he supplied neither speed nor trickery and was seldom a threat in front of goal. At a time when the club had some troublesome characters the quiet Hill appeared lost in the maelstrom and quickly moved on, with the club being unable to recoup any of the fee paid for him.

FL	34+3 apps	4 gls
FAC	2 apps	0 gls
FLC	4 apps	1 gl
Total	40+3 apps	5 gls

HILL, Keith John

Centre-back

6'0" 11st 3lb
Born: Bolton, 17 May 1969
Debut: 23 September 1987

CAREER: Blackburn Rovers May 1987; Plymouth Argyle Sep 1992 (ex with Skinner for Marker); Rochdale Jul 1996 (free); Cheltenham Town May 2001 (free); Wrexham Oct 2001-Dec 2001 (loan); Morecambe Aug 2002-Jun 2003; Chorley Dec 2003-Jun 2004.

Hill was one of several players from Greater Manchester who joined the club when a training facility was set up in Salford. Strongly built and confident, he suffered none of the frailties of youth and at twenty was made club captain. Injury prevented him establishing himself and he was never going to keep Kevin Moran out of the side. Given a spell at right-back he suffered from bad judgement in knowing when to run the ball out of defence and when the club was promoted to the Premier League was moved on. He proved a seasoned performer in the lower divisions and might have extended his career if he had not desired to keep his home in the North-West. Injuries ended his career at Morecambe although he reappeared briefly to help out his old clubmate Mark Patterson at Chorley. He then became youth-team coach at Rochdale.

FL	89 +7 apps	4 gls
FAC	5 +1 app.	0 gls
FLC	6 apps	1 gl
FMC	3 apps	0 gls
PO	0 +2 apps	0 gls
Total	103+10 apps	5 gls

HILTON, Patrick John
Forward

5'8" 10st
Born: Aylesham, 1 May 1954
Debut: 17 August 1974

CAREER: Dover GS; Aylesham YC; Coventry City; Folkestone; West Bromwich Albion Jul 1970; Canterbury Feb 1972; Brighton & Hove Albion Feb 1973; Blackburn Rovers May 1974 (free); Gillingham Sep 1975 (£3,000); Aldershot Town Mar 1977 (loan); Southport Jul 1977-Jun 1978; Folkestone Town; Dover 1978; Canterbury 1979; Folkestone Town; Margate; Folkestone Town; Thanet United; Hythe United; Gillingham 1990.

Although he was a waspish opponent and indefatigable runner Hilton lacked power and stamina and posed little threat in front of goal. Rescued by Brighton after not making the grade with West Brom, he was brought to the Rovers by Gordon Lee because, despite his limitations, he helped the cause with his effort. It was typical of the career of a man who had attended a rugby-playing school and received much rejection but always manufactured himself another chance. The opportunity at Blackburn came after he had been dismissed by Brighton for over-celebrating his twentieth birthday and breaking windows at the ground. After a decade in non-league football he was registered by Gillingham when he coached their youth team. He later worked on the Channel Tunnel and for BT.

FL	16 apps	2 gls
FLC	5 apps	0 gls
Total	21 apps	2 gls

HINDSON, Gordon
Left winger

5'9" 11st 4lb
Born: Flint Hill, Stanley, 8 January 1950
Debut: 11 October 1975

CAREER: Newcastle United Aug 1968; Luton Town Oct 1971 (£27,000); Carlisle United Sep 1975 (loan); Blackburn Rovers Oct 1975-Dec 1975 (loan); Hartford Bi-Centennials (USA) Apr 1976-Aug 1976; Evenwood Town 1976; Consett Aug 1979; Spennymoor United Jan 1981; Gateshead Nov 1981; Consett Jan 1983.

After service with Luton, Hindson was passing through a bad patch in his career when he came to the Rovers on loan. It was not a career move since the Rovers had no interest in a permanent signing and in his brief time on the Rovers' left Hindson demonstrated neither speed nor trickery, although he slotted easily enough into a system that demanded little of its wide men other than getting crosses over. As his playing days wound down he returned to his native North-East and was appointed coach and then manager of Consett.

FL	10 apps	0 gls
Total	10 apps	0 gls

HIRD, Kevin
Midfield/Full-back

5'7.5" 10st 10lb
Born: Colne, 11 February 1955
Debut: 13 April 1974

CAREER: Primet School; Sefton; Colne Dynamos; Blackburn Rovers Oct 1970 (app) Feb 1973; Leeds United Mar 1979 (£357,000); Burnley Jun 1984 (free); Colne Dynamoes; Darwen; Barnoldswick United Sep 1991; Kelbrook

A youth-team winger with pace and skill, he appeared out of place in the hustle of the Second

Division and his future appeared insecure when the club agreed to sell him to New York Cosmos for a small fee. He turned the move down and played an inadvertent hand in his own future when in the last minute of the season he missed a penalty kick against Fulham. The rebound from the goalkeeper fell kindly but, forgetting the rules, he assumed he could not touch the ball again. The extra point would have taken the club up the table sufficiently to avoid playing in the early round of the League Cup the following year. In this game John Waddington broke his wrist, Derek Fazackerley was subsequently moved back from the right-back spot and the unexpected recipient of the number two shirt was Hird. The ramifications were immediate. Hird proved sensational at right-back. With the freedom to run from deep he carved swathes down the flanks and if opponents backed off he shot explosively. His defensive qualities remained suspect, his headwork being near to non-existent, but he improvised with flexibility from the hip and unusual use of his feet. So impressive was he that departure was inevitable and a large fee took him to Elland Road where he established himself either at full-back or in midfield. Able to live at Colne throughout his career, he was made school liaison officer for Colne Dynamos when the club was at its pinnacle.

FL	129+3 apps	20 gls
FAC	8 apps	0 gls
FLC	7+1 apps	1 gl
Total	144+4 apps	21 gls

HITCHEN, Steven James

Right-back

5'10" 11st 2lb

Born: Manchester, 28 November 1976

CAREER: Blackburn Rovers Jul 1995; Macclesfield Town May 1997; Flixton Mar 1998 (loan); Shrewsbury Town Jan 2004 (trial); Bangor City Jan 2004.

Spotted playing with Salford Schoolboys, he became a trainee at Ewood and was once so promising that Celtic enquired about him. He secured a place in the reserves and occasionally travelled with the first team to away games but it was still a surprise (and a demonstration of how shallow was the depth at the club) when he was named on the bench for the European Cup game at Rosenborg. Soon after, he lost his reserve place to David Worrell and Wayne Gill and was allowed to join Macclesfield. Despite injuries, he made over 150 appearances before going to play for Peter Davenport at Bangor.

HOLDEN, Alan

Wing half

5'8" 10st 9lb

Born: Haslingden, 12 October 1941

Debut: 25 September 1963

CAREER: Haslingden County Sec Sc; Blackburn Rovers Oct 1959 (non con) Jan 1962; Stockport County Jul 1966-Jun 1967 (free); Haslingden St Mary's.

A painter from Haslingden, he came to the club as an inside forward but was converted to wing half. Being only a part-time player his development was restricted and with Clayton, McGrath, McEvoy, England, Newton and later Joyce on the staff he was lucky to have been given any opportunity. A prodigious worker, he never appeared likely to establish himself and after one barren season at Stockport he returned to his business interests.

FL	1 app.	0 gls
FLC	1 app.	0 gls
Total	2 apps	0 gls

HOLE, Barrington Gerard 'Barrie'
Wing half

5'11" 11st 4lb
Born: Swansea, 16 September 1942
Debut: 20 August 1966

CAREER: St David's School, Swansea; Cardiff City Sep 1959; Blackburn Rovers Jul 1966 (£45,000); Aston Villa Sep 1968 (£60,000); Swansea Town Jul 1970-May 1972 (£20,000).
INTERNATIONALS: Wales 30 apps.

When the Rovers were relegated in 1966 they finally converted to the 4-2-4 system that all other clubs had adopted. Crucial to the system was the acquisition of a midfield partner for Bryan Douglas and in signing Barrie Hole the club obtained a unique talent. Slim and long-legged, he could split a defence with a single raking pass and was perhaps the most devastating off-the-ball runner the club has ever had, able to cause mayhem with a judicious run that took defenders with him. The owner of a fine long-range shot, he was eventually sold when the club's finances were low, after two seasons of failure, to return to the top flight. He finished his career in his home town before becoming a shopkeeper there. Genetically he was always bound to become a footballer. His father Billy and brothers Alan and Colin all played for Swansea.

FL	79 apps	13 gls
FAC	2 apps	0 gls
FLC	7 apps	2 gls
Total	88 apps	15 gls

HOLLIDAY, Kenneth Joseph
Centre half

6'1.5" 12st 7lb
Born: Darwen, 19 August 1925
Died: Burnley, February 1999
Debut: 17 April 1948

CAREER: Spring Bank School; Darwen; Blackburn Rovers Jun 1946 (am) Oct 1946 (£4,000); Accrington Stanley Jul 1952; Barrow May 1955; Nelson 1956; Darwen; Padiham.

In 1938 Holliday played left-back in the Darwen Schools' side and during the Second World War moved to his local club. In 1946 the Rovers were sufficiently impressed by his progress that they gave him a trial. With his mop of curly ginger hair he was likely to be noticed on the field and his unusual height for a full-back of the time also made him conspicuous. The Rovers decided that this was wasted at full-back and moved him to the centre of the defence and gradually introduced him to first-team football. When Willie Kelly came from Scotland to shore up the defence his chances receded but he gave Accrington good service before the arrival of Kelly once again confined him to the reserves.

FL	29 apps	0 gls
FAC	1 app.	0 gls
Total	30 apps	0 gls

HOLMES, Matthew Jason
Midfield

5'7" 10st 7lb
Born: Luton, 1 August 1969
Debut: 19 August 1995

CAREER: AFC Bournemouth Sep 1986 (trainee) Aug 1988; Cardiff City Mar 1989 (loan); West Ham United Aug 1992 (£40,000); Blackburn Rovers Aug 1995 (ex £600,000+Slater); Charlton Athletic Jul 1997-Apr 2000 (£250,000); Dorchester Town Jul 2000.

It will forever remain a mystery why Ray Harford, newly appointed manager of the Premier League champions, and with money to spend, elected first of all to bring in Matt Holmes, a tidy, left-sided midfield man whose problem was always his size and power ratio. A finesse player, he never adjusted to life at Ewood and after a season when he never played attempted to rescue his career at Charlton. Injured pre-season, he had just gained a first-team place when a tackle from Kevin Muscat left him with an horrendously broken leg. After a valiant fight, he had to accept his ankle would never be strong enough for top-class football but he kept in the game by assisting an old friend at Dorchester.

PL	8+1 apps	1 gl
EC	2+1 apps	0 gls
Total	10+2 apps	1 gl

HOLMES, William
Centre forward

5'9" 10st 11lb
Born: Hunslet, 29 October 1926
Debut: 1 January 1952

CAREER: Morecambe 1946; Lancaster City Sep 1948; Leeds United 1948; Wolverhampton Wanderers 1948; Doncaster Rovers Oct 1950; Morecambe; Burnley Jul 1951; Morecambe; Blackburn Rovers Sep 1951; Morecambe; Bradford City Sep 1953; Southport Jul 1954-May 1956.

The story of Holmes is probably the last romantic page of an age that will never return. Although not exactly an unknown at the time (he was an amateur international) his origins were obscure. He was attending a teacher training course at Morecambe and had undergone trials with a number of league clubs but the moment he set foot in Ewood his life altered dramatically. He scored on his debut with the midweek league team, hit a hat-trick in his first game with the 'A' team and tallied 5 goals in his first 4 reserve games. Pushed into the first team, he scored within minutes of his debut. Although sometimes unavailable (he was studying) he brought zest to a struggling team with a work rate that was exceptional, roaming from side to side, a strong physical presence and a strike rate that is unlikely to be equalled. He went into the realms of folklore in a crucial local FA Cup tie against Burnley when he retrieved a ball that appeared destined to be heading for a goal kick and crossed it for a vital score. Ever a man for the big occasion, he scored a hat-trick for Southport on his wedding day. Hugely popular among the fans, he remained a talismanic figure but the Rovers' manager, Johnny Carey, was a pragmatist and he recognised the professional excellence of Tommy Briggs, who succeeded Holmes.

FL	21 apps	16 gls
FAC	4 apps	3 gls
Total	25 apps	19 gls

HOLT, David Ephraim
Centre half

5'11.5" 11st 3lb
Born: Durham, 7 January 1945
Debut: 29 March 1966

CAREER: Blackburn Rovers Apr 1963-Nov 1966.

Most footballers live out their boyhood dreams so it is a surprise to find one that gave up when still able to continue to do so. Holt, a blond-haired stylist, was brought down for trials with the youth side in 1962 and did so well that he was offered terms. Granted his debut three years later he was well in contention for a first-team place but grew disenchanted with his lack of progress and retired to help his father-in-law run his household goods company in Darwen.

FL	10 apps	0 gls
FLC	1 app.	0 gls
Total	11 apps	0 gls

HOLT, William Kenneth
Centre half

5'11.5" 12st 5lb
Born: Boldon Colliery, 31 March 1926
Debut: 7 May 1949

CAREER: Boldon CW; Blackburn Rovers Jan 1949; Weymouth 1953; Barrow Jun 1954-May 1957; Netherfield.

Holt was spotted playing full-back but had moved to centre half by the time the club got round to signing him. Recently demobbed from the Royal Engineers, he was driving a Co-op van at the time and was groomed as Bob Pryde's replacement. Although his dour defensive qualities were appreciated, he lacked height and never commanded like Pryde's eventual successor, Willie Kelly. Placed on the transfer list he moved to Weymouth so that he could continue playing, but Barrow negotiated his transfer and he gave good service on the edge of the Lake District.

FL	78 apps	0 gls
FAC	2 apps	0 gls
Total	80 apps	0 gls

HORREY, Rowland George
Winger

5'9" 11st
Born: Bishop Auckland, 9 March 1943
Debut: 13 March 1965

CAREER: Ferryhill Athletic; Blackburn Rovers Dec 1963; York City Jul 1966 (free); Cambridge United Jul 1970-Jan 1972.

When the Rovers became aware that their youth policy was not providing new recruits they targetted a number of slightly older players in the North-East. Among them was Horrey, a flying winger with slick black hair and any amount of dash. Not quite up to first-team standard, he moved to York where he performed well and was later able to prolong his league career when he was at Cambridge at the time they were elevated to the Football League.

FL	3 apps	0 gls
FLC	1 app.	0 gls
Total	4 apps	0 gls

HORTON, Henry
Wing half

5'10.5" 12st 2lb
Born: Colwall Green, 18 April 1923
Died: Hereford, 2 November 1998
Debut: 26 April 1947

CAREER: Colwall; Worcester City Aug 1946 (am) Oct 1946; Blackburn Rovers Jan 1947 (£2,000); Southampton Jun 1951 (£10,000); Bradford PA May 1954; Hereford United Sep 1955.

Horton was one of the most gifted sportsmen of all time. On leaving the Fleet Air Arm after the Second World War he was on the groundstaff at Worcestershire CCC and turned professional with Worcester City, where he played wing half. A hard-working, diligent player who combined fitness with intelligence, he caught the eye of the Rovers who paid a record fee for a non-league player. At Ewood his career was hampered by the presence of Eric Bell who played in Horton's natural left half position, but the Rovers permed the two around, using Horton occasionally on the left wing. At the time his cricket career was making no great strides (his 1 appearance with Blackburn Northern brought only 10 runs) but when he was transferred to Southampton the legendary John Arlott recommended him to Hampshire. From his debut for the county a legend was born (Arlott described him as having the ugliest stance and the straightest back in English cricket) and he went on to score 21,669 first-class runs, including 32 centuries, and gained a County Championship medal in 1961. With the demands of sport being less he combined both his sporting careers for some time before concentrating exclusively on the summer game. He even played for Worcestershire Second XI (when he was coach) at the age of fifty-five, fittingly at the Alexandria Meadows against Lancashire.

FL	92 apps	5 gls
FAC	6 apps	0 gls
Total	98 apps	5 gls

HOY, Robert
Right winger

5'7" 9st 13lb
Born: Halifax, 10 January 1950
Debut: 15 March 1975

CAREER: Huddersfield Town Jan 1966 (am) Nov 1967; Blackburn Rovers Mar 1975 (ex Endean+£5,000); Halifax Town Jun 1976; York City Aug 1977; Rochdale Dec 1977; Macclesfield 1981; Burnley (trial); Bradford City Sep 1983 (trial).

A right-wing box of tricks, he was a surprise signing on transfer-deadline day as Gordon Lee sought to freshen his team for the promotion run-in. By then his career, which had commenced with England youth caps, was sliding and he spent much time of his Ewood career on the bench, appearing too delicate for the somewhat rustic game at this level. A proficient guitarist, he earned a living as a folk singer on the Northern club circuit when he retired from football.

FL	13+6 apps	0 gls
FAC	1 app.	0 gls
FLC	0+2 apps	0 gls
Total	14+8 apps	0 gls

HUDSON, George Anthony
Centre forward

5'10" 12st
Born: Manchester, 14 March 1937
Debut: 18 April 1959
CAREER: Manchester City; Blackburn Rovers May 1955 (am) Jan 1958; Accrington Stanley Jul 1960 (free); Peterborough United Oct 1961 (£5,000); Coventry City Apr 1963 (£20,000); Northampton Town Mar 1966 (£22,000); Tranmere Rovers Jan 1967 (£15,000); Altrincham 1969.

Misjudging their own striking products is not an affliction at the club that started with James Beattie. George Hudson, a railway worker from Manchester, was considered too limited and pedestrian despite his power and eye for a goal, and was, in any case, behind Peter Dobing, Tommy Johnston and later Derek Dougan in a quest for a first-team place. Allowed to join Accrington, he immediately equalled George Stewart's scoring record, improved at Peterborough and was snapped up by Coventry to spearhead a drive that took them to the First Division. When Northampton were struggling in the top flight they turned to Hudson who proved that, despite his unpromising start, he always was capable of scoring goals whatever the level he played. He ended his career with 163 league goals scored in just under 300 appearances.

FL	4 apps	1 gl
Total	4 apps	1 gl

HUGHES, Leslie Mark* 'Sparky'
Striker/Midfield

5'11" 13st
Born: Wrexham, 1 November 1963
Debut: 25 October 2000

CAREER: Ysgol Rhiwabon; Rhos Aelwyd; Manchester United Nov 1980; Barcelona (Spain) Jul 1986

(£2,500,000); Bayern Munich (Germany) Nov 1987-May 1988 (loan); Manchester United Jul 1988 (£1,500,000); Chelsea Jul 1995 (£1,500,000); Southampton Jul 1998 (£650,000); Everton Mar 2000 (free); Blackburn Rovers Oct 2000-Jun 2002 (free).
INTERNATIONALS: Wales 72 apps 16 gls.

Spotted by Manchester United when he was twelve years old, he signed schoolboy forms two years later. During his apprenticeship he was converted by Syd Owen from midfield to centre forward where it was envisaged that he could utilise his immense strength, hold the ball and bring those around him into the game. Given an early baptism in first-team football he was immediately at home and established himself during a long United career, where he won every honour available. A spell abroad with Barcelona was not a success and on his return to United he was able to enjoy the upturn in the club' fortunes. Offloaded to Chelsea, the ravages of time started to show on his game so it was a surprise when Graeme Souness brought him to Ewood. The reason was as much for his off-field presence as his on-field play because Souness had gambled that his resilience and desire to win would rub off and so it proved, with promotion and then the Worthington Cup arriving in successive seasons. The latter proved a fitting finale for Hughes' career. Unexpectedly forced to play because of a shortage of players, he not only lasted the ninety minutes but produced an inspired display to wrest control of the midfield. Released at the end of the season, he turned his part-time managership of the Welsh national team into a full-time one and with the same team altered their achievements so that their game stood at a higher level than it had done for many years. His association with the Rovers was not at an end and in September 2004 he was offered the chance to replace Graeme Souness as manager and accepted. Despite an horrendous start that saw the club bottom near the end of November he turned the club around, instilling steel in its backbone and making them a difficult side to beat.

L	25+25 apps	6 gls
FAC	4+4 apps	0 gls
FLC	4+ 2 apps	1 gl
Total	33+31 apps	7 gls

HUGHES, William Arthur
Goalkeeper

6'2" 12st 6lb
Born: Colwyn Bay, 2 February 1919
Died: Colwyn Bay, 11 Mar 1992
Debut: 23 October 1948

CAREER: Colwyn Bay United 1935; Manchester United (trial); Larne (Northern Ireland) 1937; Newry Town (Northern Ireland); Huddersfield Town May 1939; Tottenham Hotspur Oct 1945; Blackburn Rovers Oct 1948 (ex Hayhurst+cash, total value £7,500); Nelson Aug 1950 Rochdale Sep 1950; Crystal Palace Feb 1951-Jun 1952.
INTERNATIONALS: Wales 5 apps.

When Hughes went 269 minutes from his debut to the first time he conceded a goal, the club could have been excused for believing they had unearthed a real gem. He gained a place in the Welsh national team, displacing Cyril Sidlow, a schoolmate whose ability had forced Hughes to spend his school days on the wing. Unhappily his good form did not continue. He had trouble gauging the trajectory of long shots and his defenders were never sure when he would leave his line. By the time he pulled a muscle, doubts had set in and Jack Patterson was being earmarked to succeed him. This prompted him to submit a transfer request since he was anxious about his Welsh position. He found his services were not in great demand and joined Nelson before Rochdale and then Crystal Palace rescued him. With both league clubs his experiences were identical, a magnificent start followed by a tailing-off of performances.

FL	27 apps	0 gls
FAC	1 app.	0 gls
Total	28 apps	0 gls

HUNTER, Allan
Centre-back

5'11" 12st 7lb
Born: Sion Mills (Northern Ireland), 30 June 1946
Debut: 9 August 1969

CAREER: Coleraine 1962; Oldham Athletic Jan 1967 (£5,000); Blackburn Rovers Jun 1969 (£35,000); Ipswich Town Sep 1971 (ex £50,000+Bell); Colchester United (p-m) May 1982-Jan 1983.
INTERNATIONALS: Northern Ireland 53 apps 1 gl.

Oldham appeared to have gained a fair increase when they sold Blackburn their tall, rugged centre half, but it was the Rovers who got the best of the bargain. Dominant in the air and able to use his long legs for countless last-ditch tackles, Hunter formed a partnership with Dick Mulvaney that could best be described as abrasive. However, his second season coincided with a mediocrity that brought relegation. When he shone for his country in the close-season Home International Championship it was obvious that he would not remain at Ewood and he moved to Ipswich for a large fee. He stayed in East Anglia for nearly ten years during many of the club's great seasons, capped by a FA Cup final victory. He found at Colchester he was not suitable for management and became a woodwork teacher at Belstead Special School.

FL	84 apps	1 gl
FAC	2 apps	0 gl
FLC	5 apps	0 gl
Total	91 apps	1 gl

HUTCHINS, Donald
Left winger

5'7" 10st 2lb
Born: Middlesbrough, 8 May 1948
Debut: 12 August 1972

CAREER: Stockton; Leicester City Feb 1966; Plymouth Argyle Jul 1969 (£6,000); Blackburn Rovers Jul 1972 (£10,000); Bradford City Jun 1974-Jun 1981 (ex with £5,000 for Oates); Scarborough.

Although he played as a conventional left winger, the bushy haired North-Easterner had the tricks and skill to play inside. Throughout his Ewood career he was troubled by niggling injuries and developed no consistency in his play. Traded to Bradford City, he found consistency and contributed many well-struck goals. After retiring he worked as a sales manager for Leyland Paints and was one of the leading lights in the Bradford veterans' team.

FL	37+3 apps	6 gls
FAC	1+1 app.	0 gls
FLC	2+1 apps	0 gls
Total	40+5 apps	6 gls

HUTT, Geoffrey
Left-back

5'8" 12st
Born: Hazelwood, 28 September 1949
Debut: 20 September 1975

CAREER: Huddersfield Town Jun 1966 (app.) Sep 1967; Blackburn Rovers Sep 1975 (loan); Haarlem (Holland) Jul 1976; York City Feb 1977; Halifax Town Apr 1978-Jun 1980 (£4,000).

The red-headed left-back had been a fixture at Huddersfield, making over 250 appearances and establishing himself as a tough, no-nonsense player who had a fire about his play. He came to the Rovers on loan and contributed some good displays and a thunderously struck goal, but the club could not afford the asking price and he moved to Holland. He returned after a season and served York and Halifax well before working in the sales department of Tibbett & Britten.

FL	10 apps	1 gl
Total	10 apps	1 gl

I

IRELAND, Simon Piers

Left winger

5'10" 10st 7lb
Born: Barnstaple, 23 November 1971
Debut: 30 January 1993

CAREER: Huddersfield Town Oct 1989; Wrexham Mar 1992 (loan); Blackburn Rovers Nov 1992 (£250,000); Mansfield Town Mar 1994 (loan) Aug 1994 (£65,000); Doncaster Rovers Oct 1996 (loan) Jan 1997 (£10,000); Boreham Wood Aug 1998 (free); Halifax Town Aug 1999 (trial); Guiseley Sep 1999-Dec 2000; Wisbech Town 2001.

Although he had little first-team experience with Huddersfield he discomforted Blackburn's right flank in a Rumbelows Cup tie sufficiently to convince Kenny Dalglish that he was worth an investment for the future. A player with blistering speed, he broke a bone in his foot during his first season and on recovery was allowed to go to Mansfield on loan. The move was made permanent and Ireland played nearly 100 games, the majority of which were on the opposite flank. A move to the Football League's worst club, Doncaster, was not wise and when they were relegated Ireland's career sunk into such a decline that his contract was cancelled when he was playing for Guiseley.

PL	0+1 app.	0 gls
Total	0+1 app.	0 gls

IRVINE, James Alan*

Right winger

5'8" 11st 4lb
Born: Glasgow, 12 July 1958
Debut: 28 October 1989

CAREER: Glasgow BC; Queen's Park 1977; Everton May 1981; Crystal Palace Jul 1984 (£30,000); Dundee United Jun 1987; Blackburn Rovers Nov 1989-Jul 1992 (£25,000).

A right-wing flyer with craft, he was secured by Everton after he had assisted Queen's Park to promotion. His elevation to first-team status at Goodison was slow and, despite being recognised as having good crossing ability, he was only third choice behind Trevor Steven and Terry Curran. A move to Crystal Palace brought regular football but when he returned to Scotland he could not settle with Dundee United. This enabled Don Mackay to bring him to Ewood on loan. Although he made no real impact he was signed but his Ewood career was bedevilled with injuries that prevented him playing regularly. These resulted in his retirement in 1992, although he stayed at Ewood coaching the youngsters. He kept in shape and often filled in with the reserves, his qualities being recognised by Kenny Dalglish, who asked him to join Newcastle in 1997. For four seasons he was director of the youth academy there, unearthing gems like Shola Ameobi and Michael Chopra, but was working his notice before joining the FA, to work with the England youth side, when David Moyes offered him the assistant manager's role at Everton.

FL	40+18 apps	3 gls
FLC	3 apps	0 gls
FMC	0+1 app.	0 gls
Total	43+19 apps	3 gls

ISHERWOOD, Roy Edward

Right winger

5'6" 10st 2lb
Born: Blackburn, 24 January 1934
Debut: 10 October 1957

CAREER: Griffin CE School; St Peter's CE Sec Mod; Nelson; Blackburn Rovers Jul 1956 (am) Oct 1958; Chelmsford City 1962; Altrincham Jan 1964.

If Isherwood's career had not been contemporaneous with that of Bryan Douglas he would surely have received more opportunities. A right winger of similar height but much stockier, he relied, like the master, on beating his man as often as possible. At any other club his tricks and feints might have been considered exceptional but he never escaped from Douglas's shadow. He was almost a late selection for the 1960 FA Cup final team, having deputised for Bimpson and scored two goals in the penultimate game of the season (which helped banish the spectre of relegation from Ewood). The advent of Ratcliffe and Ferguson made him surplus to requirements and as he had always been a part-time player a move into non-league football was easier. In fact joining Chelmsford, where the chairman had a plumbing firm, was ideal, since that was Isherwood's trade. He left the game in unusual circumstances, being sacked by Altrincham for failing to turn up after encountering travel hardship. He was reinstated on appeal but had had enough and retired. He is the father-in-law of another ex-Rover, Mick Rathbone.

FL	49 apps	9 gls
FAC	2 apps	0 gls
FLC	6 apps	0 gls
Total	57 apps	9 gls

J

JACKSON, Harry

Centre forward

5'8" 12st 7lb
Born: Blackburn, 30 December 1918
Died: Bury, September 1984
Debut: 1 January 1949

CAREER: Meadowcrofts; Stanhill; Darwen 1937; Burnley Jan 1942; Manchester City Jun 1946; Preston North End Dec 1947; Blackburn Rovers Dec 1948; Chester Jul 1949-1950; Hyde United; Ashton United; Nelson; Clitheroe; Lion Brewery.

In schoolboy football Jackson had no equal as a goalscorer and at Darwen he demonstrated that the gift remained. There was no shortage of league clubs interested in his services but he elected to join Burnley. When not required for Naval service he scored 105 goals in 100 appearances but when the Football League resumed he was transferred to Manchester City. Although seldom called upon in the first team, he scored 30 goals for all their teams and it was a similar story at Preston, where he scored 14 reserve goals in 12 appearances. Curiously he signed for Preston on Christmas Eve and left for Blackburn on the same day a year later. He was top scorer for the Rovers' reserves but only played the 1 league game for the first team before moving to Chester.

FL	1 app.	0 gls
FAC	1 app.	0 gls
Total	2 apps	0 gls

JANSEN, Matthew Brooke

Striker

5'11" 10st 13lb
Born: Carlisle, 20 October 1977
Debut: 30 January 1999

Matt Jansen in 2002.

CAREER: Cumwhinton PS; Newman School; Carlisle United Jan 1996; Crystal Palace Feb 1998 (£1,000,000); Blackburn Rovers Jan 1999 (£4,000,000); Coventry City Feb 2003-May 2003 (loan).

The son of a senior CID officer of Dutch descent, he was privately educated at a rugby-playing school where he took the position of scrum half. Leaving school with ten GCSEs and an 'A' level he took up a traineeship at Carlisle, where his father was coach to the youth side. In a short time he became a hot prospect. An unpredictable player with a range of tricks, he was also brave, deceptively strong in the air and impossible to intimidate, having a remarkable recovery to regain balance and keep mobile. Invited to Old Trafford for possible transfer talks he turned the proposed move down because he thought his career would develop better with the first-team football he could obtain at Crystal Palace. When Palace struck financial problems his departure was inevitable and Brian Kidd won the race and brought him to Ewood. Intended as a long-term prospect, he was immediately introduced but despite a promising start his career became side-tracked. Unfortunately, not only the opposition but also his team mates appeared incapable of anticipating his moves and he had become an isolated figure when Graeme Souness took over. He extracted greater combined involvement, fed his desire and turned him into a player who not only scored with regularity but had one of the leading tackle counts on the team. It was fitting that he should score two of the most critical goals of Souness's managerial years, the winner at Preston that guaranteed Premiership football and the first goal in the Worthington Cup final at Cardiff. Called into the English squad just before the World Cup he missed his international debut because of illness and was then controversially left out of the squad. Worse still, a motor cycle accident in the close season left him with head injuries from which his recovery has been slow and is still not guaranteed. Consequently he has played little football in the past three seasons and it remains to be seen if he will ever be the same exciting player he was.

L	104+49 apps	44 gls
FAC	8+4 apps	4 gls
FLC	9+5 apps	8 gls
UEFA	2+ 1 app.	1 gl
Total	123+59 apps	57 gls

JOHANSSON, Nils-Eric 'Nissa'

Centre-back

6'2" 12st 9lb
Born: Stockholm (Sweden), 13 January 1980
Debut: 10 October 2001

CAREER: IFK Viksjo; IF Brommapojkarna; AIK Solna; Bayern Munich (Germany) Jun 1997; FC Nurnberg (Germany) Jul 2000; Blackburn Rovers Oct 2001-Jun 2005 (£2,700,000); Leicester City Jul 2005 (free).
INTERNATIONALS: Sweden 3 apps.

At seventeen he was signed by Bayern Munich on the basis of the potential provided by his fine physique, strength and maturity. Groomed carefully through the Swedish age-group teams, he discovered that the challenge in Munich was huge and had made no impact when the club offloaded him to Nurnberg. In less demanding surroundings he excelled, helping the club to promotion and reawakening interest in him.

Most chose to wait to see how he would develop but the Rovers had injuries to Taylor and Short and needed a big man desperately. In nearly four seasons with the Rovers he had many opportunities, both at the centre of defence and at left-back, but was inconsistent. Strong and powerful, he proved error-prone and sometimes appeared slow to sense danger. Despite being given several opportunities by Mark Hughes it was decided that his contract would not be extended when it expired in 2005.

PL	59+27 apps	0 gls
FAC	8+2 apps	1 gl
FLC	8+2 apps	1 gl
UEFA	4 apps	0 gls
Total	79+31 apps	2 gls

JOHNROSE, Leonard

Striker/midfield

5'11" 12st
Born: Preston, 29 November 1969
Debut: 12 December 1987

CAREER: St Thomas Moore School; Blackburn Rovers Jan 1984 (ass sc) Jul 1986 (trainee) Jun 1988; Preston North End Jan 1992 (loan); Hartlepool United Feb 1992 (£10,000); Bury Dec 1993; Burnley Feb 1999 (£225,000); Blackpool Jul 2002 (trial); Burnley Aug 2002-Oct 2002; Bury Oct 2002-Dec 2002; Swansea City Jan 2003; Burnley Mar 2004-May 2004.

Groomed through the youth team, he made an impact at Ewood as a substitute who was capable of changing the game. Five of his first-team goals came after he left the bench, four of them in 1990/91. Explosive in the box and instinctive, he found it harder to act as a conventional target man and in 1991 underwent a conversion into a midfield player. It was discovered that he was a ferocious tackler and he could control a game, and these qualities stood him in good stead in a long career, most of which was passed locally.

FL	20+22 apps	11 gls
FAC	0+3 apps	0 gls
FLC	2+1 apps	1 gl
FMC	2 apps	0 gls
Total	24+26 apps	12 gls

JOHNSON, Athur

Goalkeeper

6'1" 13st 2lb
Born: Liverpool, 23 January 1933
Debut: 27 August 1951

CAREER: Alsop GS; Bedford Park Jnrs (Southport); Blackburn Rovers May 1949 (am) Jan 1950; Halifax Town Mar 1955; Wrexham Jun 1960; Chester Aug 1961 (loan); New Brighton May 1963; Rhyl Jul 1963; Holyhead Town Feb 1964.

When Jack Patterson was injured his logical replacement, Wilf Billington, was unable to get his release from national service. The only option was the young goalkeeper discovered in parks football in Southport, Arthur Johnson. He had a trying debut, conceded three goals, and the club went out and signed Reg Elvy. The result was that Johnson was surplus to requirements once his national service with the RAF was completed. A move to Halifax proved him to be one of the best goalkeepers in the lower division and he played over 200 games for them. He then signed for Wrexham as a part-timer, working as an accountant in the Metal Box factory in Aintree.

FL	1 app.	0 gls
Total	1 app.	0 gls

JOHNSON, Damien Michael

Right winger

5'9" 10st
Born: Lisburn, 18 November 1978
Debut: 30 September 1997

CAREER: Portadown; Blackburn Rovers 1995; Nottingham Forest Jan 1998-Mar 1998 (loan); Birmingham City Mar 2002 (£250,000).
INTERNATIONALS: Northern Ireland 41 apps.

Johnson had already played in the first team for Portadown when he became a trainee at Blackburn and therefore his progress to the fringe of the first team was not surprising. An energetic player, with real speed and seldom bested contesting a fifty-fifty ball, he suffered from uncertainty whether his best position was wide right (he was not the most accurate crosser of a ball) or inside where his hardness was a real asset. A disc problem prevented him playing for a spell, although he gained a place for the crucial weeks of the 2001 promotion campaign but thereafter dropped behind his fellow Irishman, Gillespie. When the club decided they would not renew his contract there was plenty of interest and he joined Birmingham, and thus became one of the few players to play with a promoted side in successive seasons. He has proved one of the club's best signings, a reliable worker capable of playing several roles, often in the same game.

L	43+17 apps	3 gls
FAC	3+4 apps	0 gls
FLC	12+3 apps	1 gls
UEFA	0+1 app.	0 gls
Total	58+25 apps	4 gls

JOHNSON, Jemal Pierre
Striker

5'9" 11st 6lb
Born: Patterson, New Jersey (USA), 5 March 1984
Debut: 8 January 2005

CAREER: Vale Juniors (Congleton) FC 1996; Manchester United Aug 2001 (schoolboy); Blackburn Rovers 2001; Preston North End Oct 2005 (loan).

Although born in the USA he came to live in Macclesfield at the age of five and was brought up in the Cheshire town. Signed by Manchester United, he had his traineeship cancelled for disciplinary reasons and was subsequently offered trainee terms with the Rovers. Extremely fleet of foot, his lack of physique gave concern but he coped well when promoted from the youth team. He was difficult to play against because not only was he fast and elusive but, given a sight of goal, he was extremely quick to get a shot off and this made him top scorer in the reserves in 2004. Promoted to the first-team squad at the turn of the year he displayed no nerves and scored on his full debut, in the FA Cup against Colchester.

PL	0+5 apps	0 gls
FAC	1+2 apps	1 gl
Total	1+7 apps	1 gl

JOHNSTON, Thomas Bourhill
Centre forward

5'11" 12st 2lb
Born: Loanhead, 18 August 1927
Died: Shoalhaven (Australia), 4 September 2008
Debut: 8 March 1958

CAREER: Loanhead Bluebell; Loanhead West End; Gilmerton Drumbirds; Loanhead Mayflower May 1947; Kelso United 1947 (trial); Peebles Rovers Aug 1947; Falkirk Nov 1948 (trial); Kilmarnock Nov 1949; Darlington Apr 1951; Oldham Athletic Mar 1952; Norwich City Jun 1952 (£500); Newport County Oct 1954 (£3,000); Leyton Orient Feb 1955 (ex Burgess+cash total value £6,000); Blackburn Rovers Mar 1958 (£15,000); Leyton Orient Feb 1959 (£7,500); Gillingham Sep 1961 (£3,000); Folkestone (p-c) Jul 1962; Lytham St Annes Oct 1965-May 1966.

Brought up in Midlothian, he experienced the hardships of mining and the bandage he sported on his left wrist was a daily reminder of the pit accident that almost cost him his arm.

Determined to make his feet keep him from further underground hazards, he travelled but it was not until he came to Leyton Orient that he matured into the complete player. A total of 79 goals in 102 appearances is testament to his ability with either foot and his head, but it was his all-round play that made him a great player. He led the line in the truest sense, making all those around him function and his ability to head the ball into his teammates' paths was remarkable. When Blackburn had arrived at a point where they could see promotion they paid a large fee to bring him to Ewood and he was worth every penny, guiding the team with total professionalism and contributing 8 goals in 11 games. He was equally at home in the First Division but the club needed to look to the future and a player in his thirties did not represent this. He returned to Leyton Orient, where he simply scored 40 goals in 79 games, the complete master of his craft. After retirement he moved to Poulton le Fylde on the Lancashire coast where he opened a betting shop and was even tempted out of retirement by Lytham St Annes. He never settled to the life of a bookmaker and he emigrated to Australia to live in Dapto, New South Wales, where he coached the Lysaghts' works team. Subsequently he had a house built at Sanctuary Point, surviving bowel cancer and thirteen years later open-heart surgery.

FL	36 apps	22 gls
FAC	2 apps	1 gl
Total	38 apps	23 gls

JONES, George Alexander

Striker

5'11" 12st

Born: Chapelfield, Rochdale, 21 April 1945

Debut: 13 March 1964

CAREER: Radcliffe GS; Radcliffe Amateurs; Bury Sep 1961 (am) Jun 1962; Blackburn Rovers Mar 1964 (£30,000); Bury Nov 1966 (£18,000); Oldham Athletic Mar 1973 (£10,000); Halifax Town Feb 1976 (£3,000); Southport Jan 1977; Lancaster City 1978; Radcliffe Borough Nov 1978; Stalybridge Celtic; Prestwich Heys; Hyde United Oct 1980; Prestwich Heys (p-c) Nov 1980.

A transfer fee of £30,000 for an eighteen-year-old was unusual in 1964 but the Rovers had received a huge fee for Fred Pickering and needed a replacement. Jones had burst onto the scene with Bury and had gained a European Youth Championship medal with England a year earlier but in truth he was then performing at inside forward and the Rovers required him to lead the attack. He never obtained a regular place and two-and-a-half years later was back with Bury. Here he achieved the sought-after conversion, playing as a loan striker of such prodigious energy that he was nicknamed 'the Roadrunner'. He also scored 100 goals at the rate of one every 2.5 games. He had a spell as manager at Radcliffe but went working for British Rail, eventually being tempted into coaching again at Prestwich. His son Alex was a junior at Ewood who subsequently played in the Football League with Oldham, Stockport, Preston and Rochdale.

FL	36+3 apps	14 gls
FAC	2 apps	1 gl
FLC	1 app.	0 gls
Total	39+3 apps	15 gls

JONES, Robert William

Goalkeeper

6'1" 11st 4lb

Born: Walton, Liverpool, 28 March 1933

Died: Blackburn 27 August 1998

Debut: 15 November 1958

CAREER: Meols Cop School; 4th Southport Co. Boys' Brigade; Southport Jul 1951; Chester Aug 1953; Blackburn Rovers Mar 1958 (£1,000); Great Harwood Jul 1966 (free).

The son of a Bolton goalkeeper who had coached Southport, Jones was given his league debut at that club. It was at Chester that he established himself, an ideally built player with a good temperament and sound technique but troubled by inconsistency. When he came to the Rovers he joined a club who had been managing with only one professional goalkeeper and had been relying on Harry Leyland to play when unfit. Since Jones cost little and worked as a draughtsman he fitted the club's pocket but, exposed to the first team, he proved unreliable. Even when Fred Else was in poor form he could not oust him and after relegation in 1966 both men were released. He was player-manager at Great Harwood and later continued as manager and then trainer at the club. Remaining local, he lived in Whiteacre Lane, Barrow, but was hospitalised by a stroke from which he did not recover.

FL	49 apps	0 gls
FLC	3 apps	0 gls
Total	52 apps	0 gls

JONES, Roger
Goalkeeper

5'11" 12st 4lb
Born: Upton on Severn, 8 November 1946
Debut: 20 January 1970

CAREER; Portsmouth Aug 1963 (app.) Nov 1964; AFC Bournemouth May 1965; Blackburn Rovers Jan 1970 (£30,000); Newcastle United Mar 1976 (£20,000); Stoke City Feb 1977 (free); Derby County Jul 1980 (£25,000); Birmingham City Feb 1982 (loan); York City Aug 1982-May 1985; Loggerheads.

Forced out of Portsmouth when the club scrapped its reserve side, he proved his ability in five years at Bournemouth in which he gained England Under-23 caps. With Blacklaw and Barton struggling in the Blackburn goal, his signing brought to Ewood one of their all-time great goalkeepers, a player of supreme agility, sure hands and total confidence. An athletic player who left his line with real acceleration, he could scoop the ball up with an ease that was testimony to a man in total control of his physique. In his years at Blackburn there was never a doubt that he was the star of the team and, as such, was the first man to be sold when financial constraints threatened in 1976. Even that brought frustration. Doubts about a knee condition prompted Newcastle to add an appearances rider in the contract and when they then refused to select him the Rovers did not receive the specified fee. Although they appealed they lost the case, which was a source of contention since Jones was able to play and proved it with over 200 league appearances after he left Newcastle. After some coaching experience with York he retired to become a property developer in the Midlands, continuing to play for a parks team.

FL	242 apps	0 gls
FAC	15 apps	0 gls
FLC	15 apps	0 gls
Total	272 apps	0 gls

JOYCE, Walter
Wing Half/Full-back

5'11" 12st 10lb
Born: Oldham, 10 September 1937
Died: Liverpool, 29 September 1999
Debut: 8 February 1964

CAREER: Counthill GS; Burnley Jul 1953 (am) Oct 1954; Blackburn Rovers Feb 1964 (£12,000); Oldham Athletic Sep 1967-1969 (£7,000).

In 1964 when the Rovers were challenging for the First Division title they were aware that they had a team of sufficient skill to take the prize if they did not encounter injuries. To rectify this they signed Joyce, a wing half who had been at Burnley for ten years without being any more than a much-admired stand in for Jimmy Adamson and Brian Miller. The hardest of hard men, he was a sure tackler, diligent worker but lacked flair and mobility. The foresight was immediately proved wise; the services of Keith Newton were lost for the season, but Joyce struggled to adopt to the full-back position. When the club fell into the Second Division Joyce had a brief renaissance, being used effectively as a man marker in midfield. A player who had always used intelligence to combat deficiencies in skill, it was no surprise that he took up coaching at Oldham. He moved on to Bolton where he became assistant manager and was manager at Rochdale for three years before becoming youth coach at Preston. At the time of his death he was working with the young players at Manchester United. His son Warren played in the Football League for Burnley, Bolton and Preston and later managed Hull City.

FL	119+1 apps	4 gls
FAC	9 apps	0 gls
FLC	6 apps	0 gls
Total	134+1 apps	4 gls

KEELEY, Glen Matthew
Centre half

5'10" 12st
Born: Barking, 1 September 1954
Debut: 28 August 1976

CAREER: Ipswich Town Jul 1970 (app.) Aug 1972; Newcastle United Jul 1974 (£70,000); Blackburn Rovers Aug 1976 (£25,000); Birmingham City Aug 1982 (trial); Everton Oct 1982-Dec 1982 (loan); Oldham Athletic Aug 1987 (£15,000); Colchester United Feb 1988; Bolton Wanderers Sep 1988-Mar 1989; Chorley 1989; Clitheroe 1991; Colne Oct 2000.

As a consequence of his potential with Ipswich and the England youth team he was taken to Tyneside but failed to overcome a reputation for being accident prone. His transfer to Blackburn was unusual. Roger Jones had been transferred to Newcastle but the Rovers had been unable to extract the fee due. Intending to offset it, they signed Keeley at a time when the club already had three adequate central defenders (Hawkins, Fazackerley and Waddington) but no right-back. Unfortunately, a transfer tribunal ruled against the Rovers and the club was suspended from the market until they had paid the fee for Keeley. At least they signed a good player, a hard man who dominated in physical exchanges, at his best in crowded areas where it took courage to venture and a venomous, and occasionally inaccurate, open-field tackler. Ideally complemented by the pace and strength of Fazackerley, they formed a partnership that still ranks among the best in club history and that ought to have provided the platform for tangible achievement. The man known to the fans as 'Killer' never lacked self belief and in 1982, when he decided he deserved a better setting, he was given a trial by Everton, curtailed by his first-half dismissal. Returning to Ewood, he settled down to play the best football of his career, the highlight being when he captained the side to a final victory in the Full Members' Cup. As his career wound-up his off-field activities were varied. He had his contract cancelled so that he could go to the USA in search of a commercial pilot's license. Later he set up his own catering firm, became the licensee at The Fox & Lion in Leyland and then moved to the Woodlands Hotel on Preston New Road, Blackburn. He subsequently worked for the Lancashire FA where he met John Lister, who induced him to turn out for Colne at the age of forty-six. Needless to say reports soon bracketed him with the words 'discipline' and 'referee'. He studied for a degree in Sports Administration and later was in charge of the English Federation for Disabled Sports, coached the Lancashire FA women's team and became a community development officer in Bolton.

He also found time to be a columnist for the *Lancashire Evening Telegraph*.

FL	365+5 apps	23 gls
FAC	19+1 apps	1 gl
FLC	23 apps	0 gls
FMC	5 apps	1 gl
Total	412+6 apps	25 gls

KELLER, Marc
Midfield

5'11" 12st 4lb
Born: Bulgau, Alsace (France), 14 January 1968
Debut: 13 January 2001

CAREER: (Fessenheim); Colmar; Lycee Bartoldi (Colmar); Mulhouse 1986; Lycee Montaigne; Strasbourg 1991; Karlsruhe (Germany) 1996; West Ham United 1998 (free); Blackburn Rovers Jan 2001-May 2001.
INTERNATIONALS: France 6 apps 1 gl.

Born in the wheatfield district of Alsace in a village so tiny that he and his brothers had to go to neighbouring Fessenheim to play, he was playing organised football by the age of six. By the age of twelve he was so good that he was travelling 25kms to Colmar to play and at the age of seventeen was playing for them in the French Third Division. After obtaining 'A' levels in Mathematics and Physics he was offered a contract with Mulhouse of the Second Division, which he accepted with the proviso that he could continue his studies for an Economics degree at the Lycee Montaigne. In his five years with Mulhouse he helped them to promotion and although they were subsequently relegated he had been noticed by Strasbourg and needed no inducement to join the leading club in Alsace. Desiring improvement, he moved into the Bundesliga, but remained domiciled in his beloved Alsace. By then he had gained international caps, testimony to his intelligent link-up play on the left-hand side of midfield. As his German club lost focus he seized the opportunity presented by the Bosman ruling to come to England and join West Ham. Sometimes used as a left wing-back he found it difficult to settle into the team and was signed by the Rovers as cover for their promotion push. He was already committed to a return to Alsace and as his playing days ended he was offered the chance to become director of football at the club closest to his heart, Strasbourg.

FL	0+2 apps	0 gls
FAC	0+3 apps	0 gls
Total	0+5 apps	0 gls

KELLY, Alan Thomas
Goalkeeper

6'2" 14st 3lb
Born: Preston, 11 August 1968
Debut: 14 September 1999

CAREER: St Gregory's School; Longridge St Mary's; Fulwood Amateurs; Preston North End Aug 1985; Sheffield United Jul 1992 (£200,000); Blackburn Rovers Jul 1999-Mar 2004 (£675,000); Stockport County Apr 2001 (loan); Birmingham City Aug 2001-Oct 2001 (loan).
INTERNATIONALS: Eire 34 apps.

When the father is as renowned a goalkeeper as Alan Kelly senior his sons face a daunting task in attempting to follow in his footsteps, yet both Gary and Alan junior became goalkeepers good enough to play in the Football League. For Alan the comparisons were more obvious because he joined his father's old club, Preston North End, and it is tribute to his character that he made about 150 first-team appearances. Confident and reliable, with sound judgement, he did not follow his father into the Republic of Ireland team until he had moved to Sheffield United. At Bramall Lane he became involved in a dogfight for the goalkeeping jersey with Simon Tracey, and this eventually led him to come to Blackburn, where immediately he was involved in a similar fight with John Filan. However, to a man who almost lost his career in a motor cycle accident, mere competition was no problem and, whether in or out of favour he took a philosophical attitude. When Brad Friedel arrived and reduced both Filan and Kelly to the prospect of a permanent place on the bench, Kelly stayed and extended his contract until the summer of 2004. However, during the season he suffered a career-ending injury when his finger caught in the turf and left him with a permanently damaged hand.

L	39+1 apps	0 gls
FAC	4 apps	0 gls
FLC	6 apps	0 gls
Total	49+1 apps	0 gls

KELLY, William Muir
Centre half

5'9.5" 10st 11lb
Born: Hill of Beath, 14 September 1922
Died: Darwen, 11 July 1996
Debut: 14 September 1951

CAREER: Airdrieonians; Blackburn Rovers Sep 1951; Mossley Jul 1957 (free); Accrington Stanley Sep 1957-Jul 1958: Darwen.

The small Scottish town of Hill of Beath obviously furnished some pretty substantial citizens. In the Football League there were Willie Cunningham of Preston and the Kelly brothers (Willie at Blackburn and Walter at Bury, Doncaster, Stockport and Chester). They were all stocky, square-shouldered men with faces that might have been chiselled from granite, using only straight lines. Willie was twenty-nine when he came to Ewood and a lifetime in Scottish football hardly appeared likely to have prepared him for what was to come. He met the challenge with never a false step, consistent from day one, indestructable, playing week after week, scorning injuries that prevented others playing. He was nicknamed 'Iron Man' by his colleagues and, even as age advanced, never short-changed the side. Intending to retire, he found a new challenge at Accrington but, because he had started work and the old Third Division (North) had been abolished, he retired rather than ask for time off. He lived the rest of his life in Darwen, working for fourteen years at the Lower Darwen Paper Mill. He also played for Darwen and had a spell as player rmanager.

FL	186 apps	1 gl
FAC	16 apps	0 gls
Total	202 apps	1 gl

KENDALL, Howard
Midfield

5'7" 10st 13lb
Born: Ryton on Tyne, 22 May 1946
Debut: 11 August 1979

CAREER: Preston North End Jun 1961 (app.) May 1963; Everton Mar 1967 (£80,000); Birmingham City Feb 1974 (£350,000); Stoke City Aug 1979 (£40,000); Blackburn Rovers (p-m) Jul 1979-May 1981; Everton Aug 1981 (non con).

An apprentice with Preston, he received a shock call-up to the 1964 FA Cup final when Ian Davidson was disciplined. This made him the youngest player to appear in a final and he developed into a classical wing half. A transfer was inevitable and he joined Everton where he formed, with Alan Ball and Colin Harvey, a midfield that took the club to the championship. An inspiring figure, he was deceptively efficient at imposing himself physically and had strength and energy. As he moved down the soccer ladder he commenced coaching and his potential at Stoke was recognised when the Rovers made him their player-manager. In his two seasons at Ewood he became statistically the Rovers' most successful manager of all time, taking the club into the Second Division and being prevented by goal average from progressing straight to the First Division. As part of a midfield with Parkes and Speight he helped form a defensive shield that rewrote defensive records. Inevitably he attracted attention and a move to his old club, Everton, was too good to miss. Guiding the club to the championship, FA Cup and European Cup Winners' Cup enhanced his reputation but a surprise move to Athletico Bilbao ended in failure. After that he lost the Midas touch and spells at Manchester City, two further returns to Everton, Notts County and Sheffield United as well as periods abroad with the Greek sides Xanthi and Ethnikos, brought him no further honours.

FL	79 apps	6 gls
FAC	6 apps	0 gls
FLC	7 apps	1 gl
Total	92 apps	7 gls

KENNA, Jeffrey Jude
Full-back

5'11" 11st 7lb
Born: Dublin, 27 August 1970
Debut: 18 March 1995

CAREER: St Lorcan's; Palmerston Rangers 1981; Southampton Jun 1987 (trainee) Apr 1989; Blackburn Rovers Mar 1995 £1,500,000); Tranmere Rovers Mar 2001-May 2001 (loan); Wigan Athletic Dec 2001-Jan 2002 (loan); Birmingham City Jan 2002 (free); Derby County Mar 2004 (free).
INTERNATIONALS: Eire 27 apps.

The grandson of an Irish international and son of an Irish international snooker player, Kenna's cousin Pat Scully was an apprentice at Arsenal and also went on to win an international cap. His brother Warren played in a FA Youth Cup semi-final for Peterborough and another, Colin, was ranked second-best professional heavyweight boxer in Ireland. Discovered playing for Palmerston Rangers' Under-12 side in a tournament in Southampton he was invited back for regular tuition and eventually signed schoolboy terms. Although he had a reputation for versatility he was primarily a right-back, which made it a surprise when he was a late addition to Blackburn's Premiership challenging team, which had lost left winger Jason Wilcox. In the nine games remaining that ended with the Premiership triumph he was used in both full-back positions and on both flanks, and was awarded a special medal even though he had not the requisite number of appearances. He later proved a steady right-back, able to clear under pressure and from odd angles and a dependable tackler who knew how to drift across and cover the centre. He was not comfortable on the left flank but, restored to right-back, he became an integral part of the club until in 1999 he developed Achilles tendon problems. Two operations eventually resolved these injury problems but by then he had lost his place and was allowed to join Birmingham, who he captained to victory in the 2002 promotion play-offs.

L	154+2 apps	1 gl
FAC	12 apps	0 gls
FLC	17+2 apps	0 gls
EC	5 apps	0 gls
UEFA	1 app.	0 gls
CS	1 app.	0 gls
Total	190+4 apps	1 gl

KENNEDY, Andrew John
Striker

6'1" 11st 10lb
Born: Stirling, 8 October 1964
Debut: 5 October 1988

CAREER: Sauchie Athletic; Glasgow Rangers; Seiko FC (Hong Kong) (loan); Birmingham City Mar 1985 £50,000); Sheffield United Mar 1987 (loan);

Blackburn Rovers Jun 1988 (£50,000); Watford Aug 1990 (ex Richardson); Bolton Wanderers Oct 1991 (loan); Brighton & HA; Sep 1992 (£40,000); Gillingham Sep 1994; (Hong Kong); Portadown (Northern Ireland) Jan 1995-May 1995; Witton Albion Nov 1995; Hastings Town; Hendon Mar 1996.

A free spirit, known among teammates as 'Mad Dog Kennedy', and whose reputation soared in masculine quarters when it was found that he was dating page three girl Maria Whitaker, he first came south from Rangers to Birmingham. An ideally built striker with balance and fluidity, he used above-average athletic ability to make him a presence with the aerial ball. His career became undermined by his lack of application and a series of muscle injuries that gave his appearances a staccato feel. At Blackburn he flattered to deceive, always on the point of establishing himself until removed from the line-up by a further injury. At the end of his career he played wherever he was offered an opening, at the same time being in partnership in an insurance agency with his old teammate Steve Foster.

FL	49+10 apps	23 gls
FAC	3 apps	1 gl
FLC	4 apps	0 gls
FMC	3 apps	2 gls
PO	1+1 app.	1 gl
Total	60+11 apps	27 gls

KENNEDY, Patrick Anthony
Left back

5'11" 12st
Born: Dublin, 9 October 1934
Died: Trafford, 8 March 2007
Debut: 18 September 1957

CAREER: Johnville; Manchester United Feb 1953; Blackburn Rovers Aug 1956; Southampton Jul 1958; Oldham Athletic Jul 1960.

The captain of the United team that won the inaugural FA Youth Cup, his development at Old Trafford was hampered by the presence of Roger Byrne. It was therefore puzzling why he should elect to join a club who had Bill Eckersley standing in his way, but no doubt the presence of Johnny Carey was the deciding factor. A season in the reserves established him as a steady player, sound in the tackle and without frills. Three games as Eckersley's deputy confirmed the promise but after the last he required surgery. By then Whelan and Bray had emerged to challenge Taylor and Eckersley and his spell at the club came to an end.

FL	3 apps	0 gls
Total	3 apps	0 gls

KENYON, John Francis
Striker

5'8.5" 11st 1lb
Born: Blackburn, 2 December 1953
Debut: 31 March 1973

CAREER: Emmanuel School; Witton Park School; Great Harwood; Blackburn Rovers Dec 1972 (£3,000); Wigan Athletic; Great Harwood; Runcorn; Darwen Jan 1980; Great Harwood; Feniscowles.

Few men make the transition from star player at a local non-league club to their local league side but Kenyon managed it better than most. The reason was that he was prepared to toil physically, run hard and had the eye for the half chance. Limitations in technique restricted him to use as a substitute but he was much in demand in this position because he could change the course of a game. After he left for Wigan he had a marvellous spell with Runcorn and attracted attention from larger clubs, but he refused a move to Scarborough so that he could remain in the locality.

FL	32+14 apps	7 gls
Total	32+14 apps	7 gls

KERR, James Peter

Inside forward

5'9" 11st
Born: Glasgow, 2 September 1949
Debut: 12 September 1970

CAREER: Bury Aug 1966; Blackburn Rovers May 1970 (£60,000); Highlands Park (South Africa) Mar 1972; Coventry City (reserves).

A red-haired midfield player of immense athleticism who covered acres of ground but had vision and touch, he was brought to Ewood by Eddie Quigley, the man who had discovered him for Bury. Quigley believed that he had signed a future superstar and probably he had if fate, in the form of a cruciate ligament injury, had not intervened. His career ended after 11 games, just as he had been selected for the Scottish Under-21s. After taking his insurance compensation he went to South Africa and by hard work managed to play again. Returning, he was appointed youth team manager at Coventry, came back to fitness with the reserve side but was prevented from returning to first-team football because of the insurance compensation he had received.

FL	11 apps	0 gls
Total	11 apps	0 gls

KHIZANISHVILI, Zurab

Central defender

6'1" 12st 8lb
Born: Tblisi (Georgia), 6 October 1981
Debut: 11 September 2005

CAREER: Dinamo Tblisi; FC Tblisi 1999; Lokomotiv Tblisi 1999; Arsenal (trial) 2000; Fulham (trial); West Ham United (trial); Dundee Mar 2001 (free); Glasgow Rangers Jul 2003 (free); Blackburn Rovers Aug 2005 (loan).
INTERNATIONALS: Georgia 36 apps.

Khizanishvili had attracted such attention playing junior football in Georgia that he made his international debut when he was four months from his eighteenth birthday and had made only 2 first-team appearances with Tblisi. He found that it was easier to get into the national side than his club side and moved to Second Division FC Tblisi, but had played only 9 games when he was signed by Lokomotiv. Although he still struggled to play in the first team, the international team continued to select him and his agent, Athole Still, obtained him trials with several Premiership clubs. However, his club demanded such a great transfer fee that FIFA eventually declared his contract void. This left him free to find a British club and he opted for Dundee where his international colleague, Georgi Nemsadze, was a star player. Despite a delayed start because of knee surgery, he emerged as one of the best defenders in Scotland; cool, efficient and competent in all areas. A move to Ibrox Park followed, where he took over from Amoruso, but initial contentment with his performances faded and he found himself out of the first team and looking for a new club in the summer transfer window. Several prospective moves fell down but on the eve of the deadline he signed a year-long loan move to join the Rovers with an agreement for a permanent deal if he proved satisfactory. He settled smoothly into the heart of the Rovers' defence and has been a revelation since his debut at Bolton.

PL	13+1 apps	
FLC	3 apps	1 gl
Total	16+1 apps	1 gl

KNIGHTON, Kenneth

Wing half

5'9" 11st
Born: Barnsley, 20 February 1944
Debut: 9 August 1969

CAREER: Wath Wanderers; Wolverhampton Wanderers Aug 1960 (app.) Feb 1961; Oldham Athletic Nov 1966 (£12,000); Preston North End

Nov 1967 (£35,000); Blackburn Rovers Jun 1969 (£45,000); Hull City Mar 1971 (£60,000); Sheffield Wednesday Aug 1973-Jan 1976 (£50,000).

A swashbuckling, blond-haired left-sided midfield player, he became an instantaneous idol of the crowd when he came from Preston. An aggressive player, he tackled with bone-rattling ferocity, particularly if given the opportunity to throw himself into the slide tackle. He ran hard and straight and shot with explosive power from a distance. An inspirational captain, he was far less effective in his own half and marking was never his forte. He had become a star at Deepdale and his two years at Ewood only added to his reputation. So much so, that it was no surprise when a large offer for his services was tendered and accepted. His departure had a profound effect on the club's inability to avoid relegation the same season. After coaching with Sheffield Wednesday he took a similar role at Sunderland and was promoted to manager. There and at Orient his disciplinary approach was not appreciated by the players and he was soured by the time he left the game. However, he was not long away before he was in charge again, this time at Dagenham.

FL	70 apps	11 gls
FAC	2 apps	0 gls
FLC	4 apps	1 gl
Total	76 apps	12 gls

KONDE, Oumar

Midfield

6'1" 12st 8lb
Born: Binningen (Switzerland), 19 August 1979
Debut: 14 February 1999

CAREER: SC Binningen, FC Basel 1994; Blackburn Rovers Oct 1998 (£500,000); SC Freiburg (Germany) Jun 1999 (£400,000); Hansa Rostock (Germany) Jun 2005, Hibernian Dec 2005 (trial).

The dreadlocked Swiss midfield man was first spotted by the Rovers' chief scout, John Seasman, when he was working for Tottenham and was signed by Roy Hodgson as an investment for the future. The son of a father from Guinea and a Frenchwoman he was born just over the border from France but, with a French passport, did not have to seek a work permit. He had made his first-team debut in the Swiss First Division at the age of sixteen, playing at centre-back, but was moved to a holding role in midfield. With his contract about to expire Basel thought it wise to cash-in on his potential. Konde spoke only German and French, which was not a problem when the multi-lingual Roy Hodgson was in charge, but when Brian Kidd took over he became isolated. His only first-team appearance was as a substitute in the cup at Newcastle and beyond one crunching tackle he was little visible. His position was further jeapordised when he was spotted drinking in a Preston nightclub with Kevin Davies, two days before a vital game. The following month he was transferred to a German side. His career has subsequently proved curious. Converted back to central defender he was selected in the Swiss squad for a full international against Poland but informed the selectors that he was not ready for international football.

FAC	0+1 app.	0 gls
Total	0+1 app.	0 gls

KOPEL, Frank

Left-back

5'8" 10st 12lb
Born: Falkirk, 28 March 1949
Debut: 22 March 1969

CAREER: Graeme High School (Falkirk); Manchester United Apr 1966; Blackburn Rovers Mar 1969 (£25,000); Dundee United Jan 1972 (free); Arbroath Feb 1982; Dundee United Dec 1983-1984.

The arrival of Kopel portended a familiar scenario for Rovers' fans; a cheap replacement was being signed for a star (Keith Newton) who was about to depart. There was obvious attractions to the move. Kopel had been raised at Old Trafford, had some first-team experience and had even played in Europe. He was, though, clearly not a right-back and struggled with the positional play there, but was happy on the other flank (where he was not good enough to displace Billy Wilson). His part-time accountancy studies appeared to be a wise investment and when the club dropped to the Third Division he was allowed to leave. This proved the best move of his career. He joined Dundee United, played nearly 300 games for them including their great days in Europe, and received sufficient knowledge to make the subsequent switch to coaching with Arbroath. He later set up his own business, acted as sales executive for Tay Radio and then became assistant manager at Forfar. His son Scott followed him into the Dundee United first team and Kopel still enjoys near-legendary status in the town.

FL	23+2 apps	0 gls
Total	23+2 apps	0 gls

KUQI, Shefki
Striker

6'2" 13st 10lb
Born: Vushtrri/Vucitrn (Kosovo), 10 November 1979
Debut: 13 August 2005

CAREER: Trepqa; Mikkelin Kissat (Finland); MP Mikkeliu (Finland); HJK Helsinki (Finland); FC Jokerit (Finland); Stockport County Jan 2001 (£300,000); Sheffield Wednesday Jan 2002 (£700,000); Ipswich Town Sep 2003 (free); Blackburn Rovers Jun 2005 (free).
INTERNATIONALS: Finland 42 apps 5 gls.

An ethnic Albanian, born in a war-torn and polluted area of Kosovo, he fled to Finland with his family when he was twelve years old with only the clothes they were wearing. Fortunately, an aunt had already moved to Mikkeli and the family was able to settle, and Shefki continued a footballing career that had commenced with Trepqa. An English-type striker, strong, committed and full of running, he progressed rapidly and a move to Jokerit saw him become top scorer in the Finnish League. Stockport took a chance on his potential but before the end of his first year in England the Rovers agreed a fee, subject to a week's trial at Brockhall. This was eventually truncated to a couple of days and, after a disagreement with the Stockport manager Carlton Palmer, Kuqi was sent back to Stockport. This soured his relationship with the club and he moved on, only playing to his true potential in his last season at Ipswich, when he scored 19 Championship goals. The failure of his club in the play-offs and the end of his contract allowed him to seek opportunities elsewhere and he joined the Rovers in the summer. Despite his failure to score prolifically, he had proved a popular player whose effort is always well appreciated. He also brought with him his trademark goal celebration, a flying dive, which has not yet been much seen.

PL	10+8 apps	5 gls
FLC	2+2 apps	1 gl
Total	12+10 apps	6 gls

LANGTON, Robert
Left winger

5'9.5" 11st 6lb
Born: Burscough, 8 September 1918
Died: Ormskirk, 16 January 1996
Debut: 10 September 1938

CAREER: St John's School; Burscough Victoria; Blackburn Rovers Sep 1937 (am) Nov 1937 (£50); Cooperage (Bombay); Glentoran (NI); Preston North

End Aug 1948 (£16,000); Bolton Wanderers Nov 1949 (£20,000); Blackburn Rovers Sep 1953-May 1956 (£2,000); Ards (NI) Jul 1956; Wisbech Town Jul 1957; Kidderminster Harriers 1959; Wisbech Town Sep 1959-Nov 1959; Colwyn Bay Oct 1960.
INTERNATIONALS: England 11 apps 1 gl.

When Billy Guest and his deputy Harry McShane were both injured the Rovers introduced twenty-year-old Bobby Langton, who had played for one season in the reserves. He was an instant success, a strong runner with an accurate cross and a variation in his play where he would cut in and shoot with power. Capable in the air, he would ghost in to reach right-wing crosses. The right winger, Billy Rogers, had a similar style and the pair contributed to the club's promotion in Langton's first season. The Second World War then intervened but on the bone-hard pitches in India Langton became a household name among the expatriate community. His next posting was to Northern Ireland, where he assisted Glentoran, and was also selected for the Irish League. By now a complete player, he became embroiled in a dispute with Blackburn about the nature of his club house. Coincidentally, the club had been relegated and after a long drawn-out dispute he was transferred to Preston, although the move was not a good one for either party. At Bolton he was in his element, crossing for Nat Lofthouse and taking part in the epic Matthews cup final, but soon after he was back in the blue and white, filling a position where he had never been replaced. He had three good seasons at Ewood and, even though he had always retained a poultry farm in Burscough, he wandered for a while before setting up as a plumber. Jesse Pye offered him a coaching role at Wisbech with a position as a pub landlord, and he moved to King's Lynn before settling once again in Burscough.

FL	212 apps	57 gls
FAC	18 apps	1 gl
Total	230 apps	58 gls

LAWTHER, William Ian*
Striker

5'10" 11st 9lb
Born: Belfast 20 October 1939
Died: Swindon, 25 April 2010
Debut: 19 August 1961

CAREER: Crusaders; Sunderland Mar 1958; Blackburn Rovers Jul 1961 (£17,000); Scunthorpe United Jul 1963 (£12,000); Brentford Nov 1964 (£17,000); Halifax Town Aug 1968 (£3,000); Stockport County Jul 1971; Bangor City; Great Harwood 1976.
INTERNATIONALS: Northern Ireland 4 apps.

To buy one Irishman to replace another under-performing Irishman might have been a gamble but Lawther was the complete antithesis of the mercurial, temperamental Derek Dougan. A thickset, hard-working player, capable of scoring with both head and feet, his period at Ewood was complicated by being switched from centre forward to inside forward on a regular basis. Although overshadowed by the precocious talents of Fred Pickering and John Byrom, he was always honest and reliable, if somewhat uninspired. In all he played nearly 600 league games, testimony to the fact that there was always a club who could use his qualities. Retiring, he opened a tailor's shop with his old Halifax teammate Alex Smith.

FL	59 apps	21 gls
FAC	5 apps	1 gl
FLC	11 apps	10 gls
Total	75 apps	32 gls

LEAVER, Derek
Inside forward

5'7" 10st 2lb
Born: Blackburn, 13 November 1930
Debut: 18 November 1950

CAREER: St Peter's School; Bangor St Boys; Burnley; Blackburn Rovers May 1949; Bournemouth &

Boscombe Athletic Jul 1955 (£500); Crewe Alexandra Mar 1956; Macclesfield Jul 1957; Mossley; Darwen; Wigan Athletic.

One of the finest young players to emerge from Blackburn schoolboy football after the Second World War, Leaver, with Bryan Douglas and Harry Parker, were the players groomed as the club tried to construct a youth policy. He played for the National Association of Boys' Clubs but his football was restricted to the reserves by the likes of Eddie Crossan and Eddie Quigley. Although not a consistent goalscorer, he had a knack of being in the right place although his last first-team goal was a painful affair because he broke his nose in scoring. It was to be his last game because he was released and joined Bournemouth. He next appeared at Ewood in the 1959 Lancashire Junior Cup final when his team, Wigan, lost to arch-rivals Chorley. A nephew of the Rovers' full-back Walter Crook, he played cricket for Blackburn Northern and took over the family bakery on Bolton Road.

FL	14 apps	5 gls
Total	14 apps	5 gls

LEE, Richard Anthony
Goalkeeper

6'0" 12st 8lb
Born: Oxford, 5 October 1982

CAREER: Watford Mar 2000; Blackburn Rovers Aug 2005 (loan).

Lee's chances of consolidating a career in the Watford first team have twice been terminated by injury, but it was anticipated that he would start the 2005 season in the first-team jersey. However, Manchester United bought Ben Foster from Stoke and loaned him to Watford, and Lee elected to come to Ewood on a year's loan with a view to a permanent transfer. So far he has been nominated as substitute for the first team on one occasion but has kept goal regularly for the reserve side.

LE SAUX, Graeme Pierre
Left-back

5'10" 11st 12lb
Born: Harrow, 17 October 1968
Debut: 3 April 1993

CAREER: Hautlieu School; d'Hautree School; St Paul's (Jersey); Chelsea Dec 1988; Blackburn Rovers Mar 1993 (ex Livingstone); Chelsea Aug 1997 (£5,000,000); Southampton Jul 2003 (PE for Bridge) Jun 2005.
INTERNATIONALS: England 35 apps 1 gl.

Although born in Harrow Le Saux spent most of his life in Jersey. A product of the Chelsea youth scheme, his career had reached a cul de sac as he spent his time shuttling between every left-sided position. When he joined the Rovers he came to a side who had lost their left-back, Alan Wright, to injury and so his destiny was mapped out. Nothing in his previous career had prepared anybody for the improvement he made when he specialised. Confident on the ball and happy to run at opponents from deep and cross with accuracy, he also matured into a competent defender, quick to read play and smother moves on the edge of the box, tigerish in the tackle and a natural competitor. His call up to the national side made him the first Channel Islander ever to play for England and when the Rovers won the Premiership a long, successful partnership appeared in prospect. The remainder of 1995 proved to be traumatic. He fought with his teammate David Batty on the pitch in Moscow during an ill-fated European Cup campaign. An horrific fracture and dislocation of the ankle required seven pins inserted in surgery and although he rehabilitated his heart never appeared to be back with the club. His return to Chelsea was financially profitable and he confirmed his reputation as one of the most able left-backs in the Premiership, despite an increasing reputation for violence and petulance that won him few friends outside his club. When Chelsea received their influx of Russian money Le Saux was one of the casualties, being used as trading bait when Chelsea acquired the services of Wayne Bridge.

PL	127+2 apps	7 gls
FAC	8 apps	0 gls
FLC	10 apps	0 gls
UEFA	2 apps	0 gls
EC	2+1 apps	0 gls
CS	2 apps	0 gls
Total	151+3 apps	7 gls

LEWIS, Frederick John 'Jack'

Striker

5'9" 10st 9lb
Born: Long Eaton, 22 March 1948
Debut: 24 August 1977

CAREER: Long Eaton United; Lincoln City Mar 1967; Grimsby Town Jan 1970 (£3,000); Blackburn Rovers Aug 1977 (£18,000); Doncaster Rovers Aug 1978-Jul 1980; Scarborough.

A transfer target for Jim Smith for some time, Lewis had the versatility and mobility that Smith admired. Fast, with sharp reactions and quick touches, he was most at home on the right-hand side and lacked presence when called upon to act as a central striker. In his one season at the club he seldom performed to the standard that had made him such a long servant at Grimsby and was most effective when he came off the bench. Due to his ancestry he was able to collect a Welsh Under-23 cap.

FL	24+4 apps	6 gls
FLC	2 apps	0 gls
Total	26+6 apps	6 gls

LEYLAND, Harry Kenneth

Goalkeeper

5'10.5" 13st 2lb
Born: Liverpool, 12 May 1930
Died: Meols, 7 December 2006
Debut: 20 August 1956

CAREER: Everton Aug 1950; Tonbridge Jul 1956-Aug 1956; Blackburn Rovers Aug 1956 (£600); Tranmere Rovers Mar 1961-1966; Wigan Athletic (p-m) 1966; Northwich Victoria Sept 1968..

Starting locally with Everton, he never received more than the occasional game as Bert Dunlop's deputy and was unable to find a league club when given a free transfer after six years with the club. He signed for Tonbridge but was brought to Ewood before he had played a competitive game because the Rovers had released Reg Elvy and, apart from Jack Patterson, had no other goalkeeper. A minor injury on the opening day caused Patterson to miss the next game and although Leyland was not entirely convincing he held the jersey. His morale received a real boost when his colleague from Everton reserves, Matt Woods, arrived to take control of the Rovers' defence. Woods was a magnificent player and Leyland improved markedly for his presence. Short and chunky, he was deceptively agile but inconsistent. He was, however, without peer when facing a one-on-one with an opponent, with a technique of going down at the feet that was text book. A man of great humour, he was popular with away fans, so much so that some youngsters in London named their team after him. He was an active PFA representative who later became their chairman. Although his goalkeeping was erratic he is fondly remembered for much brilliance, his semi-final display against Sheffield Wednesday in 1960 being remarkable. He did not enjoy a managerial spell at Wigan and later could not resist an appeal to make a solitary appearance at Northwich. Back in Liverpool he worked as a market trader and then built up a sports and leisure business. When retired he lived in Meols where he became chairman of New Brighton RUFC.

FL	166 apps	0 gls
FAC	18 apps	0 gls
FLC	4 apps	0 gls
Total	188 apps	0 gls

LIVINGSTONE, Stephen Carl

Striker

6'1" 12st 7lb
Born: Middlesbrough, 8 September 1969
Debut: 19 January 1991

CAREER: Coventry City Aug 1985 (trainee) Jul 1986; Blackburn Rovers Jan 1991 (£450,000); Chelsea Mar 1993 (ex Le Saux); Port Vale Aug 1993 (loan); Grimsby Town Nov 1993 (loan) Jan 1994 (£120,000); Carlisle United Aug 2003-Jan 2004.

Having gained a reputation as a goal-scorer at every level he ever played at, his transfer to Blackburn (with teammate Tony Dobson) was the first large-money gamble the Rovers had made for some years. A physical threat, particularly in the air, he was slow off the mark and had games when he failed to influence proceedings. By comparison Dobson had settled well and, when the new manager Kenny Dalglish omitted Livingstone from his squad, the end was in sight. The exchange with Chelsea for Le Saux did not work out and he eventually found ten years of employment at Grimsby, his goal-scoring record being restricted by his conversion to centre-back and also an unhappy run of serious injuries. He finished his career at Carlisle, a club his father Joe had played for.

L	25+5 apps	10 gls
FAC	1 app.	1 gl
FLC	2 apps	0 gls
Total	28+5 apps	11 gls

LORD, Frank

Striker

6'0" 12st 11lb
Born: Oldham, 13 March 1936
Died: Cape Town (South Africa), 17 June 2005
Debut: 3 December 1966

CAREER: Chadderton Sec Mod; Royton Amateurs; Rochdale Oct 1953; Crewe Alexandra Jul 1961 (£3,500); Plymouth Argyle Nov 1963 (£18,000); Stockport County Feb 1966 (£7,000); Blackburn Rovers Dec 1966 (£20,000); Chesterfield Aug 1967; Plymouth Argyle Oct 1967 (£4,000).

Born in Chadderton, the son of a wallpaper executive, he joined Rochdale at the age of sixteen. Harry Catterick converted him from centre half to centre forward and he made his league debut shortly after his seventeenth birthday. A broken leg, broken cheekbone and national service in the Royal Tank Corps limited his football and within forty-eight hours of his demob he broke the leg again. On his return he started to earn respect as a rampaging, fearless player who scored goals because of his physical presence. A move to Crewe confirmed this, although he was hindered when he broke the other leg. Eddie Quigley knew him well from his time at Stockport and paid a considerable sum for a thirty-year-old when he signed him for Blackburn. This saw him enter the least-productive spell of his career and it appeared that age was starting to restrict his power. He qualified as a coach with the FA and found immediate employment and success with Cape Town City in South Africa. He returned to work with Manchester City, Stoke City, Preston and Crystal Palace but the lure of South Africa was strong and he guided Cape Town to a double triumph. Buying a health studio and squash courts, he resolved to settle in South Africa but soon was wandering again with three years at Hereford and a spell coaching Penang State in Malaysia. A brief spell as the Rovers' chief scout followed and he returned to coach the Western

Province of South Africa. In 1995 his old Crewe teammate Dave Whelan tempted him to Wigan as caretaker manager but South Africa remained in his heart and he next turned up as coach to Cape Town Spurs.

FL	10 apps	1 gl
Total	10 apps	1 gl

LOWEY, John Anthony
Striker/Midfield

5'11" 12st 7lb
Born: Manchester, 7 March 1958
Debut: 29 November 1980

CAREER: Manchester United Jul 1974 (app.) Mar 1975; Chicago Sting (USA) Apr 1976; Port Vale Jul 1977; Blackburn Rovers Sep 1977 (non con); Port Vale Oct 1977; California Surf (USA); Sheffield Wednesday Oct 1978; Blackburn Rovers Nov 1980 (£25,000); Wigan Athletic Jul 1986 (free); Chesterfield Nov 1986 (loan); York City Mar 1987 (loan); Preston North End Aug 1987 (free); Chester City Mar 1988 (loan); Blacktown City (Australia) 1989; Brisbane Lions (Australia).

Lowey initially came to the club as a triallist in the reserves, where he instantly struck up an understanding with the mercurial Bobby Svarc that appeared likely to benefit both men. Unfortunately injury ended Svarc's career and the Rovers decided that they did not urgently require a bustling, brave striker who himself was recuperating from an ankle injury. Recruited by Sheffield Wednesday after exile in the USA it was still a measure of Howard Kendall's desperation that he paid so much money for a still-raw talent. This looked to have misfired when he scored few goals and displayed a gauche touch, but his battling qualities could never be faulted. A new manager, Bobby Saxton, saw qualities in him that no-one else could perceive and converted him to a left-sided midfield man. He forsook the physical to become a player who read angles, cutting off rather than winning in the tackle and, being acutely aware of his limited capacity on the ball, he became an exponent of the instant pass. He also was the finest corner taker the club has ever had, able to place the ball with impossible accuracy from the right corner flag. This brought a harvest of goals from the centre-backs, Fazackerley and Keeley, and gave the club an extra weapon. When he finally left he roamed around before going to Australia, where he still lives, to play for Brisbane Lions.

FL	136+5 apps	14 gls
FAC	6 apps	1 gl
FLC	9 apps	1 gl
Total	151+5 apps	16 gls

MAHON, Alan Joseph
Midfield

5'10" 11st 5lb
Born: Rialto, Dublin, 4 April 1978
Debut: 17 December 2000

CAREER: Crumlin; Tranmere Rovers Apr 1995; Sporting Lisbon (Portugal) Jun 2000 (free); Blackburn Rovers Dec 2000 (loan) Jun 2000 (£1,500,000); Cardiff City Jan 2003-May 2003 (loan); Ipswich Town Sep 2003-Dec 2003 (loan); Wigan Athletic Feb 2004 (£500,000).
INTERNATIONALS: Eire 1 app.

Although recruited by Chelsea, Leeds and West Ham, the young Dublin-born player demonstrated his maturity by electing to join Tranmere, a club within ferry distance of his home city and where he reasoned his chances would be greater. A left-sided player with good energy levels and fine control, he lacked only consistency and power but with Tranmere made a reputation for himself. Declining to sign a new contract he became one of the first players to take advantage of the Bosman ruling and left for Sporting Lisbon with another Irishman, Phil

Babb. Portugal was not paved with gold and Mahon had experienced only four minutes' play in the league when his agent negotiated him a contract to come on loan to Blackburn, where he was required to understudy Damien Duff. His opportunities at Ewood were limited and it was made known that he was surplus to requirements when he was loaned out to Cardiff for the second half of the 2002/03 season. Ipswich furthered his loan experience at the start of the 2003/04 season but their financial position precluded a permanent transfer and he joined Wigan, where he has enjoyed two glorious seasons.

L	25+ 11 apps	1 gl
FAC	10 apps	0 gls
FLC	3+3 apps	0 gls
UEFA	0+1 app.	0 gls
Total	38+15 apps	1 gl

MAIL, David
Centre-back

5'10" 11st 11lb
Born: Bristol, 12 September 1962
Debut: 25 September 1982

CAREER: Aston Villa Jul 1979 (app.) Jul 1980; Blackburn Rovers Jan 1982 (free); Hull City Aug 1990 (£160,000); Mansfield Town Mar 1995 (trial); Brigg Town 1995.

After playing in the FA Youth Cup-winning side with Aston Villa he made little progress and came to Ewood on a free transfer to understudy one of the finest pairings the club has fielded (Keeley and Fazackerley). Given immediate opportunity because of Keeley's disenchantment he slotted in well, although ultimately it was Fazackerley he displaced. Quick off the mark, able to read the player alongside him and brave in the tackle, he suffered only from lack of height, a limited heading technique and a wildness in distributing the ball. A vital component of the Full Members' Cup victory, he gelled effectively with Hendry when Keeley departed. The tragic loss of his wife at a young age created a trauma in his life and the chance for a move to Hull helped him cope with his situation. He ended his playing days with Brigg Town from Lincolnshire and appeared as substitute in the FA Vase final against Clitheroe when he replaced his brother-in-law, Neil Buckley. He later worked as a long-distance lorry driver.

FL	200+6 apps	4 gls
FAC	12 apps	0 gls
FLC	12+1 apps	0 gls
FMC	9 apps	0 gls
PO	8 apps	0 gls
Total	241+7 apps	4 gls

MAKEL, Lee Robert
Midfield

5'10" 10st
Born: Sunderland, 11 January 1973
Debut: 28 October 1992

CAREER: Springwell Jnrs; Hilda Park Jnrs; Newcastle United Feb 1987 (sch) Jun 1989 (trainee) Feb 1991; Blackburn Rovers Jul 1992 (£175,000); Huddersfield Town Oct 1995 (£300,000); Heart of Midlothian Mar 1998 (£75,000); Portsmouth Dec 1999 (loan); Bradford City Sep 2001-Dec 2001; Livingston Dec 2001; Plymouth Argyle May 2004 (free); Dunfermline Athletic Jan 2005 (free).

Tipped as the next Paul Gascoigne, Makel was a Dalglish signing intended to be groomed slowly. Sparingly used, he proved to be a neat player without great power or presence and in three years at Ewood left no lasting impression. A move to Huddersfield proved that he was an embryonic playmaker but his lack of strength remained and it was not until he moved back to the Scottish League with Livingston that he blossomed, inspiring the club to an improbable League Cup final victory. His brother Gavin was an actor on the cult TV drama Byker Grove.

PL	1+5 apps	0 gls
FLC	0+3 apps	0 gls
UEFA	0+1 app.	0 gls
EC	1+1 app.	0 gls
CS	0+1 app.	0 gls
Total	2+11 apps	0 gls

MARCOLIN, Dario
Midfield

5'11" 11st 9lb
Born: Brescia (Italy), 29 October 1971
Debut: 7 November 1998

CAREER: Cremonese US; Lazio SS 1992; Cagliari Calcio Nov 1993; Genoa 1893 1994; Lazio SS 1995; Blackburn Rovers Oct 1998-May 1999 (loan); Sampdoria UC Jul 2000; Piacenza Jun 2002 (£650,000); SSC Napoli Jan 2003 (loan); Aug 2003-Jun 2004; Germinal Beerschot (Belgium) Sep 2004 (trial); Palazzolo Oct 2004.

His 28 appearances at Under-21 level were a record for Italy at this age group. Several of these were as the over-aged captain and the Italian coach, Cesare Maldini, appeared to be grooming him for the future. Despite moving back to Lazio, where he gained a regular place, he never progressed and the arrival as coach of Sven-Goran Eriksson and the investment of £70 million in new players reduced his chances. As a consequence Roy Hodgson was able to persuade his old friend Eriksson to let the player move to Ewood in return for a loan fee of £100,000. A left-sided midfield player, easy on the ball but not dominant, he was not a favourite of the new manager, Brian Kidd, who informed him that he would not exercise the option to purchase him at the end of the season. He returned to Italy but had the misfortune to play with a Napoli side that went into bankruptcy.

PL	5+5 apps	1 gl
FAC	3 apps	0 gls
FLC	2 apps	0 gls
Total	10+5 apps	1 gl

MARKER, Nicholas Robert Thomas
Centre-back

6'0" 12st 11lb
Born: Budleigh Salterton, 3 May 1965
Debut: 26 September 1992

CAREER: Exmouth Comprehensive School; Budleigh Salterton; Exeter City Jul 1981 (app.) May 1983; Plymouth Argyle Nov 1987 (£50,000); Blackburn Rovers Sep 1992 (£250,000+Hill+Skinner); Sheffield United Jul 1997 (£200,000); Plymouth Argyle Feb 1999-Mar 1999 (loan); Cheltenham Town Nov 1999; Tiverton Town Feb 2000.

Although he had played over 400 league games for Exeter and Plymouth he was only known at Ewood as the man who gave Ossie Ardiles a painful introduction to Second Division football. Initially a midfield player, he had found use as a resolute, no-nonsense central defender. Recruited as a squad player, he remained that, although until he suffered cruciate ligament damage he was a regular on the bench. A future helping the young players develop in the reserves did not appeal and he joined Sheffield United where he appeared in a FA Cup semi-final. Arthritis in his knees and the constant need to take painkillers limited his football, however after retiring at Cheltenham his passion for the game made him stage a comeback with Tiverton.

FL	41+13 apps	1 gl
FAC	4+1 apps	0 gls
FLC	3+1 apps	0 gls
EC	1 app.	0 gls
CS	0+1 app.	0 gls
Total	49+16 apps	1 gl

MARKS, George William

Goalkeeper

5'11" 11st 8lb
Born: Figheldean, Salisbury, 9 April 1915
Died: Salisbury, 31 January 1998
Debut: 31 August 1946

CAREER: Salisbury Corinthians; Arsenal Mar 1936 (am) May 1936; Margate; Arsenal May 1938; Blackburn Rovers Aug 1946 (£5,000); Bristol City Aug 1948; Reading Oct 1948; Bulford United 1955.

Signed by Arsenal before the Second World War and farmed out to Margate, he matured sufficiently to gain 8 wartime international caps after playing only two league games. Ten days before the resumption of the Football League after the Second World War the Rovers' manager, Eddie Hapgood, returned to his old club and agreed a fee of £5,000 for their goalkeeper George Swindin. Swindin declined the move and, desperate to fill his vacancy, Hapgood negotiated a deal for Marks. The fans were aware that their new player was an afterthought but he was such a neat, tidy competent player that they soon forgot about the circumstances of his arrival. Unfortunately he received a bad facial injury in December and thereafter lost confidence. He also suffered from the club changing managers. It had been arranged that he could live in the West Country and train with Salisbury but he was made to take digs in Blackburn and train with the rest of the players. A move to Bristol City was the solution and he later played many years with Reading. He continued to live in the village of his birth where he had a smallholding and he later worked as a builder for the Defence Land Agency.

FL	67 apps	0 gls
FAC	7 apps	0 gls
Total	74 apps	0 gls

MARRIOTT, Andrew

Goalkeeper

6'0" 12st 7lb
Born: Sutton in Ashfield, 11 October 1970
Debut: 30 December 1989

CAREER: Arsenal Jul 1987 (trainee) Oct 1988; Nottingham Forest Jun 1989 (£50,000); West Bromwich Albion Sep 1989 (loan); Blackburn Rovers Dec 1989-Jan 1990 (loan); Colchester United Mar 1990 (loan); Burnley Aug 1991 (loan); Wrexham Oct 1993 (loan) Nov 1993 (£200,000); Sunderland Aug 1998 (loan) Oct 1998 (£200,000); Wigan Athletic Dec 2000-Jan 2001 (loan); Barnsley Mar 2001 (free); Birmingham City Mar 2003 (nominal); Beira Mar (Portugal) Jul 2003 (free); Coventry City Aug 2004; Colchester United Oct 2004; Bury Nov 2004; Torquay United Mar 2005.
INTERNATIONALS: Wales 5 apps.

Although he graduated through the England age group teams he failed to live up to initial assessments of his potential. His arrival at Ewood was one of a number of loan moves he experienced and in his two games he looked a tidy, agile player. It was not until he moved to Wrexham that he blossomed, a handy move because his Welsh ancestry was discovered and this brought him international recognition. Desirous of higher-grade football, he took the decision to join Sunderland but never was able to gain a first-team place and joined Birmingham in similar circumstances. A classic mistake in his only game contributed to his release and the unusual step of playing in the Portuguese Super Liga. Joining a team in the picturesque town of Aveiro he cannot have imagined that the highlight of his career was to follow shortly; participation in his small side's epic victory over Benfica in the new Estádio da Luz. Surprisingly he returned to England after a season and played for four teams in nine months.

FL	2 apps	0 gls
Total	2 apps	0 gls

MARTIN, Donnon 'Dino'
Striker/Midfield

5'10" 10st 7lb
Born: Corby, 15 February 1944
Debut: 24 February 1968

CAREER: Northampton Town Jul 1962; Blackburn Rovers Feb 1968 (£38,000); Northampton Town Nov 1975 (£5,000); Dunstable Town; Corby Town (p-m).

A promising young player who had gained youth international honours, he helped his side in the highest grade of football they ever played, an unexpected spell in the First Division. Skinny in build and with a reputation for not only being a heavy smoker but a man who liked a drink, he had silky skills, an ability to manipulate the ball, positional sense and an eye for goal. A huge investment for the Rovers, he proved worth it whether as a striker or in midfield where he could dominate with his ghosting skills. Despite a broken leg he returned and had a glorious swansong under Gordon Lee, providing the goal-scoring of a craftsman to complement the muscle of Beamish and Hickman.

Don Martin in August 1970. (Howard Talbot Photography)

FL	218+6 apps	57 gls
FAC	10+1 apps	2 gls
FLC	16 apps	4 gls
Total	244+7 apps	63 gls

MATTEO, Dominic
Defender

6'1" 11st 12lb
Born: Dumfries, 14 April 1974
Debut: 14 August 2004

CAREER: Christ the King School, Southport; Birkdale United; Liverpool May 1992; Sunderland Mar 1995 (loan); Leeds United Aug 2000 (£4,750,000); Blackburn Rovers Jul 2004 (free).
INTERNATIONALS: Scotland 6 apps.

Born in Scotland, where his grandparents had settled after leaving Italy, he was brought up in Southport. Spotted by Kenny Dalglish playing with his son Paul at Birkdale, he joined the Liverpool School of Excellence as a left-sided midfield player. It was not until he was converted to the defence that he started to become a first-team player but he made such a rapid impact that he took over from John Scales and was selected by Glenn Hoddle for the England squad. Unable to play because of injury, he later opted for Scotland. Injuries curtailed his Liverpool career but an expensive move to Leeds followed. This brought him games in European competition but he was also present at the club's relegation in 2004. With the club in financial difficulties, high wage earners like Matteo had to leave and he joined the Rovers on a free transfer. Intended for a centre-back partnership, he eventually was played in the problem position of left-back and after an unsteady start improved as the season passed.

PL	30+3 apps	0 gls
FAC	4 apps	1 gl
Total	34+3 apps	1 gl

MAY, David

Centre-back

6'0" 11st 4lb
Born: Oldham, 24 June 1970
Debut: 1 April 1989

CAREER: Blackburn Rovers Jul 1986 (trainee) Jun 1988; Manchester United May 1994 (£1,250,000); Huddersfield Town Dec 1999-Jan 2000 (loan); Glasgow Rangers Jul 2003 (trial); Burnley Aug 2003-Jun 2004 (free); Bacup Borough Nov 2004.

Not having excelled as a youth-team player, it was surprising how he adapted easily to first-team football. A quick, intuitive defender, best suited to playing alongside a big man, he was initially prevented from playing in this position because of the presence of Kevin Moran. In the promotion season of 1992 he ended by playing in the problem position of right-back but in the Premier League he developed into one of the best young defenders in the country. With his contract up for renewal he decided to join Manchester United, thus missing the Premiership-winning season of 1994/95 and, although he gained both Premiership and FA Cup winners' medals since, he also played less than 100 league games in nine seasons. The talent available at Old Trafford and a succession of injuries contributed to this and his potential remained largely unfulfilled. Returning locally, he was signed to stabilise the Burnley defence and provided excellent leadership qualities for a brief period. After resting from the game he returned at Bacup and was later appointed assistant to Brent Peters.

L	123 apps	3 gls
FAC	10 apps	1 gl
FLC	12+1 apps	2 gls
FMC	2 apps	0 gls
PO	3 apps	0 gls
Total	150+1 apps	6 gls

METCALFE, Stuart Michael

Midfield

5'7" 9st
Born: Blackburn, 6 October 1950
Debut: 27 April 1968

CAREER: Mill Hill St Peter's School; Witton Park Sec Modern; Blackburn Rovers Jun 1966 (app.) Jan 1968; Carlisle United Jul 1980 (£35,000); Tampa Bay Rowdies (USA); Carolina Lightning (USA); Baltimore Blast (USA)1981; Blackburn Rovers Oct 1982; Crewe Alexandra Jan 1983-Feb 1983; Chorley; Rossendale; Feniscowles; ROF Blackburn; Old Blackburnians.

The best young player to come out of Blackburn schools' football since the time of Bryan Douglas, he initially played on the right wing, where he beat opponents Matthews-style with close control, body swerves and assorted tricks. His competitive nature and desire to win was recognised when he was moved to the centre of midfield and he developed ball-winning skills and occasionally displayed flashes of temper. Discarded by Furphy as not being the workhorse he required, he was brought back when the club found they had no leadership without him. Despite their obvious differences he survived under Gordon Lee but as the years advanced his dependance on his right foot became more marked. In the USA he played in three different leagues (NASL, ASL (2) and MISL) but he returned home to live in Blackburn. The Rovers asked him to play with the reserves on a non-contract basis and he had one last first-team outing that produced the craziest own goal of all time. At Newcastle he started to dribble in his own penalty area but after beating several players decided to opt for better discipline and concede a corner. Unfortunately he produced a perfectly struck shot into his own net. He took up employment as a nurse and began breeding Afghan hounds as a hobby. He also proved to be one of the best contributors to Radio Rovers, the club's own radio station, giving expert opinion in a forthright and informed manner.

FL	376+11 apps	21 gls
FAC	23 apps	1 gl
FLC	22+2 apps	3 gls
Total	421+13 apps	25 gls

MILLAR, John
Left-back/Midfield

5'9" 11st
Born: Coatbridge, 8 December 1966
Debut: 5 September 1987

CAREER: Clyde Amateurs; Chelsea Sep 1984; Hamilton Academicals Oct 1986-Dec 1986 (loan); Northampton Town Jan 1987 (loan); Blackburn Rovers Jul 1987 (£10,000); Heart of Midlothian Jul 1991 (free); Raith Rovers Mar 1996 (free); Livingston United Jul 1998 (free); Stirling Albion 2001.

When his career at Chelsea was heading nowhere the Rovers paid a small fee for Millar. They found they had a left-back who was erratic and too easily beaten by skilful wingers. The following season he was moved to the left side of midfield where the change suited him. A formidable opponent who grafted hard, his release in 1991 was surprising since he had played with more spirit than most. Joe Jordan recognised a kindred spirit and took him to Hearts, where the side came within a whisker of winning the league championship.

FL	122+4 apps	1 gl
FAC	4 apps	0 gls
FLC	9+1 apps	0 gls
FMC	2 apps	0 gls
PO	8 apps	0 gls
Total	145+5 apps	1 gl

MILLER, Alan John
Goalkeeper

6'3" 14st 6lb
Born: Epping, 29 March 1970
Debut: 1 April 2000

CAREER: Arsenal May 1988; Plymouth Argyle Nov 1988 (loan); West Bromwich Albion Aug 1991 (loan); Birmingham City Dec 1991 (loan); Middlesbrough Aug 1994 (£500,000); Grimsby Town Jan 1997 (loan); West Bromwich Albion Mar 1997 (£400,000); Blackburn Rovers Feb 2000-Apr 2003 (£50,000); Bristol City Aug 2000 (loan); Coventry City Oct 2000 (loan); St Johnstone Oct 2001-Feb 2002 (loan).

Highly regarded at schoolboy and youth level, he suffered from not being able to develop his potential, constrained by the practicalities of life at a club like Arsenal where success has to be immediate. Moves to Middlesbrough and West Bromwich enabled him to escape his first-team inactivity but it is still a measure of his lack of tangible achievement that he was best known to the fans as the partner of the *Brookside* actress Claire Sweeney when Tony Parkes made the decision to sign him. The reasoning behind the acquisition remained obscure; the club had serviceable goalkeepers in Filan and Kelly, and indeed Miller's appearances were to be so limited that it underlined the conundrum. Problems with a disc in his back forced his retirement in April 2003 and he moved to live in Spain where he had business interests.

FL	1 app.	0 gls
FLC	1 app.	0 gls
Total	2 apps	0 gls

MILLER, Archibald
Wing half

5'9.5" 11st 4lb
Born: Larkhall, 5 September 1913
Debut: 22 November 1947

CAREER: Royal Albert Jun 1932; Heart of Midlothian Oct 1932; Falkirk Jan 1940; Heart of Midlothian Apr 1941; Blackburn Rovers Nov 1947; Kilmarnock Jun 1948 (£1,000); Workington (p-c) 1949; Carlisle United Sep 1950; Heart of Midlothian 1951; Workington Feb 1952. INTERNATIONALS: Scotland 1 app.

Miller spent the bulk of his career with Hearts, where he established a reputation as a constructive wing half who was capped for Scotland just before the Second World War. He lost the best years of his career during hostilities and when he came to Ewood he knew that he would only be required in emergencies. The club was anxious to develop Eric Bell but Miller did well whenever he was required. He took the first step into coaching with Workington and made a surprise return to the Football League when Carlisle signed him to play a game as an emergency measure.

FL	6 apps	0 gls
Total	6 apps	0 gls

MILLER, Ian
Right winger

5'9" 12st
Born: Perth, 13 May 1955
Debut: 29 August 1981

CAREER: Bury Aug 1973; Nottingham Forest Mar 1975 (free); Doncaster Rovers Aug 1975 (exchange); Swindon Town Jul 1978 (£25,000); Blackburn Rovers Aug 1981 (£67,000); Port Vale Jul 1989 (free); Scunthorpe United Aug 1990 (free); Stafford Rangers Jan 1992.

A sandy haired winger with one trick (he raced past full-backs on the outside and centred fifteen yards from the dead-ball line), he played over 550 league games with a variety of clubs, a tribute to his ability to maximise his talent. To do this he had to maintain his speed and strength but he was also a positive influence on the team with his capacity for hard work. When he reached the end of his Ewood career his crossing became distinctly erratic and after eight years he left for Port Vale. He turned this to his advantage since he subsequently returned to the Potteries club as youth-team coach and in 1994 was recruited by Graham Taylor to be in charge of the Wolves' reserves. His family had always professed the wish to return to the Blackburn area and an appointment as youth-team coach at Manchester City enabled him to come back north. Subsequently he joined the Rovers to look after the youth teams but, in 2004, accepted the offer to become assistant to Colin Hendry at Blackpool.

FL	252+16 apps	16 gls
FAC	12+1 app.	0 gls
FLC	10+2 apps	1 gl
FMC	5+3 apps	1 gl
PO	4 apps	0 gls
Total	283+22 apps	18 gls

MIMMS, Robert Andrew
Goalkeeper

6'2.5" 12st 10lb
Born: York, 12 October 1963
Debut: 24 January 1987

CAREER: Halifax Town Apr 1980 (app.) Nov 1981; Rotherham United Nov 1981 (£15,000); Everton May 1985 (£150,000); Notts County Mar 1986 (loan); Sunderland Jan 1987 (loan); Blackburn Rovers Jan 1987-Mar 1987 (loan); Manchester City Sep 1987-Oct 1987 (loan); Tottenham Hotspur Feb 1988 (£250,000); Aberdeen Feb 1990-Apr 1990 (loan); Blackburn Rovers Dec 1990-Jul 1996 (£250,000); Crystal Palace Aug 1996; Preston North End Sep 1996 (free); Rotherham United Aug 1997 (free); York City Aug 1998 (loan) Oct 1998; Mansfield Town Mar 2000 (free); Wolverhampton Wanderers (p-c) Jul 2001.

Ideally built for a goalkeeper, with agility and quick reflexes, he spent a long time learning the trade. High-profile moves to Everton and Tottenham did not consolidate the initial impression he had made at Rotherham but in 1990 the Rovers were fighting against relegation and were desperate for a big, reliable goalkeeper. Mimms had had a successful loan spell with the Rovers four years earlier so he was not an unknown commodity, and he proved to be sound as compared with the club's other alternatives. He was not without critics and his lack of judgement leaving his line and vulnerability from long shots was often exposed. He also was one of those most adversely affected by the change in the backpass rule, being nervous and unsure when he had to play the ball with the boot. Overall, though, he was a success and helped the club to the Premiership, although he then lost his place to Tim Flowers as the team was upgraded. He travelled often after that but gained coaching experience at York while he was playing and then joined Wolves as goalkeeping coach, the club registering him so he could play in an emergency.

L	132+2 apps	0 gls
FAC	9 apps	0 gls
FLC	15 apps	0 gls
FMC	1 app.	0 gls
PO	3 apps	0 gls
Total	160+2 apps	0 gls

MITCHELL, Albert James
Left winger

5'8" 11st
Born: Stoke, 22 January 1922
Debut: 13 March 1948

CAREER: Burslem Albion; Stoke City Apr 1939; Blackburn Rovers Feb 1948 (£4,000); Kettering Town Aug 1948; Northampton Town May 1949; Luton Town Jul 1951; Middlesbrough Sep 1954; Southport Sep 1954; Wellington Town Jul 1957; Kidderminster Harriers 1958; Stafford Rangers (p-m).

Sought as a replacement for the departed Langton, he proved a fast, direct left winger but after little opportunity was immediately released. Unable to find a league club, he was playing in the Birmingham League when Northampton rescued him. When he joined a highly talented Luton side he demonstrated that he was not only a skilful and creative player but one who ranked with the best as a finisher. During this spell he played for the England 'B' side against Holland.

FL	3 apps	0 gls
Total	3 apps	0 gls

MITCHELL, Robert
Midfield

5'10" 11st
Born: South Shield, 4 January 1955
Died: Staffordshire, April 1997
Debut: 24 August 1976

CAREER: Sunderland Jan 1972; Blackburn Rovers Jul 1976 (free); Grimsby Town Jun 1978 (free); Carlisle United Aug 1982 (free); Rotherham United Mar 1983 (free); Hamrun (Mal); Lincoln City Jan 1986-Jul 1987.

Young free-transfer signings who have failed to achieve with their first club are normally a gamble but Mitchell was hardly a risk, given his high fitness level and desire. A left-sided player who liked to support the attack, he timed his runs forward to good effect as can be gathered by his scoring record. Released because he lacked the ability to dominate, other clubs found considerable value in his presence. The highlight of his career came when a young Grimsby side won the Third Division championship in 1980. Throughout his long career no employer was ever short-changed by a man who was a model of hard work and application.

FL	17+12 apps	6 gls
FAC	2 apps	1 gl
Total	19+12 apps	7 gls

MOKOENA, Aaron Teboho (Mbazo – The Axe)
Centre-back/midfield

6'0" 12st 4lb
Born: Boipatong (South Africa), 25 November 1980
Debut: 8 January 2005

CAREER: Jomo Cosmos Jul 1997; Bayer Leverkusen (Germany) Jul 1998; Ajax (Holland) Feb 1999; Ajax Cape Town (loan); Germinal Beerschot (Belgium) Jan 2001-Jun 2003 (loan); KRC Genk (Belgium) Jul 2003 (with Kapka for Sonck); Blackburn Rovers Jan 2005 (£300,000).
INTERNATIONALS: South Africa 54 apps.

One of seven children, whose father died when he was young, Aaron was brought up by his hard-working mother in the townships where, against the odds, he kept away from the destructive forces that ruin any future for so many youngsters. A natural athlete, he was quickly signed by the Jomo Cosmos, who played in the highest division in the country. So impressive was he when placed in their defence that he became his country's youngest ever international and attracted the attention of European clubs. Still a teenager, he unwittingly signed for both Bayer Leverkusen and Ajax and was kept out of the game for nine months after FIFA ordered the clubs to sort the matter out between themselves. Mokoena's preference was for Ajax and after being loaned out to their satellite club in South Africa he made his debut in Holland. Unable to obtain a regular place, he was loaned out to Germinal Beerschot where he developed into a commanding centre half, a ferocious tackler, competitive in all aspects of the game. Even so, he was no more than trading bait when Ajax wanted Wesley Sonck and he moved to Genk. Although he had become South Africa's captain he was relatively unknown in the game when Genk agreed to let him have two days' trial with the Rovers. It was sufficient for Mark Hughes to decide to sign him in the transfer window and introduce him immediately to the first team. He struggled at centre-back, where his desire to follow the ball rather than mark space was emphasised, but he was quickly switched to a holding role in front of the back four. With Nelsen and Todd behind him he helped transform the defence into a watertight unit. Operating to instructions, he was disciplined in his positioning, razor sharp in his tackling and displayed an ideal temperament in following coaching instructions. A socially responsible young man, he owns his own team, The Birds, in the Castle League in South Africa and is a director of Sedibeng Rovers, an involvement designed to aid the young inhabitants of the townships. He also provides funding to the Busy Bee Hospice in the Vale Triangle, which helps many AIDS victims.

PL	19 +9 apps	0 gls
FAC	5+1 apps	0 gls
FLC	0 +3 apps	0 gls
Total	24+13 apps	0 gls

MOONEY, Francis
Right winger

5'9" 12st
Born: Fauldhouse, 1 January 1932
Debut: 13 February 1954

CAREER: Bathgate St Mary's; Manchester United May 1949; Blackburn Rovers Feb 1954; Carlisle United May 1956; Berwick Rangers 1960.

When Johnny Carey took over at the Rovers he had to rebuild and did not have many resources. Needing young talent, he turned to his old club Manchester United to bring in Frank Mooney, a Scot whose career had stagnated while he spent his national service with the RAF in Rhodesia. A brother of the Doncaster player John Mooney, he brought the ebullience of youth to the right wing, having fair pace and the ability to deliver a telling cross. The junior member of perhaps the greatest front five the club fielded (Crossan, Briggs, Quigley and Langton were the others) he found it easy to shine if he was prepared to run with enthusiasm. He contributed a hat-trick on the day Middlesbrough were beaten by nine goals but his time at Ewood was running out as Bryan Douglas worked his way through the youth ranks. A realist, he recognised the inevitable and asked for a transfer within a matter of weeks of losing his place. He enjoyed success at Carlisle but had only one season with Berwick, where he made just 9 appearances.

FL	58 apps	19 gls
FAC	1 app.	0 gls
Total	59 apps	19 gls

MOORE, Norman Woodliffe

Centre forward

5'10" 12st 6lb
Born: Grimsby, 15 October 1919
Died: Grimsby, 14 March 2007
Debut: 18 March 1950

CAREER: Grimsby Town 1936; Hull City Apr 1947; Blackburn Rovers Mar 1950; Bury Aug 1951; Goole Town Jul 1952; Wisbech Town Aug 1953.

The Moores have become the family most associated with Grimsby. Norman played only briefly before joining Hull and his brother Tom only fleetingly played in the black and white. However, Tom's sons, Kevin and David, became key figures in the club's history. Norman was a wing half at Grimsby but during the Second World War, where he guested for Wrexham, Chester, Charlton and Norwich, he developed skills that enabled Hull to convert him into a centre forward.

FL	7 apps	1 gl
Total	7 apps	1 gl

MORAN, Kevin Bernard

Centre-back

5'11" 12st 9lb
Born: Dublin, 29 April 1956
Debut: 27 January 1990

CAREER: Drimnach Castle CBS; Rangers Schoolboys; Pegasus (Eire); Manchester United Feb 1978; Sporting Gijon (Spain) Aug 1988; Blackburn Rovers Jan 1990-Jul 1994 (free).
INTERNATIONALS: Eire 70 apps 6 gls.

When Kevin Moran signed for Manchester United it was a huge shock for followers of Gaelic football, who had seen him develop into one of the game's great players with two All Ireland winners' medals to his credit. The qualities that made him a great Gaelic player stood him in good stead in football. Brave, willing to put his head anywhere (he perhaps spilled more blood on the field than any player ever has), a sure tackler with impeccable timing and an ability to read the game, he became the epitome of the complete clubman centre half. The decision to rebuild United caused Alex Ferguson to make the erroneous decision of allowing Moran to leave. It proved invaluable to Blackburn because, after a spell in Spain, he was happy to return to the North-West. He had business interests in card shops and pizzerias in the Manchester area but demonstrated that on the football field he had lost little as he settled into the Rovers' back four for five great seasons, during which the club was promoted to the Premiership. An economics graduate of Trinity College, he had the reputation as one of the shrewdest negotiators in the game, a talent put to good use in ProActive, the sports agency he partly owned, which was floated on the stock exchange in 2001 with Moran as financial director.

L	143+4 apps	10 gls
FAC	10+1 apps	1 gl
FLC	8+1 apps	0 gls

FMC	1 app.	0 gls
PO	5 apps	1 gl
Total	167+6 apps	12 gls

MORLEY, Brian James
Left-back

5'7" 11st 3lb
Born: Fleetwood, 4 October 1960
Debut: 10 March 1979

CAREER: Blackburn Rovers Jul 1977 (app.) Oct 1978; Tranmere Rovers Jul 1981-Jul 1982 (free); Runcorn; Fleetwood.

An apprentice left winger, Morley became another of Jim Smith's experiments that postulated that wingers and full-backs came from the same root stock. The conversion was not without merit since it was obvious that Morley lacked both speed and quick feet but with more time he was effective and could be relied upon to measure a cross and generally play with enthusiasm. Although Howard Kendall gave him opportunities and liked his attitude his defensive qualities were not great and he slipped to his home-town club, who he served for nearly a decade.

FL	20 apps	0 gls
FLC	4 apps	0 gls
Total	24 apps	0 gls

MORRIS, Peter Andrew
Winger

5'8" 10st
Born: Farnworth, 23 November 1958
Died: Bolton, 24 February 2009
Debut: 30 December 1978

CAREER: St Thomas of Canterbury Primary School; St Cuthbert's; Parkside; Preston North End Oct 1976; Blackburn Rovers Jul 1978-Apr 1980 (free); Ashton United.

A Preston apprentice full-back who failed to make the grade, he attracted the attention of Jim Smith, who saw in his quick feet and nimble carriage a man who might become a left winger. Performances in the reserves were promising but in the first team he was tentative. Given the opportunity to try out with the first team back in defence he declined, on the basis that he did not think he could handle the role. Granted a free transfer, he declined to wait until the end of the season and had his contract terminated.

FL	2+2 apps	0 gls
FAC	1+1 app.	0 gls
Total	3+3 apps	0 gls

MORRISON, Andrew Charles
Centre defender

5'11" 12st
Born: Inverness, 30 July 1970
Debut: 5 February 1994

CAREER: Plymouth Argyle Nov 1986 (trainee) Jul 1987; Blackburn Rovers Aug 1993 (£150,000+Burnett); Blackpool Dec 1994 (£245,000); Huddersfield Town Jun 1996 (£500,000); Manchester City Oct 1998-Mar 2002 (£80,000); Blackpool Aug 2000-Oct 2000 (loan); Crystal Palace Aug 2000-Nov 2000 (loan); Sheffield United Mar 2001-May 2001 (loan); Bury Dec 2002 (non con).

The son of a Scottish trawlerman, he was brought up in Kinlochbravie until his father joined the Royal Marines. This took the family to Plymouth where they remained when the father left the service and became a fisherman. Living in the notorious Stonehouse high-rise flats and crewing for his father, who ventured out when most local fishermen would not do so, gave Morrison a hard edge that youngsters of his age lacked. This stood him to good advantage on the football field, where his strength and resilience either in midfield or defence became legendary at Plymouth. Signed by Kenny Dalglish, he never prospered at Ewood where he struggled with the pace of the Premiership, but he found a good berth at Blackpool where the manager, Sam Allardyce, said 'looks like a marine, plays like a marine'. Later, Manchester City fans were equally enamoured of the bruising defender although the club struggled to cope with off-field incidents where he had been provoked and would not back down. Sending him for anger counselling endeared him even more to the fans, but he was fighting a troublesome knee injury that kept him absent for months. Unable to let the game go, he trained with Bury in a last effort to keep active.

FL	1+4 apps	0 gls
FAC	1 app.	0 gls
Total	2+4 apps	0 gls

MULLEN, James
Left winger

5'8.5" 10st 10lb
Born: Oxford, 16 March 1947
Debut: 22 October 1974

CAREER: Oxford City; Reading Nov 1966; Charlton Athletic Nov 1967; Rotherham United Feb 1969; Blackburn Rovers Aug 1974 (£8,000); Bury Jun 1976-Jul 1977 (free); Rochdale Mar 1977-May 1977 (loan); Great Harwood.

A surprise signing by Gordon Lee, he was a tricky little winger with an effervescent approach, not a normal acquisition for a route-one manager. He had gained a reputation at Rotherham as a player difficult to subdue when in form and, after a late start because of injury, his debut underlined exactly what he could add to the team. Demanding the ball, jinking and twisting, he was impossible to contain. The following week his opponent found a way. A dreadful first-minute challenge left Mullen with a broken leg, from which he never really recovered.

FL	6+4 apps	0 gls
FAC	2 apps	0 gls
Total	8+4 apps	0 gls

MULVANEY, Richard
Centre half

6'0" 12st 7lb
Born: Sunderland, 5 August 1942
Debut: 26 September 1964

CAREER: Seaham Colliery Jnrs; Cardiff City (trial); Billingham Synthonia; Peterlee Jnrs; Merton Colliery; Blackburn Rovers Feb 1964; Oldham Athletic Aug 1971 (free); Rochdale Oct 1974 (free); Gateshead 1977-1978; Chester le Street (p-c).

When the club realised that in spite of their First Division status their youth policy was ineffective they sought to bridge the hiatus by signing a few young players who were too old for traditional apprenticeships. The best of these was Mulvaney, an old-fashioned centre half, solid in every feature of the defensive game and with a mature head. He received first-team opportunities because Fred Pickering had left a gap at centre forward and the immaculate Mike England was used as a stop-gap replacement, and he made the most of his chances. The departure of England created an opening but a perforated eardrum came at an unfortunate time and the club also converted both Clayton and Sharples to the centre of the defence and then brought in Coddington. Eventually Mulvaney was called upon and formed an impressive partnership with Allan Hunter. His departure from Ewood was curious; citing his wife's desire to return to the North-East he asked for a transfer and was placed on the list. When no offers were received the fee was halved and then halved again, with the stipulation that at the end of the season he could move on a free transfer. Needless to say clubs sat back and waited and eventually he joined Oldham, a club noticeably not in the North-East. When he eventually retired he moved back to the North-East and resumed his old job of caulker in the shipyard. His brother Jimmy played in the FA Amateur Cup final for Whitby and in the Football League with Hartlepool and Barrow.

FL	135+6 apps	4 gls
FAC	2 apps	0 gls
FLC	8 apps	0 gls
Total	145+6 apps	4 gls

MUNRO, Stuart
Left-back

5'11" 11st
Born: Falkirk, 15 September 1962
Debut: 31 August 1991

CAREER: Bo'ness United; St Mirren 1980; Alloa Athletic Jun 1982; Glasgow Rangers Feb 1984; Blackburn Rovers Aug 1991 (£350,000); Bristol City Feb 1993; Falkirk Oct 1995-1996; Sydney United (Aus).

Although he had been a stalwart at Rangers for a number of years and had appeared for Scotland 'B' the blond-haired Munro was down to third choice at Ibrox when Don Mackay signed him for the Rovers. Injuries delayed his debut and when this came the writing was on the wall for Mackay. Tony Parkes was made caretaker manager and immediately backed his hunch and restored Chris Sulley at left-back. Kenny Dalglish never contradicted Parkes' assessment of the player and after an injury- plagued spell in the reserves he was released to join Bristol City. Electing to continue his career in Australia, he was on hand when Frank Arok left Gippsland Falcons in 1998 and succeeded him as coach. He was impressive and moved on to Carton SC, who he coached to victory in the Australian cup final. Misfortune then struck. The powerful side he had assembled was disbanded when they became insolvent and disappeared. He then lost most of his medals when his wife's house in Sydney burned down. Finally he was dismissed from his position as assistant coach as Paramatta Power because of economic considerations. Cited by Graeme Souness as being one of the finest professionals he has ever seen, he had talks with the Rovers about acting as an overseas scout. He was later appointed coach to South Melbourne.

FL	1 app.	0 gls
Total	1 app.	0 gls

MURPHY, Donal Patrick
Striker

5'10" 12st
Born: Dublin, 23 February 1955
Debut: Middlesbrough, 24 April 1982

CAREER: Coventry City Aug 1972; Shamrock Rovers 1973; Coventry City 1975; Millwall Oct 1977 (loan); Torquay United May 1978 (free); Plymouth Argyle Jun 1980 (£65,000); Torquay United Dec 1981 (loan); Blackburn Rovers Mar 1982-May 1983 (free); Drogheda United Oct 1982 (loan); Bohemians Mar 1983 (loan); Drogheda United 1983; UCD 1983.

A left-sided striker who threatened to break through with Coventry, he did not flourish until at Torquay he displayed a goal-scoring flair. This prompted Plymouth to pay a big fee but he disappointed and was surplus to requirements when Bobby Saxton, who signed him for Plymouth, decided that he still might have potential. He proved elegant but lacked bite, and it was not long before he finished his career in his own country.

FL	1+2 apps	0 gls
Total	1+2 apps	0 gls

MURPHY, Thomas Edwin*
Inside forward

5'7" 11st
Born: Middlesbrough, 25 March 1921
Died: 27 January 2003
Debut: 25 December 1947

CAREER: Southbank St Peter's; Middlesbrough May 1938; Blackburn Rovers Dec 1947; Halifax Town Mar 1949-May 1954; Redcar Albion Sep 1955.

Understudying the great Wilf Mannion at Middlesbrough was not the best career move and he was spotted by the Rovers in the isolated appearances he was permitted as the great man's deputy. A thoughtful, creative player, he had the difficult task of following the charismatic Alec Venters. In his first season he looked a real find but the loss of his wing partner, Langton, upset his composure. A player who brought the best out of others, he failed to cope with a procession of untalented left wingers and was transferred to Halifax.

FL	31 apps	6 gls
FAC	3 apps	1 gl
Total	34 apps	7 gls

MACLEOD, Alistair Reid 'Noddy'
Left winger

5'10" 11st 7lb
Born: Dalmuir, 26 February 1931
Died: Ayr, 1 February 2004
Debut: 18 August 1956

CAREER: Queen's Park School; Third Lanark 1950; St Mirren Sep 1955; Blackburn Rovers Jun 1956 (£6,000); Heart of Midlothian Jul 1961 (£5,000); Third Lanark 1963; Ayr United (p-c) 1965; Queen of the South Jun 1992.

A charismatic Scot, who had missed two Scottish 'B' international appearances through injury, he was an instant success when he came to Ewood in 1956. Christened 'Noddy' because of his bobbing head action when he ran, he hugged the touchline where he was deceptively fast and, despite an awkward style, was a fair craftsman. He was also a born fighter, a naturally good-humoured man who lifted the team and an achiever. Whenever asked to fill in at centre forward he was an awkwardly effective opponent. During his Ewood years the team was promoted to the First Division and reached the FA Cup final where MacLeod, in a team struggling with ten men, was immense. On a hot, humid day, he was pulled back from left wing to half-back to preserve the defensive complement and produced a display of running and effort that was outstanding. When the maximum wage was abolished he returned to Scotland and soon after embarked on a managerial career that took him from Ayr to Aberdeen to the national side. He led Scotland to the World Cup Finals of 1978 but with expectations high the team failed to deliver. Villified (Billy Connolly's remark about MacLeod believing that tactics were 'a kind of mint' became a national punch line), he returned to management at Ayr, the public choosing to ignore how MacLeod's belief and style had created the nation's optimism in the first place. He was offered the managerial role at Ewood but turned it down and moved to Motherwell. He then managed Airdrie, Ayr (for the third time) and Queen of the South. In 1992, at the age of sixty-one, he appeared for the latter's reserve side and converted a penalty. Intertwined between his footballing appointments have been spells in various hostelries in Scotland and as late as 1995 he was helping Jim Fallon at Dumbarton. He died in his adopted town of Ayr after suffering from Alzheimer's disease.

FL	193 apps	47 gls
FAC	23 apps	6 gls
FLC	2 apps	0 gls
Total	218 apps	53 gls

MCATEER, Jason Wynn
Midfield

5'11" 11st 10lb
Born: Birkenhead, 18 June 1971
Debut: 30 January 1999

CAREER: Parkside; Marine; Bolton Wanderers Jan 1992 (£1,000); Liverpool Sep 1995 (£4,500,000); Blackburn Rovers Jan 1999 (£4,000,000); Sunderland Oct 2001 (£1,000,000); Tranmere Rovers Jul 2004 (free).
INTERNATIONALS: Eire 51 apps 3 gls.

McAteer's uncles, Pat and Les, were both British boxing champions but honours appeared a long way from accruing for Jason McAteer when he was playing for Marine and then turning out in the Birkenhead League on Sunday. Playing at Horwich, he accidentally came under the scrutiny of Bolton's Phil Neal who took a chance, although he split the transfer fee in two parts with the second being conditional on achievement. An active, enthusiastic competitor, he lacked a natural position. Although he preferred to be involved in the centre of midfield he was often played wide right and he made his international debut within eighteen months of becoming a full-time professional. The Rovers, who had just become Premiership champions, agreed a fee with Bolton but Liverpool stepped in and McAteer preferred to return home. Ironically his career was restricted at Anfield by the desire to play him as a right wing-back and three years later he signed for the Rovers as Brian Kidd sought to rebuild. Despite his zest for the game his time at Ewood was not a happy one, and he was rescued by Sunderland after a widely publicised dispute with Graeme Souness.

FL	58+14 apps	4 gls
FAC	7 apps	0 gls
FLC	4 apps	0 gls
Total	69+14 apps	4 gls

McCAIG, Robert Alexander Marshall
Winger

5'6" 9st 3lb
Born: Annan, 15 August 1923
Died: Stockport, January 1986
Debut: 29 January 1949

CAREER: Lockerbie Accies; Queen of the South 1944; Carlisle United Aug 1948; Blackburn Rovers Dec 1948; Stockport County Aug 1951; Halifax Town Jan 1952; Crewe Alexandra Aug 1952; Bangor City; Wigan Athletic Aug 1957.

Although he had played only a handful of games at Carlisle he was signed to become the replacement for Langton, a difficult task in itself but made harder by the fact that he was more at home on the other flank. He displayed plenty of pace but the club was not satisfied and signed Edds to replace him. Soon after he was switched to the right and displaced Wharton, although the veteran winger fought back and regained his first-team spot. At a succession of clubs he found it difficult to hold a regular spot but his career lasted until September 1957. Sam Barkas signed him for Wigan in the close season but in a game against Southport reserves he received a bad leg injury. He aggravated it by staying on the field and complications set in, which led to his retirement.

FL	30 apps	2 gls
FAC	2 apps	0 gls
Total	32 apps	2 gls

McCLELLAND, Charles
Inside forward

5'7.5" 9st 12lb
Born: Lochgelly, 8 January 1924
Debut: 1 February 1947

CAREER: Bolton Wanderers; Droylsden; Hyde United; Blackburn Rovers Aug 1946; Droylsden Nov 1946 (loan); Hyde United Nov 1946 (loan); Exeter City Jul 1949; Portland United 1955; Cheltenham Town.

McClelland was the son of a Scottish footballer who played for Raith, Southampton, Middlesbrough, Bolton, Preston, Blackpool and Bradford and who won a FA Cup winners' medal with Bolton. On the day he was born his father scored five goals but, despite his pedigree, McClelland appeared destined not to make the Football League. Indeed, he had signed for Hyde only days before he was unexpectedly added to the Rovers' staff, which meant that he played for three different clubs in eight days. Mobile and with an eye for goal, he suffered from a lack of experience and consequently missed many goal chances. Three years later and more mature he joined Exeter where he played regularly and scored nearly 60 goals.

FL	13 apps	2 gls
FAC	5 apps	5 gls
Total	18 apps	7 gls

McDONALD, Gerard
Midfield

5'7.5" 9st 6lb
Born: Milnthorpe, 3 December 1952
Debut: 14 August 1971

CAREER: Blackburn Rovers May 1969 (app.) Aug 1971; Halifax Town Aug 1973-Jun 1974.

A stocky, right-sided player, he was thrust into the first team with his youth-team colleague David Bradford when Ken Furphy decided that a newly relegated side needed refreshing. Although Bradford received the spotlight there was much to admire about McDonald, who had good control and the ability to find openings and lose his marker. When the club signed Terry Garbett to add experience it dictated that McDonald was surplus to requirements, but it was a long spell absent through illness that led to his departure. A short stay at Halifax ensued but thereafter he was found applying his skills in the Preston & District League.

FL	19+2 apps	2 gls
FAC	0+2 apps	0 gls
FLC	3 apps	0 gls
Total	22+4 apps	2 gls

McEVELEY, James Michael 'Jay'
Defender

6'1" 12st 13lb
Born: Liverpool, 11 February 1985
Debut: 6 November 2002

CAREER: Everton (sch); Blackburn Rovers 2001 (trainee) Nov 2002; Burnley Dec 2003-Jan 2004 (loan); Gillingham Mar 2005-Jun 2005 (loan); Ipswich Town Aug 2005 (loan).

McEveley had only nine minutes of reserve experience when he was named as substitute for an understrength team in the opening rounds of the Worthington Cup. Although his experience with the youth team was at the centre of the defence he had to make an early entrance to the first team at left-back (a problem spot) and coped so well that he remained in the team until the club loaned Vratislav Gresko. Despite his inexperience he was completely relaxed, cool in possession of the ball and never struggled positionally in his new role. A fierce tackler, strong in the air and bodily strong he never appeared to be a youngster learning his trade. Able to participate in building-up play, he ran strongly down the left and proved that even occasions like the Worthington Cup semi-final held no fears for him. His reputation was established so quickly that Scotland inquired if he would declare himself for their international team, but he declined and England quickly gave him an Under-21 cap so that he could not go back on his decision. In the past two seasons his career stagnated, not aided by a serious ankle injury received when on loan at Burnley.

PL	14 apps	0 gls
FAC	2 apps	0 gls
FLC	3+1 apps	0 gls
Total	19+1 apps	0 gls

McEVOY, Matthew Andrew*
Wing half/Inside forward

5'10" 11st 5lb
Born: Bray, 15 July 1938
Died: Bray, 7 May 1994
Debut: 20 April 1959

CAREER: Bray Wanderers; Blackburn Rovers Oct 1956; Limerick Aug 1967 (free).
INTERNATIONALS: Eire 17 apps 6 gls.

Andy McEvoy in August 1963. (Howard Talbot Photography)

Spotted by Johnny Carey playing with Bray, he was offered terms by the Rovers but made no effort to accept them. In the summer Carey was on holiday in Ireland and decided to see if McEvoy could be persuaded to come to Lancashire. Reluctantly, for he was content with his life in Ireland, he accepted but his early years were punctuated by spells of homesickness and unauthorised absences when he caught the ferry home. Patiently, Carey kept on asking him back, although few could understand why he had such faith in a somewhat pedestrian inside forward. Isolated first-team appearances gave no insight but in 1960 he made an astonishing breakthrough. Ronnie Clayton was absent and he was unexpectedly moved to wing half. With a display of energy and drive he compensated totally for the Rovers' driving force and when the other wing half, Mick McGrath, was injured, confirmed that he was a wing half of the highest order. Unfortunate to lose his place, he appeared destined to be the club's best reserve player when in 1962/63 fate intervened. Unable to find an adequate inside right even though the experienced Craig and Lawther were around, the club moved McEvoy to his original position and it produced an astonishing metamorphosis. He changed from a wing half of energy and perpetual involvement to an inside forward who was the nearest thing to a Jimmy Greaves, a goal-poacher supreme who lurked on the verge of offside to use lightning acceleration to race onto the quick passes of Bryan Douglas. In front of goal he was supreme, totally emotionless, a professional assassin who scorned power for placement and found the gaps just beyond scrambling fingertips. He partnered Fred Pickering, providing the rapier to Pickering's broadsword, and in doing so finished joint top scorer in the First Division with 32 goals. Even when Pickering left, the following season he scored 29 goals but the loss of Douglas for most of the following season produced a goal drought and relegation. He might have been expected to harvest goals in the Second Division but Eddie Quigley wanted him to be a workhorse and this is never productive for thoroughbred goalscorers of the supreme quality of McEvoy. Rather than tolerate the position he returned to Ireland to play for Limerick and drive a tram, a strange outcome for a man who was still one of the game's great goalscorers. He remained in Ireland, succumbing to cancer on the final day of the season that took the Rovers into Europe for the first time.

FL	183 apps	89 gls
FAC	17 apps	10 gls
FLC	13 apps	4 gls
Total	213 apps	103 gls

McGORRIGHAN, Francis Owen

Inside forward

5'11" 12st 3lb
Born: Easington, 20 November 1921
Died: Hull, September 1998
Debut: 15 February 1947

CAREER: Easington CW; Horden CW; Eppleton CW; Middlesbrough 1943 (am) Apr 1944; Carlisle United Sep 1945; Hull City Aug 1946; Blackburn Rovers Feb 1947 (£6,000); Hull City Sep 1947; Southport Jul 1948; Scarborough Aug 1950; Wisbech Town Jul 1952-1953.

Having earned attention as a strong, constructive worker, he was brought to Ewood at a time when the club was desperate for young forwards. The transfer fee was a large one but the player was never comfortable after the move, lacking pace and not proving a threat in the penalty area. His return to Hull was in return for a conditional fee based on the games he played, a bad move since little accrued once he was back on Humberside. His career ended through an injury suffered with Wisbech.

FL	5 apps	0 gls
Total	5 apps	0 gls

MCGRATH, Michael

Wing half

5'7" 10st
Born: Dublin, 7 April 1936
Debut: 28 April 1956

CAREER: Home Farm; Blackburn Rovers Aug 1954; Bradford City Mar 1966 (free); Bangor City (p-m).
INTERNATIONALS: Eire 22 apps.

A quiet, poker-faced Dublin boy, he arrived at Ewood as something of an afterthought, a travelling companion for a highly rated teammate named Joe Wade. Player development is curious for, whereas Wade never came remotely close to making a first-team appearance, McGrath became a stalwart for years. He took over when Ken Clayton had the misfortune to break a leg and in his quiet, understated way became invaluable. A player of great positional ability, he was deceptively strong in the tackle with quick feet and a hardness that belied his stature. He had the distinction of being one of the few non-English players to play for the Football League and the misfortune to score an own goal in the 1960 FA Cup final. Following a spell with Bradford he moved into management with Bangor City but, although relatively successful, gave it up to return to live in Blackburn where he has since scouted for the Rovers and managed junior sides such as Daisyfield and Holy Souls.

FL	268 apps	8 gls
FAC	29 apps	3 gls
FLC	15 apps	1 gl
Total	312 apps	12 gls

McKEE, William Andrew

Wing half

5'8.5" 11st
Born: Burtonwood, 6 June 1928
Died: Blackburn, 14 May 1999
Debut: 21 April 1951

CAREER: Earlestown; Blackburn Rovers Nov 1959-May 1953; Newport County Jul 1953 (trial).

A solid battler, he was groomed in the reserves but had the misfortune to be around at the same time as the multi-talented Ronnie

Clayton. When Eric Bell was unfit for the penultimate game of the 1950/51 season McKee was handed his debut but he struggled. The following week the club introduced Ronnie Clayton and McKee's career was condemned to reserve football. Two cartilage operations followed and although he had a trial at Newport he never recovered from his injury, remaining in pain for the rest of his life. He continued living in Blackburn, dying in his home in St Michael's Close, Feniscowles aged seventy, which included forty-three years of marriage.

FL	1 app.	0 gls
Total	1 app.	0 gls

McKENZIE, Duncan
Midfield

5'8" 11st 3lb
Born: Grimsby, 10 June 1950
Debut: 24 March 1979

CAREER: Wintringham GS; Nottingham Forest Jul 1967 (am) Jul 1968; Mansfield Town Mar 1970 (loan) Feb 1973 (loan); Leeds United Aug 1974 (£250,000); Anderlecht (Belgium) Jun 1976 (£200,000); Everton Dec 1976 (£200,000); Chelsea Sep 1978 (£165,000); Blackburn Rovers Mar 1979 (£120,000); Tulsa Roughnecks (USA) Apr 1981 (£40,000+Busby); Chicago Sting (USA) Apr 1982-Aug 1982; Ryoden (Hong Kong).

A player of great athletic ability (able to leap over a car and throw a golf ball from one end of the field to the other) he had dexterous skills manipulating the ball, deceptive pace and an unorthodoxy about his play which was difficult to contain. A slow developer, he was taken to Leeds by Brian Clough, but found this a bad career move and took the opportunity to play in Belgium. Despite scoring 16 goals in 30 games he missed the English game and returned to Goodison Park under Billy Bingham. Much-loved on Merseyside, he was forced to move when Gordon Lee took over and demanded more effort and consistency. A move to Chelsea was unsuccessful and he became Blackburn's first six-figure player, at a time when they were destined for the Third Division. When Howard Kendall took over at Blackburn it was obvious that McKenzie's days were numbered and although Kendall was pragmatic about extracting use from the player it was obvious their approaches were always going to differ. Wisely, McKenzie took the riches available abroad before his retirement. Returning to Merseyside he became involved in the Football in the Community movement and forged a lucrative career as an after dinner speaker and radio expert.

FL	74 apps	16 gls
FAC	8 apps	1 gl
FLC	8 apps	4 gls
Total	90 apps	21 gls

McKINLAY, William
Midfield

5'9" 9st 13lb
Born: Glasgow, 22 April 1969
Debut: 21 October 1995

CAREER: Hamilton Thistle; Dundee United Aug 1985; Blackburn Rovers Oct 1995 (£1,700,000); Leicester City Oct 2000 (loan); Bradford City Nov 2000 (free); Bolton Wanderers Aug 2001 (trial); Preston North End Sep 2001; Clydebank Nov 2001-Jun 2002; Preston North End Jul 2002 (trial); Leicester City Aug 2002; Fulham Jul 2004 (p-c).
INTERNATIONALS: Scotland 30 apps 3 gls.

A rumoured target for the club for some time, he came in October 1995 but failed to make his mark, being troubled by niggling injuries and the arrival of the impressive Bohinen. The departure of Batty and an injury to Bohinen gave him the opportunity to demonstrate his qualities. A hard man, ideally suited for attrition, he brought steel and professionalism to the team but it took the departure of Ray Harford to confirm his position at the club. Tony Parkes opted for a dogs of war midfield and none came better equipped for this and a relegation fight than McKinlay. Even when the club switched from three to two midfield players he was the automatic choice at a time when Sherwood, Bohinen and Flitcroft were around. A stomach muscle problem took two surgeries to correct and a new manager, Graeme Souness, could not wait for him to recover. Surplus to requirements, his career spiralled downwards until he was finally reduced to joining financially stricken Leicester and playing for nothing until he had proved himself. This had a happy ending and McKinlay not only established himself but played a large part in the club's promotion to the Premiership. His old clubmate Chris Coleman offered him the chance to move into coaching at Fulham, and he even played in the first team in emergencies.

L	76+14 apps	3 gls
FAC	7+ 1 apps	0 gls
FLC	4 apps	1 gl
UEFA	1 app.	0 gls
Total	88+15 apps	4 gls

McKINNON, Paul John

Striker

6'2" 13st 7lb
Born: Camberley, 1 August 1958
Debut: 21 December 1986

CAREER: Chelsea; Camberley; Woking 1974; Sutton United 1977; Malmo (Sweden) 1980 (£15,000); Sutton United 1982; Ryoden Sports (Hong Kong); Sutton United 1983; Trelleborgs FK (Sweden) 1983; Sutton United 1983; TEG SK (Sweden) 1983; Sutton United 1986; Blackburn Rovers Nov 1986 (£10,000); Orebro (Sweden); Sutton United 1987; Orebro (Sweden) 1987; Sutton United 1988; Slough Town 1991; Sutton United; Walton & Hersham; Yeadon 1993; Maidstone United 1993; Fleet; Dorking; Tooting & Mitcham United Jan 1997; Sandhurst Town 1997.

It was a sign of Bobby Saxton's desperation to sign a strong striker with a proven goal-scoring record that he paid £10,000 for a twenty-eight-year-old sheet metal worker who had never played in the Football League. He had played in Sweden and won both league and cup medals with Malmo, but English clubs had never been interested in him. His short spell with the Rovers found him struggling to adapt to the pace of the game but he was never given a long run to find his feet. Released, he gained semi-professional international honours and being married to a Swedish girl found it easy to play the summer months in that country.

FL	5 apps	0 gls
FAC	1 app.	0 gls
FMC	1 app.	0 gls
Total	7 apps	0 gls

McLEAN, William

Winger

5'8.5" 11st 7lb
Born: Bootle, 14 August 1931
Debut: 9 September 1953

CAREER: Bootle GS; Liverpool jun football; Royal Corps of Signals; Bootle; Burscough; Blackburn Rovers Feb 1953; Wigan Athletic Aug 1955-May 1957 (free).

A right winger with good control who could cross with precision, he was signed to fill a position where Jack Campbell was filling in. McLean looked promising but when Johnny Carey found that Frank Mooney was available from Manchester United he preferred his potential. With Bryan Douglas also emerging McLean was faced with little prospect of a game and was given the chance to join Grimsby. Financial considerations made it more attractive to go into the non-league with Wigan where his teammate, Ronnie Suart, had taken over as player-manager. The departure of Suart after a year undermined McLean's position and he was soon released.

FL	12 apps	0 gls
FAC	2 apps	0 gls
Total	14 apps	0 gls

McLUCKIE, George Robertson
Left winger

5'9.5" 10st 7lb
Born: Falkirk, 19 September 1931
Died: Stowmarket, 1 January 2011
Debut: 1 November 1952

CAREER: Lochore Welfare; Blackburn Rovers Aug 1952; Ipswich Town May 1953 (£2,000); Reading Jun 1958-Mar 1961; Poole Town.

Given the chance to take over on the left wing he proved a stylish player, but the club preferred the proven professionalism of Wharton and Glover. The Rovers were disappointed in his achievements because they had rated him highly when they had signed him from Scottish junior football. Transferred to Ipswich, he proved a valuable player who won two Third Division (South) championship medals before moving to serve Reading well.

FL	20 apps	2 gls
FAC	1 app.	1 gl
Total	21 apps	3 gls

McNAMEE, David
Right-back

5'11" 10st 7lb
Born: Glasgow, 10 October 1980

CAREER: St Mirren Jun 1998-Feb 1999 Feb 1999-May 1999 (loan); Blackburn Rovers Feb 1999 (£500,000); Bristol Rovers Aug 2001 (trial); Livingston Aug 2002 (free).
INTERNATIONALS: Scotland 2 apps.

Signed with his close friend Burton O'Brien by Brian Kidd as an investment for the future, he was left on loan at St Mirren and suffered from the departure of the man who signed him. Only named on the bench for a League Cup tie where a weakened side was fielded, he was never under consideration for a first-team place but remained at the club because his contract was better than any he was offered. A move to Livingston brought him a League Cup winners' medal and a call up to the national team.

McNAMEE, John
Centre half

6'0" 13st 7lb
Born: Coatbridge, 11 June 1941
Debut: 26 November 1971

CAREER: Bellshill Athletic; Glasgow Celtic 1959; Hibernians Jun 1964; Newcastle United Dec 1966 (£26,000); Blackburn Rovers Nov 1971 (£12,000); Greenock Morton Jul 1973 (free); Hartlepool Nov 1973-Dec 1973; Lancaster City; Workington Jun 1975-Dec 1975.

When McNamee was signed the Rovers were sliding towards the Fourth Division. By the end of the season they were talking of promotion. Much of the transformation came from the inclusion of McNamee, the hardest of hard men, a player who brought steel and resilience to a side that was too easily intimidated, who taught the players around him never to turn the other cheek and introduced premature retaliation to Ewood. Even though he was over thirty and not in the best shape of his career his influence was immense. He gave Roger Jones and Derek Fazackerley the protection and know-how to develop into the outstanding players they subsequently became and turned a team who were pushovers when the going became rough into fighters. Difficult to control, it was not surprising that his stay was relatively brief but eventful. After a spell as manager at Workington he coached at Carlisle and continued to work in local football in Cockermouth where he was a postman. In 1988 he received injuries in a car accident which prevented him from being able to work again.

FL	56 apps	9 gls
FAC	1 app.	1 gl
Total	57 apps	10 gls

NAPIER, Christopher Robin Anthony 'Kit'
Right wing

5'11.5" 11st 6lb
Born: Dunblane, 26 September 1943
Debut: 2 September 1972

CAREER: Blackpool May 1960 (non con) Nov 1960; Preston North End Jun 1963 (£2,000); Workington Jul 1964 (£250); Newcastle United Nov 1965 (£18,000); Brighton & Hove Albion Sep 1966 (£8,500); Blackburn Rovers Aug 1972 (£15,000); Durban United (South Africa) 1974; East London United (South Africa) 1975; Durban City (South Africa) 1977-1978.

Pencil-slim and tousle-haired, he arrived at Ewood to rejoin his old manager Ken Furphy. The pair had been together with Workington on the infamous day in 1964 when the Cumbrian side defeated the Rovers in the League Cup, scoring five goals in the process. Throughout the early part of his career it was never certain whether Napier was a winger or a shifty, elusive striker but at Brighton he was confirmed as the former, using his intricate footwork to fashion space for the cross. His frail physique was accentuated by his lack of vigour and he never utilised force when the cerebral offered more reward. Clearly on the downswing of his career, he left for South Africa, remaining in the country to establish a business as a motor mechanic. His football pedigree was extensive. His grandfather was secretary of Fulham, his father was on the books of York, one uncle, Charlie, played for Celtic, Derby County, Sheffield Wednesday and Scotland and another, George, served Kilmarnock, Cowdenbeath, East Stirling and Airdrie.

FL	53+1 apps	10 gls
FAC	7 apps	3 gls
FLC	3 apps	0 gls
Total	63+1 apps	13 gls

NEEDHAM, Andrew Paul
Forward

5'11" 11st 6lb
Born: Oldham, 13 September 1955
Debut: 21 August 1976

CAREER: Birmingham City Jun 1971 (app.) Aug 1973; Blackburn Rovers Jul 1976-Mar 1977 (free); Aldershot Town Mar 1977 (loan) Apr 1977-Jun 1979.

Although born in Oldham he was raised in Harlow. Signed as an apprentice by Birmingham, he was released and offered a trial by the Rovers on a close-season tour of Gibraltar. A forceful player without great technique, he struggled when introduced to the first team but on his release settled for a long spell of nearly 100 games at Aldershot that ended because of injury. A testimonial game between Aldershot and Birmingham was played to help compensate him for his premature retirement.

FL	4+1 apps	0 gls
FLC	1+1 app.	0 gls
Total	5+2 apps	0 gls

NEILL, Lucas
Right-back

6'0" 12st 3lb
Born: Sydney (Australia), 9 March 1978
Debut: 8 September 2001

N

CAREER: Wakehurst SC 1984; Takeley Cubs (England) 1986; Wakehurst SC 1989; St Augustine's; Australian Institute of Sport Aug 1994; Millwall Nov 1995 (free); Blackburn Rovers Sep 2001 (£600,000).
INTERNATIONALS: Australia 22 apps.

The son of an Irish protestant who emigrated to Australia to work in the computer industry, Neill was only seventeen when he joined Millwall direct from the Australian Institute of Sport. He established himself as a player who could be called upon to play anywhere, both in defence or midfield and on either flank. Superbly built, naturally athletic and with a typical Australian will to win he became a vital ingredient of the side but he was ambitious enough to realise that to achieve his potential he would have to move. In dispute with his club, he was invited up for a week's trial at Brockhall soon after the start of the season that had seen Blackburn return to the Premiership. An injury to Curtis had created a vacancy at right-back and despite the fact that he had seen most of his action as a right-sided midfield player, Neill grasped the opportunity. His transition to the Premiership was achieved instantaneously. His tackling was sharp and controlled, his headwork so good that he coped comfortably at centre-back and his temperament superb. Moving out of defence, he became the vital cog in the link-up play that built attacks and his presence became crucial to the team. Over the next few years he gathered a mixed reputation, frequently disciplined by referees, but he continued to play in his own competitive style.

PL	147+4 apps	4 gls
FAC	15 apps	0 gls
FLC	9 apps	1 gls
UEFA	5 apps	0 gls
Total	176+4 apps	5 gls

NELSEN, Ryan

Centre-back

6'1" 12st 7lb
Born: Christchurch (New Zealand), 18 October 1977
Debut: 15 January 2005

CAREER: St Thomas of Canterbury College; Cashmere Wanderers; Christchurch United; Greensboro College (USA) 1997; Canterbury-Woolston 1998; Christchurch United 1998; Greensboro College 1998; Stanford (USA) 1999; DC United 2001 (USA); Blackburn Rovers Jan 2005 (free).
INTERNATIONALS: New Zealand 32 apps 7 gls.

A good enough cricketer to captain his country at youth level, he was persuaded to specialise at football because of the near-legendary status of his mother's family in New Zealand football. His grandfather Bob Smith and four of his brothers played for Canterbury; three of them and one of their sons became internationals. Nelsen started in the Canterbury Premier league but was offered a soccer scholarship in the USA. He completed his degree at the prestigious Stanford and was already a full international when he was the fourth man selected in the MLS draft. This took him to DC United, where he settled down to play on the right-hand side of a back three. He was also used in midfield and upfront as a situational player. His headed goal won his country the Oceanic Cup against Australia and, after overcoming a hernia problem, he led his club to the MLS title. Out of contract, he came for a two-week trial with the Rovers and was signed in the transfer window. An immediate success, he has proved possibly the finest signing ever, a totally dependable defender, strong in the air, fierce in the tackle and consistent. In his half season at the club he has never had a bad game.

PL	29 apps	0 gls
FAC	4+1 apps	0 gls
FLC	3 apps	0 gls
Total	36+1 apps	0 gls

NEWELL, Michael Colin

Striker

6'0" 11st
Born: Liverpool, 27 January 1965
Debut: 16 November 1991

CAREER: Liverpool; Crewe Alexandra Sep 1983 (trial); Wigan Athletic Oct 1983; Luton Town Jan 1986 (£120,000); Leicester City Sep 1987 (£350,000); Everton Jul 1989 (£1,100,000); Blackburn Rovers Nov 1991 (£1,100,000); Birmingham City Jul 1996 (£775,000); West Ham United Dec 1996-Feb 1997 (loan); Bradford City Mar 1997-May 1997 (loan); Aberdeen Jul 1997 (£175,000); Crewe Alexandra Mar 1999 (free); Doncaster Rovers (p-c) Jun 1999 (free); Blackpool Feb 2000-Jun 2001 (free).

The measure of the change of the Rovers' fortunes once Jack Walker assumed control is usually defined by the experiences with Mike Newell. When Don Mackay agreed terms for his transfer he turned the move down. With Kenny Dalglish introduced by Walker he accepted the move. Immediately he formed, with David Speedie, an attacking partnership that led the team to promotion via the play-offs. In the final Newell converted the penalty that proved to be the only goal of the game. A striker with power, mobility and passion, he was an ideal partner for anyone, a complete player underrated because the player alongside him took the headlines. When this was Alan Shearer it was perhaps understandable but Newell's quality should not be overlooked. Although he lost out when Chris Sutton was signed, he remained Shearer's ideal partner and his ten-minute hat-trick in the European Cup tie with Rosenborg still remains a record for the competition. Accepting his chances were receding he commenced to move from club to club before he started to gain coaching experience with Doncaster. A move to play again with Blackpool was ended by an injury that prompted his retirement. After a spell as reserve-team coach at Tranmere he moved into management with Hartlepool and led them to promotion from the Third Division. Dismissed in the close season he was appointed manager of Luton Town, when the club's new owners ran a public vote to elect the new man in charge, and led the side to promotion.

FL	113+17 apps	28 gls
FAC	9+2 apps	6 gls
FLC	14+2 apps	8 gls
PO	3 apps	2 gls
EC	5+1 apps	4 gls
CS	1 app.	0 gls
Total	145+22 apps	48 gls

NEWTON, Keith Robert

Full-back

5'11" 11st 2lb
Born: Manchester, 23 June 1941
Died: Blackburn, 16 June 1998
Debut: 19 September 1960

CAREER: Didsbury GS; Spurley Hey YC; Bolton Wanderers; Blackburn Rovers Apr 1958 (non con) Oct 1958; Everton Dec 1969 (£90,000); Burnley Jun 1972 (free); Morecambe 1978-1979; Clitheroe (p-m) Dec 1980.
INTERNATIONALS: England 27 apps.

Initially an inside forward who failed to make the grade at Bolton, he enjoyed a conversion during the Rovers' FA Youth Cup success in 1959. At centre half he looked an extremely promising player, athletic, aggressive and competitive and with a big-time temperament. Introduced to the first team at left half he settled in at left-back after David Whelan broke his leg. Razor-sharp in the tackle, he could bring the ball forward with authority and could have played in almost any position. He became his country's regular right-back and it was this that led to his departure to Everton. The Rovers had been relegated and Newton did not wish to allow this to jeapordise his England place. Although he earned a championship

Keith Newton in August 1963. (Howard Talbot Photography)

medal, he was never happy on Merseyside and when given a free transfer returned to give sterling service to Burnley. He later took over a newsagent's shop at Sudell Cross, living in Wilpshire. Subsequently he sold trophies, then acted as an agent selling Vauxhall trucks to small businesses. He fought a long battle against cancer but died a week short of his fifty-seventh birthday.

FL	306 apps	9 gls
FAC	21 apps	0 gls
FLC	30 apps	1 gl
Total	357 apps	10 gls

NIGHTINGALE, Albert

Inside forward

5'8" 10st 3lb

Born: Thrybergh, 10 November 1923

Died: Liverpool, 26 February 2006

Debut: 20 September 1951

CAREER: Thurcroft; Sheffield United Mar 1941 (am) Jun 1941; Huddersfield Town Mar 1948 (Ex £1,000+Bailey+Hutchinson); Blackburn Rovers Oct 1951 (£12,000); Leeds United Oct 1952-1957 (£10,000).

A member of a noted football family (a brother played for Scunthorpe and three others for Rotherham), he was a perpetual-motion inside forward who sported a dapper, Errol Flynn moustache. A hard man who never shirked a tackle, he looked frail but had a core of iron and never let opponent or referee have an easy game. He was at Ewood for only a year because his wife was unwilling to leave her teaching post in Yorkshire but he packed a great deal of experience in that time. He helped the club avoid relegation to the Third Division while at the same time mounting a cup run that came within a whisker of taking them to the final itself. A miner before becoming a professional footballer, he was glad to keep out of the pit thereafter and worked in the Huddersfield Parks Department for many years.

FL	35 apps	5 gls
FAC	7 apps	3 gls
Total	42 apps	8 gls

OAKES, John

Winger

5'8.5" 11st 12lb

Born: Hamilton, 6 December 1919

Died: Dumfries, 3 December 1995

Debut: 15 February 1947

CAREER: St Mary's School, Hamilton; Wolverhampton Wanderers 1935; Queen of the South Jan 1937-Feb 1947; Huddersfield Town (trial); Workington 1946; Blackburn Rovers Feb 1947 (£10,000); Manchester City Jun 1948; Workington Oct 1949-1951; Queen of the South Jun 1951-1952.

Although he was a schoolboy left-back who could play centre forward, he eventually made the grade as a winger. He came south to Wolverhampton at the age of fifteen but returned to Scotland, becoming a first-team player with Queen of the South at the age of eighteen. So proficient on either side that he took corner kicks with different feet, he was able to play on either flank, exhibiting the blistering speed that during the Second World War resulted in him being unbeaten over 100 and 120 yards on the professional sprinting circuit. An entrant for the prestigious Powderhall sprint, he served with the RAF and played little football during the Second World War until the officials of Hearts met him at the race track. He also guested for his home-town club and many English clubs sought his services as a guest, but he served in Belgium and Norway and only managed to fit in an appearance for Blackpool. Despite his talent he never fitted in well at Ewood, but he was better suited to Manchester City where he played for three seasons.

FL	35 apps	9 gls
FAC	2 apps	0 gls
Total	37 apps	9 gls

OATES, Graham
Midfield

6'2.5" 12st 4lb
Born: Bradford, 14 March 1949
Debut: 17 August 1974

CAREER: Tong Street; Manningham Mills; Bradford City Dec 1970; Blackburn Rovers Jun 1974 (ex £10,000+Hutchins); Newcastle United Mar 1976; Detroit Express (USA) May 1978 (£40,000); Bradford City 1981; California Surf (USA) Mar 1981-Aug 1981; Lidget Green; Dudley Hill Athletic (Bradford); Scarborough 1987; Gainsborough Trinity 1988.

One of the advantages of recruiting a manager who knew the lower divisions was that unsung talent was easier to find. Gordon Lee knew well that Oates was a fine midfield man at Bradford, strong in the tackle and more constructive than his gangling appearance might have prompted one to believe. Able to cover acres of ground almost effortlessly he was strong in the air, not just because of his height but because his timing was good and he was athletic. If he had desired he could have been a top-class centre-back (as he demonstrated in emergencies) but he preferred the centre of the pitch. His drive in the engine room was one of the reasons the club gained promotion in his first season and his manager's belief in him was sufficient for him to return to take him to Newcastle when he had joined the First Division side. Less successful at the highest level, he played most of the rest of his career in the USA, returning to play with Scarborough. Their elevation to the Football League cost Oates his job. He had taken his pension settlement and was thus unable to play again in the Football League.

FL	76 apps	10 gls
FAC	4 apps	1 gl
FLC	6 apps	0 gls
Total	86 apps	11gls

O'BRIEN, Burton 'Bobo'
Midfield

5'11" 10st 7lb
Born: Johannesburg (South Africa), 10 June 1981
Debut: 26 September 2000

CAREER: Celtic Boys' Club; St Mirren Jun 1998-Feb 1999; Blackburn Rovers Feb 1999-Aug 2002 (£500,000); St Mirren Feb 1999- May 1999 (loan); Crewe Alexandra Jul 2002 (trial); Livingston Aug 2002 (free); Sheffield Wednesday Jul 2005 (free).

O'Brien and his close friend David McNamee were signed by Brian Kidd but left to continue their development with St Mirren. Already a Scottish Under-21 cap and regarded as a gifted playmaker, he did not thus come to Ewood until six months later. Kidd had stressed that the pair were the club's future but Graeme Souness never viewed them in the same light. Often unable to gain a place in the reserves, they were available for transfer for many months but they decided to sit tight on their lucrative contracts before, once again moving together, the pair joined Livingston. Taking advantage of the change of FIFA rules that allowed age-group internationals to opt for another country to which they were eligible, O'Brien chose to represent South Africa. However, although he submitted the requisite application, the failure of the authorities to issue him a passport precluded him playing for the Bafana Bafana.

FLC	0+1 app.	0 gls
Total	0+1 app.	0 gls

O'KEEFE, James Vincent
Goalkeeper

6'0" 11st
Born: Birmingham, 2 April 1957
Debut: 13 November 1982

CAREER: Perry Common School (Erdington); Paget Rangers; Birmingham City Jul 1975; Peterborough United Mar 1976 (loan); Walsall Jul 1976; AP Leamington; Exeter City Jun 1978; Torquay United Feb 1980 (£30,000); Blackburn Rovers Aug 1982 (£15,000); Bury Oct 1983 (loan); Blackpool Dec 1986-Jan 1987 (loan) Feb 1989-Apr 1989 (loan); Wrexham Jul 1989 (free); Chorley Sep 1992; Exeter City 1992; Kidderminster Harriers 1993.

Having failed to make the league grade he earned himself a lifeline by his displays with Leamington, which brought him selection to the English semi-professional side. This induced Exeter to sign him and there and at Torquay he earned a reputation as one of the best goalkeepers in the lower leagues, particularly good at leaving his line and taking on players in one-to-one situations. Bobby Saxton knew him well from his time in the West Country and brought him to Ewood to back up the excellent Terry Gennoe. When called upon to deputise, he suffered by comparison to the regular choice but when Gennoe began to be afflicted by injuries O'Keefe became first choice, almost by default. Although the fans never could understand why Don Mackay preferred him to Gennoe, he had his finest hour in the Full Members' Cup final at Wembley when he defied Charlton with some important saves. A broken leg was to cost him his place and he moved to Wrexham where he had the unfortunate experience of being omitted from the team for the European Cup Winners' Cup competition because of the restrictions on foreign players. He returned to Ewood as one of the ex-players who acted as host in the hospitality suites and obtained an administrative post with the PFA.

FL	68 apps	0 gls
FAC	1 app.	0 gls
FLC	7 apps	0 gls
FMC	6 apps	0 gls
Total	82 apps	0 gls

O'LEARY, Donal Patrick
Left winger

5'9" 10st 9lb
Born: Limehouse, London, 24 June 1936
Debut: 17 December 1955

CAREER: Glasheen; Blackburn Rovers Oct 1954; Evergreen United Oct 1956; Blackburn Rovers Jul 1957-1957; Evergreen United (renamed Cork Celtic) 1956-1965; Cork Hibernians 1966-1967.

O'Leary had the kind of debut normally found in children's books. A left-back who had come from Ireland eighteen months previously, he travelled with the team to Lincoln as reserve, with the intention that he did nothing more than put out the team strip. When Bobby Langton was found to be unfit to play he pulled on the unfamiliar number eleven shirt and did so well that he actually received other opportunities. Like many young Irishmen he became homesick and was released and lived in the Cork area. A year later the Rovers' manager Johnny Carey was on holiday and decided to look him up. He issued an invitation to return to Ewood if he desired and to everyone's surprise O'Leary reported for pre-season training. However, there was no surprise return to the first team and he went back to Cork, where he played in the League of Ireland for a further ten seasons.

FL	6 apps	1 gl
FAC	1 app.	0 gls
Total	7 apps	1 gl

OLIVER, Neil
Left-back

5'11" 11st 10lb
Born: Berwick, 11 April 1967
Debut: 4 November 1989

CAREER: Berwick Borough; Coldstream; Berwick Rangers 1986; Blackburn Rovers Aug 1989 (£30,000); Falkirk Jul 1991; Berwick Rangers Mar 2000 (free); Hamilton Academicals Jan 2001 (free); East Fife Sep 2001-May 2002; Linthinglow Rose 2004.

A red-headed left-back signed as a development prospect, he struggled to find his feet in the first team. Noticeably one-sided, he was unfortunate to concede a penalty when forced to make a tackle on the opposite side and his final appearance was in an emergency in midfield. Strong in the tackle, he lacked judgement but helped Falkirk establish themselves in the Scottish Premier Division. In the 1997 Scottish Cup final he appeared to have equalised Kilmarnock's lead with a stunning strike but the effort was controversially disallowed. In his second spell at Berwick he broke his leg twice in less than a year but recovered and earned praise as a man-marking midfield player.

FL	5+1 apps	0 gls
FLC	0+1 app.	0 gls
FMC	1 app.	0 gls
Total	6+2 apps	0 gls

O'MARA, John
Striker

6'3" 11st
Born: Farnworth, 19 March 1947
Debut: 16 September 1972

CAREER: Bury; Gillingham Oct 1965; Dover Town Feb 1967-May 1967 (loan); Margate Jun 1967; Wimbledon May 1968; Brentford Mar 1971 (£1,000); Blackburn Rovers Sept 1972 (£30,000); Chelmsford Jul 1974 (free); Bradford City Dec 1974; Germiston Caledonians (South Africa) 1975-1976; Margate Nov 1976; Maidstone United Mar 1977; Margate Sep 1977; Dover Town Nov 1978; Ramsgate Nov 1979-1980; Oddfellows 1986.

Bought to solve a specific problem, he became one of the most reviled players in the club's history, a target of the dissatisfied fans who derided his gaucheness and his inability to use his physique to effect. The criticism was more than a little unfair. He did in fact have good speed but the team was struggling and his striking partner, Tony Field, was such a single-minded goalscorer that he was never going to form a partnership. The barracking affected his confidence and the new manager, Gordon Lee, had written him off before he took the job. After playing in South Africa he returned to England and for a time worked with a friend installing hand dryers. He was then a miner for eight years and an HGV driver.

FL	30+5 apps	10 gls
FAC	5+1 apps	2 gls
FLC	1 app.	0 gls
Total	36+6 apps	12 gls

OSTENSTAD, Egil Johan
Striker

5'11" 13st
Born: Haugesund (Norway), 2 January 1972
Debut: 21 August 1999

CAREER: Torvastad IL; Viking Stavanger 1989; Southampton Oct 1996 (£800,000); Blackburn Rovers Aug 1999-Jul 2003 (with £1,200,000 for Davies); Manchester City Feb 2001 (loan); Glasgow Rangers Aug 2003-Mar 2004 (free); Viking Stavangar Aug 2004.
INTERNATIONALS: Norway 18 apps 6 gls.

The Rovers had often been interested in the burly Norwegian striker but it was not until they were desperate to ship Kevin Davies back to Southampton that he finally signed. A hard-working but cumbersome striker, he had matured slowly in Norwegian football before he was taken to Southampton, where he played under Graeme Souness. He had enjoyed some good moments, including a famous hat-trick against Manchester United but, despite several false dawns at Ewood, he never established himself as a regular. Having been surplus to requirements for some time it was no surprise that he left the Rovers in August 2003 but his destination (Ibrox Park) took most fans by surprise. It perhaps also shocked Rangers' fans because Ostenstad was, as he later acknowledged, worn out. He sought an early release but refused a contract with Viking Stavangar, saying with refreshing honesty 'I'm no good.' However Roy Hodgson asked him to train with the side to help him recover from his Achilles tendon problems and when the club was facing relegation he played him during some parts of the last six games, of which five were won. Almost unbelievably he was recalled to the national side after a seven-year absence.

L	38+24 apps	12 gls
FAC	4+3 apps	0 gls
FLC	4+5 apps	1 gl
UEFA	2+1 apps	1 gl
Total	48+33 apps	14 gls

P

PARKER, Harry

Right winger

5'7" 10st 7lb
Born: Blackburn, 8 February 1933
Debut: 25 August 1951

CAREER: Lower Darwen Jnrs; Blackburn Rovers Aug 1951-May 1953; Chorley Jul 1953-Jun 1954.

The Longshaw local had probably the most accelerated introduction to the club of all time when he was invited to drop in for a trial before the 1951/52 season. Although not appearing in the public trial nor being selected for the opening reserve fixture, he made his reserve debut two days after the season opened. Shrewdly prompted by his inside partner, Les Graham, Parker was astonishing, running and crossing with brilliance and made such an impression that he was pushed forward to leave the field on his own so that he could take the plaudits. Immediately offered part-time terms, he replaced Chris Anderson in the first team but found the step up difficult. Before long he was overtaken by the embryonic brilliance of Bryan Douglas and was allowed to have three games with Chorley before signing for them the following season.

FL	3 apps	0 gls
Total	3 apps	0 gls

PARKER, Stuart John

Striker

6'1" 11st 9lb
Born: Preston, 16 February 1954
Debut: 14 August 1979

CAREER: St Annes YMCA; Blackpool Jul 1970 (app.) Apr 1972; Southend United Jul 1975 (free);

Chesterfield Feb 1977 (£17,000); Sparta (Hol) (£25,000); Blackburn Rovers Jul 1979 (£7,000); Halmstadt (Swe) 1980; Frecheville Com A; Bury Jul 1982; RC Mechelen (Bel); Preston North End; Chester City Sep 1983-Nov 1983; Blackpool; Drogheda United (Eir); Stockport County Feb 1984-Mar 1984; Witton Albion 1984-1985; Irlam Town 1985-1986; Runcorn; Barrow; South Liverpool; Northwich Victoria; Hyde United; Lancaster City; Blackpool Mechanics; Colne Dynamoes; Irlam Town (p-m); Blackpool Rovers.

Although Howard Kendall had never seen Parker play he signed him on a friend's recommendation in the knowledge that he had been playing top-class football in Holland. A tall, slim, gangling player, his relaxed elegance was out of place in the Third Division and although he was good in the air he only briefly ousted the more pragmatic Joe Craig.

FL	5+4 apps	1 gl
FLC	1 app.	0 gls
Total	6+4 apps	1 gl

PARKES, Anthony
Midfield

5'10" 11st
Born: Sheffield, 5 May 1949
Debut: 5 September 1970

CAREER: Buxton Town; Blackburn Rovers May 1970-May 1982 (£5,000).

No-one could have forecast that the young wall and floor tiler signed as a prospect from Buxton in 1970 would still be at the club thirty-three years later, but Tony Parkes has passed into history as one of the longest-serving employees of the club. A product of the tough Manor district of Sheffield, he was discovered by Eddie Quigley scoring goals in non-league football but initially he lacked the force and pace of a striker. The new manager,

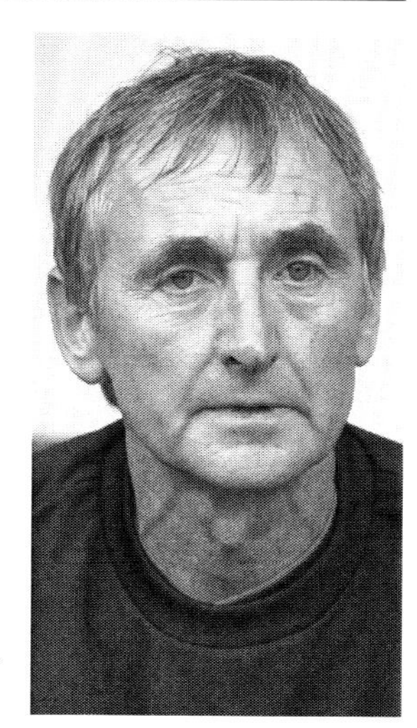

Caretaker manager Tony Parkes.

Ken Furphy, was prepared to improvise and he noticed on the training field that Parkes had skills that never translated into the first team. He moved him to midfield, where he displayed great ball-winning ability, running strongly from deep into dangerous positions and backing all this with exemplary effort. His technique on the ball was surprising, he was a difficult man to dispossess and his game was welded together with a shrewd understanding of the game itself and his own limitations. Successive managers (Furphy, Lee, Smith, Iley and Kendall) found him invaluable and no doubt Bobby Saxton would have concurred if Parkes had not made one tackle too many and broken his leg, which terminated his playing career. Fortunately he was already acting as reserve and youth-team coach, and so he had a seamless transition into a behind-the-scenes role. Saxton appointed him first-team coach and five years later, when the manager was dismissed, Parkes held the fort until Don Mackay arrived. It was to set a pattern for the future. Successive managers retained him in some capacity and when managerial changes occurred Parkes was usually drafted in to hold the ship steady. He had to do more than that when Ray Harford resigned with the club trapped at the bottom of the Premiership. While the club waited for a high-profile appointment (Roy Hodgson, though the initial intention was

Sven-Goran Eriksson) Parkes had the daunting task of keeping them in the Premiership, which he managed, to earn himself national acclaim. He acted as caretaker when Hodgson was dismissed and again when Brian Kidd went the same way, although this time he was appointed manager for the season. However, he could not arrest the decline and when Graeme Souness was brought in during February 2000 he reverted to assistant manager. He remained on the staff until the arrival of Mark Hughes in 2004 and was given a testimonial match the following year.

FL	345+5 apps	38 gls
FAC	21 apps	4 gls
FLC	21 apps	3 gls
Total	387+5 apps	45 gls

PARKIN, Timothy John
Centre half

6'1" 12st 10lb
Born: Appleby, 31 December 1957
Debut: 8 March 1977

CAREER: Appleby GS; Blackburn Rovers Dec 1974 (app.) May 1976; Fort Lauderdale Strikers (USA) Jul 1977-Aug 1977 (loan); Malmo (Sweden) Nov 1979 (£30,000); Almondsbury Greenway; Bristol Rovers Aug 1981 (£15,000); Swindon Town Jul 1986 (£27,500); Port Vale Dec 1989 (£60,000); Shrewsbury Town Sep 1991 (loan); Darlington Aug 1992 (free); Barrow Nov 1993.

It is hard to believe that the big, blond, youth-team product who was languishing in the club's reserves (with Keeley partnering Fazackerley in the first team this state of affairs had a smell of permanence) would suddenly be whisked away and find himself playing in the World Club Championship for Malmo against Olimpia of Paraguay. This was the result of catching the eye of Malmo's English coach, Bobby Houghton, a man who later rescued him from obscurity when he had returned to England and relaunched a league career that extended to more than 400 games with Bristol Rovers, Swindon Town, Port Vale, Shrewsbury and Darlington. In the process he became a journeyman defender, impressive in the air and solid under pressure. Ending back in his native Cumbria, he was appointed assistant manager of Barrow and later became Football in the Community officer in Middlesbrough before resigning to join the police force.

FL	13 apps	0 gls
Total	13 apps	0 gls

PATTERSON, John George
Goalkeeper

5'8.5" 10st 11lb
Born: East Cramlington, 6 July 1922
Died: Darwen, Octovber 2002
Debut: 8 September 1945

CAREER: North Shields; Nottingham Forest (am); Blackburn Rovers May 1945-Jun 1957; Kettering Town Jul 1957; Darwen; Great Harwood Apr 1963.

Signed after the Second World War, he was initially understudy to Marks and Hayhurst but outlasted both of them (and new signing Bill Hughes) to finally claim the first-team jersey. Sound but not showy, he lacked some authority, possibly because of lack of height. At his peak he had the misfortune to lose his place when he accidentally punched Ronnie Suart's head in training and broke a bone in his hand. The signing of Reg Elvy reduced him to odd appearances and although he actually reclaimed the jersey when Elvy was released, he surrendered it immediately by getting injured again, which permitted Harry Leyland to make his debut.

FL	107 apps	0 gls
FAC	5 apps	0 gls
Total	112 apps	0 gls

PATTERSON, Mark Andrew

Left winger

5'9" 10st 9lb
Born: Darwen, 24 May 1965
Debut: 17 September 1983

CAREER: Darwen Vale School; Blackburn Rovers Jul 1981 (app.) May 1983; Preston North End Jun 1988 (£20,000); Bury Feb 1990 (exchange); Bolton Wanderers Jan 1991 (£65,000); Sheffield United Dec 1995 (ex Blake); Southend United Mar 1997-Apr 1997 (loan); Bury Dec 1997 (£150,000); Blackpool Dec 1998-Feb 1999 (loan); Southend United Mar 1999 (free); Leight RMI; Accrington Stanley Aug 2000-Feb 2001; Darwen Mar 2001-May 2001;Rossendale United 2001; Scarborough (p-c) Nov 2001; Rossendale United Dec 2002; Leigh RMI (p-m) Dec 2002-Oct 2003; Chorley (p-m) Nov 2003-Apr 2004.

A stockily built midfield product of the club's youth system, he did not lack confidence and liked to surge forward with power and shoot with precision. Injuries and the signing of the creative Scott Sellars cost him his place but he proved a bargain signing for Preston. He roamed around all the local clubs except Burnley (he would have checked into Turf Moor but he failed a medical) but played the best football of his career at Bolton, where he helped them to the final of the Rumbelows Cup and the play-offs (although he missed both games through injury). He went into business with his brother in Blackburn (landscape gardening) but took a coaching appointment in the Conference with Scarborough. After a year the travelling became too much and he returned home and was asked to take over at Leigh RMI, where he steered them to safety after they were threatened with relegation from the Conference. Shortly into the following season he resigned after a long losing sequence but within a month was back in football as Chorley's player-manager. Success was just as elusive and he again resigned, starting work for a construction company and scouting for Colchester.

FL	89+12 apps	20 gls
FAC	3+ 1 app.	0 gls
FLC	4 apps	1 gl
FMC	2+4 apps	1 gl
Total	98+17 apps	22 gls

PEACOCK, Darren

Centre-back

6'2" 12st 6lb
Born: Bristol, 3 February 1968
Debut: 15 August 1998

CAREER: Bristol Rovers (schoolboy); Newport County Feb 1986; Hereford United Mar 1989 (free); Queens Park Rangers Dec 1990 (£200,000); Newcastle United Mar 1994 (£2,700,000); Blackburn Rovers Jun 1998-Dec 2000 (free); West Ham United Sep 2000 (loan); Wolverhampton Wanderers Oct 2000-Nov 2000 (loan).

In the early part of his career he made little progress, a serious leg injury hampering him at Newport, and it was not until he moved to QPR that he developed into a dominant, durable defender who opponents disliked playing against. A big-money transfer took him to Newcastle where, with his long hair worn in a ponytail, he became a cult figure. Surgery on a knee and the failure to agree a new contract cost him his place but Peacock held to his principals and accepted the Bosman free transfer that resulted. Anxious to replace Colin Hendry, Blackburn offered him a lucrative contract but he struggled and lost his place to Marlon Broomes. Even when the club was relegated he found that the pace of the game was becoming too much and had the rare distinction of losing his place under three different managers in one season. Placed on the transfer list he went on loan to Wolves, where he received the neck injury that ended his career.

FL	42+5 apps	1 gl
FAC	6 apps	0 gls
FLC	4 apps	0 gls

UEFA	2 apps	0 gls
Total	54+5 apps	1 gl

PEARCE, Ian Anthony
Centre-back

6'3" 14st
Born: Bury St Edmunds, 7 May 1974
Debut: 9 November 1993

CAREER: Chelsea Nov 1988 (ass sch) Aug 1991; Blackburn Rovers Oct 1993 (£300,000); West Ham United Sep 1997 (£2,300,000); Fulham Jan 2004 (ex Melville).

He was signed when only nineteen years of age without ever having started in the Chelsea first team and there was a fair degree of doubt about whether he would be a striker or a central defender. Initially used as a substitute, he established his future potential when he man-marked Romario so effectively in a friendly against Barcelona that it was decided that he would become a defender. When the veteran Tony Gale showed signs of his advancing years in the 1994/95 season, Pearce replaced him and contributed fully to the championship victory. His inexperience was exposed in the European Cup and foot surgery kept him away from the game. When he returned he found that Roy Hodgson did not value his potential and he moved to West Ham where, despite much loss of playing time with injuries, he was a physically powerful player capable of coping with the most difficult opponents.

FL	43+19 apps	2 gls
FAC	1+2 apps	0 gls
FLC	4+4 apps	1 gl
UEFA	0+1 app.	0 gls
EC	4 apps	0 gls
CS	2 apps	0 gls
Total	54+26 apps	3 gls

PEDERSEN, Morten Gamst
Midfield

5'11" 11st 6lb
Born: Vadso (Norway), 8 September 1981
Debut: 28 August 2004

CAREER: Norild 1997; Polarstjernen 1998; Norild 1999; Tromso 1999; Blackburn Rovers Aug 2004 (£2,500,000).
INTERNATIONALS: Norway 20 apps 5 gls.

Pedersen, one of only two Sami (previously known as Lapps) to play top-class football, was brought up inside the Arctic Circle, close to the border with Russia. He was in the national handball squad up to the age of sixteen and also excelled on the trampoline. However, the fact that his father Ernst had been a player for Viking Stavangar influenced him to concentrate on football. On frozen pitches in front of a handful of spectators, Pedersen commenced a career that soon took him into the top league with Tromso. Although naturally right footed, his father taught him to use his other foot so well that he became a left-sided midfield player. By 2004 he had made his international debut and had been recognised by *World Soccer* as one of the most promising young players in the game. However, there were those who questioned his durability and his arrival at Ewood appeared to confirm these doubts. After an early season debut he was left out until a shortage of players led to his inclusion at the turn of the year. During this absence Pedersen had worked hard to improve his fitness and his introduction saw him transformed. With the energy to run non-stop, he threw himself willingly into tackles, jumped superbly for the high ball, displayed confident ball control and most importantly scored goals of exquisite quality. In half a season he emerged as one of the main reasons the club survived relegation and his ability to move up front when the occasion demanded gave an added dimension to the team.

PL	37 apps	9 gls
FAC	7 apps	3 gls
FLC	3+2 app.	1 gl
Total	47+2 apps	13 gls

PEDERSEN, Per Werner

Striker

6'1" 13st
Born: Aalborg (Denmark), 30 March 1969
Debut: 22 February 1997

CAREER: Kolding BK 1974; Odense BK 1987; Lyngby BK 1990; Odense BK 1995; Blackburn Rovers Feb 1997 (£2,500,000); Borussia Mönchengladbach (Germany) Oct 1997-May 1998 (loan); RC Strasbourg (France) Aug 1998 (£750,000); Odense BK 1999-2001.
INTERNATIONALS: Denmark 6 apps 2 gls.

A tall, left-footed striker, his early career was blighted by injury that required three operations on his right knee. It was not until 1996 that he had any continuity about his football and 16 goals in the league season brought international recognition. A scoring debut followed by 4 goals against the USA in a tournament in that country alerted the scouts and he came to Ewood on trial. Desperate for a big man who could score, the Rovers signed him for a large fee, but his form was so woeful that they soon cut their losses and loaned him out. The downward spiral of his career took in an unsuccessful spell in France and then an injury ridden return to Denmark, where he finally had to face up to the fact that he would not be fit enough for top-level football. His future wife, Anja Byrial Hansen, won an Olympic gold medal with the Danish handball team. After working for several companies in the sales and marketing field he returned to football in September 2005 as sales and marketing consultant to the top-flight Danish side ACF.

PL	6+5 apps	1 gl
FLC	1+1 app.	0 gls
Total	7+6 apps	1 gl

PEDERSEN, Tore Andre

Centre-back

6'0" 12st 6lb
Born: Selbak (Norway), 29 September 1969
Debut: 17 September 1997

CAREER: Selbak Turn IF 1986; Lillestrom SK 1988; Fredrikstad FK 1989; IFK Goteborg (Sweden) 1990; SK Brann Nov 1992 (ex Bjorklund); Oldham Athletic Nov 1993-Mar 1994 (loan); Sanfrecce Hiroshima (Japan) Jul 1994 (£300,000); SK Brann Mar 1995; St Pauli (Germany) Jul 1995-Apr 1996 (loan) Apr 1996-May 1997 (£50,000); Blackburn Rovers Sep 1997 (£500,000); Eintracht Frankfurt (Germany) Oct 1998 (£225,000); Wimbledon Jul 1999-Mar 2001 (free); Trosvik Mar 2001; Fredrikstad FK Oct 2002-Nov 2003; Selbak Turn IF Dec 2004.
INTERNATIONALS: Norway 45 apps.

A calm defender, solid in all aspects of the game, he came to Ewood at a time when he was using his vast experience to camouflage the fact that his body was suffering the effects of much top-flight football. Born near Fredrikstad, he worked his way through the Norwegian divisions but it was his move to Sweden that brought him most success (two Swedish championships and a cup winners' medal). Established in the national side, where he played on the left-hand side of the back three, he wanted to enjoy the riches of the more lucrative leagues and came to England to play for Oldham in the First Division. He had helped his side to the sixth round of the FA Cup when his cruciate ligament was damaged and he was forced to return home for treatment. Spells in Japan and Germany on top of his inactivity cost him his international place but understudying Henchoz and Hendry at Blackburn did not kick-start his career. Although he left for Germany, he returned to the Premiership under Egil Olsen at Wimbledon but injury prompted the club to agree a contract termination, although it took much negotiation. During this time Pedersen considered taking up professional golf but eventually he returned to see out his career in his own country.

PL	3+2 apps	0 gls
FLC	3 apps	0 gls
Total	6+2 apps	0 gls

PELZER, Marc Sebastian*

Left-back

5'9" 12st 5lb

Born: Trier (Germany), 24 September 1980

Debut: 6 November 2002

CAREER: SV Bekond; SV Föhren; FSV Salmrohr; FC Kaiserslautern; Blackburn Rovers Jun 2002 (£300,000); SV Eintracht Trier 05 Dec 2003; FC Saarbrucken Jun 2005.

Signed despite the fact that he played only with the Kaiserslautern amateur side, he had a nightmare first season. A torn hamstring at the start prevented his inclusion and on his only first-team outing, an early round of the League Cup, he was injured early on and had to leave the field. A stocky, powerful player, he never played to his potential and when he failed to establish himself in the reserves he was released to join his home-town club.

FLC	1 app.	0 gls
Total	1 app.	0 gls

PEREZ, Sébastien

Right back/midfield

5'10.5" 11st 7lb

Born: Saint-Chamond (France), 24 November 1973

Debut: 15 August 1998

CAREER: Metiers de Lamontage (Thones); Saint-Joseph; AS Saint Etienne 1984; SC Bastia Jun 1996 (£250,000); Blackburn Rovers Jun 1998 (£2,975,000); SC Bastia Jan 1999-May 1999 (loan); Olympique Marseille May 1999-Jun 2004 (£2,500,000); Galatasaray (Turkey) Jun 2001-Jun 2002 (loan); AJ Auxerre Oct 2004 (trial); FC Istres Jan 2005 (free).

Raised in Rive-de-Ger, just 25 kilometres from Saint Etienne, it was natural that he would graduate to the famous French club. A player of massive talent, fast, skilful and with a natural high work rate, he established himself in the Saint Etienne team until knee surgery forced him to miss the best part of the season. Without him his club was relegated. Perez missed the opportunity to represent his country in the Olympic Games and a move was fashioned for him that took him to Bastia in Corsica. Best used as a right wing-back, he learned also how to play anywhere across the midfield in the 'warring jackals' style that made the club notorious. Perez's class stood out so much that for the two years he was there he was voted the best right-back in the French League by the influential *France Football*. The cosmopolitan Roy Hodgson needed considerable persuasive powers to tempt him to Ewood in the face of many offers from other clubs. He placed him on the wide right of midfield and there was no doubt that he had introduced a considerable talent. Unfortunately for Perez everything started to go wrong. Initially he was on his own in a quiet, small, Northern town. When his wife arrived with their young child they found that their daughter constantly caught colds and was unwell. He was ludicrously sent off when the innocent victim of an assault by Graeme Le Saux and then he had to undergo knee surgery to remove fragments of floating bone in his knee. By the time he returned from recuperation in France his mentor and French speaker Hodgson had been dismissed and the new manager, Brian Kidd, had already written him out of his plans. A loan move to Bastia brought him back to a climate where the sun shone and he has since performed with distinction at Marseilles and Galatasaray, where he earned a championship medal.

PL	4+1 app.	1 gl
FAC	1 app.	0 gls
UEFA	2 apps	1 gl
Total	7+1 app.	2 gls

PICKERING, Frederick

Left-back/centre forward

5'10" 12st 7lb
Born: Blackburn, 19 January 1941
Debut: 10 October 1959

CAREER; St Peter's RC School; West End; Blackburn Rovers May 1956 (non con) Jan 1958; Everton Mar 1964 (£90,000); Birmingham City Aug 1967 (£50,000); Blackpool Jun 1969 (£45,000); Blackburn Rovers Mar 1971-Feb 1972 (£10,000); Brighton & Hove Albion Mar 1972 (trial).
INTERNATIONALS: England 3 apps 5 gls.

Although he was the captain of the Rovers' side that won the FA Youth Cup in 1958, he did not appear to have the most promising career ahead of him. A former apprentice at British Northrop, he was a left-back with power and enthusiasm but was erratic. Introduced to the first team after Dave Whelan had broken his leg, he did not succeed in hiding his rawness and was sent back to the reserves, awaiting development. This might have taken forever if in one reserve game he had not latched onto a loose ball and dispatched it from the edge of the penalty area with such power and precision that the decision was made to try him at centre forward. His rawness was still evident but he demonstrated such an eye for the chance that he was introduced to the first team, leading the line, and scored two goals on his debut. Given further opportunity he matured rapidly, benefitting from the presence of Douglas to harvest goals but progressing from simply a rampaging, athletic presence to develop deft touches, subtle flicks and neat passes that brought the best out of those around him. He scored 23 goals in the 1962/63 season and when Andy McEvoy became his striking partner they formed a duo impossible to contain. He repeated the feat the following season but ended it on the books of Everton. The maximum wage had revolutionised the game and Pickering's desire to earn more than Blackburn could pay was public knowledge. His stay on Merseyside was relatively brief but productive and he earned his international debut, which brought him a hat-trick. However, he never scaled the heights he might have done. Seven years after he left the Rovers he was brought back in a last gamble to stave off relegation to the Third Division. By then he was overweight and ineffective and the next manager, Ken Furphy, quickly released him. Although he had a trial with Brighton he was not required and he returned to find driving work in Blackburn.

FL	134 apps	61 gls
FAC	10 apps	5 gls
FLC	14 apps	8 gls
Total	158 apps	74 gls

PRICE, Christopher John

Right-back

5'7" 10st 2lb
Born: Bridgnorth, 30 March 1960
Debut: 23 August 1986

CAREER: Hereford United Jan 1978; Blackburn Rovers Jul 1986 (£25,000); Aston Villa Jun 1988 (£125,000); Blackburn Rovers Feb 1992 (£150,000); Portsmouth Jan 1993 (£50,000); Dallas Sidekicks (USA); Solihull Borough; Sutton Coldfield; Cinderford Town Jun 1995; Cheltenham Town Jan 1996.

With over 300 league games to his credit at Hereford and the possessor of a balding pate, the Rovers' fans could have been forgiven for believing that the club had signed an ageing defender in the summer of 1986. In fact Price was only twenty-six and had been introduced to the Hereford first team when very young, earning a reputation as a swashbuckling, high-tempo performer who sailed into the tackle, galloped energetically down the wing and played with passion. Often lacking in strength, he played much of his best football at Ewood as a makeshift right winger, a position from which he struck several fine goals. Experiencing the disappointment of play-off defeat, he still moved into the First Division, the result of a transfer to Aston Villa. After three-and-a-half good seasons at Villa Park, he was brought back by Kenny Dalglish to provide spirit and know-how to the Rovers. Less successful this time, he did have a fine game at Wembley in the play-off victory, playing a hybrid wide-right/midfield role. When he struggled in the Premiership he was sold to Portsmouth, where he again experienced play-off disappointment. Obtaining coaching experience in Dallas, he returned to play in non-league football but found difficulty maintaining fitness. He took over as manager of Newport AFC but resigned after a few months. The following season was back in management at Cinderford.

FL	96+6 apps	14 gls
FAC	2 apps	0 gls
FLC	7 apps	0 gls
FMC	6 apps	0 gls
PO	3 apps	0 gls
Total	114+6 apps	14 gls

PRICE, John

Winger

5'4" 10st 4lb
Born: Easington, 25 October 1943
Died: Stockport, 6 May 1995
Debut: 25 September 1971

CAREER: Horden CW; Burnley Nov 1960; Stockport County May 1965 (free); Blackburn Rovers Sep 1971 (£3,000); Stockport County Mar 1974-Jun 1976 (free).

Looking smaller than his 5'4", he was a box of tricks; elusive, unpredictable and an entertainer. He had failed to build on a promising start with Burnley but at Stockport became a crowd favourite, although his lack of goals troubled his managers. When Ken Furphy hastily blended a side together, Price played a significant part in raising morale and making the team play as a unit. The next manager, Gordon Lee, had little time for players of his ilk and shipped him quickly back to Stockport. He entered the licensed trade, taking over the Grey Horse at Heaton Norris, but unhappily died by his own hand at the age of fifty-two.

FL	63+13 apps	12 gls
FAC	4+2 apps	0 gls
FLC	1+1 app.	0 gls
Total	68+16 apps	12 gls

PRIDAY, Robert Herbert

Left winger

5'9" 11st 1lb
Born: Cape Town (South Africa), 29 March 1925
Died: Johannesburg (South Africa), 30 September 1998
Debut: 19 March 1949

CAREER: Clyde (Cape Town); Liverpool Dec 1945; Blackburn Rovers Mar 1949 (£10,000); Clitheroe Aug 1951; Northwich Victoria 1952; Accrington Stanley Dec 1952; Rochdale Aug 1953-Oct 1953.

A bustling, red-haired left winger, he was one of a contingent of South Africans who arrived at Anfield as the Second World War ended. One of several left wingers (Edds, Fenton and Wharton were others) who proved it was a costly mistake when Langton was transferred to Preston, he appeared less and less likely to compensate for Langton's absence. Released, he went to work as a clerk in Clitheroe but was pulled from obscurity by first Accrington and then Rochdale, although without much effect. In 1963 he returned to work for The Tin Box Company in Cape Town but his life back in South Africa was beset by misfortune. He lost two of his six children in tragic circumstances. He also developed diabetes as a consequence of which he contracted gangrene in his left leg and had to have it amputated. Unhappily, he did not recover from the operation.

FL	44 apps	11 gls
FAC	1 app.	0 gls
Total	45 apps	11 gls

PRYDE, Robert Ireland
Centre half

6'0" 12st 4lb
Born: Methil, 20 May 1913
Died: Lytham, Jun 1998
Debut: 21 October 1933

CAREER: St Johnstone; Brechin City (loan); Blackburn Rovers May 1933 (£10); Wigan Athletic Jun 1949.

A big defensive barrier, he earned little respect in his early years at the club when people questioned his mobility and speed. It was not until the promotion season of 1938/39 that he came into his own as the rock on which the team was built and, during the Second World War, there was no finer defender in football. Selected for the Football League, even though he was a Scot, it appeared unlikely that he would return to give much service. He had, however, kept remarkably fit as an Army PT instructor and had played regularly in Italy, Greece, Yugoslavia, Czechoslavakia and Switzerland. In a poor Rovers' team he was the sole star. When age caught up with him he moved to become player-manager at Wigan, where he played on for two-and-a-half seasons. He was later a hotelier in Cleveleys and then back in Scotland, but he missed Blackburn and returned to live in Heys Close, off Livesey Branch Road. Always at the forefront of club reunions, he took an active part supporting the club until he moved to live in Lytham.

FL	117 apps	2 gls
FAC	10 apps	0 gls
Total	127 apps	2 gls
Pre-war		
FL	203 apps	9 gls
FAC	15 apps	0 gls
Total	218 apps	9 gls
Grand Total	345 apps	11 gls

QUIGLEY, Edward
Inside forward

5'8" 11st 7lb
Born: Bury, 13 July 1921
Died: Blackpool, 18 April 1997
Debut: 17 November 1951

CAREER: Radcliffe; Bury Sep 1941; Sheffield Wednesday Oct 1947 (£12,000); Preston North End Dec 1949 (£26,500); Blackburn Rovers Nov 1951 (£20,000); Bury Aug 1956 (£1,000); Mossley (p-m) Jul 1957-May 1959.

Quigley played in the pre-season trial for Bury in 1938 but made slow progress. A full-back of dubious pace, his status altered rapidly when he was moved into the attack. In his first game at centre forward he scored five goals, but it was at inside left that he proved imperious, controlling the game from deep, splitting defences with inch-perfect passes and shooting with venom. Snapped up by Sheffield Wednesday, he became a dominant influence so that Preston were forced to break the British record transfer fee to acquire his services. Curiously, the previous record had been paid by Derby County when they signed Quigley's nephew,

Johnny Morris, from Manchester United. Deepdale was a challenge he never really mastered, perhaps unhinged by the presence of the dominant force that was Tom Finney, but a move to aid Blackburn's relegation-threatened team restored his credibility. He was a major influence on the establishment of the side as a leading light in the Second Division. Eventually failure to obtain promotion led to a rebuilding of the team, but Quigley had pre-empted the decision. In his last years he had taken up a part-time salesman's job with the Renown Tyre and Rubber Co. and also applied for several player-manager's jobs. After returning to Bury he became player-manager at Mossley but returned to Bury to take charge of the youth side, developing many major talents such as Colin Bell and Alec Lindsay. A spell in management at Mossley was followed by a call to come back to the Rovers as Jack Marshall's assistant manager, which, in turn, led to him succeeding Marshall. He was relieved of his duties four years later when he exchanged positions with the club's administrative manager, Johnny Carey. Relegation cost both men their jobs but Quigley went on to manage Stockport again before becoming Saxton's chief scout when he took over at the Rovers. He later scouted for Blackpool.

FL	159 apps	92 gls
FAC	7 apps	3 gls
Total	166 apps	95 gls

QUINN, Desmond
Full-back

5'10.5" 11st 8lb
Born: Tullyverry, Co Down, 28 April 1926
Died: Liverpool, December 1990
Debut: 1 January 1948

CAREER: Royal Irish Fusiliers; Stockport County 1945 (am); Blackburn Rovers Aug 1947; Millwall Sep 1948; Bedford Town Jul 1955.

A member of the Irish Fusiliers, he joined Stockport with a fellow soldier named Clarke when they were stationed at Fulwood Barracks. A new-year posting to Ireland ended his spell with County but when he returned he was spotted by the Rovers playing for his unit on a Manchester parks pitch. He was offered amateur terms but played so well in the reserves that he was signed as a professional when he was demobbed. His only first-team opportunity came on New Year's Day, when he was required to deputise for Cook. When Millwall were reshaping their side he was offered the opportunity of first-team football and had two good seasons at The Den before Alex Jardine was signed. He is known to have died in the early 1990s.

FL	1 app.	0 gls
Total	1 app.	0 gls

QUINN, James Martin
Striker

6'0.5" 11st 6lb
Born: Belfast, 18 November 1959
Debut: 25 August 1985

CAREER: Whitchurch Alport; Oswestry Town; Swindon Town Dec 1981 (£10,000); Blackburn Rovers Aug 1984 (£32,000); Swindon Town Dec 1986 (£50,000); Leicester City Jun 1988 (£210,000); Bradford City Mar 1989 (ex Kennedy); West Ham United Jan 1990 (£320,000); AFC Bournemouth Aug 1991 (£40,000); Reading Jul 1992 (£55,000); Peterborough United Jul 1997 (free); Swindon Town (p-m) Oct 1998-Apr 2000; Weymouth Apr 2000; Hungerford Veterans; Cirencester; Northwich Victoria 2000; Hereford United Oct 2000; Highworth Town; Hayes; Northwich Victoria (p-m) Jul 2001; Shrewsbury Town (p-m) Jun 2003; Nantwich Town Oct 2004.
INTERNATIONALS: Northern Ireland 46 apps 12 gls.

Discovered by Swindon playing with Oswestry at a time when he had a job selling ice cream, he was a mobile striker who proved that he could score goals. Most of his spell at Ewood prompted harsh criticism because, although he had a fine build, took up good positions and was adept with both head and feet, he lacked charisma and dynamism. After returning to Swindon he was twice the subject of large transfers that took him to Leicester and West Ham but it was at Reading, in his veteran stage, that he reached the pinnacle of his career. His goals helped the club into the First Division and in 1995 they suffered a tragic and unfortunate defeat in the play-off final that prevented them reaching the Premier League. At that time he was joint manager with Mick Gooding. Their contracts were not renewed in 1997 but he was taken on by Peterborough as assistant manager and player. Close to forty, he still averaged a goal every other game. The chance to manage Swindon was too appealing and he retained his registration so that he could occupy the substitutes bench. He also began to appear for Hungerford Veterans and a few weeks after his dismissal by Swindon scored the winning goal at Wembley when Hungerford beat Mersey Royals in the Umbro veterans' final. When he signed for Northwich he soon found himself in charge but decided to concentrate on playing for Hereford instead. A few weeks later he had a change of heart and went back to Northwich as player-manager. In the close season of 2003 he was given the task of trying to lead Shrewsbury back into the Football League and soon restarted his playing career, leading the club back from the wilderness. When his side began to struggle at the higher level he resigned so that a new man would have ample chance to save them.

FL	58+13 apps	17 gls
FAC	4 apps	3 gls
FLC	6+1 apps	2 gls
FMC	2 apps	1 gl
Total	70+14 apps	23 gls

R

RADFORD, John

Striker

5'11" 12st 12lb
Born: Pontefract, 23 February 1947
Debut: 25 February 1978

CAREER: Hemsworth School; Hemsworth YC; Arsenal Oct 1962 (app.) Mar 1964; West Ham United Dec 1976 (£80,000); Blackburn Rovers Feb 1978-Jun 1979 (£20,000); Bishop's Stortford (p-c).
INTERNATIONALS: England 2 apps.

Twenty-four hours after he had signed amateur forms for Bradford City he was recruited by Arsenal. It was the start of a distinguished connection during which Radford collected many honours, chief of which was being involved in the double side of 1971. A robust, strong-running, high-jumping striker, his job was to physically pressure defences to help create opportunities for Kennedy and Graham. He also scored over 100 goals himself, his ability to jump early and hang in the air being reminiscent of Uwe Seeler. Struggling with injury when he moved to West Ham, he went on a lengthy barren spell, but Jim Smith persuaded him that he would have no trouble in the Second Division. Unfortunately, Smith resigned soon afterwards, Jim Iley came and went and Radford played most of his Rovers career under temporary manager John Pickering. So little of his sharpness now remained that Blackburn opted for the limited but hard-working Joe Craig and Radford retired to enter the licensed trade in Essex and then Hertfordshire. He resumed playing with the local club, Bishop's Stortford, and later coached and managed them.

FL	36 apps	10 gls
FAC	1 app.	1 gl
FLC	1 app.	0 gls
Total	38 apps	11 gls

RAMSBOTTOM, Neil

Goalkeeper

6'0" 12st
Born: Blackburn, 25 February 1946
Debut: 20 January 1979

CAREER: St Stephen's jun sc; Audley Sec Sc; St Stephen's; Blackpool (trial); Bury Aug 1963 (non con) Jul 1964; Blackpool Feb 1971 (ex £13,000+Murray); Crewe Alexandra Jan 1972 (loan); Coventry City Mar 1972 (£10,000); Sheffield Wednesday Aug 1975; Plymouth Argyle Jul 1976; Blackburn Rovers Jan 1978 (free); New Jersey Americans (USA); Sheffield United Oct 1979; Bradford City Aug 1980; AFC Bournemouth Aug 1983-Oct 1983; Chorley.

The Rovers had every opportunity to sign Ramsbottom when he was an apprentice plumber at Blackamoor School. The Rovers trained at the school but they ignored the ex-town schoolboy team representative even though the school groundsman asked them to take a look. Jack Weddle took him to Blackpool but it was Bury who signed him and introduced him to their first team. He gained a reputation as a sound rather than spectacular player but never settled with Blackpool following a high-priced transfer. At Coventry he played the best football of his career but he had become a journeyman by the time he came to his home town. The Rovers' goalkeeper, John Butcher, was erratic but it was not until he broke his nose that Ramsbottom made his debut. Slow to leave his line and erratic in judgement, he was clearly past his best and he was soon released. He continued to live locally, working in the insurance business.

FL	10 apps	0 gls
Total	10 apps	0 gls

RANDELL, Colin William

Midfield

5'9" 10st 8lb
Born: Skewen, 12 December 1952
Debut: 28 August 1982

CAREER: Lonlas YC; Coventry City Nov 1967 (app.) Nov 1970; Plymouth Argyle Sep 1973 (free); Exeter City Sep 1977 (£10,000); Plymouth Argyle Jul 1979 (£60,000); Blackburn Rovers Aug 1982 (£40,000); Newport County Jan 1984-May 1984 (loan); Swansea City Jul 1985-Jun 1986 (free); Barry Town Jan 1987.

A lookalike of the English international Ray Wilkins, he had the same tidy, involved, sideways style that always looked like it needed an injection of vigour. Born and raised in Wales in a highly successful youth set-up, he rescued his career in the West Country where he became one of the best players in a somewhat obscure area. Having served Bobby Saxton at two clubs it was not a surprise to see him follow him to Ewood, nor that he was given the playmaker's role. However, he lost his position on the right to the emerging Simon Barker and when he moved to the left lost that position to Mark Patterson. After hanging up his boots he managed Briton Ferry but resigned in March 1990 to become a PT instructor with the South Wales police force.

FL	72+1 apps	7 gls
FAC	5 apps	0 gls
FLC	4 apps	0 gls
Total	81+1 apps	7 gls

RATCLIFFE, James Barrie*

Winger

5'8" 10st 5lb
Born: Blackburn, 21 September 1941
Debut: 19 March 1960

CAREER: St James'; Blackburn Tech Coll; Blackburn Rovers 1956; Bolton Wanderers 1958 (am);

Blackburn Rovers May 1958 (am) Sep 1958; Scunthorpe United May 1964; Rochdale Jul 1965-May 1966; Clitheroe Nov 1966.

The Ratcliffe brothers, Brian and Barrie, were promising cricketers with East Lancashire and juniors with the Rovers. Brian went on to become a first-team stalwart at The Meadows but Barrie was more preoccupied with sprinting in summer (in 1957 he came fourth in the 220 yards in the All England Schools Championships) and was a better footballer. A right winger who used his explosive pace, he was happiest on the left but in the campaign when the club won the FA Youth Cup in 1959 he played on the right. During the semi-final at Old Trafford he proved he had the capabilities of making a good professional. Unprotected by the referee, he was repeatedly fouled and finished the game unrecognisable, with mud over his entire body, and later it was found his legs and body were covered in bruises. He never flinched and played his part in a dramatic victory. On first-team duty he experienced much of the same. Not the best manipulator of the ball, he put down his head and ran and full-backs of the era had few qualms about trying to intimidate such a fragile-looking youngster. His father had a butcher's stall on Blackburn market and Barrie was often behind the counter when not playing.

FL	36 apps	4 gls
FAC	5 apps	1 gl
FLC	9 apps	3 gls
Total	50 apps	8 gls

RATHBONE, Michael John 'Basil'
Full-back

5'10" 11st 13lb
Born: Birmingham 6 November 1958
Debut: 10 March 1979

CAREER: Sheldon Heath School; Sir Wilfred Martineau School, Villa Boys; Birmingham City Aug 1975 (app.) Nov 1976; Blackburn Rovers Feb 1979 (loan) Mar 1979 (£40,000); Preston North End Jul 1987 (£20,000); Darwen Aug 1991; Halifax Town 1993.

Brought on loan, he appeared to have talked himself out of a move when he got sent off for dissent, but acting manager John Pickering was able to persuade the board to finance his transfer. The following season he was joined by the man who was to be his full-back partner for years, Jim Branagan. Rathbone was a right-back but when Branagan proved demonstratively that he was not a left-back, Rathbone volunteered to play out of position. Not appreciably two-footed, he made the transition and worked on his left foot so much that he was able to favour it. Strong in the tackle and hard to shake off, he became a favourite of the crowd but a broken leg and the arrival of Chris Sulley forced him to seek first-team opportunities with Preston. As his career faded he became commercial manager at Darwen but trained as a physiotherapist and was taken on in that capacity by Halifax. He also played a little, drove the team bus and, when the club was threatened with relegation from the Football League, took over as manager from John McGrath. He continued to live in Blackburn, building up a private physiotherapist practice, but returned to football when Preston hired him as their 'physio'. In 2002 the Preston manager David Moyes left for Everton and soon came back to take Rathbone with him.

FL	270+3 apps	2 gls
FAC	15 apps	0 gls
FLC	14 apps	0 gls
FMC	4 apps	0 gls
Total	303+3 apps	2 gls

REED, Adam Maurice
Centre defender

6'0" 12st
Born: Bishop Auckland, 18 February 1975

CAREER: Darlington Jul 1993; Blackburn Rovers Aug 1995 (£180,000); Darlington Feb 1997-May 1997 (loan); Rochdale Dec 1997-Feb 1998 (loan); Darlington Jul 1998 (free); York City Jul 2003 (trial); Harrogate Town Aug 2003 (trial); Whitby Town Aug 2003-May 2004; Counden & Leeholme Jnrs.

The first signing made after they won the Premiership, he came to Ewood with the reputation of being a ball-playing defender in the Alan Hansen mould but, despite being loaned out, made little progress. His only first-team involvement was when he sat on the bench for a League Cup tie at Preston, where a weakened side was fielded. He returned to play five seasons with Darlington but remained an enigma who never achieved his potential.

REEVES, Brian Thomas
Goalkeeper

5'11" 12st
Born: Skelmersdale, 18 February 1939
Debut: 22 October 1960

CAREER: Skelmersdale Boys; Everton (am) Burscough; Blackburn Rovers Jan 1960 (non con) Aug 1960; Scunthorpe United Apr 1962 (free); Southport Jul 1965-May 1969 (free); Formby Mar 1970-Apr 1970.

Pure fortune brought Reeves to Ewood. He had gained representative honours for the Kenyan FA when serving with the RAF and had been invited for a trial with Arsenal during his next leave. He had little time and Matt Woods, whose mother lived opposite Reeves's parents, invited him to come to the Rovers. The club was hardly able to believe what they had discovered, a lithe, athletic goalkeeper with natural skills. He was signed and within a year was given a first-team debut. There his flaws came out. He could never kick a dead ball and he was inclined to nervousness, ironically suffering a lack of rapport with his mentor Woods. When Fred Else was signed he left, but played for a few years before opening an insurance agency in Southport.

FL	12 apps	0 gls
FAC	5 apps	0 gls
Total	17 apps	0 gls

REID, Nicholas Scott
Midfield

5'10" 11st 10lb
Born: Ormston, 30 October 1960
Debut: 15 August 1987

CAREER: Chorlton High School; Pudsey Jnrs; Whithall Jnrs; Manchester City May 1977 (app.) Nov 1978; Seattle Sounders (USA) Apr 1982-Aug 1982 (loan); Blackburn Rovers Jul 1987 (free); Bristol City Sep 1992 (loan); West Bromwich Albion Dec 1992 (free); Wycombe Wanderers Mar 1994 (free); Woking Sep 1995; Bury Feb 1996; Sligo Rovers (Eir) Aug 1997-May 1999.

Although he only played just over 200 games he earned himself the respect that fans reserve for special players, ones who will run all day, never shirk a tackle or concede defeat. A strong, fit man without guile or subtlety, he was added to the Rovers' staff because he, by example, made other players work harder. A natural captain, he led the team through repeatedly unsuccessful play-off campaigns, ironically losing his place when they were at last successful. The inspiration behind West Brom's play-off victory against Port Vale, he moved into management in the League of Ireland with Sligo, where they had a famous League Cup final victory over Shelbourne. Having studied for a physiotherapy qualification he was back locally in 1999 when Burnley appointed him to their backroom staff.

FL	160+14 apps	9 gls
FAC	6+2 apps	0 gls
FLC	13 apps	0 gls

FMC	5+1 apps	1 gl
PO	8 apps	0 gls
Total	192+17 apps	10 gls

REID, Steven John
Midfielder

6'1" 12st 4lb
Born: Kingston upon Thames, 10 March 1981
Debut: 23 August 2003

CAREER: Millwall May 1998; Blackburn Rovers Jul 2003 (£2,500,000).
INTERNATIONALS: Eire 16 apps 2 gls.

Born in Kingston upon Thames, Reid qualified for the Republic of Ireland because his father came from Galway. He grew up in east London, where he soon joined the schoolboy ranks at Millwall. A naturally talented player, capable of playing on either side of the pitch in defence or midfield, he played for the England Under-16 side before electing to represent Ireland at Under-18 level. A first teamer at Millwall from the age of twenty, his career was retarded slightly by persistent injury problems. His ability to play anywhere and his casual elegance evoked reminiscences of Paul McGrath from the Irish fans and a stunning goal in his second international futher endeared him. When the Rovers lost Damien Duff to Chelsea they immediately stepped up their pursuit of Reid but, the early months at Ewood, he proved that he was happier on the opposite side. Prone to injury, he did not obtain a regular first-team place until the new manager, Mark Hughes, started to use him in an advanced central midfield role.

PL	45+15 apps	3 gls
FAC	2+4 apps	0 gls
FLC	2+1 app.	0 gls
UEFA	1+1 app.	0 gls
Total	50+21 apps	3 gls

REITMAIER, Claus
Goalkeeper

6'1.5" 14st
Born: Wurzberg (Germany), 17 March 1964
Debut: 18 December 1990

CAREER: FV 04 Wurzburg; Wurzburger Kickers; Viktoria Aschaffenburg 1986; Wiener SC (Austria) 1989; Blackburn Rovers Dec 1990 (trial); Stuttgart Kickers 1991; FC Kaiserslautern 1993; Karlsruher SC 1993; Vfl Wolfsburg 1998; Borussia Mönchengladbach Sep 2003-Jun 2004; Rot-Weiss Erfurst Jul 2004; Lillestrom SK (Norway) May 2005.

With Terry Gennoe injured and Darren Collier indifferent, Don Mackay took the trouble to bring Reitmaier over in the winter continental break for a trial. The FMC tie against Everton certainly was a trial and conceding four behind a sieve-like defence left him bemused. He returned home for Christmas shortly after, the reason why he did not reappear in the New Year being explained by neither club nor player. Moving back to Germany from Austria he had a splendid career, playing regularly in the Bundesliga up to the age of forty, a player noted for his physical strength and reflexes and who acquired the consistency that once eluded him.

FMC	1 app.	0 gls
Total	1 app.	0 gls

RICHARDS, Marc John
Striker

6'0" 12st 7lb
Born: Wolverhampton 8 July 1982
Debut: 31 October 2000

CAREER: Crewe Alexandra (sch); Hednesford Town; Blackburn Rovers Jul 1999-Jul 2003 (£5,000); Crewe Alexandra Aug 2001-Sep 2001 (loan); Stoke City Sep 2001 (trial); Oldham Athletic Oct 2001-Dec 2001 (loan); Halifax Town Feb 2002-Mar 2002 (loan); Swansea City Nov 2002-May 2003 (loan); Northampton Town Jun 2003 (free); Rochdale Mar 2005-May 2005 (loan); Bristol Rovers Jul 2005 (trial); Barnsley Sep 2005.

Signed from non-league football at an early age, he achieved some success with the reserves but struggled when introduced in the League Cup. It was to be two years before he again played for the first team, again in the early rounds of the League Cup. Appearing from the bench against Walsall, he played through extra time and when the tie was decided on penalties scored the decisive one. Loaned out to Swansea, he came back a more complete player, able to hold the ball up and with abundant energy, but the club released him. An England Under-21 international, he scored one of the great goals at this level when, at the Reebok stadium, he raced half the length of the field before scoring.

FLC	1+1 app.	0 gls
Total	1+1 app.	0 gls

RICHARDSON, Leam Nathan
Full-back

5'8" 11st 4lb
Born: Leeds, 29 November 1979
Debut: 13 October 1999

CAREER: St James'; Leeds United (sch); Blackburn Rovers; Bolton Wanderers Jul 2000 (£50,000); Notts County Nov 2001 (loan); Blackpool Dec 2002 (loan) Jul 2003-Jun 2005 (free); Carlisle May 2005 (trial); Rochdale Jul 2005 (trial); Accrington Stanley Aug 2005.

The captain of the club's FA Youth Cup final side in 1998, he was given his debut in his home city in the League Cup. A sound defender with a good attitude, his career stagnated at Ewood and although he was signed by Bolton he had little more opportunity with that club. Loan moves to Notts County and Blackpool furthered his experience and he had a two-season spell at the seaside that ended with his recent release.

FLC	1 app.	0 gls
Total	1 app.	0 gls

RICHARDSON, Lee James
Midfield

5'11" 11st
Born: Halifax, 12 March 1969
Debut: 25 August 1990

CAREER: Halifax Town Aug 1986 (trainee) Jul 1987; Watford Feb 1989 (£175,000); Blackburn Rovers Aug 1990 (ex Kennedy); Aberdeen Sep 1992 (£150,000); Oldham Athletic Jul 1994 (£325,000); Stockport County Aug 1997-Sep 1997 (loan); Huddersfield Town Oct 1997 (£65,000); Livingston Feb 2000 (free); Notts County Jul 2000 (trial); Chesterfield Aug 2000 (free).

A dynamic, long-haired midfield player who relied on powerful upfield surges rather than skill, he became a favourite of the crowd once he shook off the niggling injuries that blighted his first months at the club. Although he had difficulty in sustaining the tempo for ninety minutes the game was seldom dull when he was involved. When not guaranteed a regular place he moved to Aberdeen, where he played in the Scottish Cup final and scored, despite playing with a broken toe. His services were in demand with a succession of clubs in the lower leagues, but fitness problems persisted and he eventually became assistant manager at Chesterfield, moving up to acting manager and steering them away from relegation.

FL	50+12 apps	3 gls
FLC	1+2 app.	0 gls
FMC	1 app.	0 gls
PO	1+2 apps	0 gls
Total	53+16 apps	3 gls

RIPLEY, Stuart Edward
Right winger

5'11" 12st 6lb
Born: Middlesbrough, 20 November 1967
Debut: 15 August 1992

CAREER: Middlesbrough Aug 1984 (app.) Dec 1985; Bolton Wanderers Feb 1986-Mar 1986 (loan); Blackburn Rovers Jul 1992 (£1,300,000); Southampton Jul 1998-Jul 2002 (£1,500,000); Barnsley Nov 2000-Jan 2001 (loan); Sheffield Wednesday Mar 2001-May 2001 (loan); Sheffield United Feb 2002 (trial).
INTERNATIONALS: England 2 apps.

Having spent the majority of his career with his local side, he moved to Blackburn to help establish his career and push his prospects of an England place. Capable of playing on either side but happiest on the right, he relied upon trickery rather than speed to obtain the opening for a cross. He became a vital part of the team because he was the outlet player for the defence, making himself open for the pass and retaining possession until a support player could arrive. With Wilcox he gave the Premiership championship team balance, both players knowing the value of back tracking to assist in defence if necessary. Troubled by injuries, he was seldom a force after 1995, although he added to his one England cap when he came on as a substitute against Moldova (departing a few minutes later with a pulled hamstring). His career faded when he went to Southampton, and he became a physiotherapist and fitness trainer when he retired.

Stuart Ripley in 1994.

FL	172+15 apps	13 gls
FAC	14 apps	3 gls
FLC	18 apps	0 gls
UEFA	2 apps	0 gls
EC	4+1 apps	0 gls
CS	2 apps	0 gls
Total	212+16 apps	16 gls

ROBERTS, John Thomas
Goalkeeper

5'11" 12st
Born: Cessnock (Australia), 24 March 1944
Debut: 2 May 1966

CAREER: Cessnock; APIA Leichardt; Chelsea Jan 1966-Apr 1966 (trial); Blackburn Rovers Apr 1966 (£5,000); Chesterfield Aug 1967 (loan) Feb 1968-May 1968; Bradford City Aug 1968; Southend United Jan 1971; Northampton Town Jul 1972-Jun 1973; APIA Leichardt 1973-1974.
INTERNATIONALS: Australia 1 app.

After he had taken part in a World Cup play-off game in Phnom Penh he came to England looking for a club. During a long trial at Chelsea he had been deemed promising, but the club was not in need of a goalkeeper. On the other hand they knew that Blackburn, where a part-time draughtsman backed up a fading Fred Else, were desperate for new blood, and so they advised him to try his luck further north. Playing behind a bad side he found the going hard and was stretchered off in his third game. He received no other chance. John Barton arrived the following season and, despite being in good form in the reserves, Roberts never played for the first team again. In the lower divisions Roberts proved an admirably agile goalkeeper and he rounded his career off by returning for two seasons in Australia with his first big club.

FL	3 apps	0 gls
Total	3 apps	0 gls

ROBERTS, Thomas
Left-back

5'6.5" 9st 4lb
Born: Liverpool, 28 July 1927
Died: Birkenhead, January 2001
Debut: 12 April 1952

CAREER: Skelmersdale United; Blackburn Rovers Dec 1951; Watford Dec 1954 (£1,000); Chester Feb 1956-May 1956 (free); Skelmersdale United.

Being signed by a club in the Football League is normally a happy event for players who have been playing non-league football for some time. Unhappily for Roberts, a sound if small left-back, his new club had one of the great players in the game, Bill Eckersley, in this position. If Eckersley had not had a dispute over terms Roberts might have been allowed to leave earlier than his eventual move to Watford. Even here he was unlucky for, after a promising debut, he was ineligible for the forthcoming cup tie and his deputy played well enough to retain his place. When he asked for a transfer he was allowed to join Chester, where he had problems finding accommodation and the club had no house available. The appointment of John Harris as player-manager further altered his position because Harris was a full-back. When he rejected terms offered for the following season he was given a free transfer.

FL	6 apps	0 gls
Total	6 apps	0 gls

ROBINSON, Ryan
Goalkeeper

6'2" 13st 2lb
Born: Tebay, 13 October 1982

CAREER: Blackburn Rovers 1998 (trainee)-Jun 2003; Wigan Athletic Sep 2002 (trial); Doncaster Rovers May 2003 (trial); Southend United Jul 2003-Jun 2004 (free); Wivenhoe Town Nov 2003 (loan); Morecambe Aug 2004 (free); Kendal Town Oct 2004 (loan).

A solid, calm goalkeeper who worked his way through the youth side, he was outstanding in the FA Youth Cup semi-final of 2001 when he defied Liverpool through 120 minutes and then won the tie by making saves in the penalty shoot-out. Eight times named as substitute goalkeeper for the first team, he was released in 2003 and had only 2 league appearances with Southend to his credit. Moving closer to his Cumbrian home town, he saw surprisingly little action with Morecambe in the Conference.

ROGERS, Edward Eamonn*
Midfield

5'9" 11st 5lb
Born: Dublin, 14 April 1947
Debut: 8 September 1965

CAREER: Larkview; Blackburn Rovers Aug 1962 (app.) May 1965; Charlton Athletic Oct 1971-Jun 1973 (ex £7,777+Endean); Northampton Town Nov 1972 (loan).
INTERNATIONALS: Eire 19 apps 5 gls.

The Rovers never had a more promising player than the quiet Irish lad who attended a school where they only played Gaelic games. With quick feet, acceleration, ball-winning ability and drive, he also had an eye for goal and the ability to play in any position. Nominally a midfield man, he could play on either wing, could be pushed up front and might even have developed into the best right-back the club had if he had not gone on strike and refused to play there. Successive managers failed to coax him away from his enigmatic ways or even ensure he did not turn out looking like a vagrant. He combined long unkempt hair, a beard and

Eamonn Rogers in August 1970. (Howard Talbot Photography)

moustache with the ability to make his strip look like he had slept in it after first using it for gardening but although he looked like a tramp he had the touch of an angel. Transferred to Charlton because of exasperation, his career was cut short when he was thrown through the windscreen of a car, receiving lacerations and a broken wrist. They were not career-threatening injuries but the club was losing patience and he was released. He returned to Ireland for a trial with Waterford but nothing developed and one of the potentially great players simply self destructed.

FL	159+6 apps	30 gls
FAC	4 apps	0 gls
FLC	14 apps	9 gls
Total	177+6 apps	39 gls

ROGERS, William

Winger

5'7" 10st 5lb
Born: Swarthmoor, Ulverston, 3 July 1919
Died: Barrow, February 1974
Debut: 29 August 1938
CAREER: Barrow; Preston North End Aug 1937; Blackburn Rovers Jun 1938 (free); Barrow Oct 1947-May 1953 (free).

A plasterer who played in the Lancashire Combination with Barrow, he was spotted by Preston but received little encouragement and was unloaded after one season. This was fortunate for the Rovers because they surprisingly introduced him to the right wing in place of Jack Bruton, and his strong running onto the delightful passes of Whiteside made him a force. Keen to cut inside and athletic in pursuit of high balls, he formed with Langton a young, energetic pair of wingers who did much to guarantee promotion. He lost much of his career to the Second World War and subsequently returned to help rebuild Barrow. He later became a shopkeeper in the town and served as a director of the football club.

FL	32 apps	6 gls
FAC	3 apps	3 gls
Total	35 apps	9 gls
Pre-war		
FL	41 apps	18 gls
FAC	7 apps	0 gls
Total	48 apps	18 gls
Grand Total	83 apps	27 gls

ROUND, Paul Gordon

Utility

6'0" 11st
Born: Blackburn, 22 June 1959
Debut: 26 March 1977

CAREER: St Edmund Arrowsmith School; Blackburn Rovers Jul 1975 (app.) Aug 1977; Bury Feb 1982 (free); Altrincham; Barrow; Chorley; Rossendale United; Clitheroe 1986.

Superbly built and with the talent to play in a variety of positions, he was perhaps a victim of his easy-going temperament, never achieving the intensity desired. A teenage striker, he was converted to central defence but when Howard Kendall arrived he experienced his longest spell in the first team, at right-back. The arrival of Branagan ended this run and he was in the process of being converted to midfield when he had a trial with Bury.

FL	41+10 apps	5 gls
FAC	4 apps	0 gls
FLC	5 apps	0 gls
Total	50+10 apps	5 gls

RUSSELL, Alexander
Inside forward

5'8" 11st
Born: Seaham, 21 February 1944
Debut: 15 August 1970

CAREER: Marsden CW Jnrs; Everton Dec 1961; Southport Nov 1963; Blackburn Rovers Aug 1970 (ex Calloway); Tranmere Rovers Jul 1971; Crewe Alexandra Oct 1972; Southport Nov 1972; Los Angeles Aztecs (USA) Apr 1975-Aug 1975; Bangor City 1975; Formby Nov 1975; Fleetwood Hesketh 1977-1979.

Having spent seven years toiling at Southport it was a surprise that he was rescued by Eddie Quigley. A dark, swarthy player, he produced plenty of honest effort and, at a time when the club had players with attitude problems, he was a welcome addition to the squad. The relegation that ensued was not down to him but he was moved on as the club rebuilt. After a brief spell in the USA he returned to his long-time home in Southport and went back to his former trade as a printer.

FL	22+2 apps	4 gls
FAC	1 app.	0 gls
FLC	1 app.	0 gls
Total	24+2 apps	4 gls

S

SALMON, Michael Bernard
Goalkeeper

6'2" 12st 12lb
Born: Leyland, 14 July 1964
Debut: 15 May 1982

CAREER: Farington Jun Sc; Wellfield High Sc; Blackburn Rovers Mar 1981 (non con) Oct 1981; Leeds United Aug 1982-Sep 1982 (loan); Chester City Oct 1982-Jan 1983 (loan); Stockport County Aug 1983 (free); Bolton Wanderers Jul 1986 (free); Wrexham Mar 1987 (loan) Aug 1987 (£18,000); Charlton Athetic Jul 1989 (£100,000); Oxford United Dec 1998 (loan); Ipswich Town Jul 1999 (free); Tonbridge Angels Jul 2002.

A product of the club's youth team, he was given only 1 first-team game in the last match of the season. Tall and capable, he did not develop until he was in his mid-twenties and had to step down into the lower divisions before he could gain a reputation and work his way back into the top flight with Charlton. Even here he took time to displace Bob Bolder, but eventually demonstrated himself to be a competent goalkeeper, even in the top flight.

FL	1 app.	0 gls
Total	1 app.	0 gls

SAVAGE, Robert William
Midfield

6'1" 11st 11lb
Born: Wrexham, 18 October 1974
Debut: 14 January 2005

CAREER: Bryn Alyn,Gwersyllt; Llay United; Bradley Youths; Crewe Alexandra (school of excellence); Manchester United Oct 1988 (schoolboy) Jul 1993;

Crewe Alexandra Jul 1994; Leicester City Jul 1997 (£400,000); Birmingham City May 2002 (£2,500,000); Blackburn Rovers Jan 2005 (£3,000,000).
INTERNATIONALS: Wales 39 apps 2 gls.

Brought up in the Bradley area of Wrexham, he averaged three goals a game as a junior at Llay. Spotted training at the Crewe school of excellence he was offered trainee terms at Manchester United, where he escaped notice in a FA Youth Cup-winning team that included David Beckham. An injury suffered in a car crash contributed to his release but he was rescued by Crewe and converted into a central midfield player. Two subsequent moves to Leicester and Birmingham established him a reputation as a competitive, all-action player whose energy levels and desire to tackle quickly often brought him into conflict with the opposition. Impossible to miss with his blond ponytail and incredible non-stop motor, he became probably the most notorious personality in the game to fans of the opposition. The relationship he established with his boyhood hero Mark Hughes playing with the Welsh national team led to him seeking a transfer from Birmingham. After an acrimonious series of negotiations he joined the Rovers in the January transfer window but injury restricteded his contributions.

PL	25 apps	0 gls
FAC	3+1 apps	0 gls
FLC	4 apps	0 gls
Total	32+1 apps	0 gls

SELLARS, Scott
Midfield

5'8" 10st
Born: Sheffield, 27 November 1965
Debut: 23 August 1986

CAREER: Leeds United Jul 1982 (app.) Jul 1983; Blackburn Rovers Jul 1986 (£20,000); Leeds United Jul 1992 (£950,000); Newcastle United Mar 1993 (£700,000); Bolton Wanderers Dec 1995 (£750,000); Huddersfield Town Jun 1999 (free); FC Aarhus (Denmark) Feb 2001 (loan) Apr 2001-Jan 2002; Port Vale Jan 2002 (trial); Mansfield Town Mar 2002-May 2002; Kettering Town Jul 2002 (trial); Mansfield Town Jul 2002-Jun 2003.

One of the most skilful players to represent the club, he played in midfield but liked to occupy a position very wide on the left. Although small, he was a competitor who could beat a succession of opponents with sinuous dribbles and deft flicks. He could also see the bigger picture and was capable of hitting a cross or switching play and could be relied upon to back track when necessary. Although he was involved in the promotion campaign of 1992 he had been in and out of the team under Kenny Dalglish and seized the opportunity to move back to his first team, Leeds United. Subsequent moves to Newcastle and Bolton brought him the distinction of being one of the few players to be promoted to the Premiership with three clubs.

FL	194+8 apps	35 gls
FAC	11 apps	2 gls
FLC	12 apps	3 gls
FMC	9 apps	0 gls
PO	11 apps	1 gl
Total	237+8 apps	41 gls

SHANAHAN, Terence Christopher
Striker

5'10.5" 11st
Born: Paddington, 5 December 1951
Debut: 25 September 1971

CAREER: Tottenham Hotspur Aug 1967; Ipswich Town Jul 1969; Blackburn Rovers Sep 1971-Oct 1971 (loan); Halifax Town Nov 1971; Chesterfield Oct 1974; Millwall Apr 1976; AFC Bournemouth Jul 1977; Aldershot Town Jul 1978-Dec 1979; Phoenix Firebirds (USA).

A dark-haired striker with enthusiasm and mobility, he came to the club on loan when Ken Furphy was rebuilding the side. His trial was reasonably productive but not sufficient to produce a permanent move. Soon after he moved to Halifax, and spent the next eight years playing for clubs in the lower divisions. His best years were at Chesterfield, where he scored at a rate of a goal every other game and became a firm favourite in spite of his hair-trigger temper. After a spell in the USA he was out of the game until 1987 when Harry Redknapp appointed him coach at Bournemouth. By the time he left five years later he had risen to assistant manager.

FL	6 apps	2 gls
Total	6 apps	2 gls

SHARPLES, George Frank Vincent
Wing half

5'11" 12st 11lb
Born: Ellesmere Port, 20 September 1943
Debut: 20 March 1965

CAREER: Wirral GS; Everton Jun 1959 (ground staff) Sep 1960; Blackburn Rovers Mar 1965 (£7,000); Southport Jul 1971-Jul 1972 (free).

Blond and sturdy, he had been a starter at youth level but found it difficult to break into an Everton team where he competed with internationals like Jim Gabriel, Tony Kay and Mick Meagan. The move to Blackburn gave him the opportunity to establish himself as a powerful left half who tackled hard and ran strongly. Relegation to the Second Division brought a change to 4-2-4 and Sharples's lack of mobility decreed that he would not play midfield. He made the transformation to centre-back at the same time as Ronnie Clayton, the pair dovetailing harmoniously to produce one of the tightest defences the club has had. Their lack of height, however, prompted the signing of John Coddington, leaving only one place for either Sharples and Clayton. The club was in the process of trying Sharples in midfield when he broke his leg at Derby. Recovery was slow and he never played for the first team again. For many years he lived in Pleasington and was distribution manager at the Star Paper Mill.

FL	99+4 apps	5 gls
FAC	5 apps	0 gls
FLC	4+1 app.	0 gls
Total	108+5 apps	5 gls

SHEARER, Alan
Striker

5'11" 11st 3lb
Born: Newcastle, 13 August 1970
Debut: 15 August 1992

CAREER: Gosforth High School; Cramlington Jnrs; Wallsend Boys' Club 1983; Southampton Jul 1986 (trainee) Apr 1988; Blackburn Rovers Jul 1992 (£3,300,000); Newcastle United Jul 1996 (£15,000,000).
INTERNATIONALS: England 63 apps 30 gls.

In four seasons, of which a half was lost to cruciate ligament surgery, he wrote his name indelibly into the history of the club. A complete striker with a big-match temperament, he was signed as a twenty-one-year-old in the face of competition from Manchester United. Scoring goals was entirely natural to the man; he scored on his debut and simply never stopped, but he was far more than a goalscorer. A strong man with fierce acceleration and the ability to roam wide, he could beat a man by sheer, raw power as easily as dribble past him. Out wide he was the finest crosser of the ball the club has perhaps seen; in the penalty area he had a total desire to reach the ball, which produced a harvest of goals from both head and feet. Outside the penalty area he could shoot with savage power and unbelievable accuracy. Above all his will to win was infectious,

Alan Shearer scores Blackburn's first goal against Rosenburg in 1995.

permeating through the team. As the last weeks of the 1995 Premiership season wound down and the team began to have self-doubts, Shearer was immense, a colossus making the impossible dream come true. He was equally as talismanic for his country but at Blackburn realists knew that, despite his close relationship with Jack Walker, Shearer was never going to play out his career at a small-town club tucked away in the heart of Lancashire. His departure for Newcastle, orchestrated by the media and the avaricious courting of the largest clubs, was tinged with bitterness and the feeling of betrayal that years later is only just showing the first signs of softening. He was awarded the OBE in 2001 for his services to football.

PL	132+6 apps	112 gls
FAC	8 apps	2 gls
FLC	16 apps	14 gls
UEFA	2 apps	1 gl
EC	6 apps	1 gl
CS	1 app.	0 gls
Total	165+6 apps	130 gls

SHEARER, Duncan Nichol
Striker

5'10" 10st 10lb
Born: Fort William, 28 August 1962
Debut: 28 March 1992

CAREER: Loch Harbour HS; Inverness Clachnacuddin; Chelsea Nov 1983; Huddersfield Town Mar 1986 (free); Swindon Town Jun 1988 (£250,000); Blackburn Rovers Mar 1992 (£750,000); Aberdeen Jul 1992 (£550,000); Inverness Caledonian Thistle Sep 1997; Buckie Thistle (p-m) October 2004.
INTERNATIONALS: Scotland 7 apps.

Duncan Shearer followed his brother David into the Football League but had to wait two years for his league debut. Moves to Huddersfield and Swindon established him as one of the best goal-scorers in the lower divisions (he scored over 100 goals at the rate of one every two games) and he helped the latter to promotion to the First Division (although irregularities at the club lost them this honour). A robust, old-fashioned leader of the line, he scored on his debut for the Rovers but thereafter was seldom utilised. Moving to Aberdeen, he struck the best form of his career, scoring 22 goals by the start of March and at the age of thirty made his debut for his country. Injury had a disruptive effect on the rest of his career and he returned to his roots to see out the last of it.

FL	5+1 apps	1 gl
PO	0+1 app.	0 gls
Total	5+2 apps	1 gl

SHEPSTONE, Paul Thomas Adam
Midfield

5'8" 10st 6lb
Born: Coventry, 8 November 1970
Debut: 25 August 1990

CAREER: Coventry City Jul 1987 (trainee) Nov 1987; Birmingham City Jul 1989-Mar 1990; Atherstone United; Blackburn Rovers May 1990 (free); York City Mar 1992 (loan); Motherwell Jun 1992 (£60,000); Stafford Rangers 1993; Wycombe Wanderers Jan 1994-Feb 1994; Crewe Alexandra (trial); West Bromwich Albion (trial); Halifax Town (trial); Stafford Rangers Mar 1994; Hinckley Athletic; Nuneaton Borough 1995.

A graduate of Lilleshall who had gained English youth honours, he found the transition from age group football difficult. Looking slighter than his physical measurements would imply, he operated on the left-hand side of midfield, conspicuous because of his work rate and refusal to be deterred no matter how hopeless the position of the game. His only goal for the club was a stunning effort when he threw himself full length to deflect a thunderously struck but wayward shot into the goal. Although his career never scaled great heights the Rovers made a tidy profit when they sold him to Motherwell.

FL	16+10 apps	1 gl
FAC	0+1 app.	0 gls
FLC	1 app.	0 gls
FMC	1 app.	0 gls
Total	18+11 apps	1 gl

SHERWOOD, Timothy Alan
Midfield

6'0" 11st 6lb
Born: St Albans, 6 February 1969
Debut: 22 February 1992

CAREER: Watford Feb 1986 (app.) Feb 1987; Norwich City Jul 1989 (£175,000); Blackburn Rovers Feb 1992 (loan) Mar 1992 (£500,000); Tottenham Hotspur Feb 1999 (£3,500,000); Portsmouth Jan 2003-Jun 2004 (loan); Coventry City Jul 2004-Jun 2005 (free).
INTERNATIONALS: England 3 apps.

Sherwood had lost his way at Norwich when Kenny Dalglish brought him to Blackburn, but he played little part in his first season that brought promotion to the Premiership. Improving his fitness, he became an invaluable member of the Rovers' side. A mobile performer, positionally adept, he drove the team from midfield and by the time the club won the Premiership in 1995 he was team captain. Failure to consolidate on the club's achievements led to unrest in the team and Sherwood's outspoken criticism of Roy Hodgson created a situation where in the end both men left the club. He was transferred to Tottenham but, although he managed 3 English caps, he gained less honours than might have been expected. Moving on to Portsmouth and Coventry he experienced a problem with his inner ear and, when this was corrected, he broke his leg.

L	239+7 apps	25 gls
FAC	15+2 apps	4 gls
FLC	24+1 apps	2 gls
UEFA	4 apps	0 gls
EC	6 apps	0 gls
CS	2 apps	0 gls
Total	290+10 apps	31 gls

Tim Sherwood in 1994.

SHORT, Jonathan Craig*
Centre-back

6'1" 13st 8lb
Born: Bridlington, 25 June 1968
Debut: 7 August 1999

CAREER: Lady Lumley's HS, Scarborough; Pickering Town; Scarborough Oct 1987 (free); Notts County Jul 1989 (£100,000); Derby County Sep 1992 (£2,500,000); Everton Jul 1995 (£2,700,000); Blackburn Rovers Aug 1999-Jun 2005 (£1,750,000); Sheffield United Jun 2005 (free).

Short and his brother Christian (who also played in the Football League) spent much of their childhood in Germany because their parents were teachers in Army schools. Having failed his exams, Craig was working on a building site and playing non-league football when he received the chance to turn professional with Scarborough. His play since then has displayed all the hallmarks of a man determined not to go back to manual labour. A centre-back of great determination and purpose who never flinched from a physical challenge, he has been able to remain in top-class football because of the attention he has paid to physical fitness. In the early days of Kenny Dalglish's time as manager he could have joined the Rovers but elected instead to play for Derby. Seven years later he received another chance when Brian Kidd invited him to see if he could help with the same task: get Blackburn back to the top flight. This time he agreed and was one of the few players bought by Kidd to be retained by Souness when he took over. Not expected to have the pace to survive in the Premiership, he proved all the critics wrong and formed, with Henning Berg, one of the club's best centre-back partnerships.

L	131+3 apps	4 gls
FAC	6 apps	0 gls
FLC	4 apps	1 gl
UEFA	2 apps	0 gls
Total	143+3 apps	5 gls

SILVESTER, Peter Dennis
Striker

5'11" 11st 8lb
Born: Wokingham, 19 February 1948
Debut: 9 October 1976

CAREER: West Ham United (trial); Chelsea (trial); Reading Dec 1964 (app.) Feb 1966; Norwich City Sep 1969 (£20,000); Colchester United Oct 1973-Nov 1973 (loan); Southend United Feb 1974 (£11,000); Baltimore Comets (USA) May 1974-Aug 1974; Reading Mar 1975 (loan); Baltimore Comets (USA) May 1975-Aug 1975; San Diego Jaws (USA) May 1976-Jul 1976; Vancouver Whitecaps (Canada) Jul 1976-Aug 1976; Blackburn Rovers Oct 1976-Nov 1976 (loan); Washington Diplomats (USA) Jan 1977-Aug 1977 (£7,500); Cambridge United Aug 1977-Oct 1978; Maidstone United; Peziporicos Larnaca (Cyprus); Hamilton Academicals.

The Rovers had reached such a low ebb in 1976 that they simply were catalogue shopping to find a big man who could lead the line with a modicum of intelligence and some vigour. Invited for a month to fill the vacancy was Silvester, a man who had scored nearly 100 goals in the Football League before he had decided to sample the riches available in the USA. Never a candidate for a permanent move, he looked like a journeyman, although standards were so poor that this actually upgraded the team.

FL	5 apps	1 gl
Total	5 apps	1 gl

SIMS, Harry Christopher
Full-back

5'11" 12st 6lb
Born: Liverpool, 6 December 1939
Debut: 26 October 1963

CAREER: Clitheroe; Blackburn Rovers Apr 1959-Jun 1966; Clitheroe; Great Harwood Wellington.

Although born on Merseyside he was discovered playing as an amateur at Clitheroe. In the reserves he established himself as a sound, no-nonsense right-back with a tough tackle and good attitude. His first-team debut was on the opposite side when Newton was moved to cover for England, and later in the season he won a battle with Walter Joyce for the number three shirt after Newton was seriously injured. The following season Sims started at right-back because Clayton was absent, but when the great man returned Sims lost his place in the reshuffle and never played for the first team again. He turned down moves to Rotherham and Barrow, believing that he could still make the First Division grade but, two years later, he was at Clitheroe and subsequently played in the Blackburn Combination with Great Harwood Wellington.

FL	13 apps	0 gls
Total	13 apps	0 gls

SKINNER, Craig Richard
Right winger

5'10" 11st
Born: Heywood, 21 October 1970
Debut: 3 October 1989

CAREER: Blackburn Rovers Oct 1985 (trainee) Jun 1989; Plymouth Argyle Aug 1992 (loan) Sep 1992 (PE Marker); Wrexham Aug 1995 (£50,000); York City Mar 1999-Jul 2001 (£20,000); Leigh RMI 2001; Northwich Victoria Nov 2001; Kidsgrove Town May 2002.

A strong-running right winger, capable of beating a man on the outside, he was brought into the first team when Don Mackay was dismissed and Tony Parkes acted as manager. Jason Wilcox was introduced on the opposite flank and went on to gain international honours but, at the time, there was little to chose between the two players (Simon Garner later revealing that he thought Skinner had the most potential). Injured soon after Kenny Dalglish took over, he was sent to Plymouth as makeweight in the deal to bring Nicky Marker to Ewood. He took time to establish a place in Devon but found unexpected success when converted to striker. A move to Wrexham followed, but a subsequent spell at York was punctured by hernia and knee problems. Told he would not be considered for selection he stayed away and was sacked, but later earned reinstatement after the intervention of the FA.

FL	11+5 apps	0 gls
FAC	1 app.	0 gls
FLC	0+1 app.	0 gls
FMC	3 apps	1 gl
Total	15+6 apps	1 gl

SLATER, Robert David
Midfield

5'10.5" 12st 7lb
Born: Ormskirk, 26 November 1964
Debut: 20 August 1994

CAREER: Revesby De La Salle College; Picnic Point HS; Revesby Rovers; Revesby Workers' Club; Auburn; Panania RSL; Sydney Croatia 1982-85; St George 1986; Blacktown City 1986; Sydney Croatia 1987; Nottingham Forest 1986 (trial); RSC Anderlecht (Belgium) Aug 1988; RC Lens (France) Aug 1989 (£500,000); Blackburn Rovers Aug 1994 (£300,000); West Ham United Aug 1995 (ex Holmes); Southampton Aug 1996 (£250,000); Wolverhampton Wanderers Mar 1998 (£50,000); Northern Spirit Jul 1998-2001; Manly-Warringah (p-c) 2002.
INTERNATIONALS: Australia 29 apps 1 gl.

Although not born too far from Ewood, in Ormskirk, he left the country at the age of eighteen months, when his parents emigrated to Australia. He graduated quickly from local football in the town where he lived to playing for the country's top clubs and starred in the Seoul

Olympics. Like many of his teammates he had the desire to sample the riches of Europe but a trial at Nottingham Forest produced nothing and he returned home. Having rethought his position, he returned to try continental football and was taken on by Anderlecht, but could not hold down a first-team place. Disillusioned, he left for Lens where his future was shaped. His strong running from midfield, boundless energy and appealing personality captured the hearts of the public who made the stocky redhead a cult figure. He married a local girl and was voted Oceania Footballer of the Year for 1991 and 1993, but the urge to play at a higher level was always paramount. He was on the point of agreeing terms with Aston Villa when Kenny Dalglish hijacked the move and introduced him to the team in the Charity Shield match. Intended to compensate for the missing Batty, he played in the early part of the season that brought the Premiership title to Ewood, but lost his place to the steadier Mark Atkins. His championship medal made him only the second Australian to receive this honour. Sacrificed when Ray Harford started to tinker with Dalglish's team, he moved to three other English clubs before being released by Wolves, ostensibly to return to France. He then received an offer to return to Australia to captain Northern Spirit, a team from the North Shore district of Sydney who had been elected into the Australian League. After two seasons he retired but stayed with the club to handle public relations. His opinionated views made him a chat show favourite, and he is one of the most outspoken but respected football journalists in Australia, who has a capacity for stirring up enthusiasm and upsetting the Australian football authorities.

PL	12+6 apps	0 gls
FAC	1 app.	0 gls
FLC	1 app.	0 gls
UEFA	1 app.	0 gls
CS	1 app.	0 gls
Total	16+6 apps	0 gls

SMITH, Jack

CENTRE FORWARD

5'11" 12st 2lb
Born: Batley, 17 February 1915
Died: Trafford, 21 April 1975
Debut: 31 August 1946

CAREER: Whitehall Printers (Leeds); Dewsbury Moor Welfare; Huddersfield Town Jun 1932; Newcastle United Sep 1934 (£2,500); Manchester United Feb 1938 (£6,500); Blackburn Rovers Mar 1946 (£3,000); Port Vale May 1947-1948 (£2,500); Macclesfield.

A dark-haired, energetic centre forward who was strong in the air, he was over thirty when signed from Manchester United. A scoring sensation with his first club, Huddersfield, he was at his best at Newcastle where he scored 69 goals in 104 league games. His tireless roving unsettled defences but time was catching up with him when he came to Ewood, and he did not remain long. Finishing his career with Macclesfield, he subsequently had a spell as their manager.

FL	30 apps	12 gls
FAC	4 apps	0 gls
Total	34 apps	12 gls

SMITH, William Henry

Utility

5'10" 11st 6lb
Born: East Stonehouse, Devon, 7 September 1926
Debut: 29 November 1952

CAREER: Plymouth United Aug 1944; Plymouth Argyle Aug 1945; Reading Aug 1947; Northampton Town Jul 1948; Birmingham City Feb 1950; Blackburn Rovers Dec 1952; Accrington Stanley (p-c) Jul 1960-Mar 1962.

Considered the finest utility player the club has ever had, he had played in every outfield position when he took over in goal for the reserves in a game when the goalkeeper had to leave the field. A centre half with Plymouth, he moved to centre forward at Reading but eventually settled down at inside forward. Initially used by Blackburn as an auxiliary centre forward, his supreme adaptability was recognised when he slipped seamlessly back to the right half position. Ironically, his most regular position became right-back, to which he was switched in December 1954 to replace Ronnie Suart. A didactic presence, he was used in the reserves to help with the progress of the young players, which earned him the nickname 'Colonel Bill'. Accrington noted his coaching potential and took him to Peel Park as player-coach, where he stayed until financial considerations forced them to resign from the Football League. He subsequently had a spell coaching at Queen Elizabeth Grammar School.

FL	119 apps	10 gls
FAC	9 apps	2 gls
Total	128 apps	12 gls

SPEEDIE, David Robert
Striker

5'7" 11st
Born: Glenrothes, 20 February 1960
Debut: 17 August 1991

CAREER: Ardwick School, Doncaster; Barnsley Oct 1978; Darlington Jun 1980 (free); Chelsea Jun 1982 (£70,000); Coventry City Jul 1987 (£750,000); Liverpool Feb 1991 (£675,000); Blackburn Rovers Aug 1991 (£250,000); Southampton Jul 1992 (P Ex Shearer); Birmingham City Nov 1992-Jan 1993 (loan); West Bromwich Albion Jan 1993-Mar 1993 (loan); West Ham United Mar 1993-May 1993 (loan); Leicester City Aug 1993 (free); Crawley Town Aug 1995-Jan 1996 (free); Atherstone United Apr 1996-May 1996; Hendon Aug 1996-Sep 1996; Stamford; Kirby Muxloe; Guiseley Mar 1997; Crook Town Sep 1997.
INTERNATIONALS: Scotland 10 apps.

After ten months as a miner he received the opportunity to play football with Barnsley. A midfield player, he had a waspish personality and a tenacious, abrasive presence, but did little to suggest there was not to be a return to the pit. Released to join Darlington, he had the fortune to be moved up front when John Stalker was injured, and proved an instant success, niggling, hustling, always on hand for the half chance. Despite his lack of physique he had the approach of a hard man and scored goals. Big money transfers to Chelsea and Coventry established him a reputation at the top level and brought him international honours. Kenny Dalglish spotted his potential to be better than he was achieving at Coventry and, to the surprise of many, took him to Anfield. However, the manager resigned and his successor, Graeme Souness, had no time for him. With the first traces of the Jack Walker millions, Don Mackay agreed transfer fees for Speedie and the Israeli international Rosenthal. Rosenthal declined to drop a division, but Speedie just wanted to play and an Ewood legend was born. He was already in the scoring groove when Kenny Dalglish took over and harnessed him to an ideal partner, Mike Newell. He scored goals all season, his final day hat-trick at Plymouth earning a play-off spot. A few days later he was fouled in the penalty area at Wembley and Newell stepped up to score the most vital penalty kick in the club's history, earning them promotion to the Premier League. It was a personal disaster for Speedie, who had to be immediately expended so that the club could obtain Alan Shearer from Southampton. No club ever again held the same appeal for the permanently ill tempered, disgruntled Speedie, and only three years later he was contemplating playing for the Chetwynd Arms in Nuneaton when Crawley offered him a chance. Problems with referees that had bedeviled his career intensified in the non-league. He parted company with Crawley over their interpretation of his disciplinary record, was sent off on his debut for Guiseley

David Speedie in 1992.

and survived one other game before his next red card. After applying for a PFA course for future referees he took sounder advice and became an accredited FIFA agent.

FL	34+2 apps	23 gls
FAC	2 apps	1 gl
FLC	2 apps	0 gls
PO	3 apps	2 gls
Total	41+2 apps	26 gls

SPEIGHT, Michael
Midfield

5'10.5" 12st 7lb
Born: Upton, 1 November 1951
Debut: 9 August 1980

CAREER: Sheffield United Jan 1968 (app.) May 1969; Blackburn Rovers Jul 1980 (£60,000); Grimsby Town Aug 1982 (£25,000); Bury Mar 1983 (loan); Chester City (p-c) Jul 1983-Dec 1985; Flekkefjord (Norway) (p-m) Jan 1986.

A vastly experienced midfield man who had been on a tour of New Zealand with the England 'B' side, he was brought to Ewood because of his known ability to man mark and distribute accurately. With Kendall and Parkes he formed the hardest engine room the club has ever possessed, contributing to an excellent defensive record. Able to fill in at centre-back, he assisted fully in a first season in which promotion to the First Division was lost on goal difference. The immediate exit of Kendall signalled Speight's departure. Incompatible with Bobby Saxton, he chose to air his grievances and was advised to find another club. At Chester he received a brief opportunity to be acting manager and enjoyed the experience but, forthright as ever, proved too strong a character for the next manager. He therefore left his position as player-coach to take up a similar appointment in Norway. He stayed in the country for nearly twenty years, acting as coach for Drobak/Frogn, Vidar, Moss, Sogndal and Mjondalen.

FL	50+1 apps	4 gls
FLC	6 apps	0 gls
Total	56+1 apps	4 gls

STAPLETON, Francis Anthony
Striker

5'11" 13st
Born: Dublin, 10 July 1956
Debut: 19 August 1989

CAREER: St Martin's; Bolton Athletic; Wolverhampton Wanderers (trial); Manchester United (trial); Arsenal Jun 1972 (app.) Sep 1973; Manchester United Aug 1981 (£900,000); Ajax (Holland) Aug 1987; Derby County Mar 1988 (loan); Le Havre (France); Blackburn Rovers Aug 1989-Jul 1991 (free); Aldershot Town Sep 1991 (free); Huddersfield Town Oct 1991 (free); Bradford City (p-m) Dec 1991-May 1994; Brighton & Hove Albion Nov 1994. INTERNATIONALS: Eire 70 apps 20 gls.

By the time he came to Ewood he had amassed over 400 league appearances and scored 135 league goals for Arsenal and Manchester United. He had also many cup medals from both clubs and well over fifty international caps for the Republic of Ireland. At his best he had been a mobile striker, a threat with both head and either foot, and was regarded by many as the model of a modern striker. He had spent the tail end of his career chasing pay days on the continent but was brought back to England by the Rovers in the hope that his experience would rub off. He arrived with fitness problems and had a wretched first season, but appeared to have played himself back to something more acceptable in his second season. Nevertheless, he was released and soon was pursuing a managerial career at Bradford. Dismissed in May 1994, he briefly played for Brighton but left because he had the desire to manage. In 1996 he was appointed coach of the New England Revolution in the MLS but his lack of empathy with Latin players led to his dismissal. He returned home to supervise his business interests around Stockport and has been brought in by Sam Allardyce to act as coach to the Bolton strikers.

FL	80+1 apps	13 gls
FAC	4 apps	1 gl
FLC	5 apps	1 gl
FMC	1 app.	0 gls
PO	2 apps	0 gls
Total	92+1 apps	15 gls

STARBUCK, Philip Michael

Striker

5'10" 11st
Born: Nottingham, 24 November 1968
Debut: 8 September 1990

CAREER: Nottingham Forest Jun 1984 (app.) Aug 1986; Birmingham City Mar 1988 (loan); Hereford United Feb 1990-Mar 1990 (loan); Blackburn Rovers Sep 1990 (loan); Huddersfield Town Aug 1991 (£80,000); Sheffield United Dec 1994 (loan) Jan 1995 (£150,000); Bristol City Sep 1995-Oct 1995 (loan); RKC Waalwijk (Holland) Feb 1997-Mar 1997 (loan); Oldham Athletic Mar 1997 (loan) Aug 1997 (free); Plymouth Argyle Mar 1998-Jun 1998 (ex Littlejohn); Halifax Town 1998; Cambridge City 1998-Mar 1999; Burton Albion Mar 1999; Hucknall Town (p-m) Dec 1999-Jun 2003; Leigh RMI (p-m) Oct 2004-Nov 2004; Arnold Town Dec 2004.

Considered a prospect by Brian Clough, his career never took off and his loan spell at Ewood was just one of many around the Football League. Hard-working and applied, he never looked sharp in front of goal, although his spell at Huddersfield partially disproved this diagnosis. With Kevin Street of Crewe he founded the Christians in Sport group, who meet in Wythenshawe for Bible readings. The most famous players connected with this movement are Matt Jansen and Gavin Peacock. His career has been littered with oddities. He headed a goal for Huddersfield against Wigan within three seconds of coming on as substitute. At Sheffield he took the field plastered with stickers, printed locally, that questioned their notorious chairman's intelligence. When he moved to join his former teammate Nigel Clough at Burton he became interested in coaching and was employed as a part-time coach by Leicester. When appointed to manage Hucknall he made a step perhaps unrivalled in the game's history; he appointed his father-in-law, Sammy Chapman, to be his coach. He became number two to Mark Patterson at Leigh RMI and, when Patterson resigned in October 2003, he replaced him, but resigned when their playing budget was cut by two-thirds.

FL	5+1 apps	1 gl
Total	5+1 apps	1 gl

STEAD, Jonathan Graeme

Striker

6'3" 11st 7lb
Born: Huddersfield, 7 April 1983
Debut: 7 February 2004

CAREER: Hepworth United; Huddersfield Town Nov 2001; Blackburn Rovers Feb 2004 (£1,000,000), Sunderland Jan 2005 (£1,800,000).

As a youngster, Stead concentrated on swimming as his main sport, but he was spotted by Huddersfield playing for Hepworth United on the left wing. Naturally enough, given his height, the club converted him to a striking position and when he was given an opportunity with the first team he quickly scored goals. In 2003/04 he was top scorer in Division Three with 16 goals when the Rovers secured his services in the January transfer window. The club had intended to sign the American international Brian McBride but at the last minute he opted for Fulham and, with time running out, the Rovers had to move hastily to sign him before the deadline. The youngster made a sensational impact, scoring on his debut, and most of his 6 goals secured the club wins. Without them the Rovers would have certainly been relegated. The following season he struggled but kept working at his game, never giving anything but solid effort.

PL	32+10 apps	8 gls
FAC	1+3 apps	0 gls
FLC	0+1 app.	0 gls
Total	33+14 apps	8 gls

STEPHAN, Harold William

Inside forward/wing half

5'5.5" 9st 10lb
Born: Farnworth, 24 February 1924
Died: Bingley, 11 June 2011
Debut: 16 May 1942

CAREER: Blackburn Rovers Sep 1942 (am) Dec 1943; Mossley Aug 1948; Chorley Jul 1951.

A small, dark-haired player who sported a moustache, he arrived in the Second World War years and earned a reputation for doggedness and determination. An inside forward for two seasons, he was converted to wing half and had a spell in the first team replacing Arnold Whiteside. Hardly required in 1948, he joined up with his old teammate Len Butt at Mossley. The Rovers retained his registration and Carlisle offered their asking fee, but Stephan turned the move down. Soon after, Accrington Stanley agreed a fee for Stephan and Bob Tomlinson, who was in an identical situation. The transfer was lodged with the Football League but Butt refused to sign their release forms. The matter went to a FA Commission of Inquiry but neither player joined Accrington.

FL	13 apps	1 gl
FAC	2 apps	0 gls
Total	15 apps	1 gl

STEPHENSON, Roy

Inside forward

5'5" 10st 7lb
Born: Crook, 27 May 1932
Died: Ipswich, 4 February 2000
Debut: 9 November 1957

CAREER: Sunniside Jnrs; Crook Colliery Welfare; Burnley Jun 1949; Rotherham United Sep 1956; Blackburn Rovers Nov 1957 (£5,000); Leicester City Mar 1959 (£7,500); Ipswich Town Jul 1960; Lowestoft Town Jun 1965.

When, in 1957, Tommy Briggs was displaying signs of age, the Rovers thought that an economical way of replacing him would be to move young Peter Dobing to the centre and sign Stephenson to play inside. A veteran who might have made more appearances for Burnley if he had not worked as a coal board draughtsman, he had moved to Rotherham. He slotted easily into the team but, despite his great pace, he was not a natural goalscorer, nor was Dobing a leader of the line. As promotion became a possibility Tommy Johnston was signed to play centre forward and Stephenson was reduced to back-up appearances, although he was also a vital part of the cup team that reached the semi-final stage. In the First Division he was utilised little, which turned out to his advantage. He signed for Ipswich, was used more logically on the right wing and ended with a Second and then a First Division championship medal. He put down his roots in East Anglia, remaining there until he died of stomach cancer in 2000.

FL	21 apps	5 gls
FAC	6 apps	0 gls
Total	27 apps	5 gls

STEWART, Gareth John
Goalkeeper

6'0" 12st 10lb
Born: Preston, 3 February 1980

CAREER: Brownedge St Mary's; Blackburn Rovers May 1997; Bournemouth May 1999 (free).

Stewart's father and uncle were well-known local goalkeepers, so it was no surprise that he became a competent goalkeeper who represented England at several age-group levels. He kept goal when the club reached the final of the FA Youth Cup but always appeared suspect because of his lack of height. Probably the best kicker of the ball ever seen, he was born to cope with the back-pass rule. A move to Bournemouth brought him two seasons of regular play before he lost his place. He was named as substitute goalkeeper on just one occasion, when Flowers was injured and the third goalkeeper Williams was on loan at QPR.

STONEHOUSE, Kevin
Striker

5'11" 11st 10lb
Born: Bishop Auckland, 20 September 1959
Debut: 29 September 1979

CAREER: Shildon; Blackburn Rovers Jul 1979; Huddersfield Town Mar 1983 (£25,000); Blackpool Mar 1984 (£25,000); Darlington Aug 1987 (free); Carlisle United Mar 1989 (loan); Rochdale Jul 1989-Jan 1990 (free); Bishop Auckland 1990; South Bank, Northallerton Town; Willington.

A slim redhead who liked to strike from the wide-left position, he was an unexpected find made by Howard Kendall's scout in the North-East. With pace and a screaming shot, he was a shifty player who was difficult to mark. A superb penalty taker, he missed only one of eleven he took for the Rovers. He left the Rovers following a misguided attempt to convert him into a midfield player, but continued to give value to several clubs, during which he took his league goal-scoring total to 72. Despite his slender frame, he proved to be a durable player and he was still playing in 1996 at Willington, where he was assistant manager and physiotherapist. By the millenium he was manager at Ossett Town.

FL	77+8 apps	27 gls
FAC	2 apps	0 gls
FLC	3+1 apps	2 gls
Total	82+9 apps	29 gls

SUART, Ronald
Full-back/centre half

5'11" 12st 6lb
Born: Kendal, 18 November 1920
Debut: 24 September 1949

CAREER: Netherfield; Blackpool Jan 1939; Blackburn Rovers Sep 1949 (£10,000); Wigan Athletic (p-m) Jul 1955-1956.

Having spent his youth playing in the Barrow area, he was discovered by Blackpool playing for Netherfield. If this had not happened Suart might have followed his brother, Ken, who became a rugby league professional with Barrow. He progressed rapidly with Blackpool and would have played in the 1948 cup final if he had not been injured, but the presence of Shimwell and Garrett limited his opportunities. A move to join the Rovers promised more playing time, and this proved to be the case. Initially he played centre half, but later he took over at right-back from David Gray. The dome of his balding head hinted at the cerebral and this was exactly what he brought to the game, positioning well and being unruffled by pressure. At full-back he was an ideal foil for the élan of Eckersley, the pair being one of the best full-back partnerships at the club. As age caught up and he lost his place to Bill Smith he decided to move into management with Wigan. Masterminding them to the Lancashire Junior Cup, his star was on the ascendancy and he moved on to Scunthorpe before having nine years with Blackpool. He later moved to Chelsea, who he served in a variety of roles (including manager) for sixteen years.

FL	176 apps	0 gls
FAC	11 apps	0 gls
Total	187 apps	0 gls

SUKER, Hakan
Striker

6'3" 12st 11lb
Born: Adapazari, Sakarya (Turkey), 1 September 1971
Debut: 1 March 2003

CAREER: Sakaryaspor 1987; Bursapsor 1990; Galatasaray 1992; Torino (Italy) 1995; Galatasaray Oct 1995; Inter Milan (Italy) Jun 2000 (£10,000,000); Parma (Italy) Jan 2002-May 2002; Blackburn Rovers Dec 2002-May 2003 (free):Galatasaray Jul 2003 (free).
INTERNATIONALS: Turkey 102 apps 46 gls.

Lionised in his own country as 'the bull of the Bosphorus', he was a teenage prodigy who played for his home town at the age of sixteen. A man of great athleticism, he allied boundless energy to an ideal physique and used constant movement to undermine defences. Supreme in the air, he became a legend in Turkey although his personal life was not without tragedy. His wife died in the 1999 earthquake and even though he was a national hero in his own country, he failed to impress with three Italian clubs. It was when the last of these released him, soon after he had helped his country take third place in the 2002 World Cup, that Graeme Souness had the opportunity to bring him to Ewood. Having worked with him at Galatasaray he knew the man well but, before his plans could bear fruit and before his debut, Sukur broke a leg during training. Working unbelievably hard to achieve fitness, he finally made his debut but, beyond a couple of clinically executed goals against Fulham, he made no impact and returned to Turkey at the end of the season. Although Turkey did not qualify for the World Cup Finals, Sukur was recalled to the national side for the final qualifying games and in playing became only the third Turk to play 100 games for his country.

PL	7+2 apps	2 gls
Total	7+2 apps	2 gls

SULLEY, Christopher Stephen
Left-back

5'9" 11st
Born: Camberwell, 3 December 1959
Debut: 11 March 1987

CAREER: Chelsea Jul 1976 (app.); AFC Bournemouth Mar 1981; Dundee United Jul 1986 (£15,000); Blackburn Rovers Mar 1987 (loan) Apr 1987 (£15,000); Port Vale Aug 1992 (free); Preston North End Jul 1993-1994 (free).

A sound left-back who liked to move forward, he tackled well, distributed the ball with precision and was one of the few full-backs who would support the attack inside the winger in the manner of an old-fashioned left half. After over 200 games for Bournemouth he joined Dundee United, but never settled and joined the relegation-threatened Rovers on loan. He quickly replaced Rathbone and won a winners' medal within weeks when the club was victorious in the Full Members' Cup final. Injuries removed him from the scene but acting manager Tony Parkes immediately restored him to the team when Don Mackay was dismissed. The arrival of Alan Wright ended this run of appearances and he joined Port Vale and played in the play-off final for them at Wembley. A noted coach with youth players, he has held positions at Preston, Blackburn and currently he is in charge of the Bolton youth side.

FL	134 apps	3 gls
FAC	6 apps	0 gls
FLC	6 apps	0 gls
FMC	5 apps	0 gls
PO	5 apps	0 gls
Total	156 apps	3 gls

SUTTON, Christopher Roy
Striker

6'2" 11st 12lb
Born: Nottingham, 10 March 1973
Debut: 20 August 1994

CAREER: Norwich City Jul 1989 (trainee) Jul 1991; Blackburn Rovers Jul 1994 (£5,000,000); Chelsea Jul 1999 (£10,000,000); Glasgow Celtic Jul 2000 (£6,000,000); Birmingham City Jan 2006 (free).
INTERNATIONALS: England 1 app.

Sutton's father Mike played in the Football League for Norwich, Chester and Carlisle, and he was the person responsible for taking Chris to Norwich. In his early days there was considerable discussion about whether he would be a better player in defence or

Chris Sutton in 1994.

up front, but he had no doubts that his future was to score goals. When he obtained 28 in the 1993/94 season he guaranteed that his future lay away from Carrow Road, but it was a surprise when the Rovers defeated Manchester United and Arsenal in obtaining his transfer. He was the final piece in the jigsaw that saw the club become Premiership champions, designed to take the weight off Alan Shearer and provide a double-pronged spearhead that clubs would have difficulty defending against. Perhaps the finest holder of possession in football, he had the rare ability to link play and was an efficient if unspectacular striker, able to score without every using excessive force. As the championship season wore on he was sacrificed more and more to shore up midfield if needed, which explains why he only totalled 15 goals. The following season, when Ray Harford took over, Sutton found himself in the wilderness because Shearer had a preference for playing with his close friend Mike Newell and Harford was not inclined to dissuade him. Once Shearer and

Harford left Sutton blossomed and, under Roy Hodgson, played the finest football of his career, a roving goalscorer with an exceptional work rate. Relegation caught the club and the player by surprise but it was no shock to the fans that he opted to leave in a huge transfer deal with Chelsea. A disappointment at Stamford Bridge, he settled into the Celtic team as a vital component in their successful renaissance, won honours season after season and has displayed no desire to return to England.

PL	125+5 apps	47 gls
FAC	9 apps	4 gls
FLC	11+1 apps	7 gls
UEFA	3 apps	1 gl
EC	3+3 apps	0 gls
CS	1 app.	0 gls
Total	152+9 apps	59 gls

SVARC, Robert Louis

Striker

5'7" 11st 2lb
Born: Leicester, 8 February 1946
Debut: 4 October 1975

CAREER: Linwood Lane School; Leicester City Oct 1961 (app.) Mar 1963; Lincoln City Dec 1968; Barrow Sep 1970-Nov 1970 (loan); Boston United Oct 1971 (loan) Dec 1971 (£1,750); Colchester United Dec 1972; Blackburn Rovers Oct 1975-Jan 1978 (£25,000); Watford Sep 1977 (loan).

Born in Leicester of Czech descent, he was a stocky striker with an eye for goal. His initial promise disappeared during a period of his life when he lost all discipline. Rescued by his conversion to the Jehovah's Witness faith, he was signed by Jim Smith to provide goal-scoring potential. Amazingly strong in the air for a small man, he was a great opportunist but was hampered by injuries. He had recovered much of his old zest in the reserves but a disastrous loan move to Watford resulted in a career-ending injury on his debut. He remained in the Blackburn area and opened his own business installing burglar alarms.

FL	42+8 apps	16 gls
FAC	4 apps	1 gl
FLC	3+1 apps	3 gls
Total	49+9 apps	20 gls

SWINDELLS, John

Centre forward

5'9" 11st 9lb
Born: Manchester, 12 April 1937
Died: St Kew, Cornwall, 23 June 2009
Debut: 28 September 1957

CAREER: Manchester City May 1955 (am); Blackburn Rovers Jun 1957 (am) Nov 1957; Accrington Stanley Dec 1959 (£1,250); Barnsley Jun 1961; Workington Feb 1962; Torquay United Jul 1963; Newport County Jul 1964-Mar 1965; Altrincham Aug 1965-May 1971 (£550); Radcliffe Borough 1971-1972.

Swindells played left half for the Manchester City youth side in the FA Youth Cup of 1954, but the presence of Mike Doyle prompted a switch to the left wing. A year later he played for the England youth side against Ireland in the international youth tournament in Italy. City never offered him professional terms, so he came to Ewood on trial and was offered a contract. In the reserves he was converted again to centre forward and, in two-and-a-half seasons, scored 56 goals. His first-team outings were disappointing and he was allowed to join Accrington. Together with his Rovers' reserve teammate George Hudson, he formed a deadly partnership only broken when he was transferred to Barnsley. After a few moves, he requested that Newport cancel his contract so that he could return north to look after his father, who was sick. It enabled him to play with Altrincham where he achieved legendary status. In his first season he scored 86 goals and when his career ended had more than 250 to his credit.

FL	9 apps	1 gl
Total	9 apps	1 gl

T

TALIA, Francesco 'Frank'
Goalkeeper

6'1" 13st
Born: Melbourne (Australia), 20 July 1972

CAREER: Knox City 1985; Australian Institute of Sport; Melbourne Victory 1990; Sunshine George Cross 1992; Blackburn Rovers Sep 1993 (£115,000); Hartlepool Jan 1994-Mar 1994 (loan); Manchester City Aug 1995 (trial); Swindon Town Sep 1995 (loan) Nov 1995 (£125,000); Gillingham Jul 2000 (trial); Wolverhampton Wanderers Aug 2000 (free); Sheffield United Sep 2000-Jun 2001 (free); Benfica (Portugal) Aug 2001 (trial); FC Antwerp (Belgium) Oct 2001; Reading Feb 2002 (trial) Mar 2002-Jun 2002; Bristol City Aug 2002 (trial); Wycombe Wanderers Aug 2002.

The Australian, who possessed an Italian passport, was signed for a small fee, which subsequently was raised in the House of Commons by the Labour MP Kate Hoey as an example of the convoluted workings of the transfer system, since apparently his club received only £8,500 of it. With many goalkeepers at the club he played only for the reserves, although he was substitute for the first team on 28 occasions. Serious shoulder injuries kept him out of the game for a year and he travelled widely in his search for first-team football. During twelve seasons he has played regularly only at Swindon and Wycombe, but has looked competent at these levels.

TALLON, Gerrit Thomas 'Gary'
Left-back

5'10" 11st 7lb
Born: Drogheda 5 September 1973

CAREER: Drogheda United; Backburn Rovers Nov 1991 (£25,000); Kilmarnock May 1996; Chester City Mar 1997 (loan); Barnsley 1997 (trial); Mansfield Town Dec 1997-Aug 2001 (free).

A popular player at Drogheda, he came to Ewood as a midfield player but was converted to a left-back. Not sufficiently equipped defensively to cope in a flat back four, he spent a long time at the Rovers but was only promoted to the bench in the 1995 Charity Shield game at Wembley. Ultimately he found a home at Mansfield until arthritis ended his career and sent him back to Ireland, working in his father's decorating business. He attempted a comeback when he thought his knee was improving, but settled eventually for coaching Ardee Celtic in the Meath and District League.

TAYLOR, Andrew
Left-back

5'11" 11st 7lb
Born: Blackburn, 14 March 1986

CAREER: St Philip's; St Bede's; Blackburn Rovers 2003 (trainee).

A classy left-back with a sweet left foot who runs well and overlaps willingly, he was born locally, living in the Preston New Road area. He was a member of the side that reached the semi-final of the FA Youth Cup and the following season progressed into the reserves. Given a first-team squad number in May 2005, he was promoted to the bench for the final home game of the season.

TAYLOR, Gordon
Winger

5'6" 11st 2lb
Born: Ashton under Lyne, 28 December 1944
Debut: 13 March 1976

CAREER: Mossley Rd Co Primary; Ashton under Lyne GS; Curzon Ashton; Bolton Wanderers Jun 1960 (am) Jan 1962; Birmingham City Dec 1970 (£18,000); Blackburn Rovers Mar 1976 (£20,000); Vancouver Whitecaps (Canada) Jun 1977-Aug 1977 (loan); Bury Jun 1978-Jul 1980.

At his peak he was a chunky, thrusting winger who could play on either flank and cut in and shoot powerfully. By the time he arrived at Blackburn he had played over 400 league games for Bolton and Birmingham and his best days were long gone. Utilised primarily on the right flank, his one tactic of trying to outrun his man on the outside was nullified by his lack of speed. Unable to get ahead of his man, he employed the tactic of doubling back and crossing from a deeper position with his other foot. The resultant crosses were generally easily dealt with. Only the need for experience allowed him to play in so many games for the club. His contribution to the game was to increase when he retired. He obtained an external degree in Economics from London University and in 1981 was elected secretary of the PFA, a post that made him the highest paid executive in the trade union movement.

FL	62+2 apps	3 gls
FAC	2+1 apps	0 gls
FLC	2 apps	0 gls
Total	66+3 apps	3 gls

TAYLOR, Kenneth Gordon

Full-back

5'7.5" 11st
Born: South Shields, 15 March 1931
Debut: 4 December 1954

CAREER: North Shields; Blackburn Rovers Jan 1950-Jun 1964; Morecambe Jul 1964-May 1965.

Brought to Ewood by the same scout who discovered Eric Bell, he had perhaps the longest apprenticeship of any Rovers player. With Suart and Smith at the club there was no pressure to find a new right-back and it took Taylor four years to graduate from the 'A' side to the reserves. Given his first-team debut, he proved surprisingly adept, calm in temperament, steady in his positioning and sound but unspectacular in all aspects, although he might have been the fastest back-pedalling player of any age. With his close friend Ronnie Clayton, he shared a dedication that included an emphasis on fitness and an avoidance of the excesses detrimental to professional footballers, which was not common at the club at that time. The emergence of Bray and Whelan restricted his appearances but his ability to play on either flank enabled him to reach 200 league appearances. When he retired he returned to his old job as a baker.

FL	200 apps	0 gls
FAC	22 apps	0 gls
FLC	11 apps	0 gls
Total	233 apps	0 gls

TAYLOR, Martin 'Tiny'

Centre-back

6'4" 14st
Born: Ashington, 9 November 1979
Debut: 29 September 1998

CAREER: Cramlington Jnrs; Blackburn Rovers 1996; Darlington Jan 2000-Feb 2000 (loan); Stockport County Mar 2000-May 2000 (loan); Birmingham City Feb 2004 (£1,250,000).

A massive central defender discovered in the North-East and developed through the youth team, his potential was always huge. The possessor of amazingly quick feet and comfortable on the ball, his defects were those his physique ought to have made strengths. His heading improved steadily, but he lacked aggression and the will to use his natural power. His appearances were restricted by the team's need to include dominating presences such as Berg and Short, but he played anywhere across the defence and up front in an emergency. When his career appeared gridlocked he joined the exodus of Rovers players to Birmingham City.

L	68+20 apps	5 gls
FAC	13+2 apps	1 gl
FLC	17 apps	0 gls
UEFA	3+2 apps	0 gls
Total	101+24 apps	6 gls

TAYLOR, Royston
Midfield

5'8" 10st 11lb
Born: Blackpool, 28 September 1956
Debut: 16 September 1978

CAREER: Preston North End May 1972 (app.) Oct 1974; Sunderland (trial); Blackburn Rovers Nov 1976-Jul 1979 (free); Lincoln City 1979 (free); Barrow; Workington; Barrow; Wren Rovers.

An energetic midfielder, his potential was recognised by many managers but he never succeeded in converting his promise to achievement. After serving his apprenticeship at Preston, he was taken on by Sunderland on non-contract terms but failed to make it into the first team. Given another opportunity by the Rovers, he failed to capitalise on some energetic performances in the reserves. His third and final game with the first team was curious. Before the last game of the season he had already been informed that he would be released, but he was selected for the game and responded with his only league goal.

FL	3 apps	1 gl
Total	3 apps	1 gl

THOMAS, Edward
Inside forward

5'9" 10st 5lb
Born: Newton le Willows, 23 October 1933
Died: Allestree, Derby, 12 November 2003
Debut: 13 February 1960

CAREER: Everton Oct 1951; Blackburn Rovers Feb 1960 (P Ex Vernon); Swansea Town Jul 1962 (£6,000); Derby County Aug 1964 (£5,000); Orient Sep 1967-Jun 1968; Nuneaton Borough Feb 1968 (loan); Heanor Town Aug 1968.

His misfortune was that he served to remind the fans of their status, a makeweight in the deal that took the ambitious Roy Vernon to Everton but destined to replace him in the Blackburn first team. A neat player who toiled hard but without inspiration or punch, he failed to prove that he was a player the club could develop. He had one unforgettable game in the League Cup against Bristol Rovers, when every ball appeared to drop at his feet and he scored four goals. Leaving the club brought the development that escaped him in his early years. He played for Swansea in the FA Cup semi-final and was a real goal-scoring asset to Derby.

FL	37 apps	9 gls
FAC	2 apps	1 gl
FLC	5 apps	5 gls
Total	44 apps	15 gls

THOMAS, James Alan
Striker

6'0" 13st
Born: Swansea, 16 January 1979
Debut: 15 September 2000

CAREER: Blackburn Rovers Jul 1996; West Bromwich Albion Aug 1997-Sep 1997 (loan); Blackpool Mar 2000-May 2000 (loan); Sheffield United Nov

2000-May 2001 (loan); Bristol Rovers Sep 2001 (trial) Mar 2002-May 2002 (loan); Swansea City May 2002-Jun 2005 (free).

A product of the youth team and the most capped player at Welsh Under-21 level, he was a natural leader of the line, able to hold the ball and bring others into play, but suffered from an inability to score regularly. He was twenty-one before he was given his debut and within seconds managed to miss an open goal from two yards. Undeterred, he scored twice on his full debut and celebrated it with a first-minute goal. The transfer of Marcus Bent cost him a squad place with the first team, and he went on loan to help compensate the transferring club, Sheffield United. A frequent injury victim, he was eventually released and joined his home town club. On the last day of the season he became the local hero when his hat-trick helped the club avoid relegation from the Football League. Persisrent knee problems forced him into retirement in 2005.

FL	1+3 apps	1 gl
FLC	1 app.	2 gls
Total	2+3 apps	3 gls

THOMPSON, Christopher David

Striker

5'10" 11st 6lb
Born: Walsall, 24 January 1960
Debut: 27 August 1983

CAREER: Bolton Wanderers Jul 1977; Lincoln City Mar 1983-May 1983 (loan); Blackburn Rovers Jul 1983 (free); Wigan Athletic Jul 1986 (free); Blackpool Jul 1988-Mar 1990 (free); Cardiff City Mar 1990-Jul 1990; Walsall Feb 1991 (non con)

It is curious that a striker who played 250 league games for seven teams and was a youth international should never command a transfer fee, but no-one ever lost by including Thompson in their line-up. He arrived at the Rovers in time to replace the injured Norman Bell and seamlessly achieved a partnership with the irrepressible Simon Garner. This master goal-scorer required a blunt instrument alongside, a courageous man who would run and challenge and cause the confusion Garner could use to his advantage. A quietly hard man, the selfless Thompson mastered the role and scored a few goals himself in the process. He was superseded by Jimmy Quinn, who had more footballing potential, but the club never experienced the same symbiosis upfront. After retirement he remained living in Blackpool, selling insurance for an American company.

FL	81+4 apps	24 gls
FAC	10 apps	2 gls
FLC	5 apps	0 gls
Total	96+4 apps	26 gls

THOMPSON, David Anthony

Midfield

5'7" 10st
Born: Birkenhead, 12 September 1977
Debut: 31 August 2002

CAREER: Liverpool Nov 1994; Swindon Town Nov 1997 (loan); Coventry City Aug 2000 (£3,000,000); Blackburn Rovers Aug 2002 (£1,900,000).

Part of a successful Liverpool youth team, he was hugely popular on Merseyside but found that did not guarantee him first-team selection often enough. A move to Coventry took him to a poor side and, although he was the star of their First Division side, he was desirous of playing top-flight football. A natural Souness choice, he is a footballer who plays with aggression for ninety minutes, a fierce tackler and harrier who, despite his lack of stature, never backs down. Nominally positioned wide right, his natural position is probably in the centre of the field, but he is equally at home on the left flank. Not a prolific goalscorer, he is still a threat from distance. Before knee surgery curtailed his season he had forced his way into the England squad for international matches but, in three seasons at Ewood, he has seldom been fully fit.

PL	46+18 apps	5 gls
FAC	7+1 apps	2 gls
FLC	5+1 apps	2 gl
UEFA	5 apps	1 gl
Total	63+20 apps	10 gls

THORLEY, Dennis
Midfield

6'0" 11st 4lb
Born: Stoke, 7 November 1956
Debut: 12 April 1980

CAREER: Roebuck FC; Stoke City Jul 1976-Jul 1982; California Surf (USA) (loan); Blackburn Rovers Mar 1980-Apr 1980 (loan).

When the transfer deadline of 1980 approached and promotion to the Second Division was a possibility, Howard Kendall was concerned about the lack of cover for several positions. Having coached at Stoke he knew about Thorley, a tall midfield player who could be utilised in the defence. Bringing him on loan was a safeguard but he was little utilised and, apart from a neat, tidy approach, made little impact. He had guested in a similar fashion for California Surf but failed to make the first team. Two years later he had to retire from the game because of injury.

FL	2+2 apps	0 gls
Total	2+2 apps	0 gls

THORNE, Peter Lee
Striker

6'0" 12st 2lb
Born: Manchester, 21 June 1973
Debut: 14 August 1994

CAREER: Blackburn Rovers Jun 1991; Swindon Town Jul 1997 (£200,000); Stoke City Jul 1997 (£350,000); Cardiff City Sep 2001 (£1,600,000); Norwich City Jul 2005 (free).

Taken on as a trainee after being rejected by both Manchester clubs, he made himself a reputation as a goalscorer with both the youth and reserve teams. With Shearer, Newell, Wegerle and Gallacher ahead of him, he was never given an opportunity until an injury crisis before the 1994/95 season. After a good display in a pre-season friendly he was on the bench for the Charity Shield and when brought on made an impression with his quick skills and strength. Kenny Dalglish allowed him to join Swindon to help his old friend Steve McMahon and Thorne has since proved one of the most reliable goal-scorers in lower division football, scoring the winning goal in the 2000 Auto Windshields Shield final.

CS	0+1 app.	0 gls
Total	0+1 app.	0 gls

TODD, Andrew John James
Centre-back

5'10" 12st 3lb
Born: Derby, 21 September 1974
Debut: 19 September 2002

CAREER: Middlesbrough Mar 1992; Swindon Town Feb 1995 (loan); Bolton Wanderers Aug 1995 (£250,000); Charlton Athletic Nov 1999 (£750,000); Grimsby Town Feb 2002-Apr 2002 (loan); Blackburn Rovers May 2002 (£750,000); Burnley Sep 2003-Oct 2003 (loan).

The son of the elegant England international Colin Todd, he played in his father's position but without the panache. A tough, no-nonsense defender with a notoriously short fuse, he was moved on by two club for his physical altercations with the assistant manager Phil Brown at Bolton and his goalkeeper, Dean Kiely at Charlton. Souness was undeterred by these pecadilloes, seeing in him a man who could bring in experience and know-how in a position where they are often required. As previously in his career, he was his own worst enemy. Although supported by his manager after one memorable dismissal, he commenced an irreversible confrontation with Souness when Amoruso was restored to the side in the relegation fight in 2004. Instructed to look for another club and excluded from the pre-season tour, he was fortunate that he was injured and could not obtain a move. The arrival of Mark Hughes transformed his situation. He was recalled to the side, made captain and ended as the club's Player of the Year. Maturity has aided his ability to read play and as a stand-up tackler he has few equals, as he uses great body strength and timing to win the ball.

PL	63+7 apps	3 gls
FAC	9 apps	0 gls
FLC	7 apps	0 gls
UEFA	2 apps	0 gls
Total	81+7 apps	3 gls

TODD, Paul Raymond

Inside forward

5'11.5" 12st 7lb
Born: Middlesbrough, 8 May 1920
Died: Boston, Ocober 2000
Debut: 19 August 1950

CAREER: Wolverhampton Wanderers (trial); Leicester City (trial); Doncaster Rovers Aug 1945; Blackburn Rovers Jul 1950 (£10,000); Hull City Oct 1951 (£6,500); Kings Lynn (p-m) May 1953; March Town (p-m) 1959.

After unsuccessful attempts to obtain a club in the Football League when he was a teenager, he was spotted playing in Ceylon and was signed by Doncaster. He quickly made the first team and scored over fifty goals for them, a powerful player who had a natural talent for spotting a chance. His arrival at Blackburn came at a time when he was starting to slow, and this impacted upon his game. It was a shrewd piece of business for the Rovers to unload him to Hull while he still had a transfer value, because his career deteriorated rapidly. He was subsequently player manager at King's Lynn, manager at Worksop and made a brief playing comeback when manager at March Town.

FL	46 apps	13 gls
FAC	1 app.	0 gls
Total	47 apps	13 gls

TOMLINSON, Robert Windle

Full-back

5'10.5" 10st 6lb
Born: Blackburn, 4 June 1924
Died: Blackburn, January 1996
Debut: 1 September 1945

CAREER: Feniscowles; Blackburn Rovers Jan 1943-Jun 1951; Mossley Aug 1948; Halifax Town Jun 1951-May 1952; Ashton United.

A calm full-back who came out of local football, he would have made more appearances if he had not suffered a broken toe, followed by a broken wrist that took time to heal. By then his career had stagnated and his chances of a game were not great. He joined Mossley, where his ex-teammate Len Butt was manager, but the Rovers retained his Football League registration. Accrington made an attempt to bring him back to the Football League but Mossley intervened and the subsequent FA inquiry nullified the move. He subsequently played a few games at Halifax before retiring to become a foreman fitter at a paper mill in Feniscowles.

FL	25 apps	0 gls
FAC	4 apps	0 gls
Total	29 apps	0 gls

U

TUGAY KERIMOGLU

Midfield

5'8.5" 11st 7lb
Born: Istanbul, 24 August 1970
Debut: 8 September 2001

CAREER: Trabzanspor 1984; Galatasaray 1986; Glasgow Rangers Jan 2000 (£1,300,000); Blackburn Rovers May 2001 (£1,300,000).
INTERNATIONALS: Turkey 92 apps 2 gls.

The son of a Turkish international and brother of a Turkish First Division player who became a respected coach, his skill levels were visible from an early age but his initial progress was slow, partly because of his reputation for enjoying the nightlife in Istanbul. Straightening himself out, he moved to the top club Galatasaray and gained a regular place in the national team. Souness knew all about the Turkish playmaker from his time at Galatasaray and, when Rangers could not find a first-team place for him, began to work on plans to bring him to Ewood. Tugay sensibly waited until the side was in the Premiership before signing, but he quickly became the club's dominant creative force. Operating from deep midfield, he dictated the tempo of the game, was skilled on the ball and possessed a subtle variety of passes that switched the ball either way. Doubts were expressed about his ball-winning ability but he was mobile, covered large areas of the pitch and brought a deep will to win. For a man who had played for two clubs who have followers that are among the largest and most passionate in the world, his close relationship with the Blackburn fans has been remarkable. Never a man not to acknowledge the support he receives, he is always the last man off the pitch and his smiling good humour had endeared him to all the Rovers' fans. His wife Etkin was an international basketball player back in Turkey.

PL	121+21 apps	6 gls
FAC	10+2 apps	1 gl
FLC	14+1 apps	0 gls
UEFA	6 apps	0 gls
Total	151+24 apps	7 gls

TURNER, David John

Midfield

5'9" 11st 12lb
Born: Retford, 7 September 1943
Debut: 2 September 1972

CAREER: Newcastle United Aug 1960 (am) Oct 1960; Brighton & Hove Albion Dec 1963 (free); Blackburn Rovers Aug 1972-Jul 1974 (free).

Sheer lack of numbers forced Ken Furphy to bring Turner to Ewood. He was available on a free transfer after completing 300 games for Brighton and had a proven reputation for reliability and intelligence. Introduced, he steadied the side but the following season succumbed to long-term injury that ended his playing career. He followed Furphy to Sheffield United, where he became the youth-team coach, and then coached Aldershot. For ten years he lived in Canada, where he coached Toronto Blizzard, but in 1990 he returned to live in Aldershot although he subsequently moved to Nottinghamshire.

FL	23+2 apps	0 gls
FAC	1 app.	0 gls
Total	24+2 apps	0 gls

ÜNSAL, Hakan

Left-back

5'10" 12st 8lb
Born: Güzelyali, Uzmir (Turkey), 15 June 1973
Debut: 2 Mar 2002

CAREER: Ayancyk, Lisesi'nden 1991; Emlak Bankasy, Istanbul 1991; Karabükspor 1993; Galatasaray 1994; Blackburn Rovers Feb 2002 (£350,000); Galatasaray Aug 2002 (£350,000); Caykur Rizespor Jun 2005-Dec 2005.
INTERNATIONALS: Turkey 33 apps.

Born in a fishing village on Izmit Bay he started playing locally but at eighteen was taken to Istanbul. Two years later he was playing in the Turkish League and was signed by one of the three giant clubs, Galatasaray. He made rapid progress, initially as a holding midfield man, but his prospects improved when he was converted to left wing-back. Quick on his feet, able to participate in crisp passing movements and with a sweet left foot that could hit the ball powerfully, he established himself in the national side. The European Championships of 2000 established him as a seasoned international but it also unsettled him when he saw the greater rewards in other countries. Refusing to re-sign, he fell out of favour and had been left out of the first-team squad when his transfer to Blackburn was negotiated. The move meant that he had joined a club who did not use wing-backs and he played both at left-back and wide left in his first-team appearances. His keen tackling had adversely affected the attentions of English referees without much cause, and in the World Cup of 2002 he was again in the spotlight, sent off against Brazil when the referee was totally deceived by Rivaldo's cheating, for which the Brazilian was subsequently fined. He came back from the tournament with a third-place medal and the need for arthroscopic surgery. Despite recovering pre-season, it was suddenly announced that he was unable to settle in England and he was sold back to Galatasaray.

PL	7+1 apps	0 gls
Total	7+1 apps	0 gls

V

VALÉRY, Patrick Jean Claude
Full-back

5'11" 11st 7lb
Born: Brignoles (France), 3 July 1969
Debut: 9 August 1997

CAREER: AS Brignoles; AS Monaco 1984; Toulouse FC Oct 1995-1996 (loan); SC Bastia 1996; Blackburn Rovers Jun 1997 (free); SC Bastia Jul 1998 (£80,000); Olympique Marseilles Jul 2001 (trial); Aris Salonika (Greece) Dec 2001-May 2002 (free); AS Cannes Jun 2002-Jul 2002.

Taken to Monaco at the age of fifteen, he gained a French championship medal when Arsene Wenger guided the side to the title. He also played in the final of the European Cup Winners' Cup. A tough, intimidating defender with a predilection for the two-footed tackle, he was a strictly stay-at-home defender and at Monaco he struggled to obtain a regular place with the likes of Claude Puel, Eric de Meco, Patrick Blondeau and Emmanuel Petit challenging for places. Even a move to Bastia caused him to play on his weaker left side because the highly talented Sebastien Perez played right-back. Brought to Ewood on a Bosman free by Roy Hodgson, he soon lost his first-team place and moved back to Bastia when the Rovers signed Perez. Back home with the notoriously tough Corsican team he was in his element and, after receiving cautions in his first three games, had served two suspensions before the end of November. Released by Bastia, he played briefly in Greece but was delighted to return to his home area and sign for Cannes. A month later he was out of the game because the transfer body (DNGC) refused to ratify his transfer and those of Yoan Bouchard and Gregory Noto because of irregularities at the club.

V

PL	14+1 apps	0 gls
FAC	1+1 app.	0 gls
FLC	2 apps	0 gls
Total	17+2 apps	0 gls

VENTERS, Alexander
Inside forward

5'8.5" 11st 7lb
Born: Cowdenbeath, 9 June 1913
Died: Cowdenbeath, 30 Apr 1959
Debut: 15 March 1947

CAREER: Southend Rovers; St Andrews United 1930; Cowdenbeath 1930; Glasgow Rangers Nov 1933; Third Lanark Feb 1946; Blackburn Rovers Feb 1947 (£2,000); Raith Rovers Feb 1948-May 1948 (£300).
INTERNATIONALS: Scotland 3 apps.

Venters joined the Rovers when he was thirty-three, having won all the honours the Scottish game had to offer. Thirteen years earlier, after his first Scottish cap, the Rovers had agreed a fee for the player and found him a job in town as a compositor with the *Northern Daily Telegraph*. Venters decided to join Rangers instead, and came to East Lancashire at a time when the club was fighting against relegation to the Second Division. He was a licensee north of the border and was reluctant to come, but was sufficiently intrigued by the past to eventually assent. Although he had lost his speed he was a huge onfield influence, organising the team and proving to be still a real hard man. In the vital relegation game against Brentford he produced a solo goal of such vital and epic proportions that his memory was etched forever in the annals of the club.

FL	25 apps	7 gls
Total	25 apps	7 gls

VERNON, Thomas Royston*
Inside forward

5'8.5" 10st 2lb
Born: Ffynnongroew, Holywell, 14 April 1937
Died: Blackburn, 5 December 1933
Debut: 3 September 1955

CAREER: Rhyl GS; Mostyn YMCA; Everton (trial); Blackburn Rovers Mar 1954 (ground staff) Mar 1955; Everton Feb 1960 (£27,000+Thomas); Stoke City Mar 1965 (£35,000); Halifax Town Jan 1970 (loan); Cape Town FC (South Africa); Great Harwood.
INTERNATIONALS: Wales 32 apps 8 gls.

Vernon arrived at Ewood after he had failed to be taken on by Everton. He was taken on the ground staff because he declined professional terms until he received a Welsh amateur international cap. A whipcord inside forward with dazzling feet, greyhound speed and a shot that had traces of cordite, he assisted the club to promotion to the First Division. Completely at home in this environment, he was a good ball winner and could trade knocks with the hardest players. In February 1960 the manager who had nurtured his Rovers career, Johnny Carey, returned to take him to Everton for a large fee. In return he got a man who was top scorer for four out of five seasons and led the club to the league title. After service with Stoke he returned to Blackburn, where he dealt in antiques. A keen follower of the greyhounds he also was one of the most prolific smokers in football, often taking his cigarette into the shower. He was even spotted by sharp-eyed fans in the Paddock returning after half-time still finishing his cigarette.

FL	131 apps	49 gls
FAC	13 apps	3 gls
Total	144 apps	52 gls

WADDINGTON, John

Centre-back

5'10" 11st 7lb
Born: Darwen, 16 February 1952
Debut: 6 October 1973

CAREER: St Mary's College; Darwen (am); Liverpool May 1970; Blackburn Rovers Aug 1973 (free); Vancouver Whitecaps (Canada) Jul 1977-Aug 1977; Bury Aug 1979-Apr 1981 (£10,000); Great Harwood Town 1981-1983.

Darwen-born and a member of the town's schoolboy side, he preferred to sign for Liverpool and became a regular in their reserves. Ken Furphy contacted his club with a view to loaning him and using him in the attack, but a severe glandular illness ended this speculation and appeared to have ended Waddington's career. Granted a free transfer, he arrived for three months' trial with the Rovers, during which he was converted to the defence. The club's failure to replace John McNamee gave him the opportunity to play in the first team alongside Fazackerley, although the subsequent arrival of Hawkins and Keeley limited his appearances. An intelligent reader of the game, he lacked speed and mobility but tackled well and used the ball to good effect. A regular member of the squad for six seasons, he was not always guaranteed a place but was versatile enough to play in several defensive positions and as a striker. By the time he finished his career at Bury he was building up a retail business in the area. Starting with a shop in Mill Hill, Waddington and his partner built up a chain of seventy shops and a cash-and-carry outlet that they subsequently sold at a vast profit in 1999. In his younger days he opened the bowling for Rishton in the Lancashire League, sharing the new ball with the great Michael Holding for one season.

FL	139+9 apps	18 gls
FAC	12 apps	1 gl
FLC	7+1 apps	0 gls
Total	158+10 apps	19 gls

WAGSTAFFE, David

Left winger

5'8" 10st 8lb
Born: Manchester, 5 April 1943
Debut: 1 January 1976

CAREER: Manchester City May 1960; Wolverhampton Wanderers Dec 1964; Blackburn Rovers Jan 1976 (£5,000); Blackpool Aug 1978 (£5,000); Blackburn Rovers Mar 1979-Oct 1979 (£2,000).

He had played over 450 league games for Manchester City and Wolves before Jim Smith brought him to Ewood on loan, yet he remained a sublime artist. A classic winger who took on his full-back and beat him with feints and sinuous dribbles and then played teammates into scoring positions with quick flicks, he was a joy to watch even as advancing years drained the stamina from his legs. It is ironic that such a purist became the first man in the Football League to receive a red card (on the day the system was introduced in 1976). After two good seasons it was a surprise that he took the advantage that freedom of contract represented to leave for Blackpool, where he also took over a boarding house. Neither of the moves worked for him and John Pickering gambled on his return towards the end of the season. However, a heel injury was difficult to cure and he finally retired. He moved back to live in the Midlands and for a time was steward of the Old Wulfrunians at Castlecroft and later ran Waggie's Bar inside Molineux.

FL	74+3 apps	7 gls
FAC	4 apps	0 gls
FLC	4 apps	0 gls
Total	82+3 apps	7 gls

WARD, Ashley Stuart
Striker

6'1" 13st
Born: Middleton, 24 November 1970
Debut: 9 January 1999

CAREER: Manchester United (sch); Cheadle Town; Manchester City Aug 1989; Wrexham Jan 1991 (loan); Leicester City Jul 1991 (£80,000); Blackpool Nov 1992 (loan); Crewe Alexandra Dec 1992 (£80,000); Norwich City Dec 1994 (£500,000); Derby County Mar 1996 (£1,000,000); Barnsley Sep 1997 (£1,300,000); Blackburn Rovers Dec 1998 (£4,500,000); Bradford City Aug 2000 (£1,500,000); Sheffield United Aug 2003 (free) Jun 2005.

He attended William Hulme Grammar School in Manchester where he played only rugby union and lacrosse, but overcame the lack of opportunity to be taken on as a trainee at Maine Road. He twice broke his leg during his early years and later at Barnsley contracted meningitis. For several seasons in the lower divisions he proved himself to be a hard-working, orthodox trier who would wander to either flank and never gave up. Quite why this pedigree prompted Brian Kidd to pay the asking price of over £4 million and play him in the Premiership is hard to explain. He proved to be one of the worst buys the club has ever made, lacking mobility, pace and panache in front of goal. During one barren spell he went 837 minutes without a goal and ended with a record of a goal every four-and-two-thirds games. When his contract ran out at Sheffield United he joined his wife in running her business, which designs and builds speciality houses for the very affluent.

L	52+2 apps	13 gls
FAC	4+1 apps	0 gls
FLC	2 apps	0 gls
Total	58+3 apps	13 gls

WARHURST, Paul
Utility

6'1" 12st 7lb
Born: Stockport, 26 September 1969
Debut: 12 September 1993

CAREER: Davenport HS; Manchester City Jul 1986 (trainee) Jul 1988; Oldham Athletic Oct 1988 (£10,000); Sheffield Wednesday Jul 1991 (£750,000); Blackburn Rovers Aug 1993 (£2,750,000); Crystal Palace Jul 1997 (£1,250,000); Bolton Wanderers Nov 1997 (loan) Jan 1999-Jun 2003 (£800,000) Sep 2003; Stoke City Mar 2003-Apr 2003 (loan); Chesterfield Oct 2003-Nov 2003; Barnsley Nov 2003 (trial) Dec 2003-Jan 2004; Carlisle United Feb 2004-Mar 2004; Grismby Town Mar 2004-May 2004; Chester City Jul 2004 (trial); Preston North End Sep 2004 (reserves); Blackpool Nov 2004-Feb 2005; Forest Green Rovers Apr 2005-May 2005; Wrexham Aug 2005.

The son of the old Manchester City player Roy Warhurst, he was transferred to Oldham when still in his teens. He formed a centre-back pairing with Earl Barrett that had pace and finesse, and they were projected on the national scene when the club reached the semi-final of the FA Cup and the final of the League Cup. He was switched by his club to right-back and then to striker, but he was able to take every change in his stride. This was possible because he instantaneously controlled the ball and this gave him time to look up and assess passing opportunities. A move to Sheffield Wednesday took him back to the centre of the defence until he reluctantly had to deputise for David Hirst up front. Although he disliked the role, he scored 12 goals in cup competitions and 6 in the league during a season when the club reached the final of both cup competitions. Signed by Blackburn and promised a chance in midfield, he broke his leg within a month of breaking into the first team. On his return he was used more and more as a utility player, covering at right-back, central defence and even wide on the left. Injuries continued to bedevil his career and have done ever since his departure. He holds one special place on the affections of the fans – all his goals for the first team at the Rovers were scored against Manchester United!

PL	30+27 apps	4 gls
FAC	2+1 apps	0 gls
FLC	6+2 apps	0 gls
UEFA	0+1 app.	0 gls
EC	4+1 apps	0 gls
Total	42+32 apps	4 gls

WATT, Michael
Goalkeeper

6'1" 11st 10lb
Born: Aberdeen, 27 November 1970

CAREER: Cove Rangers; Aberdeen; Blackburn Rovers Aug 1997 (loan); Norwich City Aug 1998 (trial) Sep 1998-Jun 1999 (free); York City Jul 1999 (trial); Kilmarnock Aug 1999-Jun 2000 (free).

Although he had gained 12 Under-21 caps and played for Scotland 'B', Watt played only 79 first-team games in eight years at Aberdeen. When he fell down to fourth choice he came to Ewood on a month's loan because Tim Flowers was recovering from hernia surgery. After sitting on the bench for two games, he broke his jaw in two places playing for the reserves, which ended his chances of a permanent move. Released by Aberdeen, he was training with Forfar when Norwich asked him to come for a trial because Robert Green was injured. He played 7 games for the Canaries but with Andy Marshall and Green both fit he was not required and moved back to Scotland with Kilmarnock.

WEBBER, John Vincent
Centre forward

5'9" 11st 1lb
Born: Blackpool, 2 Jun 1918
Died: 1989
Debut: 22 March 1947

CAREER: Blackpool 1939 (am); Hyde United; Blackburn Rovers Feb 1947-May 1948; Ashton United 1948.

Prior to the Second World War Blackpool had an enlightened youth policy that discovered, among others, Stanley Mortensen. In the early months of 1939 Webber, a local lad, began to appear on the left wing for the 'A' team. Hopes of a smooth transition to the first team were halted by war and, after enlisting with the East Lancashire Regiment, he played his football in Madagascar and India. Chance took him to Hyde, where the Rovers had been keeping an eye on Charlie McClelland. Even though Webber was then twenty-six they decided to take a chance on him. Signed in February, the club had decided by the close season that he would not make the grade, but he was granted a reprieve. He came back for the following season so full of running and power that he was immediately installed in the first team, but the purple patch was short-lived. Injury necessitated a cartilage operation and he had only just recovered when at the season's end he was released.

FL	8 apps	1 gl
Total	8 apps	1 gl

WEGERLE, Roy Connon
Forward

5'11" 11st
Born: Johannesburg (South Africa), 19 March 1964
Debut: 7 March 1992

CAREER: Pretoria Boys HS; Arcadia; University of South Florida 1982; Tampa Bay Rowdies (USA) 1984; Tacoma Stars (USA) 1984; Chelsea Jul 1986; Swindon Town Mar 1988 (loan); Luton Town Jul 1988 (£75,000); Queens Park Rangers Dec 1989 (£1,000,000); Blackburn Rovers Mar 1992 (£1,000,000); Coventry City Mar 1993

(P Ex Gallacher); Colorado Rapids (USA) Oct 1995; Washington DC United (USA) 1997; Tampa Bay Mutiny (USA) Apr 1998-Oct 1998 (ex Lassiter)
INTERNATIONALS: USA 30 apps 7 gls.

When his brothers Steve and Geoff left for the USA to play football (Steve with Tampa Bay and Geoff with Oakland) Roy went with them, attending the University of South Florida. Not surprisingly, given his range of subtle ball skills and athletic approach, he was the first player selected in the 1984 NASL draft. After a year with the Rowdies, his skills were further sharpened by his exposure to the hard surfaces of the MISL. He developed into an audacious, unpredictable player, a free spirit who played football with a flourish. Chelsea spotted his potential but it was not until he joined QPR that he finally blossomed. Playing up front, often wide right, he displayed such unconventional skills that his assimilation into the English national team was broached. As ever he was his own man and elected to make himself available to the USA, the country of his wife. Signed by the Rovers to bolster a promotion challenge in 1992, he was frustrated by the fact that he was never a regular, a decision made easier by the fact that his teammates were as confused as the opposition by his eccentricities. After he had appeared in the 1994 World Cup in the USA he decided that he would return to the country and see out his career in the MLS. He had a spell at Colorado as caretaker coach but did not enjoy it and when he had finished playing worked for ESPN, commenting on the game. A superb sportsman, he high-jumped 2 metres when he was with the Rovers, a height no athlete in Blackburn achieved until 1997. Introduced to golf by Dalglish and Shearer, he used his time after retirement to improve his game and in January 2002, when on holiday in South Africa, made history by qualifying for the Alfred Dunhill Championship, a European tour event.

L	20+14 apps	6 gls
FAC	4+1 apps	2 gls
FLC	3+3 apps	4 gls
Total	27+18 apps	12 gls

WEIR, John Britton
Centre forward

5'8" 11st
Born: Fauldhouse, 20 October 1923
Died: Glasgow, 9 January 2003
Debut: 1 February 1947

CAREER: Leith Renton; Hibernian 1941; Blackburn Rovers Jan 1947 (£10,000); Glasgow Celtic Feb 1948 (£7,500); Falkirk Oct 1952; Llanelly Jun 1953; Dumbarton Dec 1953.

Weir joined the Royal Navy soon after signing for Hibs and served in the Fleet Air Arm. For three years he guested for Cardiff. The Rovers chased his signature for some time; a deal was set up months before the transfer but initially fell through. Initially the fans were delighted with his speed and fire, although it was noticed that ball control was not his forte and he tended to stumble past rather than beat opponents. Injury and loss of form unsettled him and when Celtic asked about him a transfer appeared wise for all parties. It certainly was for the Scottish club for, on the last day of the season, he scored a hat-trick that dispelled fears of relegation. He suffered from dementia, believed to have been caused by heading the heavy ball, in the last years of his life.

FL	23 apps	7 gls
Total	23 apps	7 gls

WESTCOTT, Dennis
Centre forward

5'11" 12st 7lb
Born: Wallasey, 2 July 1917
Died: Stafford, 13 July 1960
Debut: 21 August 1948

CAREER: Wallasey Grocers; Leasowe Rd. Brickworks; Everton Jan 1935-Dec 1935; New Brighton Dec 1935 (am) Jan 1936; Wolverhampton Wanderers Aug 1936 (£300); Blackburn Rovers Apr 1948; Manchester City Feb 1950 (£12,500); Chesterfield Jun 1952; Stafford Rangers.

A product of Wallasey football, he found that signing for Everton at a time when they had goal-scorers such as Dean, Cunliffe and Stevenson was unfortunate. New Brighton gave him a stage and this was sufficent to attract the attention of the Wolves, who found they had acquired a scoring sensation. In 71 league and cup games he scored 56 goals and led them to the final of the FA Cup. After the Second World War, in which he gained wartime international honours, he resumed scoring with the same nonchalance (37 in 35 appearances). However, the Wolves were developing Jesse Pye and when they also wanted to bring more youngsters into the reserves, he assented to a move to Blackburn. He proved to be everything that had been promised, a simple, uncomplicated footballer who moved through the centre and thumped away chances. He scored 21 goals in his first season and the following season had 16 by February, when Manchester City made an offer the Rovers could not refuse. For the rest of his career he continued to display the scoring methods that made him one of the most underrated goalscorers of all time. He became a publican in Stafford when he retired but died suddenly when still young.

FL	63 apps	37 gls
FAC	3 apps	0 gls
Total	66 apps	37 gls

WHALLEY, Jeffrey Hugh

Winger

5'9" 10st 6lb
Born: Rossendale, 8 February 1952
Debut: 21 March 1970

CAREER: Blackburn Rovers Aug 1967 (app.) Feb 1970-Jun 1972; South Sydney (Australia); Accrington Stanley; Croatia (Australia); Great Harwood Feb 1977; Colne Dynonoes 1978; Oswaldtwistle Emmanuel.

A blond-haired winger with an abundance of pace and reasonable skills, he was prominent on the 1968/69 youth team, which was an unusually successful one. His first-team appearances were limited, some of his coaches believing that he lacked discipline. Spells abroad only served to hide him from potential clubs in England and he also suffered from inactivity, caused by delays in receiving international clearance.

FL	2 apps	0 gls
FLC	1 app.	0 gls
Total	3 apps	0 gls

WHARTON, John Edwin

Winger

5'6" 10st 3lb
Born: Bolton, 18 June 1920
Died: Worcester, May 1997
Debut: 28 August 1948

CAREER: Pikes Lane School; Peace St UM; Bolton Wanderers; Plymouth Argyle Oct 1935 (am) Jun 1936; Preston North End Jul 1939 (£5,000); Manchester City Mar 1947 (£4,000); Blackburn Rovers Aug 1948; Newport County Feb 1953 (£1,500); Wigan Athletic Jun 1955.

It took a long journey to the West Country to make Wharton a Football League player but, at Plymouth, he attracted the attention of those clubs who could have spotted him at school and guaranteed that, for the next fifteen years, he did not need to leave his native North-West. His spell at Preston included the war years and his time at Maine Road was ended when Blackburn decided that they were desperate for someone of his ebullient character. Capable of playing on either flank, he liked to take on the full-back and whip over a centre, but he also liked to cut into areas where his capacity for falling under challenge became legendary. His son Terry was perhaps an even better winger than his father, making nearly 350 appearances, primarily for Wolves and Bolton. Jackie moved to the Midlands to be near his son and for twenty-one years was head barman at a hotel in Wolverhampton.

FL	129 apps	15 gls
FAC	9 apps	2 gls
Total	138 apps	17 gls

WHEALING, Anthony
Left-back

5'9" 10st 4lb
Born: Worsley, 3 September 1976

CAREER: Blackburn Rovers 1993-Jun 1998; Burnley Feb 1998 (trial); Leigh RMI Sum 1998; Radcliffe Borough Sum 1999; Staybridge Celtic Jun 2004.

An athletic left-back, he rose rapidly through the youth ranks to secure a spot in the reserves just after the club had become Premiership champions. Even so, he was not in a contention for a first-team place and his nomination as substitute in the European Cup in Moscow and at home against Rosenborg was a sign of how few squad players the club possessed. When he moved into non-league he played for Leigh RMI in the FA Cup at Fulham. His sweetly struck free-kick brought a draw in the tie, which forced Fulham into a replay at Hilton Park.

WHEELER, Alfred John
Winger
–5'6.5" 9st 12lb
Born: Fareham, 6 April 1922
Debut: 27 March 1948

CAREER: Portsmouth (am); Blackburn Rovers Apr 1947; Swindon Town Jul 1949; Boston 1951; Weymouth Town Aug 1953; Chippenham Town 1955.

Spotted playing in services football on Salisbury Plain, he was, at the time, an amateur on Portsmouth's books. Impressed by his two-footed craftsmanship, the Rovers offered him professional terms, but exposure to the first team proved that he lacked thrust. When he moved to Swindon he was used irregularly and was one of five forwards released in 1951 when the club had to pay for its floodlight system.

FL	21 apps	5 gls
Total	21 apps	5 gls

WHELAN, David
Full-back

5'6" 11st 3lb
Born: Bradford, 24 November 1936
Debut: 27 August 1956

CAREER: Wigan BC; Blackburn Rovers Dec 1953; Crewe Alexandra Jan 1963-Jun 1966.

Born in Yorkshire but raised in Wigan, he played with the club's youth team and was a member of the side that reached the quarter-finals of the FA Youth Cup in 1955. His future did not appear assured and he had trials with Wigan Athletic, but remained in the Rovers' fold and was eventually the successor to the great Bill Eckersley. His first love was rugby league and he brought the passion and zest of that game to his play, sailing into tackles, chasing hard and hustling throughout. When the club reached the FA Cup final in 1960 he was in the side, but Wembley was to be his last first-team game. A broken leg saw him depart in the first half and, although he recovered sufficiently to play over 100 games for Crewe, his window of opportunity at Blackburn had closed. Keen to go into business, he took a market stall at Wigan, where his fight against officialdom brought him much local goodwill. Capitalising, he opened supermarkets in Wigan, St Helens and Chorley. When he sold this chain to the William Morrison group he became a millionaire. Some of the proceeds were invested in JJB Sports, which he built up to the point where he had 110 stores nationwide. A stock exchange flotation in 1994 raised £8.5 million but still left him with a controlling interest. He has utilised his wealth to gain control of Wigan Athletic and Wigan Rugby League Club, which he moved in to share the newly built Robin Park. He also had control of the best local rugby union club, Orrell, and countless other business investments. In 2005 he achieved a cherished ambition when he saw Wigan Athletic promoted to the Premiership. On the latest *Sunday Times* Rich List in the UK he is ranked 213th with an estimated fortune of £227 million.

FL	78 apps	3 gls
FAC	9 apps	0 gls
Total	87 apps	3 gls

WHITESIDE, Arnold
Wing half

5'6.5" 9st 8lb
Born: Calder Vale, 6 November 1911
Died: Chorley, 12 September 1994
Debut: 12 November 1932

CAREER: Woodplumpton Jnrs; Blackburn Rovers Jan 1932 (am) Mar 1932; Wigan Athletic 1949.

Whiteside spent an entire career proving that a frail, boyish appearance did not prevent him competing with the tough dray horses who were customarily found at wing half. Deft and tidy, he applied himself with artistry but he had the stamina to remain effective. A weaver from Calder Vale, his early years were so inauspicious that the club decided to let him go in 1938. When no-one came to sign him, Bob Crompton had another look and decided that his positional skills and ball-playing ability could be used. The result was his contribution to the club's promotion and a long association that saw him unexpectedly return after the Second World War and play on. He briefly helped his old friend Bob Pryde at Wigan but, contemplating a new means of earning a living, spotted an advertisement in a Southport paper from a chimney sweep who was selling his brushes. He taught himself the technique and set up in business in the Preston-Blackpool area, living in Penwortham. He plied the trade for twenty-five years, leaving the business to his son Terry.

FL	35 apps	0 gls
FAC	5 apps	0 gls
Total	40 apps	0 gls
Pre-war		
FL	183 apps	3gls
FAC	16 apps	0 gls
Total	199 apps	3 gls
Grand Total	239 apps	3 gls

WHITTLE, Maurice
Wing half

5'8" 10st 11lb
Born: Wigan, 5 July 1948
Debut: 21 August 1968

CAREER: Blackburn Rovers Jun 1963 (app.) Oct 1966; Oldham Athletic May 1969 (free); Fort Lauderdale Strikers (USA) Apr 1977-Aug 1977; Barrow Oct 1977; Wigan Athletic; Fort Lauderdale Strikers (USA) Apr 1978-Aug 1978; Southport; Fort Lauderdale Strikers (USA) Mar 1979-Aug 1979; Stafford Rangers 1979; Wigan Athletic Mar 1980-Oct 1980; Barrow (p-m); OSB (Finland) (p-m) 1984; Lytham.

Taken on from school, he was an old-fashioned wing half who was caught in the transition to 4-2-4. A better defender than attacker who was sound in the tackle, he could also strike a ball with venom and was useful at long-range set pieces.

It was obvious that he would play defence rather than midfield but it was a surprise that Oldham made him into such an effective left-back, who made over 300 league appearances. For a time he commuted across the Atlantic to play and later had managerial experience with Barrow before becoming manager of a JJB store in Chorley.

FL	5+2 apps	0 gls
Total	5+2 apps	0 gls

WIGHTMAN, John Renton 'Jock'
Wing half

5'8" 12st 4lb
Born: Duns, 2 November 1912
Died: Blackburn, 20 April 1964
Debut: 23 January 1937

CAREER: Duns Athletic; Scarborough (trial); York City Aug 1933; Bradford PA Jul 1934; Huddersfield Town Jan 1935; Blackburn Rovers Jan 1937; Carlisle United Aug 1947; Shrewsbury Town.

A left winger who played in Scottish junior football, he moved to Yorkshire in an attempt to progress. He had a trial with Scarborough but then moved on for the pre-season trial with York, who were in the Football League. They made him play left half and immediately offered him terms. Promoted to the first team in an emergency, he played well but the club decided that he would be better at left-back. It was not until he joined Huddersfield that he was moved back to wing half, where he was said to play 'an unhurried, typically Scottish style'. He was brought to Ewood so that Pryde could move to centre half and helped transform a team that was heading for relegation into one that lost only 4 of the last 17 games. He missed out in the promotion season of 1938/39, losing his place to Frank Chivers, but returned after the Second World War to regain his first-team place. When age caught up with him he returned to the Rovers as coach to the 'A' team and was in charge of the reserves at the time of his death.

FL	23 apps	1 gl
FAC	4 apps	0 gls
Total	27 apps	1 gl
Pre-war		
FL	43 apps	1 gl
FAC	1 app.	0 gls
Total	44 apps	1 gl
Grand Total	71 apps	2 gls

WILCOX, Jason Malcolm
Left winger

5'10" 11st 6lb
Born: Bolton, 15 July 1971
Debut: 16 April 1990

CAREER: St Bede's School; Blackburn Rovers Jul 1987 (trainee) Jun 1989; Leeds United Dec 1999 (£3,700,000); Leicester City Jul 2004 (free); Blackpool Nov 2005 (loan).
INTERNATIONALS: England 3 apps.

A graduate of the club's youth scheme, he gained a black belt in judo and represented England at age level. A left winger with speed, he took time to develop and his introduction was delayed until Tony Parkes was made caretaker manager after the dismissal of Don Mackay. He gradually developed into a vital part of the team, able to track back, competent enough in the tackle to occasionally play left-back, but above all able to make ground down the left and deliver a wicked diagonal ball that defences found it hard to deal with. His loss through injury in the final months of the Premiership-winning season was the only reason the club lost momentum and finally struggled, his service to Alan Shearer being crucial to the game plan. The development of Damien Duff challenged his long-standing role in the number eleven shirt but Brian Kidd considered Wilcox the best left winger in England, and it was only after his dismissal that Duff was in the team regularly. Reserve football was not an option for a man who had worked his way into the

Jason Wilcox in 1994.

England squad and he moved to Leeds, where he contributed to a side that finished third in the Premiership.

L	241+27 apps	30 gls
FAC	18+2 apps	2 gls
FLC	17+1 apps	1 gl
FMC	1 app.	0 gls
UEFA	4 apps	0 gls
CS	1 apps	0 gls
Total	282+30 apps	33 gls

WILKINSON, David Lemon
Winger

5'8" 9st 2lb
Born: Ryhope, 28 May 1928
Debut: 6 September 1948

CAREER: Silksworth Jnrs; Blackburn Rovers Jul 1948; Bournemouth & Boscombe Athletic Jun 1950; Berwick Rangers 1951 (£500); Ashington 1955; Horden CW; Ryhope CW.

Spotted by the scout who discovered Eric Bell, his progress was monitored while he was in the RAF and he was offered terms when he was demobilised. His one opportunity with the first team was as Wharton's deputy, and he had little chance to make an impact. He joined Jack Bruton in Bournemouth but he never settled and when his wife became ill asked for a move back north. He joined his brother Alan in the Berwick side that played in the Scottish 'C' Division, but broke his leg and missed a great deal of football. He ended his career in the Wearside League and scouted for the Rovers for two years before he decided he would rather play golf.

FL	1 app.	0 gls
Total	1 app.	0 gls

WILKINSON, Neil
Full-back

5'7" 10st
Born: Blackburn, 16 February 1955
Debut: 11 November 1972

CAREER: Witton Park School; Blackburn Rovers Aug 1971 (app.) Feb 1973; Hellenic (South Africa); Cape Town City (South Africa) Mar 1977; Great Harwood; Port Vale Jul 1978; Crewe Alexandra Oct 1978-Mar 1981.

As befitted a cousin of Bryan Douglas he was one of the best players to come out of local football. He had a natural presence, playing right-back with power and authority and tackling strongly. Competition from Mick Heaton reduced his chances and eventually led to the club listening to an offer from Grimsby. When Wilkinson found no fee was involved, he negotiated a more lucrative move to South Africa. On returning, he sought out some football with Great Harwood but was able to move on and play regularly at Crewe.

FL	27+3 apps	0 gls
FAC	2 apps	0 gls
FLC	5+1 apps	0 gls
Total	34+4 apps	0 gls

WILLIAMS, Anthony Simon
Goalkeeper

6'1" 13st 5lb
Born: Ogwr, Bridgend 20 September 1977

CAREER: Blackburn Rovers Jul 1996; Queens Park Rangers Feb 1998-May 1998 (loan); Macclesfield Town Oct 1998-Nov 1998 (loan) Jan 1999-Mar 1999 (loan); Huddersfield Town Mar 1999 (loan); Bristol Rovers Mar 1999-May 1999 (loan); Gillingham Aug 1999-Oct 1999 (loan); Macclesfield Town Feb 2000-Mar 2000 (loan); Hartlepool United Jun 2000 (free); Swansea City Nov 2003-Dec 2003 (loan); Stockport County Jan 2004-Apr 2004 (loan); Grimsby Town Jul 2004 (free); Carlisle United Jun 2005.

A goalkeeper who worked his way through the youth side, he was agile and calm and appeared certain to become a regular player in the Football League. He made 15 appearances for the Welsh Under-21 side but never graduated to the national side. He was named substitute for Blackburn 14 times but was often absent on loan. Eventually he found at Hartlepool the regular football people had thought him capable of.

WILLIAMSON, John
Inside forward

5'11.5" 12st 13lb
Born: Manchester, 8 May 1929
Debut: 30 March 1955

CAREER: Manchester Corp Transport Dept; Newton Heath; Oldham Athletic (am); Manchester City Aug 1949; Blackburn Rovers Mar 1956-May 1957 (£1,000).

In the early 1950s Manchester City baffled football by introducing the 'Revie' plan. This was a psychological rather than tactical masterpiece, since it consisted of nothing more than handing the centre forward shirt to a creative inside forward and allowing the inside forward to push up in compensation. The system was tried out first in the reserves, where playing the pivotal role was Johnny Williamson, a player so unpopular with the Maine Road fans that Don Revie wrote to the *Manchester Evening News* in his defence. The move to Blackburn came two years after he had played this significant role but he was too slow for first-team action and lacked edge. By 1957 he was so disillusioned that he walked away from the game and took an off licence in Ashton.

FL	9 apps	3 gls
Total	9 apps	3 gls

WILLIAMSON, Philip James
Defender

5'9" 10st 10lb
Born: Macclesfield, 19 June 1962
Debut: 5 September 1981

CAREER: Macclesfield Town; Blackburn Rovers Jul 1979 (app.) Sep 1980-Jul 1982.

In 1979 at the age of sixteen he was added to the Macclesfield squad for first-team games. The Rovers monitored his progress and offered him terms but he failed to develop. Best suited to playing centre-back, he was restricted by lack of height but received a first-team opportunity in the third game of the season, when a threadbare squad was down to its limits. He received no other chance and was released at the end of the season.

FL	0+1 app.	0 gls
Total	0+1 app.	0 gls

WILLIS, John Johnson
Inside forward

5'10.5" 12st
Born: Boldon, 28 May 1934
Debut: 1 October 1955

CAREER: Boldon Colliery; North Shields; Blackburn Rovers Aug 1954; Accrington Stanley Jul 1957 (trial); Mossley Dec 1957; Aston Villa Aug 1958; Nelson; Grimsby Town Aug 1959 (trial); Mossley Oct 1959; Boldon Colliery.

Offered a month's trial in 1954, he made good use of his chance by scoring two goals for the junior side in the pre-season practice game. Places in the forward line were hard earned because the club was fielding their golden five (Mooney, Crossan, Briggs, Quigley and Langton) and his only opportunity was as Briggs's deputy. After failing in a trial with Accrington, he was unexpectedly recruited by Aston Villa and played in his second game in the Football League. He returned to live in Billington and play for Nelson but he lost his place to Peter Woosnam and returned to Mossley.

FL	1 app.	0 gls
Total	1 app.	0 gls

WILSON, William

Left-back

5'9" 11st
Born: Seaton Delaval, 10 July 1946
Debut: 13 February 1965

CAREER: Blackburn Rovers Sep 1963; Portsmouth Jan 1972-Jul 1979 (£15,000).

Blond and towheaded, he arrived from the North-East and was introduced to the team at a time when they were struggling in the First Division. As Keith Newton's partner in the Second Division, he formed quite the best pairing in the division and if the swashbuckling Newton took the eye there was no mistaking the quality of Wilson. He tackled with precision, combining great speed of strike with sheer power, and his speed and athleticism was allied to a doggedness that eroded the opposing winger's confidence. After several good seasons his form and attitude altered when Newton was sold and the club deteriorated. When they fell into the Third Division he had already made his outlook plain and the club transferred him to Portsmouth, where he found a new lease of life and eventually a new occupation as the landlord of the public house contained within Fratton Park.

FL	246+1 apps	0 gls
FAC	14 apps	0 gls
FLC	16 apps	0 gls
Total	276+1 apps	0 gls

WITSCHGE, Richard Peter

Midfield

6'0" 11st 7lb
Born: Amsterdam, (Holland), 20 September 1969
Debut: 30 April 1995

CAREER: SDW (Amsterdam); Ajax; Barceloan (Spain) 1990 (£3,000,000); Girondins de Bordeaux (France) 1993 (£1,650,000); Blackburn Rovers Mar 1995-May 1995 (loan); Ajax May 1996-May 2003; Deportivo Alavés (Spain) Jun 2001-Feb 2002 (loan); ADO 20 Aug 2003; Oita Trinita (Japan) Feb 2004; Glasgow Rangers Aug 2004 (trial).
INTERNATIONALS: Holland 31 apps 1 gl.

A talented left-sided player who was a natural playmaker, he followed his brother Rob to Ajax and into the national side. A player of vast talent, his career was chequered with disagreements with coaches and clubs and his potential to be one of the great players in Holland has never been achieved. He was brought to Ewood on loan to cover the side as they entered the final stretch of the run in that brought the championship to Ewood. In fact he was only used once, and his record of causing disruption was in evidence as he soon described the English game as just like rugby. Wisely, Dalglish spotted his potential to damage a cause and ignored him. It is somewhat curious that Witschge has since stated that he was offered a Premiership winners' medal because one losing appearance would appear to be somewhat short of league guidelines for qualification for a medal. After being exiled for a spell in Spain he returned to Ajax to bring down the curtain on a controversial but talented career and had an emotional send-off in his last game from the home fans. In demand with other Dutch clubs, he refused to compromise on his wage demands and instead played as an amateur for a team coached by his brother.

PL	1 app.	0 gls
Total	1 app.	0 gls

WOOD, Michael John

Full-back

5'11" 10st 13lb
Born: Bury, 3 July 1952
Debut: 31 January 1970

CAREER: Blackburn Rovers Jul 1968 (app.) Feb 1970; Bradford City Feb 1978 (£10,000); Halifax Town Aug 1982-Jul 1984 (free); Dudley Hill Athletic; Guiseley.

A wing half not mobile enough to play midfield, he found a solution to his positional problems at left-back. He had many good qualities, a steady positional sense, a strong tackle and a rare ability to chip the ball large distances with unique accuracy. Seldom having a long stretch as a starter, he was useful insofar as he could be moved into the centre, where he was sound in an emergency. His two goals for the first team were scored in the same game, although on this occasion he was enjoying a rare outing in midfield. After he finished playing he became a physiotherapist at the FA School of Excellence at Scholemoor.

FL	140+ 8 apps	2 gls
FAC	10+1 apps	0 gls
FLC	6+1 apps	0 gls
Total	156+10 apps	2 gls

WOODS, Maurice 'Matt'

Centre half

6'0" 12st 6lb
Born: Burscough, 1 November 1931
Debut: 24 November 1956

CAREER: Burscough Oct 1946; Everton 1947 (am) Nov 1949; Blackburn Rovers Nov 1956 (£6,000); Hakoah (Australia) 1963; Luton Town Jul 1965; Stockport County Jul 1966; Drumcondra (Eire).

Of all the transfers in Blackburn Rovers' long history none ever benefitted the club more than the day they paid £6,000 for Everton's reserve centre half Matt Woods. Kept out of the Merseyside team by Tommy Jones, Woods was an immense talent, totally sure of himself, an inspiration to those around him and a dominating presence. It is still unbelievable that he never gained an England cap because for at least four years he was the nation's leading defender, but the presence of Billy Wright in the England team prevented him from gaining honours. In between Clayton and McGrath he formed a dynamic half-back line that took the club to promotion and to a FA Cup final, and Woods was as key to success as those Ewood legends Douglas and Clayton. The

Matt Woods in April 1960. (Howard Talbot Photography)

emergence of Mike England prompted him to take a player-coaching job at Hakoak in Australia and he played for Australia in a non-international game. He returned to see action for Luton and Stockport and was hired, with John Bray, to play in the European Cup with the Irish side Drumcondra. Returning to Australia, he coached Hellas before returning to Merseyside to do the same at Southport. After moving to Stockport he had a spell as manager before running his own transport firm in the Manchester area, eventually retiring to Heald Green, Cheadle.

FL	260 apps	2 gls
FAC	30 apps	1 gl
FLC	17 apps	0 gls
Total	307 apps	3 gls

WRIGHT, Alan Geoffrey
Left-back

5'4" 9st
Born: Ashton under Lyne, 28 September 1971
Debut: 26 October 1991

CAREER: Wrexham (non con); Blackpool Aug 1988 (trainee) Apr 1989; Blackburn Rovers Oct 1991 (£500,000); Aston Villa Mar 1995-Jun 2003 (£900,000): Glasgow Rangers Jul 2003 (trial); Middlesbrough Aug 2003 (free); Sheffield United Oct 2003 (loan) Jan 2004 (free).

One of Kenny Dalglish's first signings, he made the transition to the First Division and then the Premier League without trauma. Tiny defenders are always considered suspect but he was fleet of foot, capable of covering huge areas on the left and intelligent with his crosses. Despite his height he was difficult to victimise, coping well with the aerial ball. His career at Blackburn might have been longer, but two hernia operations kept him out and Graeme Le Saux was signed in the meantime. Not a man to be content with mere squad status he moved to Aston Villa, where he played over 250 games.

L	67+7 apps	1 gl
FAC	5+1 app.	0 gls
FLC	8 apps	0 gls
PO	3 apps	0 gls
Total	83+8 apps	1 gl

WRIGHT, Archibald Watson
Inside forward

5'6" 11st 3lb
Born: Glasgow, 23 November 1924
Died: 1990
Debut: 18 August 1951

CAREER: Rutherglen; Glencairn Jnrs; Hamilton Academicals 1946; Clyde 1946 (£6,000); Falkirk 1949; Blackburn Rovers May 1951 (£10,000); Grimsby Town Jul 1953; Accrington Stanley Jun 1954 (£1,000); Netherfield 1957.

A former ball boy at Ibrox Park, he came to prominence with Clyde, who he helped to the final of the 1949 Scottish Cup. A dapper, quick-footed player with a waspish touch near goal, he had attracted the Rovers' attentions when they came across him in a friendly. He found his opportunities at Ewood were limited by the presence of two great players, Crossan and Quigley, and he soon submitted a transfer request. He finished his playing days with Netherfield but subsequently managed Horwich RMI before in 1963 he was appointed manager of Airdrie.

FL	22 apps	10 gls
Total	22 apps	10 gls

WRIGHT, Glenn Mark
Inside forward

5'11" 11st
Born: Walton, Liverpool, 27 May 1956
Debut: 16 April 1974

Y

CAREER: Blackburn Oct 1972-Jun 1975; Clitheroe Academicals; Clitheroe; Chatburn.

Wright was born in Walton, when his father worked as a water-well borer, but the family subsequently moved to the Ribble Valley. The Rovers signed him from school in Clitheroe. Originally he played up front, where he had a good eye for an opening, was quick to react and was elusive. His ball skill led the club to try and move him into midfield, and he received his only first-team chance at the end of the season when he played wide on the left. The following season he was released and returned to amateur football in the Ribble Valley Amateur League until Jimmy Birkett persuaded him to move to a higher standard.

FL	1 app.	0 gls
Total	1 app.	0 gls

WYLES, Thomas Cecil*
Centre forward

5'9" 11st 7lb
Born: Dunsby Fen, 1 November 1919
Died: Liverpool, 10 October 1990
Debut: 13 October 1945

CAREER: Peterborough United Apr 1935; Kettering Town; Everton Feb 1938 (£300); Blackburn Rovers Oct 1945; Bury May 1946 (free); Southport Oct 1946; Bangor City 1950; Spalding United 1952-1953.

A winger capable of playing on either flank, he made only 11 appearances with Peterborough but displayed enough potential to attract Everton. Gradually switched to centre forward, he had little opportunity on Merseyside but was recruited by the Rovers as a precursor to rebuilding their war-damaged side. In his only season with the club he scored 16 goals in 22 Football League (North) appearances, but the arrival of Eddie Hapgood changed the direction and Wyles did not figure in his plans. He later became a stalwart for Southport, scoring more than fifty goals for them, and he remained in the town when he retired. For a time he was manager of Prescot Cables.

FAC	2 apps	1 gl
Total	2 apps	1 gl

YELLDELL, David
Goalkeeper

6'4" 13st 8lb
Born: Stuttgart (Germany), 1 October 1981

CAREER: Vaihingen; TSG Backnung; Stuttgart Kickers Sum 2002; Blackburn Rovers Jun 2003 (£120,000); Brighton Jan 2005 (loan); Stuttgart Kickers Jun 2005 (£65,000).

The son of a Texan serviceman and a German mother, he was brought up by his mother near Stuttgart and worked his way up to play for Stuttgart Kickers, the smaller of the city's two Bundesliga clubs. Brought over for trials, his transfer to the Rovers was eventually negotiated and he made a first-team debut on tour in the USA. A huge man, he played for the reserves and was named as substitute for the first team on eight occasions without being required to play. In January 2005 he was loaned to Brighton but, after an impressive debut at Leeds, looked nervous in his next two games and returned to Ewood, but could not replace Steve Drench in the reserves.

'YORDI' JORGE GONZÁLEZ DIAZ
Striker

6'1" 12st 12lb
Born: San Fernando, Cadiz (Spain), 2 September 1974
Debut: 24 February 2002

CAREER: Inf. Sevilla BC; Sevilla FC (B) 1993; Sevilla FC 1995; Atletico de Madrid (B) 1996; Real Zaragoza 1997; Blackburn Rovers Feb 2002-May 2002 (loan); Getafe CF Jul 2004; RCD Mallorca Aug 2005 (free).

A tall, energetic, English-type striker who bustled and challenged, he made an astonishing debut, coming on in the Worthington Cup final in Cardiff in the same week that his loan signing had been registered and ending the day with a winners' medal. The previous season he had gained his first medal when Zaragoza won the Spanish cup. Yordi became available because Zaragoza had signed Savo Milosevic, a target for Souness, who then switched to the displaced Yordi to fill a gap in his striking squad. Although he contributed two valuable goals in the club's fight against relegation, Souness had decided not to keep the player beyond his loan period. In 2004 he gained another cup medal as a substitute, but this time he did not get onto the field in the Spanish cup final. It was, though, his goal in the quarter-final against Barcelona that set up his club's epic cup campaign.

PL	5+3 apps	2 gls
FLC	0+1 app.	0 gls
Total	5+4 apps	2 gls

YORKE, Dwight Eversley

Striker

5'9" 12st 11lb
Born: Canaan (Tobago), 3 November 1971
Debut: 17 August 2002

CAREER: Bon Accord Gov Sc; Scarborough High School; Signal Hill Comp; St Clair's Coaching School; Aston Villa Dec 1989; Manchester United Aug 1998 (£12,600,000); Blackburn Rovers Jul 2002 (£2,000,000); Birmingham City Aug 2004 (£500,000); Sydney FC (Australia) Apr 2005.
INTERNATIONALS: Trinidad & Tobago 69 apps 23 gls.

It was a huge stride from being one of nine children raised in a two-bedroom bungalow on the tiny island of Tobago to becoming a world-class footballer, respected throughout the game. Yorke achieved this, on his own terms, refusing to curtail the fun-loving side of his personality and his inclination for the company of beautiful women. Spotted by the chief of the Trinidadian FA, Jack Warner, by virtue of the fact that he was playing in the national age group teams when he was two years younger than the other players, he was taken to the larger island to live with Warner and to be placed for future development under the national coach, Bertie St Clair. When Aston Villa visited the island for a friendly, they noticed his talent and after trials and a negotiation Yorke was introduced to English football. After a slow start, he became one of the game's leading strikers, a mobile, speedy player with the coldness in front of goal of the true assassin. A move to Manchester United brought him all the game's honours in a four-year stay, but increasing friction between him and Alex Ferguson eventually erupted and Graeme Souness brought him to Ewood to renew his partnership with Andy Cole. There were few signs that the almost telepathic understanding that was legendary at Old Trafford had survived the years, but he had the distraction of coping with the fact that the baby he had fathered with the celebrity Jordan had serious health problems. It was a relief to the fans when he was sold to Birmingham in 2004, but his stay in the Midlands was short-lived and equally barren.

PL	42+18 apps	12 gls
FAC	3+1 apps	3 gls
FLC	5 apps	4 gls
UEFA	4+1 apps	0 gls
Total	54+20 apps	19 gls

FA Cup Winners 1884
From left to right, back row: J. Lofthouse, H. McIntyre, J. Beverley, W. Arthur, F. Suter, J. Forrest, R. Birtwistle (Referee). Front row: J. Douglas, J. Sowerbutts, J. Brown, G. Avery, J. Hargreaves. The trophies in the picture are the East Lancashire Charity Cup (left), The FA Cup (centre) and the Lancashire Cup.

FA Cup Winners 1885
From left to right, back row: McIntyre, Suter, Haworth, Brown, Arthur, Fecitt. Front row: Lofthouse, Turner, Sowerbutts, Forrest, Douglas, Inglis.

FA Cup Winners 1886
From left to right, above: Turner, Walton, Strachan, Fecitt. Middle: Sowerbutts, Suter, Forrest. Below: McIntyre, Brown, Aruthur, Douglas.

FA Cup Winners 1891
Back row: Brandon, Pennington, Barton, Southworth, Dewar, Forrest. Front row: Lofthouse, Walton, Forbes, Hall, Townley.

FA Cup Winners 1928. Three days after winning the FA Cup the Blackburn team returned to Ewood Park to display the trophy and beat Portsmouth 6-0. From left to right, back row: J. Walsh (Chairman), R. Crompton (Director and Manager), T. Mitchell, D. Campbell, J. Eddleston (Director), W. Rankin, J. Crawford, J.Chadburn (Director), J. Hutton, R.Roxburgh, H. Jones, M. Atherton (Trainer). Front row: G. Thornwell, S. Puddefoot, J. Roscamp, H. Healless (Captain), T. McLean, A. Rigby.

The FA Cup Winning Squad 1928 (before the cup final). The 14 players who appeared in the seven cup ties during the 1927/28 season. From left to right, back row: A. Barritt (Secretary), W. Rankin, R. Roxburgh, J. Hutton, J. Crawford, A. Campbell, H. Jones, T. Mitchell, M. Atherton (Trainer). Front row: G. Thornwell, S. Puddefoot, J. Roscamp, H. Healless (Captain), T. McLean, A. Rigby, P. Holland.

The
History
Press